ONNAGATA

Onnagata

A LABYRINTH OF GENDERING IN KABUKI THEATER

Maki Isaka

UNIVERSITY OF WASHINGTON PRESS
Seattle and London

Epigraph to part 1: Lynda Hart, "Motherhood According to Finley: 'The Theory of Total Blame,'" *TDR* 36, no. 1 (Spring 1992): 124–134, published by MIT Press.

Parts of chapters 1, 2, 3, and 5 appeared previously in my article "The Gender of *Onnagata* as the Imitating Imitated: Its Historicity, Performativity, and Involvement in the Circulation of Femininity," *positions: east asia cultures critique* 10, no. 2 (Fall 2002): 245–284.

Parts of chapter 7 appeared previously in my article "Women *Onnagata* in the Porous Labyrinth of Femininity: On Ichikawa Kumehachi I," *U.S.-Japan Women's Journal*, nos. 30–31 (2006): 105–131.

Parts of the epilogue appeared previously in my article "What Could Have Happened to 'Femininity' in Japanese Stagecraft: A Memorial Address to Yamada Isuzu (1917–2012)," *positions: asia critique* 21, no. 3 (Summer 2013): 755–759.

© 2016 by the University of Washington Press
Printed and bound in the United States of America
Composed in Warnock Pro, typeface designed by Robert Slimbach

All rights reserved. No part of this publication may be reproduced or transmitted in any form or by any means, electronic or mechanical, including photocopy, recording, or any information storage or retrieval system, without permission in writing from the publisher.

University of Washington Press
www.washington.edu/uwpress

Library of Congress Cataloging-in-Publication Data
Isaka, Maki.
　Onnagata : a labyrinth of gendering in kabuki theater / Maki Isaka.
　　pages　cm
　Includes bibliographical references and index.
　ISBN 978-0-295-99510-6 (hardcover : alk. paper)
　1. Kabuki—History.　2. Actors—Japan—History.　3. Female impersonators—Japan—History.　I. Title.
　PN2924.5.K3I77　2015
　792.0952—dc23   2015033571–

The paper used in this publication is acid-free and meets the minimum requirements of American National Standard for Information Sciences—Permanence of Paper for Printed Library Materials, ANSI Z39.48–1984. ∞

To Ako-san

Contents

Preface and Acknowledgments . . . . *ix*
Note on Textual Conventions . . . . *xiii*

PART I. FUNDAMENTALS: INVITATION TO
    LABYRINTHS OF GENDERING

Introduction: A Labyrinth of Onnagata 5
1. Geneses of a Maze: Androgyne Fatale 22

PART II. FEMININITY INSIDE OUT: ONNAGATA WHO PASS

2. Denial of Transience: Forfeiting the Androgynous Charm 33
3. Prescription for Femininity: Onnagata Who Pass 37
4. Canonization: Creating Onnagata Traditions 58
5. Femininity in Circulation: Texts in Kabuki, Kabuki in Texts 64

PART III. MARGINALIZED CENTERS: BODIES AND PERSONNEL

6. Naturally Disciplined: Moving Real on Procrustean Beds 87
7. Female Onnagata in the Porous Labyrinth: The Enunciated
   Femininity and the Enunciating Masculinity 112

PART IV. ORIGINS OF ONNAGATA: MODERN REFORMATION

8. Toward Contemporary Onnagata: Art in Their Blood 141
   Epilogue: The Journey Continues 159

Notes *165*
Bibliography *221*
Index *249*

Preface and Acknowledgments

THIS book comprises two primary ingredients: gender studies and *onnagata*, actors playing women's roles in all-male kabuki theater in Japan. This combination alone is rather mundane today, but *how* the book combines them and *what* the combination generates are not. It will discuss, for example, gender as gait, gender as adoptees, and female *onnagata* in modern times as legitimate participants in men's world of kabuki: proven to be capable but obliterated from historiography nevertheless. The conclusion of this book is simple. Far from popular images of *onnagata* as the creators of some extraordinary femininity independent of women's everyday femininity, the labyrinth of gendering they show us is rather an ordinary one: intricate yet porous, precarious but binding, and codependent on the labyrinths of others.

As they are arguably the most radical "cross-gender" performers, female *onnagata* are capable of showing us an exemplary labyrinth of gendering. Furthermore, they deserve special attention not so much because they are an underestimated periphery invisible in kabuki historiography today—which is true in its own right—as because they belonged to an abjected part of the mainstream, which was obliterated due to the advent of a modern gender economy and for the sake of the mainstream's survival amid it. (They were dismissed not merely on their own merits. Their existence in the mainstream threatened its own cultural identity and, by extension, existence. Female *onnagata* had to be erased for that precise reason. In short, they were not simply rejected but abjected.) Ultimately, this phenomenon concerns the question of who is made to pay the price for establishing, naturalizing, and maintaining a system, a significant question indispensable to gender studies.[1]

This book's commitment to not only male but also female *onnagata* does not indicate lack of appreciation for kabuki or *onnagata*. On the contrary, I am a kabuki admirer who relishes *onnagata* acting. I just see no need to deny female *onnagata* in order to appreciate male *onnagata*, just as we can appreciate both contraltos and countertenors at the same time. I count myself lucky to have witnessed quite a few impressive *onnagata*, including Kataoka Gadō XIII (1910–1993), Nakamura Utaemon VI (1917–2001), Nakamura Shikan VII (1928–2011), Sawamura Sōjūrō IX (1933–2001), and Bandō Tamasaburō V (b. 1950). They are, in one way or another, *onnagata* of moment for kabuki history. Arguably, Utaemon and Tamasaburō have been two epochal *onnagata* in the post–World War II era, representing two radically new types of *onnagata* respectively ("radically new" at their respective times), while Gadō, Shikan, and Sōjūrō have demonstrated ways in which contemporary *onnagata* negotiate between present-day kabuki dramaturgy and the seemingly *ancien* taste of *onnagata* acting. Theirs is not simply individual acting. For example, when he was deeply engaged in training under the tutelage of Shikan, Tamasaburō vividly demonstrated the power of training by which one creates a being. Although not related by blood to Shikan, Tamasaburō at that time looked and sounded as if he were a loyal "son" who resembles his "father" very much. It has been my good fortune to witness the performances of these *onnagata* not only as a kabuki fan but also as someone who writes about it. This book, however, has almost nothing to do with my own theatergoing experiences, primarily because this project is a textual analysis of discourse on and by *onnagata* and also because the book covers a time period that is much longer than my lifetime.

This book would have been impossible had it not been for foundational library research in Japan, generously made possible by a Charles A. Ryskamp Research Fellowship from the American Council of Learned Societies, for which I am sincerely grateful. I would also like to express my gratitude to the University of Minnesota, whose awards generously supported the several stages of this project. I am also lucky to have interacted with audiences who contributed to the development of this project through their much appreciated interest as well as questions and comments. I am thankful to them and to hosting institutions including Carleton College, Duke University, Midwest Japan Seminar, Northern Michigan University, University of Michigan, University of Minnesota, University of North Carolina at Chapel Hill, and Western Michigan University.

Published works on the topic of gender and *onnagata* have enabled me to develop my conceptualization of the subject. I am thankful to the editors, anonymous reviewers, and readers of the following pieces: "The Gender of *Onnagata* As the Imitating Imitated: Its Historicity, Performativity, and Involvement in the Circulation of Femininity," *positions: east asia cultures critique* 10, no. 2 (Fall 2002): 245–84, reprinted in vol. 4 of *Gender and Japanese Society*, edited by Dolores P. Martinez, in the Critical Concepts in Asian Studies series (London: Routledge, 2014), 31–60, which became the seeds for chapters 1, 2, 3, and 5; "Women *Onnagata* in the Porous Labyrinth of Femininity: On Ichikawa Kumehachi I," *U.S.-Japan Women's Journal* 30–31 (2006): 105–31, from which chapter 7 grew; and "What Could Have Happened to 'Femininity' in Japanese Stagecraft: A Memorial Address to Yamada Isuzu (1917–2012)," *positions: asia critique* 21, no. 3 (Summer 2013): 755–59, which informs the epilogue. Two other short essays in anthologies contain ideas that are now developed and spread throughout this book: "Box-Lunch Etiquette: Conduct Guides and Kabuki *Onnagata*," in *Manners and Mischief: Gender, Power, and Etiquette in Japan*, edited by Jan Bardsley and Laura Miller (2011), 48–66; and "Images of *Onnagata*: Complicating the Binarisms, Unraveling the Labyrinth," in *PostGender: Gender, Sexuality and Performativity in Japanese Culture*, edited by Ayelet Zohar (2009), 22–38. Each of these earlier works has been significantly expanded here with the addition of new material and translations, more questions and arguments, and even different conclusions on some occasions. The same is true of the present book as well: my hearty thanks go to Lorri Hagman, executive editor at the University of Washington Press, and two anonymous reviewers, for their helpful comments. I also extend my thanks to the future readers of this book.

This book would have been impossible had it not been for the following people, whose support and guidance have been greatly appreciated: Ayako Kano, Linda H. Chance, William R. LaFleur, Jennifer Robertson, Tani E. Barlow, Ann Waltner, Josephine Lee, Jason McGrath, Anna Clark, Jigna Desai, Jan Bardsley, Rika Saitō, Patricia Schiaffini-Vedani, Haneda Sumiko, Lynda Hart, Dorry and Red Thomson, Ro Fava, Uncle Ton, Kondō Ikuko, Matsuzawa Satoko, Nemoto Yoshiko, Hori Keiko, and Ako Sahara.

Note on Textual Conventions

THIS book deals with both premodern and modern actors, which led to the decision to leave it unillustrated so that readers could focus on the *idea* of gender as it was manifest in the context of kabuki theater. Had the book contained two types of images—premodern woodblock prints and modern photographs—the grammar of the images (such as painting with no vanishing point) would have demanded substantial argument so that we would not be misled by our own sense of "naturalness," a concept of great moment here.

Unless otherwise noted, all translations from Japanese are mine. I have tried to make them as literal as possible. When original texts favor repetitious rhetoric, I preserve it, even though readers may well understand the meaning of a sentence without such reiteration.

TERMINOLOGY

In this book, the term "modern times" refers to the Meiji era (1868–1912) onward and "premodern times" refers to the period before and through the Edo era (1600–1867). The Edo era is also called the "Tokugawa period," as this was the time when Japan was ruled by the Tokugawa shoguns and the shogunate was located in the city of Edo, the site of present-day Tokyo. In the interest of consistency, this book uses "Edo" when referring to this period.

While female performers were banned throughout nearly the entire the Edo era, modern times in Japanese-theater history are characterized by their return. Regardless of the time, the present book uses the words "female performer," "female actor," and "woman performer" as generic terms. In turn, specific terms are used for female performers playing kabuki, "theater-master" for premodern times and "woman-actor" for modern times, reflecting the original Japanese words *okyōgenshi* and *onna yakusha* respectively. Another specific group of modern female actors is the actress (*joyū*), who, unlike the woman-actor, performed a new type of theater and embodied a new understanding of femininity that considered females the sole matrix of femininity. Because of this historical specificity, the gender-specific word is suitable for discussion in this context.

Because women performed kabuki, there were also female *onnagata*. In relation to issues regarding norms and markedness, one theoretically should use the phrase "male *onnagata*" as a logical contrast to "female *onnagata*." Such usage, however, would nullify the insidious reality of the two, especially the asymmetry between them, and thus make invisible the important questions that female *onnagata* can raise. Accordingly, in order to reflect the politics surrounding the term "*onnagata*," I follow the convention of using the unmodified term to refer only to male actors and use the term "female *onnagata*" for female actors. This is to avoid making invisible and naturalizing the problems and is not intended to endorse the hierarchy. When the distinction between male and female *onnagata* calls for emphasis, I use "male *onnagata*."

Among four traditional Japanese theaters (noh, *kyōgen*, bunraku, and kabuki), bunraku-puppet theater has several related appellations (*ningyō jōruri*, *gidayū*, etc.). In the interest of lucidity, this book uses the terms "puppet theater" and "bunraku," although "bunraku" is relatively new nomenclature that has not existed for the entire history of this theater, raising the possibility of anachronistic usage of the term. When focusing on the musical and audio aspect (e.g., chanting), however, either the terms "*jōruri*" or "*gidayū*" will be used. *Jōruri* chanting is a broader category that subsumes *gidayū* chanting; the two terms are sometimes used interchangeably, however, especially in the context of the latter. In bunraku, a *gidayū* chanter—accompanied by a shamisen [three-stringed instrument] player—provides narration and the voices of all puppets playing theatrical characters onstage.

When these traditional performing arts appear in kabuki discourse, they more often than not signify authentic traditions from which kabuki cites. In this context, noh and *kyōgen* are called *hongyō*, and bunraku is called *honmon*, both of which mean authentic traditions.

PREMODERN AND MODERN CUSTOMS

This book uses the term "fourth month" for dates before 1873 and "April" for dates after that year, to reflect the particular calendar in use, namely, the lunar calendar before 1873 and the solar calendar after 1873.

The way of counting a person's age also changed in 1873. Before that, the traditional East Asian age-counting method was used, in which a newborn was considered one year old during the calendar year of his or her birth. For example, a baby born in the twelfth month would be one year old through the end of the month and become two years old the following month when a new year began. Yet, even after the Meiji government introduced the new method in 1873, the old custom remained predominant in society as late as the mid-twentieth century. When calculating ages, this book follows the traditional East Asian age-counting method during the time the method was used in Japan so that the text will be consistent with quotations.

The way in which personal names appear in this book also reflects the difference between premodern and modern customs. Upon introduction, all Japanese names are given surname first, followed by the given name. In subsequent references, a single element is used: the family name for those living in modern times (1868 onward) or the given name for those who lived before that. For example, Ihara Saikaku (1642–1693) is referred to as Saikaku, and Ihara Toshirō (1870–1941) as Ihara. Exceptions are commonly known names (e.g., Zeami, not Motokiyo; Chikamatsu, not Monzaemon) and authors who have published in English using Western name order.

This book follows a specific rule for the names of kabuki actors, whether before or after 1868. Not only do they have generation numbers, but they also change their names (usually first names but sometimes last names as well) as their acting careers progress. When a kabuki actor is introduced, the most well-known name (i.e., the one that is considered most critical for her or his acting career) is used, along with a generation number. In later references, only the first name is used, occasionally including the generation number for clarity. For example, Nakamura Utaemon VI (1917–2001) was Nakamura Kotarō III from 1922, Nakamura Fukusuke VI from 1933, Nakamura Shikan VI from 1941, and Nakamura Utaemon VI from 1951 onward. He appears in this book as Nakamura Utaemon VI on first mention and as Utaemon afterward. When his father, Nakamura Utaemon V (1865–1940), is discussed in proximity, the generation numbers are added so as to distinguish between them: Utaemon VI and Utaemon V. An actor's most well-known name is usually the latest name, but there are some exceptions. For instance, Matsumoto Kōshirō VIII (1910–1982) changed his name to Matsumoto Hakuō I just a few months before his death, with his son succeeding to the name Kōshirō. He appears in this book as Matsumoto Kōshirō VIII on first mention and Kōshirō or Kōshirō VIII afterward. When citing works by actors, however, I use their last names in notes and the bibliography, with generation numbers in parentheses if necessary for clarity.

ONNAGATA

PART I

Fundamentals

Invitation to Labyrinths of Gendering

> Ideology, as we know, often works this way: an appropriation of ideas from one group is made functional by another, even though their interests are in conflict.... The solution is of course not to push for a rigid adherence to either position [of essentialism and constructionism], but to continually problematize, and *historicize*, the essentialist/constructionist binary.
>
> —LYNDA HART, "Motherhood According to Finley"
> (125, 132; emphasis in original)

Introduction

A Labyrinth of Onnagata

QUATERCENTENARY kabuki theater in Japan is a "queer" theater. That is not so much to say that kabuki is an all-male theater, in which male actors play women's roles, as to note how radically this art form has altered the connotations of the word "kabuki." Just as with the word "queer," the implication of which has changed fundamentally over the years, the meanings of the word "kabuki"—nominalized from a verb, *kabuku* (to lean; to act and/or dress in a peculiar and queer manner)—have transformed dramatically. Not only did it shift from a generic word (that which is eccentric, deviant, queer, and the like) to a proper noun (this theater), but its connotations also altered tremendously from something negative to something positive. That is, kabuki theater was born as a kabuki thing—merely another stray entertainment among many, which was considered akin to prostitution—and ended up proudly styling itself *the* kabuki theater. With a checkered past marked by bans, shutdowns, exile, and even capital punishment for the parties concerned, kabuki—once a theater of rebellion for the common people—is now one of four classical genres of Japanese theater that the nation proudly presents to the world, along with noh (a medieval Buddhist theater a few centuries older than kabuki), *kyōgen* (a theater of mime and speech that accompanies noh), and bunraku (a puppet theater), all of which are all-male theater.

Kabuki is well known for its exaggerated acting, flamboyant costumes and makeup, and unrealistic stories filled with ghosts, women who are actually birds or flowers, men who can transform themselves into toads or rats, and so on. With the aid of wires, actors playing magical foxes, supernatural samurai, or ghostly ladies-in-waiting literally fly through the air in playhouses. Kabuki is a fantasy theater. That said, unlike other genres of classical Japanese theater, kabuki appears amorphous, resisting concise definition. Some kabuki productions might remind spectators of *jingju*, a traditional form of Chinese theater also referred to as Peking Opera, with their highly stylized choreography and masklike faces heavily painted with bold lines in primary colors. Others come very close to straight theater, based on realistic movement and elocution. Some kabuki plays are nearly identical to its contemporaneous bunraku. Still others pay homage to noh, in terms of both dramaturgy and performance style based on dance and chanting.

One famous aspect of kabuki is its use of *onnagata* actors who specialize in women's roles and are admired for their beauty and artistry. *Onnagata* are considered indispensable in the world of kabuki, which is clearly "male"-centric, or, more precisely, masculinity-centric. For example, at the end of a play, a protagonist performed by a male-role troupe leader sometimes uses the "three-steps" (*sandan*), a mobile staircase that emphasizes pictorial stage effects and amplifies the presence of the troupe's top actor. The three-steps is reserved for male-role players (*tachiyaku*); when a leading *onnagata* (*tate-oyama*) does a similar performance, he uses the "two-steps" (*nidan*) instead, visually materializing the gender hierarchy. Likewise, since stage left (*kamite*) is charged with superiority compared to stage right (*shimote*), an *onnagata* seldom stands left of a male-role partner when they are dancing, except when performing a couple such as a princess and her retainer. For that matter, terminology itself is quite telling. While the initial meaning of the term "*onnagata*" meant "those in charge of women's [roles]," enunciating the marked gender of the characters to be performed, *tachiyaku* (lit., "standing role") is a privilege unmarked by gender. Closely related to the noh *tachikata* (lit., "those standing"), *tachiyaku* are simply "actors." Within this masculinity-centric picture is the *onnagata*, the flower of kabuki.[1]

With the increasing availability of DVDs and YouTube, images of internationally renowned *onnagata* such as Bandō Tamasaburō V (b. 1950) have been abundantly available worldwide, which further stimulates discourse on *onnagata*. It is no exaggeration to say that the topic of *onnagata* is among the most often discussed in both academic and popular discourse.

Taking a bird's-eye view of discussions of the *onnagata*'s performance of femininity, one cannot help but recall the quote from Karl Marx that serves as the epigraph for Edward W. Said's *Orientalism*: "They cannot represent themselves; they must be represented."[2] This sentiment is echoed in a remark on *onnagata*'s performance of femininity in *The Kabuki Theatre*, a book published in the 1950s: "Yoshizawa Ayame (1673–1729), a famed player of women's roles, wrote in his book *Ayame-gusa*, 'If an actress were to appear on the stage she could not express ideal feminine beauty, for she would rely only on the exploitation of her physical characteristics, and therefore not express the synthetic ideal. The ideal woman can be expressed only by an actor.'"[3] Among materials written in English, this book is one of the basics of kabuki studies in its early days, which dates to immediately after World War II and the subsequent American occupation of Japan. The quotation is well circulated in works on *onnagata* and beyond. The idea that *onnagata*'s performance of femininity is unavailable to women is nearly ubiquitous in works on *onnagata* today. Moreover, this remark is also a rare example of the use of Japanese performance outside the confines of Asian studies. The notion that *onnagata*'s femininity construction is unavailable to women has thus been attractive and influential.

The predominance of this idea is intriguing. It is understandable, for it corresponds to a current basic understanding in gender theory that gender and biological sex are not in a binding relationship. Topics relating to *onnagata* also speak to the contemporary phenomenon of "beautiful-boy" (*bishōnen*) culture. However, it is ironic that the possibility of *onnagata* artistry is regarded as residing in male actors alone, considering that the art of *onnagata* is, in both theory and practice, made possible by the very presupposition of "femininity [being] separable from women's anatomical sex."[4] If *onnagata*'s gender performance were possible only in male actors, a rigid binding relationship would connect sex and gender, albeit in an opposite way. *Onnagata* artistry is never limited in such a manner, and the fixation—despite its attractiveness—has constrained the potential for the analysis of *onnagata*'s gender performance to contribute to our thinking on gender.

This potential is not merely possible but urgently needed. First, the purported remark of Yoshizawa Ayame in *The Kabuki Theatre* cannot be located in "The Words of Ayame" (Ayamegusa), an eighteenth-century *onnagata* treatise. In fact, the text in its entirety strongly suggests the opposite. The *onnagata*'s performance of femininity was not the exclusive property of male actors; rather, *onnagata* constructed it by approximating women through observation and training and by circulating it with women. This notion was not idiosyncratic to this specific text but rather was representative at the time it was written. Furthermore, although *onnagata* artistry has changed radically over its four-century history, even in recent years (that is, after the idea of considering *onnagata* art available only to male actors became dominant in modern times), quite a few *onnagata*—including major *onnagata* such as Tamasaburō—have left words signifying otherwise. For master practitioners, it is not so much the biological sex of a body as talent, training, and dedication to the art that matter for the performance of gender. The alleged statement, which does not exist in "The Words of Ayame," has thus hindered effective analysis of *onnagata*'s gender performance in not only premodern but also modern times. In particular, what has been grossly underrated is the impact *from* females on *onnagata*'s performance of femininity. The impact includes both compatibility between women in general and male *onnagata*, which was materialized in history as *onnagata* passing as women, and female *onnagata*'s contributions to the art and traditions of *onnagata*.

PARADOX? "CROSS-GENDERING FEMININITY IN SOCIAL CURRENCY"

I earlier said that kabuki was a fantasy theater. In this theatrical space, consistent verisimilitude seems insignificant on the level of both drama texts and acting. There is no need for a butler to enter, for whatever plausible reasons, to clean up a mess on the floor. That can be handled automatically by stage assistants who may appear seemingly freely during the performance. The entrance door of a house, likewise, can simply be taken away by the assistants when more space becomes necessary for characters to interact inside the house. If a character reveals something, such as a hidden identity or an emotional state, he or she can change costume or add makeup in front of the audience, reflecting the transformation (e.g., change in emotion). Literally as well as metaphorically, deus ex machina can appear at any moment in this fantasy space of singing (*ka*), dancing (*bu*), and acting (*ki*), all performed by male actors. To all intents and purposes, being realistic hardly seems to be a virtue of kabuki.

Yet after female performers were legally expelled from performance activities in 1629, male actors in charge of women's roles, *onnagata*, came to have much influence on how to materialize womanliness not only in the fantasy world of kabuki but also in society. Through circulation and emulation, *onnagata*'s theatrical gender practice even affected how women manifested femininity outside the theater,⁵ an example of gender and sex being divorced from each other. This societal phenomenon involving *onnagata* and women lasted explicitly until the return of modern actresses in the Meiji era and continued implicitly afterward. The modern restoration of actresses was strongly associated with new, scientific discourses that grounded femininity in women's bodies alone and thus drastically transformed how gender was defined,⁶ yet *onnagata* and their methodology of femininity construction and articulation somehow managed to survive this change. Along with modern actresses, there existed in late-nineteenth- and early-twentieth-century Japan a specific group of female performers called "women-actors" (*onna yakusha*), whose performance of femininity was closely associated with male-*onnagata* traditions in kabuki. Although women-actors themselves became extinct soon afterward, such a phrase as "not so much an actress as a 'woman-actor' [imitating *onnagata*]" still amounted to a compliment for female actors, as playwright Enomoto Shigetami lamented as late as 1984.⁷ Even today, this is not an obsolete mind-set. In the fall of 2008, a cosmetics company released commercials featuring narration by Tamasaburō, explaining, for example, how women can be beautiful, and, as the interviewer specified, women were the target audience.⁸ The same *onnagata* was invited in 2011 to talk about his quest for "eternal female beauty" (*eien no joseibi*) at an event in Tokyo promoting healthy living in menopause, and women, this time in a particular age group, were again the target audience.⁹

As far as *onnagata* were concerned, fantasy did not remain inside playhouses, not to mention on the stage, for long but had a substantial impact on society. Why did actors have such an influence? Was it an example of *theatrum mundi* (the world as stage)? Did women in Edo-era Japan display festive womanliness in everyday life? Certainly, "Sex was perceived as subordinate to gender; females were to approximate—or bring their innermost temperaments in accord with—female-likeness."¹⁰ This was, however, a female-likeness defined not by actors, especially those who were part of flamboyant festivities, but by theorists of an educational movement called Shingaku (Heart learning).¹¹

This conundrum reaches several levels. First, kabuki is diverse, and the examples in the opening paragraphs represent merely the most eye-catching aspects of this theater. There certainly exists a repertoire of kabuki plays that depict a "slice of life" at that time. What is more, kabuki dramaturgy by definition appreciates conflicting methods that are employed simultaneously. This is related to kabuki's definition of itself. Kabuki synchronically contains two contradicting types of impulses: to *kabuku* ("to deviate from the norm") and to be faithful to "authentic traditions"(*hongyō* or *honmon*, depending on the genre of the preceding tradition). Etymologically, it is a generic term nominalized from the verb *kabuku*. Accordingly, the common noun *kabuki* can refer to anything eccentric. What would later be known as kabuki theater styled itself as such. No wonder inclinations toward *kabuku* penetrate this theater as one of its vital impulses. In turn, there also exists in kabuki-theater dramaturgy another incentive, to rely on authentic traditions, that is, earlier traditions that one cites as authentic. (Born at the very beginning of the Edo era, kabuki inherited many features from preceding performing arts.) These kinds of contradictory urges—the passion for deviation and for legitimacy—constitute the dynamic kabuki dramaturgy, and they are dynamically amalgamated in kabuki theater on many levels, ranging from drama texts to stage setting, to costumes, to music, and to choreography and performance.[12] In this regard, supposed oppositions such as overacting and realistic performance coexist easily on the kabuki stage.

This does not explain, however, why theater practitioners can be models of behavior for people beyond the theater or in society at large. Ultimately, it entails the question of theatricality. In general, theater tends to be *made* to associate with negative attributions, such as falsehood, which is tellingly displayed not only in many English terms[13] but also in the Japanese lexicon (e.g., *kyōgen gōtō* [theater robbery] means "sham robbery"). It is not only that people have likely separated onstage performance from offstage behavior in their understanding of a world,[14] but it is also assumed that the two *must* be separated. In the final analysis, this is an aporia, with which this book will deal in its entirety, along with another aporia of what "being realistic" means.

Furthermore, regardless of this conundrum of theatricality and reality, the question "Why actors?" brings about another riddle: Why *onnagata*? Aside from the seemingly simple question of why women had to be taught anything about womanliness by men, a problem sometimes associated with patriarchy,[15] *onnagata* were not the first to be engaged in "cross-gender" performance in the history of Japanese theater. If kabuki, born in the seventeenth century, provided women offstage with "exemplary models (*kata*) of 'female' (*onna*) gender . . . to approximate,"[16] could not the same be said of noh theater, which preceded kabuki by a few centuries? Kabuki emerged as a hybrid entertainment at the dawn of the Edo period, inheriting various elements from noh and other antecedent performing arts, and noh constitutes authentic traditions of significance for kabuki. Noh is also an all-male theater, so women characters in noh are performed by men. If *onnagata* in kabuki theater amount to models of womanliness in the Edo era and beyond, were noh actors performing women's roles also regarded as the epitome of the feminine? This question could apply to many other examples: boy players in English Renaissance theater; *nandan* players in Chinese traditional theater, such as *jingju* and *kunqu* (also called *kunju*); and, expanding beyond femininity and into gender, even male-role actors in all-female Takarazuka theater.[17] What is so special about *onnagata*?

Although comparative studies are beyond the range of this book, even a glance at such an incomplete inventory suggests the relatively unique, not to say *the* unique, position from which *onnagata* have dealt with "cross-gender" performance.[18] Noh actors are classified in terms of the theatrical *functions* they perform in a play: *shite* and *waki*. *Shite* (lit., "the one who does") refers to the principal character in each noh play as well as to actors performing *shite* roles, and *waki* are the "side" character and actors playing *waki* roles. *Shite* actors, thus, should be capable of performing all principal roles, such as deities, warriors, women, crazed persons, and demons. Accordingly, noh actors need a wide range of training in what noh actor-playwright Zeami Motokiyo (1363–1443) termed the "two techniques and three bodies" (*nikyoku santai*), that is, the two arts of dancing and chanting and the three role types of the old person, the woman, and the warrior.[19] In comparison, kabuki actors are classified in terms of the *categories* of characters they perform: for example, *tachiyaku* and *onnagata*, and further, *oyaji-gata* (those in charge of old men's roles) and *dōke-gata* (those in charge of the clown), to name just a few. Unlike women characters in noh plays, who are performed by "generalists" who have mastered all three role types, women in kabuki are performed by specialists. Furthermore, unlike Takarazuka male-role actors—and many, if not all, boy players elsewhere—who are expected to "graduate" after a certain period of time, *onnagata*'s acting is virtually a lifetime vocation. Segawa Kikunojō I (1693–1749), for example, is said to have been on his deathbed in full dress in accordance with the *onnagata* garb code.[20] There is a similar anecdote about Onoe Baikō VI (1870–1934). While performing the role of Enju, a dignified old woman, in November 1934, Baikō had a stroke onstage and died a few days later. Although on the verge of a coma, he is said to have made a great effort to fix his disheveled costume, a testament, according to Matsumoto Kōshirō VII (1870–1949), who was with him at the time, to Baikō's perfection as an *onnagata*.[21]

Onnagata have dealt with femininity as its specialized doers, just like another group of specialized doers of femininity, namely, women. (As long as gender is a doing, people have to *do* their gender.) For both, the duration of such a mission is indefinite. Moreover, both women and *onnagata* were circulating femininity in the Edo period. Unlike most women, however, *onnagata* have been engaged in femininity in the form of "cross-gender" performance. The male identity of the actors offstage is equally as important as their performance of femininity onstage. It was so for early *onnagata* after the 1629 ban on female performers for obvious legal reasons, and it is still so for present-day *onnagata* albeit for a different reason.[22] Taken together, these conditions situate *onnagata* in a special position in dealing with gender. Subsequently, analyses of *onnagata* can furnish a useful aperture through which to contemplate femininity construction and the gender economy. This is a vantage point, as the gender economy—its construction mechanism included—is usually naturalized and made invisible under "normal" circumstances in many societies and cultures or, more precisely put, under successful circumstances in which constituent members of a community have internalized the norm held by their community. An inquiry into *onnagata* artistry can show what is usually invisible.

The term "cross-gender" demands our attention. I have used quotation marks for it so far, and the same theoretical caution will be maintained even though quotation marks are dropped simply for the sake of readability. The phrase "cross-so-and-so" presupposes separate—and, more often than not, stable—categories. Only with such a presupposition can one be engaged in an action called "to cross (over)," although there is always a possibility that the action of crossing (over) creates a new space. Furthermore, when it comes to gender, demarcation tends to be based on dualistic principles, which in itself is not unique to gender but is especially visualized in cognitive practices associated with gender. Strictly speaking, it is risky to adopt the term "cross" for analyses of subject matter involved in gender. The map of gender is a dynamic spectrum, not a cluster of two mutually exclusive, static, polarized categories of femininity and masculinity. For one thing, gender is concomitant with "acts" that we constantly perform, as demonstrated by the concept of performativity. For another, the concepts of gender and sex operate in a slippery way. The number of sexes has never been two, as developmental geneticist Anne Fausto-Sterling calls our attention to intersexuality by using the phrase "five sexes."[23] Nevertheless, in the realm of gender, femininity and masculinity have long been conceptualized as a pair, making each the constitutive other of the other. The constitutive other is the notion that explains our perception that differentiation between A and B is always functional, and we can distinguish A only with the aid of B-which-is-not-A. Theoretically, therefore, the constitutive other has no essential, innate characteristics. The relationship between masculinity and femininity entails this characteristic of *différance*.[24] Far from the popular notion to regard gender as societal roles or meanings attached to preexisting sex, gender *on the contrary* resides in the act of perception that *gives* meanings to the object of perception, that is to say, sex. Here, what cognitively makes sex sex-as-we-know-it is none other than gender, and not the other way around. There is no such thing as preexisting sex in this sense.

In short, classification into categories here is formidable in practice but elusive in theory. Here, groups (to cross over) do not exist a priori but emerge as people conceive borders in accordance with criteria in operation and behave in line with—or in some cases against—the norms thus defined. Categories are simultaneously the conditions and the results of cognitive praxes related to classification. In this sense, the phrase "cross-gender performance" is insidious precisely because it contains this theoretical slippage, if not contradiction, that is, it presupposes dichotomized concepts that it itself helps polarize and stabilize: male and female, femininity and masculinity, nature and nurture, and the like. None of these exists a priori, and no "pair" here is symmetric. *Onnagata* have been engaged in cross-gender performance defined as such.

For this reason, an investigation of *onnagata* can remind us that we are dealing with not so much a labyrinth of gender (noun) as a labyrinth of gendering (verb). By that I do not mean to associate gender with a being and gendering with an action in a mutually exclusive way. Existences and actions do not categorically divide in the realm of gender. Insights from gender studies have already revealed that gender is not just a being. Existences and actions work together, in complicity, in generating further existences and provoking further actions. Rather than assuming an illusionary clear-cut boundary between existences and actions, this book, by using the verb "gendering," foregrounds skepticism that "gender" is capable of pretending (disguising) its nature as an existence. In doing so, it will also help us realize how undependable the doomed dualism of masculinity and femininity is in theory although formidably unflinching in practice. Its theoretical elusiveness does not offset the fact that gender is extremely binding in reality.[25]

Among many ideas proposed and utilized in the rich and diverse fields of gender studies, the present book relies particularly on the concepts of performativity and contingency,[26] as the *onnagata*'s way of dealing with gender is informative of these ideas. Simply put, performativity explains how a *doing* participates in the construction of a *being* (that an iterative doing creates a being). The performativity notion is significant for gender as it is based on the criticisms of similarities, *and not differences*, between biological determinism (biology is destiny) and cultural determinism (gender is a social product). They both presuppose the modern subject conceptualized by the metaphysics of substance and retain the same structure of gender-giving narrative. In this model, a human being is considered the metaphysical locus of agency, and to this human subject, Nature gives gender in biological determinism and Culture in cultural determinism. The notion of performativity reveals that this structure of gender giving, based on the presumption of the metaphysics of substance, is illusory. Gender is not automatically bestowed on us, by either Nature or Culture, but is constructed through our doing, that is to say, by citing other people's doings of gender, which are already citations. It is in this regard that gender is culturally constructed and extremely precarious. For in the light of citationality, neither a pure original (a hypothetical original that cites nothing) nor a rigorously exact imitation (a perfect copy that does not differ from its original in any way) is realistic. Citation does not occur in such a form that one hands gender to another, as an intact object. Unwittingly or otherwise, each transaction involves revision to one degree or another, accidental or otherwise. With countless, constant, and mutual transactions, such an illusionary idea as origins vanishes in the aporia of which one of innumerable copies came to exist first. Gender is thus both culturally binding and contingent. In this sense, cross-gender performance (i.e., doing gender across the boundary of previously defined gender categories) is capable of creating a new space, a new way, and a new effect of gendering.

Certainly, *onnagata*'s cross-gender performance has kept producing new sites, methods, and results regarding how femininity is materialized, conceptualized, and naturalized. *Onnagata* artistry has been deployed in a way that is far from monolithic over four centuries. Moreover, the changes in question are not simply development in the sense of improvement or refinement. Considering the dynamic nature of crossing, it is to be expected that the definition of *onnagata* artistry has changed dramatically over time, along with the definition of femininity itself. Even the topic of cross-gender performance, a theme that seems to permeate the entire history of *onna-*

gata, is never straightforward. For instance, the meaning of an actor's male identity has totally changed. The 1629 ban on female performers meant that *onnagata* legally had to occupy the straddling position between male and female (male identity offstage and feminine performance onstage). In contrast, *onnagata* these days are no longer bound by such legal constraints but are now subject to the latest definition of *onnagata* artistry, which is that it is the exclusive property of male actors. For another example, the history of kabuki does have examples of female *onnagata*, that is, female actors engaged in the performance of femininity as cross-gender performance, using the same methodology and techniques as do male *onnagata*. They provide an exceptionally visible or visualized example of an operation faithful to a binary that ends up revealing the very incompleteness of the dualism.[27] (In this sense, ironically, female *onnagata*, who seemingly are not crossing the alleged boundary of gender, are more revealing about the complicated features of cross-gender performance. Likewise, female *onnagata* are more capable of telling nuanced stories about the divorce of gender and sex.) No wonder *onnagata*'s art and their gender performance have been defined and redefined intermittently in a way that is almost dialectical and furnishes many instances of femininity construction. Everything is cross-gender performance in a broad sense, but *what* to cross, *how* to cross, and *why* to cross differ from one case to another.

The following three examples, taken from the discourse on *onnagata*, serve as a sneak preview of the diverse history of *onnagata*. The term "*futanarihira*" (androgynous beauties) was used to compliment early *onnagata* on their beauty, while, from the early eighteenth to late nineteenth centuries, "suffering from gynecological disorders" (*chi no michi ga okorishi*) was the epithet for skillful *onnagata* who systematized and theorized their gender performance.[28] The understandings and expectations of their gender performance were drastically differentiated between them. Both concepts and their respective presuppositions are also significantly foreign to the more recent epithet for modern *onnagata*: "even more womanly than women are" (*onna yori mo onna-rashii*). As these examples hint, the history of *onnagata* is dynamic, and the landscape of *onnagata* artistry is complicated. What follows examines these and inquires into how the gender performance of *onnagata* has been understood, conceptualized, and theorized. By extension, it also explores how the concepts and mechanisms of femininity, along with the economy of gender construction, are configured in a localized context. It is a case study of how gender has been constructed and naturalized, defined and redefined, theorized and practiced. It is a case study on gendering, yet its implications go well beyond disciplinary or geographic cloisters. It is not merely *their* story.

PREVIEW: MISE-EN-SCÈNE AND METHODOLOGY

Kabuki was born at the dawn of the Edo era as a people's theater. While it inherited many features from earlier performing arts, this emerging hybrid entertainment was first and foremost that which is eccentric. It was considered by the social elite to be a depraved theatrical entertainment until the Meiji period, when it transformed itself into a classical theater. Playhouses and brothels were regarded in the same negative light, and kabuki remained subject to the shogunate's interference and suspicion.[29] Intervention in the form of repeated bans did in fact determine the development of kabuki. The first cluster of kabuki performing arts is usually called *onna kabuki* (women's kabuki),[30] although it was not exclusively performed by only women. Cross-gender performance (women's performance in the roles of men, and vice versa) was already a signature feature of kabuki from the outset, and one type in particular (men playing women's roles) became indispensable for kabuki after 1629, when female performers were banned from the stage on the grounds that they were associated with prostitution. Women's kabuki had been popular until then, and the ban resulted in a shift of popularity from women's kabuki to *wakashu kabuki* (young boys' kabuki). This form of kabuki—an all-male entertainment—featured young boys playing female roles, which emphasized their feminine beauty. The term *"wakashu"* refers in general to male minors before initiation into adulthood and, more specifically, to junior partners in male-male relationships. The Way of *wakashu* (*Wakashudō*) had already been well established in Japan, with a long tradition in the relatively prestigious samurai class. *Wakashu kabuki* inevitably entailed sexual connotations and became the target of censorship due to an allegation similar to the one that had been made against women's kabuki. It was finally banned in 1652. The disappearance of *wakashu* players filling women's roles created a demand for actors capable of female impersonation not solely through somatic characteristics but, more importantly, through the artistic skill of acting. Thus *yarō kabuki*, kabuki performed by adult men, came into being, the prototype of today's kabuki, with adult male actors playing women's roles virtually for a lifetime, relying not just on transient beauty but on artistic acting techniques.[31] They are *onnagata*.

Onnagata, hence, epitomized the development of kabuki as a theatrical art in relation to political adversity. Much like the checkered history of kabuki, the process of establishing *onnagata* artistry was full of vicissitudes. It began as androgynous aesthetics nurtured in *wakashu kabuki*, then transformed itself into the imitation of women, and finally overcame imitation and achieved artistic femininity. This précis stands for what might be called the greatest common divisor between studies of kabuki and *onnagata*. There is hardly a hypothesis yet proposed that completely contradicts the three-stage trajectory itself, and yet that fact does not point to a single understanding of *onnagata* artistry. What defines artistic-artificial femininity is already cumbersome, allowing many proposals including the following: it symbolizes, idealizes, and emphasizes feminine qualities, which actresses cannot do;[32] it is "a profound symbol of the mystery of metamorphosis";[33] it is "a fiction of female-likeness based on a male 'body beneath.'"[34] Furthermore, many studies regard *onnagata* artistry as independent of the imitation of women. According to them, only nascent *onnagata* were engaged in imitation, as makeshift female-role players filling in for the expelled women performers, and their performance is summarized as imitations, impersonations, and descriptions of women. They regard the art of *onnagata* as something that was made possible later by overcoming these characteristics.[35] Nascent *onnagata* are here characterized as surrogates, and later *onnagata*—"real" *onnagata*—as metamorphoses.

The concept of imitation clearly was key to the establishment of *onnagata* artistry. Imitation was not something to be overcome but the very foundation of the methodology and techniques of *onnagata*. Eighteenth-century *onnagata* distinguished themselves from their predecessors through their successful imitation of women. Imitation enabled them to participate in the circulation of femininity, whence the paragons of womanhood,[36] and served as the basis for conceptualizing gender training and thereby reaching artistic perfection. This way of conceptualizing imitation is related to the theory and practice of cultivation (*shugyō*) that have been established by those involved in Japanese arts in general. Repetitive training based on the act of imitating not only improves the physical and mental conditions suitable for a particular form of art; rather, the training creates the very human being. This is a performative mechanism (repetitious actions create a being), although this version sets an intriguingly high value on essentialism and constructionism, offering rich room for discussion on the concept of performative. Practitioners of cultivation conceptualize a "second nature," achieved through cultivation, in an intimate relationship with "nature." The proximate pair of second nature and nature would later form a striking contrast to the modern polarized pair of the Artificial and the Natural. Cultivation thus concerns the cognitive problem of what defines a being, and its importance is comparable to that of the linguistic turn in gender studies and, by extension, Western philosophy. It is in this sense that imitation helps *onnagata*-artistry analysis contribute to the discussion of performativity.

It is thus a great loss to ignore this matter. The concept of imitation was not stigmatized until the relegation of the notion in modern times vis-à-vis the notion of an original.[37] In modernity, originality is given a privileged status, and imitation is the constitutive other in this paradigm. Given the inferior attribution of imitation, it is little wonder that *onnagata*'s femininity, once it came to be categorized as artistic femininity, could no longer afford to be associated with imitation. The denial of the association between imitation and *onnagata* artistry—and thus the solid demarcation between the "natural" femininity of women and the artistic-artificial femininity of *onnagata*—is vicious in at least two ways. In a theoretical sense, it hinders the effective perception of *onnagata* artistry, for it inevitably entails the closure of a citation circuit, which in turn nullifies the validity of performativity. It has both misinformed our understanding of *onnagata* artistry and helped thwart career building in this vocation by women. Theoretically as well as historically, the popular discourse in academia and beyond, which isolates the concept of imitation from *onnagata* artistry, has done more harm than good. Consequently, one of the tasks in the present book is to revisit the meanings of imitation in the context of four centuries of *onnagata* artistry.

This project, however, does not intend to present the comprehensive history of *onnagata* or kabuki. Many *onnagata* important to the history of *onnagata* and kabuki are omitted here in order to focus on themes related to femininity construction and the gender economy.[38] Methodologically, this book is characterized by several choices.

First, this is mainly an analysis of literature, such as theater reviews, *onnagata* treatises and interviews, and other kabuki-related publications. As a study of performance, its heavy reliance on literary texts would be peculiar were it not for several reasons. The circulation of femininity between *onnagata* and women is crucial for this analysis, meaning that not only the performance but also its reception, perception, and evaluation are of great import. Also, a genre of literary texts called "accounts-on-*gei*" (*geidan*) has played a vital role in communities involved in *gei* (acquired artistic technique). *Gei* is a blanket concept for nearly any technique, be it martial, literary, musical, or theatrical. The notion of acquisition is indispensable to the concept of *gei*, and practitioners are expected to master *gei* by internalizing it as second nature through long-term—often lifetime—training. Many *gei* practitioners (especially those in involved in theatrical *gei*) have expounded prolifically on the vocation to which they devote their lives. These literary texts make up the famous genre of accounts-on-*gei*. Hence, literary texts are of great importance for *gei* culture, and kabuki is no exception. If anything, kabuki has a specific connection with texts, as the kabuki culture during the Edo period was deeply integrated with the theater industry and publication culture.

Second, I pay much attention to female *onnagata*, who performed in public from the late nineteenth to the early twentieth century.[39] Even before that, female performers—including female *onnagata*—existed not only in the initial phase of kabuki's history (i.e., women's kabuki) but also in a marginalized, hidden quarter thereafter. Nevertheless, as kabuki had firmly established itself as an all-male theater by the mid-seventeenth century, female *onnagata* who performed in accordance with the established norms of kabuki dramaturgy have not attracted enough scholarly attention,[40] as they are not considered the mainstream of kabuki or *onnagata*. However, an analysis of female *onnagata* reveals the complexity of femininity construction in the discourse of *onnagata*, male and female. Moreover, the abjection of female *onnagata* in modern times is key to understanding the modern definition of *onnagata* artistry. In other words, the chief purpose of this book's inquiry into female *onnagata* is not so much to supplement kabuki historiography as to explore and expose what was made abjected and sacrificed for the sake of a system as a whole. Ultimately, what is worth probing is not just a periphery in and of itself but *how* it became marginalized (by what, on what grounds, and so on).

The highest compliment for female *onnagata* was "favorable" comparison to their male counterparts, saying, for instance, that once Actor X was on stage, it was impossible to tell that she was not a male. Such a female *onnagata* is a typical "honorary man," seemingly adapted to the men's world of kabuki. One can easily find her trapped in "the master's way of seeing."[41] Her excessively masculinized rendering of stereotyped femininity, however, helps us perceive the "historical constructs" of women.[42] These are especially visible when one contrasts her with her male counterpart. The best compliment that her contemporary male *onnagata* could win was identification with women in society, such that nobody noticed that Actor Y was not an actual woman in the restaurant. Moreover, *onnagata* artistry was, for both female and male actors, heavily based on masculinity, and yet both male and female *onnagata* found the highest sense of accomplishment in performing the role of a young, innocent, "truly feminine" princess. Despite their assimilation with male *onnagata*, female *onnagata* performed women's roles far beyond the confines of witches, bitches, and britches. With the aid of female *onnagata*, the labyrinth before us becomes visibly complicated. Accordingly, the juxtaposition of female and male *onnagata* enables us to contemplate several things. First, it helps emphasize the elusive nature of the *onnagata*'s cross-gender performance. In kabuki, female *onnagata* engage in the performance of femininity as cross-gender performance, revealing that the female "impersonation" of kabuki is not merely a stage phenomenon by the opposite sex but, rather, part of the mechanism of femininity construction in society. Furthermore, it helps problematize key concepts in gender theory. The *onnagata*'s gender practice is informative on the concept of performativity, one of the most powerful concepts in understanding gender: performativity negates both essentialism and constructionism. The discourse of *onnagata* seems to demonstrate, however, not only conformity with performativity but also interesting similarities with constructionism and essentialism, although neither constructionism nor essentialism alone is effective individually in the discourse of *onnagata*. In order to embody ideal femininity, Actor X, whose biological sex is female, has to attain the status of being indistinguishable from a man onstage. Likewise, in order to radiate ideal femininity, Actor Y, biologically male, has to pass as a woman in everyday life. In this discursive paradigm, constructionism and essentialism coalesce in creating ideal womanhood. Is it possible to assume, then, a case that exemplifies performativity and yet accords with constructionism and essentialism?

Another feature of the present book is a methodological prioritization of *how* over *what*. Echoing a strategic preference for gendering over gender, I pay attention to *how* femininity is constructed and perceived rather than *what* femininity is generated, because *how* questions can visualize the complicated mechanism of femininity construction that *what* questions would blur. For example, "The Words of Ayame" prescribes a method of femininity construction for *onnagata* similar to the ways in which its contemporary

Greater Learning for Women (Onna daigaku), a popular primer on womanhood, prescribes an approach to ideal femininity for women beyond the theater. The two texts detail attire, posture, attitudes, and daily chores. They share the process of creating gender (*how*), if not a specific form of gender in and of itself (the illusionary *what*). The nineteenth-century female *onnagata* Ichikawa Kumehachi I (ca. 1846–1913), for example, left an intriguing anecdote: she is said to have bound her breasts and deformed her vocal cords through rigorous voice training so that she could be a perfect kabuki actor, yet she was highly acclaimed for an *onnagata* performance that was said to be "truly feminine." This parallels frequent reviews of male *onnagata* by the time of Kumehachi: for instance, Actor Z is a genuine woman from the bottom up, no matter what exists under the loincloth. Here, both actors are acclaimed because they have attained a being (what we may want to call identity) through a doing (performance and training) independent of their physical conditions before their training, whether under a loincloth or a breast-binding cloth. What they share is the system of gender construction, that is, *how* to construct gender. Thus, *how* questions can aid in visualizing this mechanism of femininity construction, which defines femininity in terms of acquisition: that which is obtained through arduous training, whether onstage or offstage, by both men and women.

It is noteworthy that when they came into being in the seventeenth century, *onnagata* modeled themselves on the *wakashu* of the samurai class. Until the advent of *onnagata*, samurai *wakashu* were characterized as robust adolescents in male-male relationships who were diligently learning the samurai's way of manhood from partners who were both their seniors and their superiors. Starting from this military masculinity, *onnagata* eventually reached artistic perfection in the eighteenth century, when they were considered a reification of femininity. At that time, women and *onnagata*, as the doers of femininity, began circulating femininity through reciprocal imitation. Thus, within the short span of about a century, *onnagata* demonstrated a radical transformation from military masculinity to ideal femininity via what might be called androgynous aesthetics.

CHAPTER 1

Geneses of a Maze

Androgyne Fatale

I F Ayame is considered the "founder" (*kaisan*) and a "tutelary deity" (*uji-gami*) of *onnagata*,[1] then Ukon Genzaemon (b. 1622?) is known as the ancestor of *onnagata*.[2] Certainly, early-eighteenth-century theater-related publications use him as a point of reference when talking about the inception of *onnagata* traditions.[3] Regardless of whether it is possible to pin down one individual as the progenitor, a valid question in its own right, it is nevertheless quite revealing that Genzaemon has been considered a pioneer *onnagata*, for documents record his performance at the Ichimura-za Theater as early as 1648,[4] and thus his career covers both *wakashu kabuki* and *kabuki*, exemplifying continuity between the two. Furthermore, he is said to have devised methods of using a kerchief as a significant ornament for *onnagata* (*oki-tenogoi*, also *oki-tenugui*, which would later become *bōshi* [cap]), an accessory of epistemological importance.[5] His performance was also acclaimed by being associated with the name of an aristocratic poet of a bygone era, Ariwara-no Narihira (825–880). What was significant about a kerchief, or about Narihira?

A statement like "As actors playing women's roles, *onnagata* perform femininity" might appear plain and simple, but an analysis of *onnagata* of the seventeenth and early eighteenth centuries contradicts it. It would be somewhat far-fetched to say that the combination of the concepts "*onnagata*" and "femininity" was made possible by serendipity, but the combination was equally far from something natural that can be taken for granted. *Onnagata* transformed their gender from military masculinity to the androgynous gender and then to ideal femininity.

This trajectory was by no means linear. Initially, *onnagata* appeared to embody a practical continuity with their immediate predecessors, *wakashu*, but this continuity concealed an insidious yet radical theoretical discontinuity. The ensuing changes would be merely time-lag reifications of this theoretical discontinuity, which was overruled in practice when it happened and instead generated paradoxes as symptoms. The *onnagata*'s overdue reactions to this impasse resulted in the said trajectory. The most fundamental paradox lies in the fact that *onnagata* were made possible only by the theoretical negation of *wakashu*, yet they nonetheless depended on the practices and aesthetic of *wakashu*. This theoretical negation is the initial hidden discontinuity in the gender-formation trajectory of *onnagata*. Had it not been for this discontinuity, *onnagata* would never have become doers of womanhood, much less its paragons.

The said theoretical denial concerned two key characteristics of *wakashu*: transience, which was explicitly nullified in eighteenth-century *onnagata* methodology, and homogenderity, which was negated in the seventeenth century. The term "homogenderity" refers to the fact that *wakashu* (junior partners in male-male relationships) shared, or aimed at, a gender similar to that of their senior partners. The emergent popularity of androgynous aesthetics dramatically changed the *wakashu* gender itself, however, from military masculinity to something floating between feminine and masculine. This made the gender formation of *onnagata* in the seventeenth century elusive. *Wakashu* were transforming themselves into a new model, while nascent *onnagata*, themselves former *wakashu*, thus inherited the *wakashu* gender, which was in a state of flux.

To all intents and purposes, kabuki's *onnagata* had a strong continuity with *wakashu kabuki*'s female-role players, and neither *onnagata* nor *wakashu* modeled themselves on the purged female performers or, by extension, on women in general. We have seen that kabuki historiography pays much attention to the bans on female performers in 1629 and on *wakashu kabuki* in 1652. It might look as if the female-performer ban caused *wakashu* to replace women players, and the *wakashu-kabuki* ban resulted in the birth of *onnagata* as artists. The bans, however, did not create such a vacuum but provided a loophole, allowing continuity between *wakashu* and *onnagata*. This is not to negate the fact that the two bans required a long time to take root, as they certainly did.⁶ More important for our agenda is that the bans, even when successfully executed institutionally, conceded some continuation in practice, despite popular narratives that present the birth of kabuki (as theater) as totally divorced not only from women's kabuki but also from *wakashu kabuki* (as entertainment-cum-prostitution). This was to be expected due to the temporal overlap between women's kabuki and *wakashu kabuki* and the continuation of personnel—that is, actors—from *wakashu kabuki* to kabuki.

Wakashu kabuki's female-role players were not successors to ostracized women players in the strictest sense.⁷ *Wakashu kabuki* and its female-role players existed long before the 1629 female-performer ban. Kabuki performed by young boys was recorded as early as 1603, although it is not known when the term "*wakashu kabuki*" came into use.⁸ This temporal overlap suggests that the female players of women's kabuki and the female-role players of *wakashu kabuki* had been on stage as potential rivals for several decades. *Wakashu kabuki* certainly overtook women's kabuki in popularity after the female-performer ban, but it did not come into being because of it.⁹

Continuity of personnel would also be expected, considering the disparate implications of the female-player ban and the *wakashu-kabuki* ban. In 1652, *wakashu kabuki* faced a sweeping ban as had women's kabuki before it: "The twenty-third day of the tenth month [of 1629]. A notification issued by the Honorable Shimada [of the Edo Police Department]. Those activities of women's kabuki and the like performed these days at Edo are strictly prohibited. Thus, stop doing these hereafter."¹⁰ On closer examination, however, one cannot help but notice a radical difference between the two bans in terms of targets. Before the overall interdiction of their kabuki in 1652, *wakashu* were frequently "deprived" of their forelocks: "The twenty-seventh day of the sixth month [of 1652]. . . . Since *wakashu kabuki* is prohibited, [some] young boys' forelocks are forcibly shaved in the city."¹¹

The *wakashu-kabuki* ban targeted the forelocks of performers, emphasizing the significance of the *wakashu* forelock as a signifier: that is, the wearer's status as a male minor and, by extension, possibly (i.e., actual or eligible) a junior partner in a male-male relationship. Upon reaching adulthood—the exact age varied depending on many factors—*wakashu* shaved their foreheads and became non-*wakashu*. The *wakashu* found a loophole in this custom that was not available to the female performers who had been barred from performing. Whereas the female players could not officially return to the stage after the ban, *wakashu* were able to circumvent the ban by shaving off their forelocks regardless of their actual age and claiming that they were non-*wakashu*. Early *onnagata* were, in fact, ex-*wakashu* who were already playing female roles in *wakashu kabuki*.[12] They shaved off their forelocks, put purple kerchiefs on their foreheads, and returned to the stage. For example, Genzaemon is first mentioned in documents in 1648, and after the ban on *wakashu kabuki*, his performances are recorded in 1657, 1662, and 1676.[13] Therefore, it is not surprising that, as far as performance typology was concerned, kabuki had a strong congruity with *wakashu kabuki* and not with women's kabuki.[14] Rather, kabuki was "essentially a developed form of *wakashu kabuki* [with a shift in interest from dance to theater]."[15] Since kabuki's *onnagata* had substantial continuity with *wakashu kabuki*'s female-role players,[16] an exploration of *wakashu* will contribute to an effective understanding of the gender of *onnagata*.

Historically, male-male relationships already had a long tradition in the samurai class as well as the Buddhist community.[17] In this tradition, the Way of *wakashu* was not only a "normal component of male sexuality"[18] but also something by which townsmen, wealthy yet socially humble, could somehow identify with the prestigious samurai class. In this context, *wakashu* were initially characterized by two features in relation to *nenja*, their adult and superior partners: *wakashu* aimed at acquiring an appropriate gender similar to that of their partners, and *wakashu* were strictly transient beings. In this practice, a *wakashu* and his *nenja* would form a tight relationship analogous to a conjugal relationship, in which "sex was only one element."[19]

Importantly, an adolescent member of the samurai class would form a marriage-like relationship with an adult member of the class in order to internalize ideal samurai manhood: "The adult male lover ... was supposed to provide social backing, emotional support, and a model of manliness for the boy. In exchange, the boy was expected to be worthy of his lover by being a good student of samurai manhood. Together they vowed to uphold the manly virtues of the samurai class: to be loyal, steadfast, and honorable in their actions."[20] When the *wakashu* attained adulthood, which was symbolized by several changes in his appearance including a shaved forehead, "he was no longer available as a wakashu for sexual relations with adult men like himself but was now qualified to establish a relationship with a wakashu."[21] In this regard, the Way of *wakashu* somewhat corresponds to what Luce

Irigaray calls the exemplary homosexual relationship: "*father-son relationships*, which guarantee the transmission of patriarchal power and its laws, its discourse, its social structures."[22]

The father-son metaphor is effective in analyzing this samurai *nenja-wakashu* relationship and, by extension, for perceiving the gender of *wakashu* in this context, for two reasons. First, like father and son, this *nenja-wakashu* couple seems to be oriented toward the same gender. *Wakashu* were expected to learn (read copy) the samurai identity of *nenja*. Figuratively, *The Great Mirror of Male Eros* (Nanshoku ōkagami) by Ihara Saikaku (1642–1693) describes, and thus prescribes, many *wakashu* who are ostentatiously violent and thus manly.[23] This type of *wakashu*, though younger and "inferior" to his *nenja*, should not be weak or feminized. One who was so beautiful in a womanly manner that "nobody thinks of him as a male" could not even expect to have a *nenja*.[24] Second, just as the son is expected to become a father himself in order to transmit patriarchy from generation to generation, this *wakashu* is to become a *nenja* in order to transmit samurai manhood. The attribution of *wakashu* is thus strictly time-sensitive.[25] These two features of the samurai *wakashu-nenja* relationship originally determined the "nature" of the *wakashu* gender: homogenderity and transience. It is this *wakashu* with whom *wakashu* in the theater world, namely *wakashu kabuki*, were initially identified, as *The Great Mirror of Male Eros* "describes" (that is, prescribes in disguise) the commonality.[26]

It must have been a long journey for a copycat of a diligent student of samurai manhood to become a reification of ideal womanhood. To repeat, early *onnagata* were themselves formerly *wakashu* of *wakashu kabuki*. Their journey of radical transmutation consists of several phases, the first of which had already been in progress during the time of *wakashu kabuki*, when the homogenderity of the "original" *wakashu-nenja* relationship was denied. *The Great Mirror of Male Eros*, published in 1687, seems to have grasped the change in the gender of *wakashu*:

> In the past, the Way of male eros was rough, putting up a bold front. They spoke abrasively. *Wakashu* of large build were popular, and scratches on bodies were the sign of this Way of male eros. Even *wakashu* in the theatrical world inherited this [disposition].... Now is the time when even warriors do not need any armor. Then, there is no need for even a small knife at pleasure parties. Watermelon can be cut in the kitchen and served on plates, that's all. Those who are called *wakashu* are simply fragile.[27]

The text goes on to say that the names and clothing of *wakashu* in the theater circles of its day were feminized and compared them with those of female prostitutes.[28] Thus, the late seventeenth century saw a radical change in the characteristics of *wakashu*, whose gender, which used to be prescribed as homogendered in relation to that of their *nenja*, became something else.

The new way of playing with gender exemplifies a phenomenon of the time called *futanarihira*, from *futanari* (intersex; androgyny) and Narihira, the aristocratic male poet of the ninth century, who has been treated in the literary tradition as the quintessential beauty. "*Futanarihira*" means, therefore, "androgynous beauties." Imao Tetsuya defines the criteria for *futanarihira* as follows: "They are floating between the polarities of male and female, synthesizing *an sich* [in itself] the principles of both sexes, thereby radiating neutral ravishing sexuality, and thus pleasing both men and women."[29] As an actor-critique booklet published in the first month of 1720 put it, "In the time of Ukon [Genzaemon], *onnagata*'s appearance was vague and confusing (*omokage wa magirawashiku*)."[30]

The prevalence of *futanarihira* aesthetics is usually attributed to the end of a long period of war.[31] This change from multigenerational domestic belligerency to politically stable peacetime occurred slowly but definitely, and several battles in 1600, 1614–15, and 1637–38 served as milestones. This entailed not only social but also epistemological transformations, which were especially drastic for the samurai class. Simply put, in a battle-free society, the ruling warrior whose vocation lay in combat was an oxymoron. Various inversions occurred in reaction to this paradox, such as turning fighting skills into martial *arts*.[32] *Futanarihira* came to reify the criteria of trendy *wakashu* at this historical moment, and *wakashu*, including early *onnagata*, were bound by this aesthetic. The oft-quoted *kyōka*-poem by Nakarai Bokuyō (1607–1678) reads, "If you think it's a woman, it's a man, Mannosuke. Such is indeed an illusion of *futanarihira*."[33] Likewise, it was said in the *The Tales of Actors through All Ages* (Kokon yakusha monogatari), of 1678, that Genzaemon himself "look[ed] like a woman but he is in fact a man. His appearance is just like that of Narihira."[34] Sunaga Asahiko regards this as evidence that the connotations of the name Narihira were transformed from "noble prince" to "androgyny" around that time.[35] This appreciation of such vague *futanarihira* also appears foreign to the aforementioned remark in *The Great Mirror of Male Eros* indicative of what is expected of a desirable *wakashu*. It reads, should he be so beautiful in a womanly manner that "nobody thinks of [him] as a male," he could not even expect to have a *nenja*, which must have been ultimate failure for *wakashu*.[36] *Futanarihira* aesthetics remained dominant even among early-eighteenth-century *onnagata*.[37]

The term "*futanarihira*" requires an exegesis. It may impress some readers that a peaceful society embracing intersexuality is liberal and admirable.[38] The *futanarihira* phenomenon is not that innocent, however. First, a component of the term, *futanari*, implies that this understanding of intersexuality is strongly anchored to the dualistic notion of sex.[39] *Futa* means "two," and *nari* refers to either a "figure" or a state of "becoming."[40] What is more, the dualism in question manifests itself in these concepts in several ways.

Furthermore, *futanari* and *futanarihira* must be differentiated in the strict sense. Unlike *futanari*, *futanarihira* virtually points to males and resists being reduced to intersexuality. (Narihira, the poet, was male after all.) Also, considering the *wakashu* tradition, the age limitation must be a vital characteristic for beautiful *futanarihira* but not for *futanari*. The relationship between the concepts of *futanarihira* and *futanari* is intricate: proximate in some elements and yet totally differentiated in others. This elusive relationship reveals insidious notions about intersexuality behind the seemingly innocent idea of the beauty of androgyny. While *futanari* referred to intersexuality, *futanarihira* was used mainly to indicate the popular image of male minors and, by extension, desirable junior partners in male-male relationships. Boys who are attractive in a specific way cannot be equal to the intersex in general. Their gender aside, the sex of *futanarihira* must have been taken as male.[41] Simply put, they were "androgynous" but not androgyny. With the reification of the popular criteria for *wakashu*, their sex was (considered) male and their gender floated between femininity and masculinity. Both concepts still equally presuppose dualistic perception, and as language indicates, the society embracing "androgynous" beautiful boys had an unmistakably dualistic understanding of sex. *Futanari* builds on the binary understanding of sex, and *futanarihira* is based on the concept of *futanari*.

It is in this context that *futanari* were included in an anonymous late-twelfth-century scroll painting, *The Book of Disease* (Yamai no sōshi),[42] and *futanarihira* were considered beautiful *wakashu*. In this paradigm, *futanari* falls into the category of disease, along with anal fistulas, pyorrhea, lice, and so forth, whereas *futanarihira* amounts to a certain aesthetic. The contrast assigns a negative attribute to *futanari* and a positive attribute to *futanarihira*. Somewhere between *futanari* and *futanarihira*, there must have existed a boundary of abjection, from which *futanarihira* might have been "rescued" (by the princely Narihira?).[43] Significantly, the *futanari* depicted in *The Book of Disease* wears an *eboshi*, a hat worn by men after initiation into adulthood, signaling that the person, shown with a beard and a mustache, has been freed from the age limitations of *wakashu*.[44]

Dualism manifests itself diversely in the notions of *futanari* and *futanarihira*. *Futanarihira* in Bokuyō's poem cited earlier points to that-which-is-between, and such an idea is in line with the above-mentioned *futanarihira* criteria summarized by Imao. There also exists another understanding of *futanari* as that-which-has-two-extremes. The *Encyclopedia of the Heaven, Earth, and Humans in Japan and China* (Wakan sansai zue) (ca. 1712) defines *futanari* with characters meaning "half," "man," "woman," as well as those meaning "two" and "forms," and lists several types of *futanari*: those who have both male and female bodies; those who spend a half day (from midnight until early afternoon) as men and the rest of the day as women; and those who spend the first half of a month as men and the latter half as women.[45] The encyclopedia also introduces another term as its synonym, *haniwari* (half-month), which had already been included in the tenth-century *Classified Glossary of Japanese Nomenclature* (Wamyō ruijūshō, also Wamyō ruijushō): "One theory says that *haniwari* [spend] fifteen days out of thirty days per month as men and [another] fifteen days as women."[46] If the that-which-is-between is a dualistic understanding of sex that tries to unite the extremes, the that-which-has-both-extremes is another dualistic notion attempting to observe a split in the human body, be it diachronically or synchronically.

We should not regard these concepts of "between" and "both" as mutually exclusive, however, nor can we reduce their dissimilarity to the distinction between the terms "*futanarihira*" and "*futanari*." Occasionally, the term "*futanarihira*" is interchangeable with "*futanari*." A collection of *kayō*-song, *Collected Fallen Leaves* (Ochibashū) (1704), illustrates these issues, expressing the "both" idea in the context of a story about two long-necked persons. One night, Tokusai and his wife detach their heads from their bodies. The heads are sitting on an architrave (*nageshi*) high up in the room, exchanging soft words of love. When a friend surprises them, the husband and wife mistakenly go back to the other's body and thus become *futanarihira*.[47] Here, it is the body, instead of time, that is divided into two, just like one type of *futanari* in the eighteenth-century encyclopedia. Importantly, the genitalia do not really matter here, as is explicit in Tokusai's case. Behind the concept of *futanarihira* are such persistent attempts to understand intersexuality in a dichotomized sense; furthermore, the dualistic principles at work are not themselves monolithic.

Such reconfirmation might well seem clichéd, given that "the concept of intersexuality is rooted in the very ideas of male and female."[48] It is necessary to verify this point, however, because *futanarihira* aesthetics dealt with gender in a way that could potentially threaten dichotomized notions related to gender. *Wakashu*'s playing with gender appeared to obey and reinforce dualistic understandings of gender on the surface but in effect revealed its incompleteness and hence complicated the labyrinth of gendering.[49] *Futanarihira* maintained the sex identity of male and the gender identity of androgynous, implying that the two types of identity were not necessarily in a binding relationship.[50] Such a demarcation of sex identity and gender identity was also inherited by later *onnagata*, who overcame *futanarihira* aesthetics through rigorous gender training and thereby established the artistry of *onnagata*. They were both, in a sense, playing with the allegedly two "basic" genders. While retaining one that endorses male identity, *futanarihira* did another gender that was located between the two, and *onnagata* performed the two genders simultaneously. *Wakashu* at this historical moment were about to lose an important defining characteristic, that is, the shared gender of their partners in male-male relationships. Likewise, the other feature of the *wakashu* gender, transience, was also at stake.

PART II

Femininity Inside Out

Onnagata Who Pass

> If expressing diversity in creation is burdensome, then making an abso-bloody-lutely exact copy of something is also taxing to the same extent. Raphael would be troubled if he were forced to paint two completely different paintings of Madonna, with no resemblance whatsoever between them, but he would be equally at a loss if someone put in an order for two identical paintings of the Holy Mother. Come to think of it, it might be way more bothersome to paint two identical ones. Kōbō Daishi would be in trouble if somebody requested, "Your autograph, 'Kūkai,' in exactly the same brushstrokes as yesterday's, would you please, sir." Who knows, that might be much more trying than "Please totally change the style"? . . . Humans have no ability of perfect imitation.
>
> —NATSUME SŌSEKI, *Wagahai wa Neko de Aru* (164–65)

CHAPTER 2

Denial of Transience

Forfeiting the Androgynous Charm

IN the Edo era, kabuki was so popular that many publications about it circulated. One such popular genre (and indeed critical for kabuki studies) were actor-critique booklets. Several actor-critique booklets in the early eighteenth century contrast *onnagata* of their time with *onnagata* at the nascent stage. An issue published in the first month of 1720 reads:

> [Women these days are careful in their appearances.] Nobody other than their mirrors, which they use day and night, knows their innate disgraceful features.... This is also the case for *onnagata*.... In the time of Ukon [Genzaemon], the *onnagata*'s appearance was vague and confusing [*omokage wa magirawashiku*]. They made themselves up roughly, placing just kerchiefs [*oki-tenogoi*, also *oki-tenugui*] on their heads. Audiences back then accepted [this rough-and-ready appearance], and, compared to what we have today, there were also weird things in plays' plots.[1]

The implication here is intriguing. Unlike early *onnagata* such as Genzaemon, *onnagata* in the early eighteenth century made themselves up carefully (just like their female contemporaries), and their appearance was no longer vague or confusing. The writer seems to suggest that the makeup

[33]

technology had now become much more meticulous. What had become "clear," and according to what? What differentiates eighteenth-century *onnagata* from their predecessors? If Genzaemon and his fellow *onnagata* were ambiguous in appearance, what was unmistakable about the likes of Ayame?

During the eighteenth century, the art of *onnagata* was brought to perfection. Two *onnagata* treatises produced at that time, which express the ideas of two renowned *onnagata* including Ayame, have long been referred to as the foundation of *onnagata* artistry, and their ideas are still used as points of reference for discussions of *onnagata* performances. By examining the configuration of how the *onnagata*'s performance was theorized at that time, we can expect to understand the foundation of *onnagata* artistry and to see the logic and operation of femininity construction in this localized context.

The gender of *onnagata* in the eighteenth century relied on training seeking prolonged femininity in order to overcome the transient nature of the *wakashu* gender. Compelled by social conditions to remain *wakashu*—that is, *young* boys—yet prohibited from doing so by the imperative of transience of the *wakashu* aesthetic, eighteenth-century *onnagata* were in need of protracting their stage lives by training themselves to be doers of another gender, namely, femininity. The allure of ambiguity, so characteristic of *futanarihira*, was canceled—forfeited if not relinquished—through the *onnagata*'s solution to this paradox of perpetual transience. Their prescription for femininity completed the transformation of the *onnagata* gender, brought the art of *onnagata* to perfection, and thereby made possible *onnagata* as paragons of womanhood.[2] Interestingly, even at this decisive moment of radical departure from *wakashu*, *onnagata* were haunted by memories of *wakashu*, which showed how dramatic—radical yet insidious—the transformation was.

This newly acquired perpetuity had particular implications. Theoretically, "perpetual male minors" are a contradiction in terms, and "perpetual *wakashu*" were thus logically impossible. Paradoxically, however, becoming "perpetual *wakashu*" was the only possible strategy if *wakashu* in theater circles were to survive. In practice, this strategy initially appeared to be a blessing, albeit a tricky one. *The Great Mirror of Male Eros* reads:

> When [*wakashu*] *kabuki* was prohibited and *wakashu* had to become fellow men by shaving their forelocks, not only they but also their masters grieved

as if buds had fallen before their time. In hindsight, however, nothing could have been luckier. No matter how wonderful male eros is, it is impossible for anyone over twenty to perform the *wakashu* part, keeping his forelock. It is possible for fellow men in their mid-thirties, however, to be hugged, pretending they are *wakashu*. The Way of eros seems peculiar.... Actors can play on a dimly lit stage.... As far as performance is concerned, it is no problem that *wakashu* over seventy wear long-sleeve *kimono* [an outfit exclusively for youth].[3]

This "timelessness" was precarious, because somatic youth was considered the source of *wakashu* beauty. The same text also teases a thirty-eight-year-old *wakashu*, who is embarrassed when his age is disclosed.[4] After all, "the peak of *wakashu* lasts only four or five years, [which is much shorter than women's]."[5] *Onnagata* may have opened a Pandora's box, but they had no alternative in the society in which they lived.

Socially, overcoming transience was imperative for *wakashu* in the theatrical world. Those who were assigned the *wakashu* part in the *wakashu-nenja* economy of the samurai class would someday become *nenja* themselves, but their equivalents in theater circles did not have such mobility. As defined by the shogunate, theater was contiguous—or even synonymous—with prostitution. Playhouses were categorized as "evil places" (*akusho*) along with brothels. *Wakashu* in the catamite teahouses could not become *nenja*, that is, buyers, unless they changed their financial, and probably social, status quite dramatically. Ayame talks about Tachibanaya Gorozaemon, an important patron and no doubt his *nenja*, in great detail in his treatise,[6] but there was no *wakashu* figure with whom Ayame would have had a relationship had he become a *nenja* himself. Ayame is said to have been born into a samurai family, and around the age of five, he was sold as an *iroko* (child of eros), that is, a boy prostitute for pederasts, due to his father's adversity or death.[7] Had he remained a samurai-class member, he would no doubt have become a *nenja*. Thus, those like Ayame were most likely destined to be *wakashu* for as long as they remained within the confines of the *wakashu-nenja* economy.

By definition, a *wakashu* aims to achieve what Zeami calls a "temporary bloom," and an *onnagata* aspires to obtain "the true Flower."[8] Importantly, a *wakashu*'s temporary bloom is not as something that will someday turn out to be the true Flower, making transience the decisive feature that defines *wakashu*. Buddhism might also have contributed to the emphasis on the transient nature of *wakashu* aesthetics. Impermanence is an important premise for the Buddhist cosmology, and male-male relationships also flourished in the Buddhist community.

The *wakashu-kabuki* ban could not help but create a loophole in the law of transience, which presented *onnagata* with an insidious paradox, as the *wakashu*'s pseudosignifier, namely, the kerchief covering the shaved forehead, not only substituted for the lost forelock but generated "perpetuity." The importance of the kerchief, later refined as the *bōshi*-cap, is so great that the cap eventually came to indicate *onnagata* metonymically. The new regulation required that all actors cut their forelocks earlier than *wakashu* custom required, and because anybody over the age of fourteen had to dress his hair in the adult masculine style, without the forelock,[9] all actors, including those who otherwise were qualified to be considered *wakashu*, lost the signifier, the forelock. Now that nobody could claim to be a *wakashu*, ironically, anybody could claim that he would have been one were it not for the regulation. The purple kerchief that an *onnagata* donned after shaving his forelock was the pseudosignifier of the youth, and the *onnagata* putting on the kerchief was a paradoxical being in the sense that he was a perpetual *wakashu*, a reified impossibility. It took a while for this theoretical paradox to make itself visible.

With no compulsory retirement age, *onnagata* now had to perform indefinitely. The ephemeral *futanarihira* aesthetic of *wakashu* could no longer be the principle of *onnagata*. Something had to change so that a temporary bloom could transform himself into the true Flower, a male actor who represented ideal femininity through his art. It was the early-eighteenth-century virtuosos—Ayame, Kikunojō, and the like—who, by meticulous gender training, made the shift final, bringing the art of *onnagata* to perfection.

CHAPTER 3

Prescription for Femininity

Onnagata Who Pass

THE art of the *onnagata* is said to have been brought to perfection by Ayame, who came to be regarded as "the guardian deity of the Way" of *onnagata*.[1] "The Words of Ayame" has long been treated as one of the most important and influential *onnagata* treatises. Of secondary importance is the so-called "Secret Transmissions of an *Onnagata*" (Onnagata hiden), which contains the ideas of Kikunojō, who allegedly followed the Way paved by Ayame.[2] These two texts play a significant role in our quest for the logic and operation of femininity construction by *onnagata*.

"The Words of Ayame," included in *The Actors' Analects* (Yakusha banashi) (1776),[3] contains broad analyses of not only technique but also the underlying thought of *onnagata* art, and "The Secret Transmissions of an *Onnagata*," included in *The Pioneering Analects from Past and Present Actors* (Kokon yakusha rongo sakigake) (1772),[4] focuses on technique.[5] They are both situated at the interesting juncture where the *onnagata* gender was transformed. Scholarship on *onnagata* tends to regard the *onnagata* art of perfection at that time as a metamorphosis and not sheer mimicry, a disposition said to be evident in "The Words of Ayame." The two treatises, however, do not aim at such a metamorphosis; rather, they suggest that the foundation of the *onnagata* art of perfection was meticulous gender training in which the performative for *onnagata* was based on what the likes of Ayame considered the constative of women.

In contrast to the transient nature of *wakashu*, perpetuity is proposed as the imperative in both texts. The last section of "The Words of Ayame" discusses the importance of remaining young for *onnagata*: "For one thing, for those who are called *onnagata*, there is the appellation of *waka-onnagata* [or *waka-oyama* (young *onnagata*)] [which may be used] even when one is over forty. It is reasonable to call him simply an *onnagata*, but the character *waka* [young] is added. Therefore, he should not let a flowery feeling go. Even though it is a small thing, this character of *waka* amounts to an issue of great moment for *onnagata*. I humbly overheard him say this to someone in a lesson session" (section 29).[6] "The Secret Transmissions of an *Onnagata*" is even more ambitious, asserting that an *onnagata* should not cease his efforts to remain young for his entire life. It suggests that an *onnagata* dress himself on his deathbed and put on the *bōshi*-cap, the signifier of *onnagata*, which began as a surrogate signifier of youth. Kikunojō himself is known to have done this on his deathbed in 1749.[7] Indeed, a 1750 document describes him as follows: "It was unbelievable that beautiful long-sleeve *kimono* [for youth] suited him very well even when he was merely two or three years shy of sixty."[8]

Kikunojō and Ayame were both faithful to the principle of perpetual youth, although Ayame's case is more nuanced. An actor-critique booklet published in the first month of 1719 describes Ayame as "peerless in all the three cities [*sangoku musō*]" when he was forty-seven.[9] He retained similar—or even higher—rankings and reputation for a year or two ("number one in all the three cities" in the third month of 1719, and "number one in Japan" in the first month of 1720),[10] but remarks indicating an imminent crisis began to creep into reviews. For instance, another issue of the booklet in the first month of 1720 began by describing Ayame as an "incomparable virtuoso" but ended with "Even if [Ayame were] made [the rank of] the number one of all actors [beyond *onnagata*], Granny would be trustworthy indeed."[11] In the ensuing month, it became more than an allusion: Ayame, ranked as "peerless in all the three cities," was critically acclaimed as a virtuoso, yet some asked whether he should be called the incomparable virtuoso among *kashagata* (those specializing in old women) and not among all *onnagata* (including *waka-onnagata*) any longer, as he was no longer good at love scenes.[12] This review was presented in the format of a round-table discussion, and it was furiously denied ("Nonsense! Say one more word, and I'll cut you down like a gourd!"), but Ayame's age was clearly an issue. Eventually, in 1721, he quit playing women's roles and tried to shift his career to male-role acting against the prohibition of his own *onnagata* instruction.[13] His decision was lamented in an actor-critique booklet issued in the first month of 1722: "The *onnagata* celebrated in all the three cities has now become a male-role actor, in view of the times. It is as if Nachi had lost the moon and all the flowers had vanished from Kōya."[14] After failure as a male-role actor, he resumed his part as an *onnagata* soon afterward, and subsequent reviews again praised him as "incomparable" (the third month of 1723, and the first and third months of 1724).[15] His entire acting career exemplifies the paradoxes and contradictions resulting from the imperative of perpetuity.

For the sake of perpetuity, the treatises methodize meticulous, conscious, long-term gender training that aims at achieving "womanliness," which is categorically foreign to the former popularity of *futanarihira*. Whereas Bokuyō appreciated an androgynous boy, writing, "If you think it's a woman, it's a man, Mannosuke. Such is indeed an illusion of *futanarihira*,"[16] "The Words of Ayame" now declares the opposite: "[Thinking about Ayame's point], I was humbly impressed that, according to the principle [of things], there is no such being-body [*mi*] that can become a woman and a man [alike]" (section 10).[17] Likewise, while a *wakashu* could not afford to be so beautiful in a womanly manner to the extent that "nobody thinks of [him] as a male" because, according to *The Great Mirror of Male Eros*, such *wakashu* would not be able to have a *nenja*,[18] "The Secret Transmissions of an *Onnagata*" asserts to the contrary: "An *onnagata* must wish as follows. He must have many male admirers who wish, 'If only there were a woman like this'" (section 9).[19] It is an illusionary or surrogate female eros (*joshoku*) that this *onnagata* should aim for, rather than a "genuine" male eros (*nanshoku*), as defined in *The Great Mirror of Male Eros*.[20] In this paradigm, male eros is set in opposition to, and superior to, female eros, and in that context, a *wakashu* is the preferable partner for a man. The shift from transient beauty to perpetual art thus involves a shift to the projection of a surrogate female eros set in a surrogate context of male-female relationships.[21] The two *onnagata* treatises similarly provide a striking contrast to *futanarihira*.

"The Secret Transmissions of an *Onnagata*" continues: "As for women admirers, an *onnagata* should make them adore the fashions he likes—such as combs, hairpins, the [forehead] cap, clothing, and sashes. You should wish that your fashions would be imitated by women at samurai's residences, courtesans, and young [nonprofessional] girls. Make them think that you are a woman just as they are. [That is the most important point] when it comes to female admirers" (section 9).²² "The Words of Ayame" advises *onnagata* not to play men's roles, relating the incompatibility between women's and men's roles onstage to that of women and men offstage:

> For one thing, if he who is an *onnagata* thinks of male-role acting as the alternative to *onnagata*, the alternative in case he cannot make it as an *onnagata*, his *gei* [acquired artistic technique] would turn into debris. He should understand that a real woman [*hon no onago*] would not become a man. Is it possible for an actual woman [*hon no onna*] to become a man when something goes wrong [with her life as a woman]? If he thinks that way, he proves himself ignorant about women's sentiments. So it was said [by Ayame], and it was compelling. [Section 11]²³

This incompatibility of men's and women's roles is, according to Ayame, analogous to that of men and women offstage: "For one thing, if he who is an *onnagata* thought that he might be good at male-role acting, that would be a shame among shames. If an *onnagata* is acclaimed when becoming a male-role actor, he must have been bad when he was an *onnagata*. If an *onnagata* becomes a male-role actor and is poor at it, he must be good as an *onnagata*. Ayame used to say this, and when Ayame became a male-role actor, he was certainly bad at it" [section 10].²⁴ Cynical though it is, therefore, Ayame's failure at switching to male-role acting proves his point effectively.²⁵ The two texts methodize scrupulous, heedful, and lifelong gender training that aims at liberation from the strict time limit imposed on *wakashu*.

The two texts catalog the behavior of female humans. "The Secret Transmissions of an *Onnagata*" contains ten mostly technical sections,²⁶ which show that women under various conditions, such as in a specific emotional state or in a particular social class, manifest different appearances. These sections prescribe how to look like women in different situations by using props and makeup for a womanly appearance (sections 1, 2, 6, and 7); paying attention to the interaction between women's appearance and states, whether emotional or social (sections 3, 4, and 5); and using cosmetics to keep an *onnagata*'s face wrinkle-free (section 8).²⁷

In comparison, "The Words of Ayame" is a much longer document, containing twenty-nine narrative sections.²⁸ Far more detailed than the terse instructions in "The Secret Transmissions of an *Onnagata*," the contents of "The Words of Ayame" also appear relatively more philosophical. The text is full of what Imao calls "ethics."²⁹ Ayame requires that *onnagata* keep their appearance mischievous and coquettish yet their minds chaste (section 3); live as women in their everyday lives (section 7); hesitate to perform strong women's roles (section 8); avoid trying to make the audience laugh (section 9); give the highest priority to chastity (section 13); remain *onnagata* even in the dressing room (section 22); hide their wives and children (section 23); try not to deviate from women's sentiments (section 24); and remain young (section 29).³⁰ Emphasis on the physical and formal is not limited to "The Secret Transmissions of an *Onnagata*," nor is a focus on the mental and conceptual exclusive to "The Words of Ayame." Rather, the physical and the mental are adjacent, and so are the formal and the conceptual in this context. The mental conceptualization of a womanly appearance in "The Words of Ayame" is also coupled with practical instructions on bodily movement (sections 2, 6, 12, and 24).³¹ *Onnagata* should always remain conscious of a womanly appearance, physically as well as mentally.

At first glance, these instructions seem to show that this "womanliness" is specifically constructed as "femininities that should be opposed to masculinity." Such an idea in and of itself is rather mundane as a cognitive praxis, that is, femininity is being conceptualized as the constitutive other of masculinity, and vice versa, for that matter, and thus masculinity and femininity are in the relation of *différance*. The way in which the texts prescribe femininity for *onnagata* to that end is intriguing in what they reveal about their presuppositions concerning gender and femininity, although the ideas in these texts are not entirely original, unprecedented, or unique. In the traditions and communities involved in *gei*, or acquired artistic technique, the concept that one's artistic creativity is inseparable from the act of internalizing—and being internalized in—a tradition in which one is located was already firmly established.³² Such texts as "The Words of Ayame" and "The Secret Transmissions of an *Onnagata*" demonstrate ideas on what *onnagata* must materialize in terms of gender. These ideas, which are radically differentiated from those of their predecessors (i.e., *wakashu*), established *onnagata* artistry and thus helped determine *onnagata* traditions down through the ages.

Their prescription for femininity for *onnagata* involves several issues. First of all, "The Words of Ayame" comments positively on the alleged natural masculinity inside *onnagata*'s bodies, despite the much-quoted section 7: "It is hardly possible for an *onnagata* to be considered proficient unless he spends his everyday life as a woman."³³ Masculinity is taken for granted: "If an *onnagata* is good at a high-ranking courtesan role, then all other [women's roles] come easily. This is because [an *onnagata* is] originally [*moto ga*] a man, so that he possesses from birth something stern and sharp [*kitto shitaru koto*]" (section 1).[34] Their masculinity is also regarded as something they must utilize for certain roles: "For one thing, [there are points about when] one becomes a samurai's wife who handles a sword. One must manage the sword in a mannish way, when, for instance, you play the role of someone who, chased by a large force, tries to protect a princess" (section 6).[35] Ayame further suggests that *onnagata* conceal their wives and children but seems not to question whether to have them in the first place: "For one thing, an *onnagata* should hide that he has a wife. He could not act as an *onnagata*, much less go up in the world, if he did not blush when asked about his wife. No matter how many children he may have, he feels as if he were a child himself. That is the nature of a skillful *onnagata*" (section 23).[36] In this regard, even in their radical departure from *wakashu*, *onnagata* share an intriguing feature with them. They both retain "masculinity" in one way or another, yet this positive evaluation of masculinity did not immediately result in the present-day understanding of *onnagata* artistry, namely, that only men can genuinely enact this artistry.[37] The reason for that is related to another point in their prescription of femininity for *onnagata*.

Positing these masculine features as the opposite criteria, "The Words of Ayame" presents the performative for *onnagata*, which is often tagged as the "constative" of women: weak (section 8); bad at making people laugh (section 9); likely to flinch in front of many people (section 12); chaste (section 13).[38] "The Words of Ayame" and "The Secret Transmissions of an *Onnagata*" justify *onnagata* instructions on the grounds that "real women (*hon no onna*) do it this way," that is, the "constative" of women. (Should it be a constative statement that "woman is chaste," however, how are we supposed to interpret the various codes against adultery that can be found in many societies?) On the non-comical attribute of women, "The Words of Ayame" reads: "For one thing, I heard Ayame tell Jūjirō [another *onnagata*] as follows. Good for you, [your performance was] very well received. But you should cease desiring to make the audiences laugh. It will be fine if they laugh spontaneously, seeing the action. It is not women's feelings [*onna no jō*] to attempt to make [people] laugh on purpose. [At that time] Jūjirō looked slightly upset, but when I saw him later, he said that he thought of Ayame as the guardian deity of this Way [of *onnagata*]" (section 9).[39]

Likewise, "The Secret Transmissions of an *Onnagata*" bluntly "observes":

"For one thing, when they are upset, women first cry before a speech" (section 4).[40] Here, the latter sentence or clause in each case is presented as (if it were) the objective truth about women (constative), which is *made* to support Ayame's or Kikunojō's point. A pure hypothetical constative statement is one in which a speaker removes all the possible variables and simply and objectively describes a fact. Postmodern examinations of performativity have revealed the formidable difficulty of this. Therefore, we should rather regard constative as performative in disguise, unwittingly or otherwise: The A-is-B type of statement is most likely to assign the B attribute to A. Given this, one may consider the statements (that women first cry when upset and that it is not women's feelings to make [people] laugh on purpose) to be bracketed by the unstated, or even unrecognized, remark "I pronounce that." Therefore, the *onnagata*'s conceptualization of a womanly appearance is an observation of how they look and at the same time a prescription of how they should look. This ambiguous relationship between performative and constative has a flip side: the possibility that the performative for *onnagata* can technically amount to the "constative" of women, whence the paragons of womanhood.

Regardless of theoretical precariousness, the concept of constative is important in two ways. It affects readers, as constative statements imply expectation, regulation, and prohibition. And if *onnagata* theorize femininity based on what they claim as constative, even if illusionary, it is impossible to dissociate "imitation" from their construction of femininity. Whether in scholarly or popular writings, the dominant understanding of *onnagata* holds that the femininity *onnagata* present differs from women's femininity (however it may be defined). This notion coexists with several statements that are now almost taken for granted: that *onnagata* do not imitate women and that *onnagata* create artificial and artistic femininity independent of, and unavailable to, biological women. For example, Katherine Mezur states: "Imitation of real women was never the goal [of *onnagata*]"[41] and "women cannot enact the onnagata fiction of female-likeness because they do not have a male sexed body beneath."[42] These may apply to contemporary *onnagata*, but even they nevertheless build their theorization of femininity construction on what Ayame and others established in the eighteenth century. Certainly, female *onnagata* would later be abjected, but that was due to a historical circumstance and not because the *onnagata*'s constructed femininity was foreign to, or impossible for, women's performance of the gender. Rather, they were abjected precisely because they were capable of enacting *onnagata*'s femininity and because their ability to do so was perceived as "inconvenient" in the historical circumstances. Such historicity was foreign to eighteenth-century *onnagata*. On the contrary, the persistent usage of constative statements in such texts as "The Words of Ayame" and "The Secret Transmissions of an *Onnagata*" suggests that they conceptualized womanliness based on what they believed to be the objective truth about women, which they simply "observe."

Ayame and his treatise "The Words of Ayame" have played a major role in English-language writings about kabuki and *onnagata*. Earle Ernst wrote in his 1956 book *The Kabuki Theatre*: "Yoshizawa Ayame (1673–1729), a famed player of women's roles, wrote in his book *Ayame-gusa*, 'If an actress were to appear on the stage she could not express ideal feminine beauty, for she would rely only on the exploitation of her physical characteristics, and therefore not express the synthetic ideal. The ideal woman can be expressed only by an actor.'"[43] Based on this claim, allegedly made by Ayame, Ernst continues: "From this point of view of the design of the production, the *onnagata* is necessary because, according to the Japanese, although the surface of the woman portrayed should be soft, tender, and beautiful, beneath this surface there should be a strong line, which can be created only by a man. A man of eighty plays the role of a girl and, because of his mastery of the vocabulary of Kabuki acting, creates before the audience a stronger theatre reality of her essential qualities than could any woman."[44]

Thus far no phrase in "The Words of Ayame" bears out, however slightly, the words he is alleged to have said,[45] and considering Ayame's constant observation of those whom he calls "actual women," which appears in the form of unrelenting "constative" statements, it is difficult not to conclude the opposite—that is, this text did not propose that *onnagata* artistry was unavailable to women. (Female *onnagata* would later prove that he was indeed correct.) This does not efface the fact, however, that the idea in Ernst's book—disguised as Ayame's—impinges on the images of the text, the *onnagata*, and *onnagata* as a whole in English-language works. It has had a lasting effect, not only in the context of Japanese theater or culture,[46] but also in gender studies and theater studies beyond the confines of Japanese materials.[47] Figuratively, one work cites "The Words of Ayame" itself but nonetheless adds the said excerpt Ernst attributed to Ayame in his monograph.[48] This image of Ayame created by Ernst might not necessarily be the most typical or dominant understanding in English-language kabuki studies today,[49] but the lingering references prove its popularity.

The popularity of Ernst's idea is informative not so much of *onnagata*'s theorization of femininity construction in eighteenth-century Japan as of the speakers' conceptualization of *onnagata* and, by extension, of female impersonation. The prevalence of the narrative that eighteenth-century *onnagata* artistry was conceptualized as an artistic artifact unavailable to women indicates that people have so internalized the popular image of contemporary *onnagata* that it is difficult for scholars to problematize it as that which plays a role in the presupposition of their perception. In addition, Ayame's supposed statement bears an uncanny correspondence to Roland Barthes's lyrical remark on the "Oriental transvestite": "The Oriental transvestite does not copy Woman but signifies her: not bogged down in the model, but detached from its signified; Femininity is presented to read, not to see: translation, not transgression."[50] This also neatly fits into feminist attention to female impersonation: "the fictionality of the patriarchy's representation of the gender."[51] It appears, therefore, that this alleged "eighteenth-century-*onnagata* notion" can well support, and has been made to help support, our knowledge in gender studies and women's studies that Woman is a cultural product, specific to each societal and historical environment, that is rigorously constructed through the "male gaze" of society.[52] The purported words of Ayame were a perfect fit for this narrative.

Then, do the absence of the said citation—and furthermore the abundant counterevidence in the text—cancel the potential contribution that the discourse of *onnagata* once seemed to promise for gender studies? I do not think so. The discourse of *onnagata* did eventually materialize the concept of constructed, artistic Woman detached from women, which happened much later in the early twentieth century. However, even modern *onnagata*'s theory and practice were not totally independent of their Edo-era predecessors', as they were created "anew" but in relation to the traditions. Just as early *onnagata* relied on *wakashu* in practice while refusing them in theory, the modern *onnagata*'s relationship with eighteenth-century *onnagata* is complicated and ambiguous. In the time of Ayame and Kikunojō, moreover, their involvement in the construction of femininity in society was far more elusive and dubious than a static model of patriarchy's—or men's, for that matter—fiction of femininity. It might certainly be damaging for women if patriarchy is to impose its fiction of femininity on them in an illocutionary speech act, but conceptualizing a specific definition of femininity as the illusionary constative of "real women" could have been more so.[53]

Another characteristic of the prescription for femininity in the two *onnagata* treatises is the weight of "class" and "degree." "The Words of Ayame" conceptualizes femininities according to these two criteria, which intermingle in an intriguing way. As Jennifer Robertson puts it, class was, along with sex and age grades, a binding factor in determining one's female-likeness: "This hierarchy of ideal social and occupational statuses was further complicated by coexistent operations of a separate sex-gender system, which effectively bisected each of the four social classes into female and male divisions. Age grades provided additional denominators."[54] Socially, the male-female distinction had been a lesser difference than class differences in premodern times, that is, before the Meiji period.[55] Class was, therefore, one of the factors *onnagata* had to take into account in order to decide what kind of femininity was necessary for a particular role. Ayame focuses his attention on this issue (sections 2, 3, 6, and 12), and so does Kikunojō (section 5).[56]

Moreover, "The Words of Ayame" adds another criterion for prioritizing femininity, the degree of femininity:

> For one thing, a certain *onnagata* inquired of Mr. Yoshizawa the following. Of what had *onnagata* better take heed? Mr. Yoshizawa replied as follows. As long as an *onnagata* is good at a high-ranking courtesan role, then all other [women's roles] come easily. This is because [an *onnagata* is] originally a man, so that he possesses from birth something stern and sharp. Were it not for special attention, it would be impossible for him as a man [or with a man's body] [*otoko no mi nite*] to [embody] the characteristics of a high-ranking courtesan, that is, naive [*adome mo naku*] and soft [*bonjari*]. Accordingly, give priority to the lessons in a high-ranking courtesan's role. [Section 1][57]

The argument is seemingly simple. The courtesan is considered challenging to perform because she has something that is located at the furthest extreme from what *onnagata* have from birth. The discrepancy is understood to be a matter of distance, a degree of space, metaphorical or otherwise (setting aside the problems of what this "something" is that the courtesan is said to have and of another "something" claimed to be an inborn property of the *onnagata*).

Imao defines what "The Words of Ayame" says as "something stern and sharp" as "the masculine principle" (*dansei-teki genri*) and "naive and soft" as "the opposite idea" (*taikyoku no idē*), and he praises as acute Ayame's idea that men possess the former and lack the latter. Accordingly, he states: "It is no coincidence that 'The Words of Ayame' begins with this clause. This is the most important part [of this treatise], which is the opening and at the same time the conclusion of the entire twenty-nine clauses."[58] Similarly, Samuel L. Leiter introduces this section as follows "The [high-ranking courtesan] is the antithesis of masculinity, being soft instead of hard, gentle instead of rough, delicate instead of strong."[59] On the whole, this understanding seems not to have been seriously questioned in kabuki studies.[60] Kawatake Toshio gives a more detailed and nuanced account:

> The meaning [of section 1] should be obvious. A man disguises himself as a woman as that which is the opposite [hankyoku no onna]. Originally, men and women alike possess some elements of their opposite sexes. But she who is a high-ranking courtesan is, regardless of her true nature, at least on the level of outward appearance, an existence that is completely made up for the sake of men, the existence collecting all the elements of female-likeness and eliminating any element of male-likeness. At least, she should be like this. Accordingly, as far as a male actor is concerned, it is the ultimate transformation [to perform this], the difficulty of which lies in the fact that he has no clue in his everyday experience. If he masters it, [Ayame says,] other things should be easy.[61]

Thus, for Kawatake, not only the role but also the model for it is already a role that the *onnagata* is performing.

> She who is a high-ranking courtesan is a woman in a different world than the ordinary world of such mundane women as the wives of samurai and townsmen, their daughters, maids, and the like. She lives solely for the purposes of winning men's favor and providing them with sexual satisfaction. She shouldn't be argumentative or stiff, and she ought to embody sex appeal, charm, tenderness, modesty, that is, all those things that regular men do not have. Thereby, she has to be an incarnation of "that which is a woman in and of itself" as the opposite of men. That which is the ideal opposite sex, from men's viewpoint, [is a high-ranking courtesan]. And it is the biggest transformation for a male actor to disguise himself as such. If he can do it, the rest must be easy. Therefore, *onnagata* [such as Ayame] examined, in the existence of a high-ranking courtesan as a model, the value of women that is not recognized by women themselves and the whereabouts of their beauty, which can be found only through men's perspective. They analyzed these in terms of forms and reconstructed them with emphasis [kyōchōteki ni saikōsei] by negating their own selves as men. It is how they tried to overcome the biggest challenge of their bodies, that is, they cannot become women after all.[62]

Two qualifying points specified here indicate that *onnagata* reconstruct what is already constructed and that the latter—that is, what is already constructed by a high-ranking courtesan—can be differentiated from the ordinary world. (However, is this "ordinary world" a site where ordinary women evince what is not constructed?)

Ayame holds that this "naive and soft" feature is a characteristic applicable, to one degree or another, to all other women, and that the courtesan has more of it than other women do. She is *more* feminine, and "thus" *less* masculine, than other women are. (The word "thus" is in quotation marks because femininity and masculinity are placed in a certain relationship here, but one should not take the presumed correlation for granted.) Other women share this essence (the core of femininity) to a lesser extent, so that they are relatively easy to perform for a person who resides at the opposite end of the spectrum (i.e., an *onnagata*). The correspondence between the argument in "The Words of Ayame" and the readings of modern scholars, however, appears too natural.

That kabuki scholarship thinks highly of this naturalness and takes it for granted without much questioning implies that this notion of the degree of femininity has been (until recently) too natural for us to problematize.[63] It must have been radically new in the past, however. It was quite different from, for instance, Zeami's fifteenth-century idea of performance theory regarding the difficulties of performing a woman. For Zeami, it is difficult to perform a lady-in-waiting in royal service, not because she is more feminine, but because she is hardly seen. From Zeami's point of view, Ayame should have had difficulty playing the role of a high-ranking samurai's wife and not that of a courtesan, to whom Ayame no doubt had easier access. Despite that, the difficulty, Ayame argues, depends on the degree of femininity. Ayame even implies that the role of a samurai's wife is somehow closer—thus arguably easier—to *onnagata* because she has something stern and sharp (*kitto shitaru*), a propensity Ayame thinks *onnagata* possess from birth.[64]

The notion of femininity as that which is at the furthest extreme within the spectrum of masculinity/femininity (in section 1 of Ayame's text) has affinities with the modern idea of gender, which may explain why it comes so naturally to modern scholars. It was not necessarily always natural in the context of Japanese theater. This notion of the degree of femininity is an interesting herald of the modern understanding of femininity in that it hints at the modern binary opposition of femininity and masculinity. The clear-cut opposition of masculinity versus femininity was foreign to the gender economy of Edo-era Japan, as femininity in premodern Japan was highly class-oriented. The femininity that a peasant woman internalized was totally differentiated from that of an aristocratic woman, and there was no central or essential femininity that applied to all women across classes. The active participation of *onnagata* in the creation of womanhood, however, heralded a single femininity that, together with masculinity, constituted the clear-cut sex dichotomy, or an illusion of it, in modern Japan. The gender theory articulated in "The Words of Ayame" hints at this phenomenon.[65]

Not only the definitions of what one has, be it masculinity or femininity, but the courtesan section of "The Words of Ayame" is concerned with the distance between the two. This principle per se—the more distant the character's feature, the harder to perform—sounds simple. In the paradigm of performance theory in Japanese theater, however, masculinity and femininity had not necessarily set up standards for measuring the extent of proximity. (After all, noh, *kyōgen*, bunraku, and kabuki are all-male theaters.) As for a general principle of dramatic performance in noh theater, Zeami states:

> There are many kinds of role-playing [*monomane*; lit., "mimicry"], and it is hardly possible to write them down exhaustively. Nevertheless, role-playing is vital to this way [noh artistry], and one must explore it no matter what.
>
> On the whole, it is fundamental to make [one's performance] resemble [the subject in question], whatever role it is. Be aware, however, of the gradations [that are appropriate] depending on the subject.
>
> In the first place, the demeanor of the likes of nobles and warriors, the first and foremost of which begins with rulers and ministers. It is impossible [for the likes of us] to reach their state, so sufficient resemblance is hardly possible. However, do work hard to study their parlance and gestures, and humbly seek audiences' honorable opinions. In addition, one had better imitate in detail when it comes to ways in which people of decent vocations do things and the beauties of nature. When it comes to those engaged in physical labor in rice paddies and field, do not meticulously imitate their vulgar manner in detail.[66]

In short, upper-class demeanor is difficult to imitate, whereas the manner of laborers should not be imitated in detail. It is noteworthy that Zeami regards the former alone as formidable. Though tacit, it is obvious that the latter is considered possible in terms of the actor's ability. It might seem possible, accordingly, to reduce his point to social standing. When Zeami proceeds to particular points, however, it starts to look different, as in the "Woman" section: "When it comes to high-ranking women in royal service, we can hardly see their behavior in person, so one needs to examine it greatly. Personal preference is out of the question for the way in which the clothing [for these women], such as *kinu* and *hakama*, is donned. Make inquiries. The appearance of ordinary women should come easily, as one is used to seeing them in everyday life."[67] Here the difficulty is certainly related to societal tiers, but Zeami appends another factor—whether or not one can actually see the subject of imitation in person. Distance thus consists of the proximity of social standing and of physical existence. It is a matter of familiarity and not of the essence of being, such as the masculine principle and its opposite.[68]

Another interesting factor of distance, namely, race-ethnicity, would later be introduced due to the internationalized performing arts industry. Tamasaburō recollects arguing against Andrzej Wajda (b. 1926) when he was working with the Polish director for *Nasutāsha/Nastazja* (Nastasya), a play based on *The Idiot* (1868) by Fyodor Dostoevsky (1821–1881). The play premiered in 1989 in Tokyo and subsequently was staged in 1993 in Warsaw, where it was also shot as a film, released in 1994. The theater productions and the film featured the same contemporary *onnagata* in the roles of both Prince Lyov Myshkin and Nastasya Filipovna. In an interview about this serial work, the interviewer asked about some scenes from the film version, in which Tamasaburō is surrounded by Polish supernumeraries. Tamasaburō replied:

> Originally, there were more scenes [that had been planned] in which many more Polish extras [would] appear. Like [the director was thinking about] shooting the last scene with the crowd surging into the room, shouting, "Idiot!" But then I insisted that I wasn't confident about playing a European woman in Europe, you know. And then he said, "You're wrong" [laughter]. But, seriously, it's weird, isn't it? That I [would] ask something in Japanese, and yet the other party [would] respond in Polish. Anyway, it's already strange enough that a man acts [*yaru*] a woman, but not only that, it's also a Westerner that I become [*nari*], and on top of that, it's down there, their place that I go to [*iku*].[69]

The distance of familiarity is conceived here by the present-day virtuoso to be the holistic phenomenon of "doing," "becoming," and "going," as well as that of "language," "gender," "race-ethnicity," and "balance"[70] among the actors involved. The validity of a clear-cut division between distance and quality thus evaporates.[71] (Yet another overlapping proximity for audiences should be taken into consideration, that between them and the "reality" they witness. This is also critical, as they, too, participate in the creation of "reality.")

While certainly a herald of the modern binary, the way in which "The Words of Ayame" approaches the performance of women's roles is not a mutation of this paradigm of performance theory in Japan, as the criterion of social standing is being interwoven with the criterion of the degree of femininity. On this point, Ayame's text is also supported by "The Secret Transmissions of an *Onnagata*," which brusquely commands: "For one thing, whenever performing the role of the wife of a chief retainer, think that you are ugly and play that part" (section 5).[72] "The Words of Ayame" objects: "For one thing, Mr. Yoshizawa said as follows. The manner of *onnagata* performance is that one should make his appearance mischievous and coquettish while keeping his mind chaste. However, it is unsightly to behave stiffly, even [when playing] the wife of samurai" (section 3).[73] Objection though it is, the presupposition is the same as that of "The Secret Transmissions of an *Onnagata*." Both texts presume that female members of the samurai class are assigned such features as unattractiveness (*bukiryō*) and clumsiness (*gikotsunaru*). The difference is that "The Words of Ayame" holds that it is unsightly to present it *as is* onstage. "The Words of Ayame" continues: "When gesturing the manner of a woman who is stern and sharp [*kitto shitaru*], one must keep his mind tender" (section 3).[74]

Logically, this prescription is suspect, for, should the problem be inelegance, one possible solution—not only logically possible but also compelling given the traditions of male beauties—would have been to make the role beautiful in masculine terms, such as "gallant" (*ririshii*). "The Words of Ayame" rejects this as well, however. The real issue probably is not beauty or attractiveness or unattractiveness but a discrepancy in the degree of femininity, which must be offset by its antithesis, which Ayame considers softness.

A few things draw our attention in this solution of "soft-feminine performance for strong-masculine women's roles." The text openly admits that women can be stern and sharp, the predisposition that the text has previously assigned to men (section 1), and thereby candidly recognizes that the association of femininity with softness, an association that the text proposes as a methodology, is arbitrary. Furthermore, the "manly" feature is allocated to high-ranking female members of the samurai class, thus mingling gender and class. Of equal importance is that this characteristic should be offset by another feature of tenderness (*yawaraka*), again pointing to the presence of a spectrum of "sharp" to "soft." Considering the fact that this treatise uses the adjectives "stern" and "sharp" for masculine and "soft" for feminine traits (e.g., section 1), it is no wonder that this spectrum of "soft/sharp" overlaps with that of "femininity/masculinity":

> Mr. Yoshizawa said as follows. When, as the wife of a chief retainer, cornering an enemy in a dispute, one without exception behaves in a dignified manner with his hand placed on his sword. It is bad acting, though, to make [the role] too gallant [*ririshi sugitaru*] because, for all that she is the wife of a chief retainer, she would not carry the sword all the time. It is enough if one's action shows that she is not afraid of a sword. It would be a male-role actor wearing a cap if he pressed the enemy too hard, with his hand on the hilt, saying, "What, what, what is that?" while slapping the stage. [Ayame] must have said this frequently. [Section 2].[75]

The cap here is the ornament initially invented as a kerchief by the *wakashu* when they were required by law to have their foreheads shaved; hence it was initially the pseudosignifier of youth and in due course became the very signifier of *onnagata*. The phrase "male-role actor putting on a cap" can thus be paraphrased as an actor merely wearing *onnagata* clothing but having no *onnagata* skill. Another section on the same role—the wife of a chief retainer—again uses this wording:

> For one thing, there is the role of a female [version of a] chief retainer, who, on behalf of her husband, is granted an audience with the lord. There she would dispose of matters. [When performing this role,] one must do [her tasks] insecurely. It would be a male chief retainer wearing a cap if one behaves securely. Differently put, for all that she is the wife of a chief retainer, there is no reason why [a woman] does not flinch when she is surrounded by many people. Behave timidly, so much so that one trembles with fear. Only after the enemy role heaps abuse [on you] must you become stern and sharp. At the eleventh hour, women [do not hesitate to] say what they want to say, much more so than men. Nevertheless, do the action somewhat flushed. So [Ayame] said. [Section 12][76]

In short, "The Words of Ayame" requires soft (read "feminine") performance for strong (read "masculine") women's roles.

The text comes back to this case of a "soft-feminine performance for strong-masculine women's roles" several times, more frequently than to the case of a high-ranking courtesan. This reflects the text's recognition of the importance and difficulty of such roles and echoes scholarly works on Ayame's acting career and reputation based on actor-critique booklets and other theater publications. Masaki Yumi concludes that Ayame established in kabuki dramaturgy a certain psychological acting technique (called "meditative pose with hidden sorrow") vital for "samurai women" (*onna budō*) and that this technique was made possible by Ayame's mixture of acting techniques for love scenes and for "samurai women" per se.[77] This shows how Ayame materializes his own prescription of a "soft-feminine performance for strong-masculine women's roles." Masaki adds that, not only was Ayame praised for this technique, but this psychological acting technique was adopted by other virtuosos of "samurai-women roles" (*onna budō no meijin*).[78] Takahashi Hiroko also states that Ayame's previous experience in the roles of women in the samurai class—some of whom are cross-dressing—helped contribute to the change in his career from an *onnagata* to a male-role actor,[79] although the transition in and of itself was not successful. Likewise, Inoue Nobuko states that Ayame was not necessarily highly praised for his performance in courtesans' roles but was critically acclaimed for his performance of "samurai women," which he did not necessarily like to perform.[80] Inoue writes that Ayame was reluctant to play the roles of samurai women,[81] and "The Words of Ayame" certainly shows such sentiments ("A role in which one corners an enemy in a dispute is a nuisance for *onnagata* to play, but if one cannot decline it due to the overall production, one does accept the role" [section 8]).[82] It nevertheless seems that these remarks imply that Ayame regarded this type of role as significant.

The samurai-woman role is formidable in its delicate gradations, as stated in "The Words of Ayame":

> For one thing, [there are points related to when] one becomes a samurai's wife who handles a sword. One must manage the sword in a mannish way, when, for instance, you play the role of someone who, chased by a large force, tries to protect a princess. She's the wife of a samurai, and when it comes to the moment that loyalty overwhelms her, she surely acts like one. When one corners an enemy in a dispute inside the room, [however], it is not yet a critical moment. The manner in which one handles a sword should be gentle. I heard [Ayame] say this to Tamagashiwa repeatedly. [Section 6][83]

Indeed, distinguishing a beige toothbrush from a light brown toothbrush might be considerably harder than differentiating a navy-blue toothbrush from a pink one. Therefore, from Zeami's point of view (in terms of distance), Ayame should have had difficulty playing the role of a high-ranking samurai's wife and not that of a courtesan, to whom Ayame must have had easier access. The implication from this perspective is that Ayame must not have felt that way, because Ayame suggests that the role of a samurai's wife is somehow closer to *onnagata* (in terms of the degree of femininity). While the role of a high-ranking courtesan is difficult for *onnagata*, the role of a high-ranking samurai woman is also tricky because it is too close in degree of femininity. In this specific paradigm of the prescription for femininity, the constitutive other of a high-ranking courtesan is *never* a man, as declared by the text itself and as taken for granted by modern scholars, but is in fact a high-ranking samurai woman.

The method of approaching femininity seen in section 1 of "The Words of Ayame" is thus critical in several ways. It hints at the impending modern binary of masculinity and femininity, and it is also situated within the context of performance theory of Japanese theater in that it attempts to meet the challenge of acting by "measuring" the distance between an actor and his role holistically. Although it introduces the relatively new issue of "degrees of femininity," it still maintains the issue of class by which such degrees are explained. Femininity here is situated between a force that makes it a quantifiable feature and another force, nonetheless part and parcel of the former force, that makes it unquantifiable. While the courtesan is more feminine and *hence* less masculine, the samurai's wife is more masculine and *hence* less feminine. The femininities thus prioritized, of which that of a high-ranking courtesan marks the uppermost and that of a samurai's wife the least, demonstrate the spectrum in which gender and class are deeply intertwined. Ayame's choice of the eros spectrum over class diversity (as pronounced categorically in section 1) is complicated, if not offset, by the sections on women in the samurai class.

Without taking these factors into consideration, we cannot effectively perceive Ayame's positing of the femininity of a high-ranking courtesan as the extreme degree of femininity, performing samurai women by adjusting the parameters, and still conceptualizing his gender performance as grounded in the "constative" features of women. It is this constructed essential femininity that his contemporaries accepted as realistic imitation of women: "A genuine woman from the bottom up, dunno what's there under the loincloth. . . . Regardless of which person he is made to imitate, from a high-ranking lady-in-waiting, to a samurai's wife, and to a maidservant, [Ayame] completely reproduces the figure [of the woman] intact, without any element of fabrication."[84] The prescription for femininity methodized in the *onnagata* treatises offers an intriguing way of understanding "gendering" in which femininity cannot be reduced to the constitutive other of masculinity.

These accounts of the prescription for femininity not only reveal the *onnagata* gender, on or off the stage, but also hint at some broader aspects of gender and its economy. First, gender identity can be divorced from sex identity. Second, the gender dichotomy is actually based on the gender spectrum. Third, gender is presentation and not representation. The haunting shadow of *wakashu* is still recognizable in these issues, even when *onnagata* distinguished themselves as perpetual performers of femininity and thus non-*wakashu*.

The *onnagata*'s way of doing gender is radically isolated from *futanarihira*'s way of doing gender, and yet the two are uncannily complicit. While retaining the one that endorses male identity, *futanarihira* did another gender located between the two genders, and *onnagata* did the two genders simultaneously. For this "unnatural" situation, both did gender in an exceptionally visible manner.[85] This was not so visible in the case of the original samurai *wakashu* and the intersex person teased in *The Book of Disease*, whose genders they were made to believe were neatly aligned with their sex identity.[86] *Onnagata* and *futanarihira* upset the putative stability of sex identity and gender identity and thereby questioned its validity. This demarcation of identities theoretically precedes the possibility that someone whose sex identity is male, namely *onnagata*, can represent the ideal gender identity of female.

The way in which "The Words of Ayame" prioritizes femininity according to its degree again displays a slippery complicity in a gender economy between *futanarihira* and *onnagata*. The notion of gender as dichotomy necessitates what appears its counter-notion: gender as a continuum. In prioritizing femininity and assuming that its essence exists in the high-ranking courtesan, "The Words of Ayame" hints at the possibility of the formidable dualism of femininity and masculinity. This complicity demands our attention for several reasons. The dynamic movement toward dualism theoretically relies on the presence of a continuum. In section 1 (the courtesan section), more feminine is *made* interchangeable with less masculine, revealing that the two entities, as polarities, share the same pivot. This indicates that *onnagata* were likely to carve out a new direction based on what the estranged *futanarihira* had built—that is, a continuum (a *wakashu* spectrum of gender) plus a centrifugal force (degree of femininity by *onnagata*) equals dualism. In this intimate relationship between a spectrum and a polarity, the "complicity" between *onnagata* and *futanarihira*, or haunting memories of the latter, is apparent.

This complicity also turns out to be illustrative of the future direction of the gender economy in Japan. Scholars have pointed out that there was no monolithic femininity before modern times in Japan and that it was considered in relation to not only sex but also class and age. The notion of prioritized femininity, however, implicitly anticipated *the* femininity to be created by aligning diverse femininities according to the priority of eros. The notion of the eros spectrum can theoretically overrule class diversity, although in practice the prescription proposed in the text demonstrates that the spectrum incorporates not only gender but also class. A continuum must have been useful in the alignment process. The spectrum-polarity oscillation of gender must have been about to swing to the latter, but this dynamic would have been impossible had it not been the former in the first place. The origins of "Ayame's choice," the eros spectrum over class diversity, at this particular moment is extremely intriguing. On the one hand, it envisioned the impending condensed historicity of monolithic femininity in the dichotomized gender economy; on the other, it was reminiscent of a historicity of its time, and of the past as well.

The accounts of gender training present a severe challenge to the validity of kabuki historiography's metamorphosis hypothesis as well. The two notions, metamorphosis and lifelong training, seem rather incongruous in the context of eighteenth-century Japan. Metamorphoses here inevitably entail a Buddhist understanding of the world,[87] in the cosmology of which metamorphoses can be understood as enlightenment, be it gradual or sudden.[88] The two texts are filled with painstaking instructions on matters ranging from body movement to deathbed manners, which any enlightened being would be unlikely to need. In addition, Ayame seeks femininity without erasing what he says is his natural masculinity. Even on paper, he does not renounce masculinity, which he thinks is useful for the art of *onnagata*, and in their everyday lives, *onnagata* have no problem fathering children. Ayame himself had at least four sons who became famous enough as kabuki actors to be recorded in documents. This "residual" masculinity contradicts the metamorphosis hypothesis, which implies a complete transformation from one being to another.

The *onnagata* figure Ayame points to is far more elusive. He lives as a woman offstage (sections 7 and 22), always retains womanly sentiments and chastity (sections 13 and 24), and physically blushes when asked about his wife (section 23).[89] He blushes but is not surprised when asked, for his marriage and offspring are public knowledge through the vast network of popular periodicals, such as actor-critique booklets, that link kabuki to its fans. (Ayame's four sons are also mentioned in these publications.)[90] That an *onnagata* remains male although he has to live as a woman signifies less a metamorphosis than a superimposition.[91] In this sense, it is presentation and not representation.[92] Yet this presentation was based on a deeply worked "constative" conceptualization of femininity and did not remain inside a playhouse but circulated in society.

CHAPTER 4

Canonization

Creating Onnagata Traditions

THE reputations of two *onnagata*, Ayame as the epochal *onnagata* who determined the nature of *onnagata* artistry down through the ages and Kikunojō as a faithful follower of Ayame's who consolidated the *onnagata* traditions, are firmly established in kabuki studies. Hattori Yukio writes:

> It was none other than Yoshizawa Ayame who established the acting technique that one devotes his entire life wholly to women's feelings [*onna no jō*] and their structures. Unlike *onnagata* before him, he did not attempt to approach the *futanarihira* aesthetic, a common element shared by *wakashu* and those earlier *onnagata*. In addition, he was also different from other mediocre *onnagata* who sought easy success with comical acting or [samurai women]. He did nothing like that and, instead, established the acting technique of *waka-onnagata* [*waka-oyama*, or young *onnagata*], which is devoted to the imitation of women [*onna no monomane*]. It must have been that such an acting technique was established by none other than Ayame and was developed by Kikunojō.[1]

Their *onnagata* treatises are also highly regarded. Yamamoto Jirō states:

> [In the clause quoted from "The Words of Ayame,"] Ayame taught younger actors that realistic art is the main part [of kabuki] and dance the decorative

part. Here, too, we can observe Ayame's intelligence, which grasps the quintessence of kabuki.... The accounts-on-*gei* in [the text] are only twenty-nine items, only a small quantity, but every single one of them derives from his sincere training in *gei*. [A theater-related book has an account saying that Kikunojō] told his disciples [about a certain instruction in "The Words of Ayame"] and added that he has never forgotten it, nor has he anything to teach other than that. No wonder that it has been treated in this part of society as the textbook of *gei*.[2]

Accordingly, "The Words of Ayame" and "The Secret Transmissions of an *Onnagata*" have been treated as the two most important and influential treatises to date on the art of *onnagata*.

Because the two *onnagata* and their texts have been so canonized, they in effect determined the ensuing history of *onnagata*. Whether or not a text was righteously canonized on its own merits is an aporia in the final analysis, but one can still examine whether it has functioned as an imperative in a localized context.[3] When reading the history of *onnagata*, one can find the aforementioned narrative on the two texts literally anywhere,[4] not only in modern scholarship but also in the Edo era. Their contemporaries and succeeding *onnagata* are especially critical because they were directly involved in the process of defining *onnagata* artistry in the first place.

"The Secret Transmissions of an *Onnagata*" is of significance here. The contents of this treatise were originally published in 1772 as part of the anthology about kabuki theater, *The Pioneering Analects from Past and Present Actors*. While the anthology's table of contents lists the treatise under a different, lengthy title, there is no clear indication in the main text itself that the ten items, which record the words of Kikunojō, constitute an independent unit (e.g., a chapter). They are simply included in the section devoted to thirteen actors' accounts-on-*gei*.[5] Later, Ihara Toshirō (alias Seiseien) (1870–1941) excerpted the ten items by Kikunojō and published them in 1904 in his *History of Japanese Theater* (Nihon engekishi): "There also exists what is called 'The Secret Transmissions of an *Onnagata*' by Kikunojō. I hereby publish it."[6] Ihara, the compiler of *The Chronological Table of Kabuki* (Kabuki nenpyō) and author of a theater history trilogy starting with his *History of Japanese Theater*, was a prominent philologist who introduced extensive primary sources, and Imao proposes that the title was most likely chosen by Ihara himself.[7] Ihara may well have canonized and thus valorized what was originally an untitled text by picking particular passages from a collection of thirteen actors' narratives and giving the cluster a title. That a modern philologist was instrumental in textual history has not undone the canonization of "The Secret Transmissions of an *Onnagata*,"[8] but we should be aware of the possibility that this text has been overrated and that other passages in theater-related publications deserve equal, if not more, attention in terms of *onnagata* artistry.

Onnagata themselves have also been involved in the history making of the pair. Even *onnagata* in modern times, while situated in a cultural milieu that has changed drastically starting from the Meiji era, are not isolated from the two treatises, especially "The Words of Ayame." Nakamura Utaemon VI (1917–2001), the leading *onnagata* of his time, says of his training as an *onnagata*: "When it comes to mental preparation as an *onnagata*, there are many anecdotes left by great actors in the past, as well as texts that preserve a golden rule of *onnagata*, such as 'The Words of Ayame' of Yoshizawa Ayame."[9] Utaemon does not necessarily agree with everything in it, such as Ayame's recommendation that *onnagata* live as women in everyday life (section 7). He grounds his disagreement in the transition of the times, saying, "Now is the time when man goes to the moon," although adding that everyday life nevertheless carries significance for kabuki actors, *onnagata* included.[10] Onoe Taganojō III (1887–1978) is more easygoing: "There're two ways of *onnagata*, you see. One is like what [my master, Onoe Kikugorō VI (1885–1949),] used to say, ['One just needs to be a woman onstage']. And then, like Yoshizawa Ayame-san's instructions. From everyday life, *onnagata* can't say, 'I have diarrhea.' [Patting his stomach.] You gotta say, 'Oh my, female disorders [*chi no michi*]. . . .' There are even stories like that. But try that today, and you'd get a punch [laughter]."[11]

Taganojō's words hint at new ways for *onnagata* in modern times, epitomized here as Kikugorō's opinion, but it is nonetheless noteworthy that Ayame and "The Words of Ayame" are still used as a point of reference. Baikō, the brother of Kikugorō and one of the two top *onnagata* in the early twentieth century, along with Utaemon's father, left a substantial number of accounts-on-*gei*, in which he mentions the remarks of Ayame and Kikunojō.[12] Baikō wrote: "This Kikunojō is said to have passed away [in a remarkable manner]. It is said that he took a bath, having his hair set, and dressed himself, with the [*onnagata*] cap on his head. Then he had the million-time Buddhist invocation [*hyakumanben*, also *hyakumanben nenbutsu*] chanted around his deathbed and bade farewell to the people in the theater. It seems to me that he was extremely sensible all the time. Though

I can't equal [the likes of him], I'd like to learn from the behavior of such a great actor."[13] Readers will recall the account of Baikō's death at the beginning of this book. Ayame's influence was such that later *onnagata*—including those in modern times—refer to texts from the past such as "The Words of Ayame" and thereby keep reinforcing the canonization.

The reputation of the Ayame and Kikunojō already existed in eighteenth-century theater publications. *The Complete Book of Actors through All Ages, the New Edition* (Shinsen kokon yakusha taizen) (1750), by Hachimonji Kishō and Hachimonji Zuishō, juxtaposes Ayame and Kikunojō, who was two decades younger than Ayame: "The success of [Kikunojō] was unprecedented for the actors from Kyoto and Osaka after the late Ayame. . . . [Kikunojō] passed away in the seventh month of last year, and it was unbelievable that beautiful long-sleeve *kimono* [for youth] suited him very well even when he was merely two or three years shy of sixty. He was a sheer beauty *even when he did not wear makeup*, not to mention onstage. It was as if all the colors and eros of the entire world had been condensed [in him]."[14] In this moment, the two actors are posited as the "twosome" in *onnagata* traditions, which paved the way for the canonization of the two *onnagata* treatises.

Similarly, *The Pioneering Analects from Past and Present Actors* contains summaries of actors' reputations from actor-critique booklets and other publications. It introduces Ayame as "peerless in all the three cities," "incomparable through all ages" (*kokon murui*), and so on,[15] and speaks of Kikunojō as follows:

> In the revival period, the late Segawa Kikunojō was recorded in the introduction of *Encyclopedia of Actors* (Yakusha daizen) as too good at dancing to be skillful in drama. This remark must have been about somebody else. Or it must have been about the roles of samurai women. [Kikunojō] lacked nothing as far as women's technique was concerned. One does not need to explain how good the high-ranking courtesans he performed were, as were any scenes of lamentation he played. *Unlimited Bell* (Muken no kane) and *Saint Narukami, the Woman Version* (Onna Narukami), which he played, have become the heirlooms of the house for his lineage, and he was also famous for his performance in *Dōjōji Temple* (Dōjōji) and *Stone Bridge* (Shakukyō). Most *onnagata* become sexually unattractive as they age, but Kikunojō was extremely good at love scenes in *furisode* [long-sleeve *kimono* exclusively for youth] until he was over sixty years of age [sic]. He was not only beautiful but also skillful. He was nothing other than a founder [*kaisan*] of *waka-onnagata* in recent history.

In addition, his younger brother Segawa Kikujirō was also a master. . . . Kikujirō's acting was in accordance with "The Words of Ayame." It was maestro Ayame who left the thirty-item [sic] sayings. Also, Kikujirō did not act like a man for his entire life. The Segawa brothers truly mastered the woman's way, *from everyday life to mind-set*, and to various techniques [suitable for women].[16]

The anthology afterward presents the words of Kikunojō, namely, "The Secret Transmissions of an *Onnagata*."[17] Hence, it was eighteenth-century theater-related publications that initially proposed, and arguably helped establish, the "information" of the twosome. This was the moment when "The Words of Ayame" was canonized in discourse as well as the moment when the canon helped define *onnagata* artistry.

It was therefore Kikunojō's contemporaries, long before the modern philologist, who initially helped the process of canonization. Whether overrated or not, the knowledge that Kikunojō and his words were almost as important as Ayame and his words was integral to the formation of *onnagata* artistry in the eighteenth century. An enthusiastic fan of Kikunojō's went so far as to run down Ayame, just to praise Kikunojō. *The Famous-Product Journal, Actors' Sleeves* (Yakusha meibutsu sode nikki), a theater-related book published in 1771, has this to say about Ayame:

> When he was young, Kikunojō is said to have asked great Ayame how *onnagata* should train themselves. Ayame is said to have answered, "An *onnagata* only need do the gesture of a high-ranking courtesan from the bottom of his heart. It's easy to do things in everyday life." There is a theory that it was a golden saying and that Kikunojō managed to become a skillful actor thanks to this advice. My stupid heart cannot follow that. . . . I'm not convinced that the said instruction holds any truth. [Come to think of it,] even though Ayame is great, there is no theory that he kept *women's feelings in his daily life*. [In turn,] there is no one who doesn't know that Kikunojō's behavior is that of a woman *in everyday life*. He is the only one in all ages.[18]

This criticism of Ayame is intriguing because, as Hattori correctly observes in defending him,[19] it was after all an important point made in "The Words of Ayame": "It is hardly possible for an *onnagata* to be considered proficient unless he spends his everyday life as a woman" (section 7).[20] In any case, it is apparent that these eighteenth-century theater publications were active in creating the definitions of *onnagata* artistry and traditions.

Canonization is thus a powerful self-fulfilling prophecy. These two texts are significant in the history of *onnagata* not simply because they have been canonized in the scholarship but more fundamentally because their canonization has determined the field. It is in this sense that the evaluations of Ayame and Kikunojō by their contemporaries and by their successors are of great moment. Furthermore, it calls attention to the fact that this canonization took place in publications, that is, before the eyes of many kabuki admirers. Of equal significance is that their reputation is justified not only by their performance onstage but also by their conduct offstage, as is obvious from such phrases as "not wear[ing] makeup," "for his entire life," and "everyday life." All of that concerns not only *onnagata* but also women.

CHAPTER 5

Femininity in Circulation

Texts in Kabuki, Kabuki in Texts

IN exploring the extent to which eighteenth-century *onnagata* constructed femininity by imitation and citation, secured their knowledge, and achieved the femininity of perfection as second nature, a consideration of kabuki as a literary experience is useful. Of central concern here are the meaning of the term "real women" (*hon no onna*), encountered in texts such as "The Words of Ayame" and "The Secret Transmissions of an *Onnagata*," and the nature of kabuki as a literary experience and as performing art.

Dependent on song (*ka*) and dance (*bu*), kabuki is actors' theater. It is the theater in which drama texts (plays) are perceived as subordinate to performance (acting), and the history of kabuki consists of traditions transmitted through actors. In this sense, kabuki is not so much the theater of drama texts as the theater of performance. Seeing kabuki is a theatrical experience, and it might well be puzzling to think of it as a literary experience. Furthermore, kabuki is people's theater and was much more so in the Edo era. While the shogunate treated it as a depraved theatrical entertainment subject to suspicion and interference, it was deeply loved by the common people. The *Audience-Critique Booklet at the Three Theaters* (Sanshibai kakusha hyōbanki) (1811), by Shikitei Sanba (1776–1822),[1] vividly describes theater lovers as spectators who participate in the creation of theatrical effects.

Their antithesis is modern audiences, defined as "students" by Osanai Kaoru (1881–1928),[2] one of the founders of modern Japanese theater: that is, students who *sincerely* learn the theater onstage. Far from being sincere and quiet students, spectators in Edo-era kabuki playhouses shout the actors' *yagō* (shop name)[3] to praise performances, eat snacks and box lunches, and enjoy themselves in what Hattori calls the "site of a fete" (*shukusai kūkan*), a site shared by actors, musicians, staff members, and audiences alike. None of these things happen, however, without the theater being performed in a specific place and audiences going there. As Josette Féral states, "Space seems fundamental to theatricality, for the passage from the literary to the theatrical is first and foremost completed through a spatial realization of the text."[4]

Hattori is one of the earliest kabuki scholars to pay special attention to kabuki playhouses in terms of the meanings of the space, producing a landmark study on the weight of a theater as a physical site of performance and reception. Building on preceding studies in theater architecture, he examines the effect of architectural features on kabuki acting, the actor-audience relationship, and, by extension, people's kabuki experiences as a whole. He states that, while it is a flexible theatrical entertainment that can be performed almost anywhere, kabuki is most appropriately produced at an original site, which he calls "the native provinces of kabuki," meaning "a site that was used when kabuki was actually alive [i.e., the Edo era], when it kept generating one new play after another for about two centuries, and when actors constantly performed [these new plays]. There must be no doubt that the [original] form of such a site is most appropriate [for Edo-era kabuki plays]. This is because every single kabuki play is made presupposing the very existence of a playhouse of that particular size and with that particular structure. Acting and direction have been refined presupposing these as well."[5] One of Hattori's major achievements is thus to reconstruct the original sites in monographs,[6] a picture book,[7] and reproduction models of an Edo-era kabuki playhouse exhibited at the Edo-Tokyo Museum, one of which is a scale model of an entrance of the playhouse and the other a miniature model of its entire structure. (Hattori himself considers these his major work.)[8] The museum reproductions are modeled after the Nakamura-za Theater, one of the three "big theaters" (*ōshibai*) in Edo, and the *Picture Book of Dream Kabuki in Edo* (Ehon yume no Edo kabuki) meticulously reproduces a typical theatrical production from historical documents, starting from the preparation through the actual stage performance, which is set in Nakamura-za in the first decade or two of the nineteenth century.[9] In actuality, the Kanamaru-za Theater, located in Kotohira-city, Kagawa prefecture, is the only extant playhouse in contemporary Japan that was built in the Edo era.[10]

One of the reasons that the space is of uppermost importance is its direct impact on acting.[11] For example, the kabuki stage has been enlarged significantly, especially in modern times,[12] and Hattori quotes Kataoka Nizaemon XIII (1903–1994), who noted in a public lecture that the lyrics a chanter recites to accompany an actor's movements are made for an Edo-size stage, and playhouses nowadays cannot accommodate the choreography. Therefore, the actor must run even when the drama requires him to walk or the chanter must prolong the music, either of which destroys the timing (*ma*) of kabuki.[13] The space is also important because a kabuki playhouse was originally the site of a fete, which has religious connotations. In his *Extraordinary Playhouse* (Ōinaru koya), Hattori associates a "mouse-gate" (*nezumi-kido*), an extremely small entrance for audiences in Edo-era kabuki theaters, with the following remark in a noh-theater treatise: "For one thing, one enters into a dressing room, where even the color of an object is invisible. This is the form that one dwells in a womb. For another, one appears on stage, raising the curtain. This is the form that humans are born."[14]

According to Hattori, the mouse-gate is not just an entrance that prevents admittance without paying the fare. More important, spectators squeezing themselves through the mouse-gate go through a process similar to the experience of a noh actor described above or that of a tea practitioner, who enters a tea room through an equally small entrance (literally a square hole approximately two feet by two feet). Hattori states that those who pass these thresholds are reborn into an extraordinary world completely differentiated from the ordinary world outside.[15] There are many other examples of architectural features used to similar effect, with cultural significance.[16] Kabuki is thus a religiously charged fete.[17] These issues of great moment are all irrelevant to kabuki as a literary experience.

What is a "text" in the context of kabuki? Can bibliophiles be theater-lovers? The answer is yes, as a theater-related book in 1829 claims,[18] but why, and how is it possible? "Texts" are awkwardly situated in the context of kabuki. Although drama is perceived as subordinate to performance in kabuki, this does not mean that drama texts do not carry importance in kabuki theater. The works of many Edo-era writers are still performed today, including Chikamatsu Monzaemon (1653–1724),[19] Namiki Shōzō (1730–1773), Nagawa Kamesuke (dates unknown), Namiki Gohei (1747–1808), Sakurada

Jisuke (1734–1806), Tsuruya Nanboku (1755–1829), and Kawatake Mokuami (1816–1893). Had it not been for these writers and their works, kabuki would not have been possible.

Rather, drama is subordinate to performance in the sense that the former is unequivocally located in the middle of enunciation and cannot be, or cannot disguise itself as, the enunciated itself. The enunciated is that which is produced; enunciation is an act by which one produces the enunciated. A kabuki script is floating through the process of enunciating a theatrical production and is hardly recognizable as an enunciated text in and of itself. In a sense, any drama text theoretically entails this slippery problem as long as there is a chance that it will be performed, and kabuki simply highlights the elusive relationship among the important concepts of drama, theater, and performance. Gunji Masakatsu summarizes this phenomenon as follows: "There are reasons why a complete version of a kabuki script is hardly possible [at any given moment]. A kabuki script increases its value only after it is performed repeatedly. Furthermore, every time it is produced, it is the principle that the script is revised. By nature, kabuki scripts are differentiated from drama that presupposes its own literary value. Differently put, the *gei* [acquired artistic technique] of actors takes priority over drama [in kabuki]."[20] Figuratively, even actors, not to mention audiences, did not have access to a play script in its entirety for a long time. An actor was merely given an "extract" (*kakinuki*), a note containing his or her part alone. The status of a script changed somewhat in the Meiji era, when kabuki plays began to be published. Gondō Yoshikazu states that one of the earliest such works was a collection of Mokuami's plays published in 1888.[21] This is a relatively a recent phenomenon in the history of kabuki, and even after that, it remains valid on the whole that drama is subordinate to performance in the context of kabuki.

Drama texts are not the only kind of text in kabuki culture, however, and other texts might well have been far more significant for kabuki as a societal phenomenon in Edo-era Japan. The kabuki culture in the Edo period deeply integrated the theater industry and publication culture. There were many types of publications on kabuki at that time, which can be roughly classified into actor-critique booklets, playbills (*banzuke*), and other theater-books (*gekisho*).[22] Actor-critique booklets and playbills provided readers with updates on kabuki and its actors. Topics covered by theater-books include "introduction to kabuki," "the history of kabuki," "introduction to kabuki plays," "actors, present and past," and "actors' treatises." While drama texts were confined to the backstage, both literally and metaphorically, these periodicals, books, and playbills were actively published and consumed. Quite a few other enterprises in Edo-era Japan were equally important, such as lighthearted prose literature that went hand in hand with kabuki's popularity,[23] rental library businesses,[24] and advertising businesses.[25] All these literary cultures operated in people's kabuki experiences, that is to say, the kabuki culture.

The historical significance of theater-related publications is apparent in the 1829 theater-book *Theater under the Microscope* (Gekijō ikkan mushimegane) by Kimura Mokurō (1774–1856): "There are so many theater-lovers in the world these days but very few theatergoers."[26] These publications not only provided information on kabuki for playgoers but also functioned as virtual theatergoing for other theater-lovers. Playgoers were a minority of kabuki lovers, as epitomized physically by the limited capacity of kabuki playhouses. For example, in the city of Edo, kabuki could be officially performed at only three licensed theaters, called "big theaters," simultaneously after the 1714 regulations following an incident that totally shut down the theaters for a while.[27] One playhouse hosted approximately five or six performances per year. Kabuki playhouses of this time had no modern lighting facilities and were much smaller than kabuki playhouses today. The size of a kabuki theater kept increasing in line with that of a kabuki stage, but even the latest ones in the Edo era were diminutive compared to modern theaters. Partially due to the seating system, it is impossible to pinpoint the number of people that a playhouse could have accommodated in the past,[28] but, considering the size of a stage, we can assume that seating capacity was also limited, estimated at between seven hundred and a thousand people.[29] All these factors indicate that there was only a small number of actual theatergoers. In addition, it was difficult for social elites to attend a theatrical entertainment that was considered depraved.[30] Since it was expensive, the poor could not afford it either. Those who could attend the performances were mainly people of means with a relatively low social status (e.g., merchants).

Those kabuki "spectators" who did not go to the theaters were faced with a wide range of options. The most opulent were private performances staged at the residences of theater patrons, which were, however, even more limited than actual theatergoing. Instead, the majority of theater-lovers had a variety of inexpensive modes of virtual theatergoing, such as voice mimicry, unlicensed little theaters called "small theaters" (*koshibai*), and the audio-only theater called "shadow theater" (*kage-shibai*), which combined voice mimicry and sound effects. Theater-related publications provided information on actors and kabuki via both pictures and narratives. Publications even included a popular genre called "parrot stones" (*ōmuseki*), how-to voice-mimicry books that used lines from kabuki plays.[31] In this way, the voices, accents, postures, gestures, movements, attire, and ornaments of popular actors became public knowledge through any number of publications, such as Hachimonji Jishō's *The Complete Book on Actors* (Yakusha zensho) (1774).[32] Speaking figuratively, the introduction to the 1829 theater-book concludes: "This book will explain these points [points mentioned in the introduction] for the inexperienced viewers. This is the reason why this book is titled *Theater under the Microscope*."[33] This is the context in which the concepts of womanliness theorized in such texts as "The Words of Ayame" and "The Secret Transmissions of an *Onnagata*" circulated well beyond playgoers. Of equal significance is that the audience for these various types of hybrid virtual theatergoing was by nature limitless.

Publications not only constituted a substantial part of the kabuki experience for spectators but also generated a considerable site where the definitions of kabuki artistry and acting were debated and legitimized (as when *onnagata* artistry presented by the likes of Ayame was canonized in this manner). This phenomenon was most visible and obvious in actor-critique booklets and theater-books that evaluated performance, for evaluation inevitably entailed establishment of norms. Kabuki theater in the Edo era was thus greatly involved with the publication industry, which made possible a major channel through which women and *onnagata* circulated femininity.

If *onnagata* conceptualized womanliness in detail, and even if women read their ideas via theater-related publications, did they take "lessons" from actors? Information about popular actors, ranging from their accents to their theorization of womanliness, was published in detail, but how might women's imitation of *onnagata* have been complicated by the fact that the actors' social status was *made* so low? After all, "no matter how luxuriously they might have lived, kabuki actors were not [treated as] 'human beings.'"[34]

It is no wonder, then, that *Greater Learning for Women*, a popular book of precept literature for women first published in the early eighteenth century, emphasizes that women "must not feed their eyes and ears with such stupid things as kabuki, *jōruri*, and the like."[35] Likewise, *Women's Treasury* (Onna chōhōki), a reference book for daily life published in 1692, judged that, while the clothing *onnagata* prefer or wear is all the vogue, it is not decent to follow such a trend,[36] which suggests that women were imitating *onnagata* fashion. For example, the cloth called Edo-*kanoko* (*kanoko* pattern of Edo) was known as Kodayū-*kanoko* in Edo, named after Itō Kodayū II (d. 1689), a popular *onnagata* who was active in the late seventeenth century.[37]

Kikunojō's wish that *onnagata* be involved in the chain of citation was thus granted: "As for women admirers, an *onnagata* should make them adore the fashions he likes—such as combs, hairpins, the [forehead] cap, clothing, and sashes" (section 9).[38] One could see Kikunojō's consciousness of his "to-be-looked-at-ness" as the object of the male gaze, especially because "The Secret Transmissions of an *Onnagata*" reads that an *onnagata* "must have many male admirers who wish, 'If only there were a woman like this.'"[39] In terms of femininity circulation, however, it is far more important that the text pays attention to female admirers as the target audience capable of attesting the *onnagata*'s femininity: *onnagata* must "make them think that you are a woman just as they are."[40] Here, an *onnagata* is aware that he is an important part of the chain of citation among the doers of femininity and that the citation traffic of femininity is visibly reciprocal. It is quite intriguing that the cap, which initially constituted a pseudo—or surrogate at best—sign of *wakashu* beauty, here amounts to the sign of *onnagata* beauty in its own right and is to be copied by women. In any case, *onnagata* treatises were thus instrumental in proposing an influential femininity to women as well, even if not the ideal version in the eyes of "decent" people. *Greater Learning for Women* might have indeed prohibited women from seeing kabuki, and *Women's Treasury* scorned the vogue created by *onnagata*, but as Robertson effectively puts it, "During the Tokugawa period (and beyond), the paragons of female-likeness were *onnagata*."[41] This paragon here might not have been officially designated but was a powerful, de facto one.

Onnagata such as Kikunojō and Ayame devoted themselves to faithful imitation of "real women," who in turn followed trendy *onnagata* fashions. Imitation was thus a mutual act by which all the doers of femininity, women and *onnagata* alike, reciprocally cited each other and thereby effaced the illusionary starting point of citation. They were all simultaneously citers and citees to a certain extent, equally confined to a certain Möbius strip of citation. This mutuality was made possible by several historical factors realized in eighteenth-century Japan, such as the mediums of circulation and the possibility of separating gender identity from sex identity. The latter was further reinforced by a notion of femininity independent of the woman's biological body per se. Incorporating male actors into the citation chain of femininity, let alone enthroning them as paragons, requires a notion that does not regard femininity as grounded in a woman's body along with mediums of gender interaction between *onnagata* and women. The term "imitate," used thus far regarding the establishment of *onnagata* artistry in the eighteenth century, refers to an act of *attempting* to copy something that is posited as the object of imitation. The aim of imitation is not to copy *the* original, and it does not produce exactly the object of imitation.

The bilateral nature of femininity citation between *onnagata* and women helps highlight the elusive relationship between an original and a copy, which has long been proposed—and fairly established—in such a field as gender studies. Imitation generates the mirage of an origin, and its repetition constructs and simultaneously builds on a condensed historicity. An origin is by no means an innocent illusion, however. Albeit in a different context, Judith Butler demonstrates that endless copies create the illusion of an origin by unfolding how "heterosexuality . . . presupposes homosexuality": "Logically, this notion of an 'origin' is suspect, for how can something operate as an origin if there are no secondary consequences which retrospectively confirm the originality of that origin? The origin requires its derivations in order to affirm itself as an origin, for origins only make sense to the extent that they are differentiated from that which they produce as derivatives."[42] In terms of degree of originalness or copyness, therefore, "gay is to straight *not* as copy is to original, but, rather, as copy is to copy."[43] As Butler's example illustrates, an illusionary origin comes to carry the authority of the origin once it comes into being. The repetition of our own doing, past and present, creates the illusion of the original, and we make ourselves believe that it exists a priori. Whether appropriately or inappropriately, we act according to norms, and the norms are the product of repeated acts of copying.

It is only by imitation that *onnagata* could participate in the creation of femininity as that which can pose as an authority, which is to be cited by others. This also involves the concept of "copy" in premodern Japan and the cultural value thereof in contrast to the widespread value system in use today. Originality has been given a privileged status in modernity. Although the Author has been discovered dead and we now regard endless citationality as the demiurge of the "origin,"[44] we are not freed from the myth of originality completely, for, as Mark Rose puts it, "We are not ready . . . to give up the sense of who we are,"[45] a sense that each of us can think something original. The discourse of *onnagata* resides in a regime that is theoretically incongruous with modernity, however.

The regime in question is that of esotericism (*hiden*; lit., "secret transmission"). Esoteric practices in Japan were initially institutionalized by Kūkai (774–835), the de facto founder of Japanese esoteric Buddhism, and later adopted in various arenas ranging from literature to martial arts. In theater, Zeami is said to have introduced esoteric practices, and they have been conducted ever since. Esoteric practices are actions by which people secretly transmit, within a group, particular knowledge, such as the choreography of a play, along with what signifies the legitimacy of the knowledge (e.g., a ritual of transmission and a symbolic object such as a prized sword or fan). By these practices, "knowledge" would be conceptualized and commodified. The regime of esotericism justifies a particular type of knowledge by first being authorized by the subject of the enunciated, such as the mystic figure who first bestowed teachings upon the founder of a school. Then the subject of the enunciation, that is, the successive mentors in the said school, would be incorporated into the tradition of teachings and thereby into the collective subject of the enunciated. This "backward" process— "backward" seen from the psychoanalytic viewpoint—keeps legitimizing the subject of the enunciated and, by extension, the enunciated, that is, the knowledge per se. Importantly, legitimization is tantamount to rationalization in this paradigm. For instance, in his noh treatises, Zeami claims that he received the teachings rather than created them himself.[46] Modern scholarship has often interpreted this statement as proof of filial piety or of modesty, but Zeami's discourse, situated in the regime of esotericism, operates according to hearsay dynamics, by which the "truth" is disclosed as hearsay from the imagined past.[47] In this regime, if Zeami wishes to justify his teachings, he must legitimize them by proving that the teachings have long been in proper hands and by stating his status as a recipient. In this regime, therefore, imitation, repetition, and transmission are the moment when knowledge is created, legitimized, and reinforced. Only with this understanding can we appreciate the positive implications of imitation in the discourse of *gei* practitioners such as Zeami, Ayame, and Kikunojō in contrast to the popular concept of knowledge today, which grants a privileged attribute to originality.[48]

It is of equal importance that the act of imitating results in countless copies, each of which theoretically can function as an original. Each citation transaction involves revisions and sometimes an accidental bug. (Here lies additional counterevidence of originality. With countless, constant, and mutual transactions, the illusionary idea of origins vanishes in the aporia of which came first.) Given this, although real and virtual theatergoing were not mutually exclusive, the latter type let people participate more actively in the circulation of citation through the imitation of elocution, locomotion, and decorations.[49] Mediated imitation is more likely to efface the putative original being imitated. The longer the circuit of citation, the more diverse the copies. This process makes it far harder to pinpoint the alleged original. Suppose, for example, the wife of a merchant in a rural town in eighteenth-century Japan buys the aforementioned Edo-*kanoko*, called Kodayū-*kanoko* in Edo, as a token of the popular *onnagata* Kodayū. Is the wife following the metropolitan vogue prevalent among Edo women, or is she following the individual *onnagata* himself? This labyrinth epitomizes how they did femininity in eighteenth-century Japan: they were simply *passing*. Onnagata and women together participated in the labyrinth of citationality, which was made possible by the mediums of circulation. Imitation was, thus, an elusive act that helped construct femininity and yet nullified the boundary of "women," the alleged matrix of femininity. This further reinforced and, at the same time, was reinforced by the notion of femininity independent of a woman's body.

In the light of circulation, let us revisit the idea of the "constative," one of the principles by which "The Words of Ayame" and "The Secret Transmissions of an *Onnagata*" methodize their prescription for femininity: *onnagata* should aim at X, because X is the way in which real women exist. For instance, "The Secret Transmissions of an *Onnagata*" deciphers what it considers actual women's constative body language, based on which it offers concrete instructions for *onnagata*: "For one thing, when a woman hugs a man while faking love, she will hug him over both his arms and [will] face sideways. If it is with true affections, she will cling to him, with her arm deeply under his left arm; [follow this principle], then, you will appear realistic" (section 3).[50] Likewise, "The Words of Ayame" posits various qualities for the woman in the above formula: soft (section 1), naive (section 1), weak (section 8), not good at making people laugh (section 9), timid in front of people in great numbers (section 12), more vocal than men when cornered (section 12), and chaste (section 13).[51]

Incidentally, the remark in "The Words of Ayame" that women are more verbally effusive than men seems to contradict a point made in "The Secret Transmissions of an *Onnagata*": "when they are upset, women first cry before a speech" (section 4).[52] This is not necessarily an inconsistency, however, as, unlike "The Secret Transmissions of an *Onnagata*," "The Words of

Ayame" is concerned with gradations, in this case, the degree of emotions and corresponding physical expression. It reads that any woman flinches "when she is surrounded by many people.... Only after the enemy role heaps abuse [on you] must you become stern and sharp. At the eleventh hour, women [do not hesitate to] say what they want to say, much more so than men" (section 12).[53] Also, it is clichéd but intriguing that womanliness is defined as a deficiency and an excess at the same time (e.g., lacking a penis but abundant in liquid). If femininity is to be defined as the constitutive other of masculinity, a long-standing and omnipresent cognitive praxis in human history, then what is really meaningful is the comparative quantity (i.e., lack, deficiency, abundance, excess, etc.) and not what it claims to modify, that is to say, the quality (e.g., penis, liquid, and verbal fluency). Moreover, if such a comparison depends on a constitutive-other concept that is in a state of flux, seemingly opposite modifiers (deficient and abundant) can coexist in discourse even when the quality in question is the same (verbal fluency), let alone when there are multiple qualities to modify (penis and liquid).

Constative rhetoric has tremendous potential as discursive power and violence. The implications of constative statements are expectation, regulation, and prohibition. Given this, it is noteworthy that *onnagata* treatises propose what most probably is ideal femininity in the guise of "real femininity" in a tactful even insidious manner. Expectation here includes what is usually considered incapability, such as that a woman cries before explaining verbally when she is upset. This is a classic example of "damned if you do, damned if you don't." As a virtuous woman, you cannot explain emotion in language effectively, and, should you be capable of that, you are not considered a real woman. Women are (that is, must be) soft, naive, weak, emotional, chaste, timid, and unable to manipulate people, such as by making them laugh on purpose. When a text dictates conduct, one effective way to do so is to put it in the constative mode. While these texts were explicitly binding on the primary preachee (*onnagata*), they were perhaps far more implicitly and insidiously binding on the secondary preachee (women). What the constative does is not descriptive but definitive, proclaiming the definition as a "simple, truthful fact." Such a definition stabilizes the norms of the object of imitation.

The prescription for femininity in the *onnagata* treatises is also directed toward women in everyday life. In fact, it is characteristic of many *gei* to place an emphasis on everyday life, well beyond the artistry of *onnagata*. It is no wonder that "The Words of Ayame" repeatedly brings up offstage conduct in the interest of performance onstage: "For one thing, an *onnagata* remains an *onnagata* even inside his dressing room. He should take this to heart. When he takes a box lunch, for example, he should do so out of sight of the people in the room. If he gobbles it up, alongside a [male-role actor with whom he is about to do a love scene], and goes straight to the stage, then the male-role actor cannot truly empathize [with the role and love the partner]. That is the reason both parties will fail in it" (section 22).[54] This section seems to be concerned mainly with the partner's feelings, but elsewhere the treatise recommends that an *onnagata* spend his everyday life as a woman, precisely because "the usual state [*tsune*] is critical" (section 7).[55] At the end of the day, there is no clear offstage-onstage boundary, since the role of a woman onstage (as an *onnagata*) is analogous to—or even interchangeable with—the role of a woman offstage (as a woman). It is for this reason that an *onnagata* should not regard male-role acting as an alternative career, just as "a real woman would not become a man . . . when something goes wrong" with her life as a woman (section 11).[56]

Such an emphasis on offstage actions is not unique to "The Words of Ayame." "The Secret Transmissions of an *Onnagata*" presents an extreme case, stating that Kikunojō on his deathbed was in full dress in accordance with the *onnagata* garb code.[57] *The Pioneering Analects from Past and Present Actors* reads: "For one thing, the duty of *onnagata* is first and foremost to imitate women. If an *onnagata* goes to a bad neighborhood after dark, he should take sufficient care to wear a new loincloth. [This is far more important] than carrying a sword. He would look beautiful even when he was stripped."[58] Other theater-books canonizing "The Words of Ayame" and "The Secret Transmissions of an *Onnagata*" evince the same mind-set through such words as "with no makeup," "everyday life," "in his entire life," and other phrases to this effect. Theories on *onnagata* artistry in these texts are quite similar in their attention to everyday life as the base of *onnagata* artistry, whether it is nocturnal walking, eating, or even dying.[59] These texts do not recognize a decisive boundary between onstage performance and daily conduct offstage but anchor the foundation of acting to everyday life. (This point is still endorsed in the twentieth century by the *onnagata* Utaemon, who said that everyday life is important for kabuki actors, *onnagata* or otherwise.[60])

The flip side of this acting principle is the importance of verisimilitude in evaluating performances. Theater-related publications, such as actor-critique booklets, present plausibility as one of the most important criteria for acting. For *onnagata*, this translates as whether or not he can pass as a woman, whence come the praises of Ayame as "a genuine woman from the bottom up"[61] and Kikunojō as "a person who doesn't need the character *kata* [i.e., *gata*] out of the [noun] *onnagata*."[62] (*Onnagata* – *gata* = *onna* [woman]. Here, the compound word "*onnagata*," derived from *onna*, returns to its origin, *onna*; the performer of womanliness [*onnagata*] is restored to her "rightful" position, that is to say, "woman as is" [*onna*].)[63] Another *onnagata* called Kokan Tarōji (d. 1713) left an intriguing anecdote that illustrates this point. Dressed as a married woman of about thirty, he was standing in front of the stage during an interlude in the performance. Audience members nearby moved to make room for him, thinking that a female audience member was looking for an open seat. "Sequel to 'The Dust in the Ears'" (Zoku "Nijinshū"), the text that includes this anecdote, presents it as irrefutable proof that "Tarōji was such a maestro."[64]

Attention to everyday life as well as plausibility as a criterion of acting are not unique to *onnagata* artistry but informative of a basic understanding of acting in kabuki (and arguably in premodern Japanese theater beyond kabuki). "The Dust in the Ears" (Nijinshū) records an illustrative anecdote, in which an obscure *onnagata*, Sugi Kuhei, is said to have told Sakata Tōjūrō I (1647–1709), a renowned male-role actor: "Since I am an *onnagata*, I work hard to imitate women. Because you are a male-role actor, you should work hard to imitate men."[65] Acting is thus nothing other than imitating, regardless of the gender of the characters to be played.

In addition to the constative rhetoric and emphasis on everyday life, another point also epistemologically enhances the discursive power of the *onnagata*'s prescription for femininity. In the paradigm of *gei* culture, the physical and the mental, the formal and the conceptual, and the body and the mind cannot be separated, let alone dichotomized. The exterior and the interior are contiguous, and they will become one if one completes a specific type of training called cultivation (*shugyō*), a Buddhist term meaning "a pragmatic enterprise aiming at spiritual training and improvement of character *through training of one's body*."[66] Along with esotericism, cultivation is a critical concept in the *gei* paradigm, in which there is no appreciation for an idle genius or uncultivated prodigy. A person can be extremely talented, even divinely gifted, but he or she nevertheless needs to go through arduous, physical, long-term (typically lifetime) training. Defined as such is cultivation, whence the significance of the acquisition process for the concept of *gei*.⁶⁷ In diverse *gei* communities, *gei* practitioners engage in cultivation to acquire *gei* and in esotericism to transmit it to later generations. The notion of cultivation is not limited to the realm of arts narrowly defined, which is simply one site where the concept has been refined and theorized. Just as femininity for *onnagata* is *gei*, womanliness for women is also somewhat *gei*-like, in the sense that it is to be acquired as second nature through proper living. If what you appear externally equals who you are internally, then there can be no logic to support such a remark as "I didn't mean it."

"The Words of Ayame" and "The Secret Transmissions of an *Onnagata*" put great emphasis on the body (e.g., its posture and movements). Yet training the body, despite its obvious importance to acting, is not an end itself; more important, the body signifies the state of the being, whether through posture or movements. For instance, according to "The Secret Transmissions of an *Onnagata*," the way in which a woman hugs a man signifies her true emotions toward him. Likewise, the way in which she speaks shows how much she is emotionally charged. One's exterior can explain one's interior.⁶⁸ Rather, one's exterior *is* one's interior.

There are several levels in the body-mind connection between physical appearances and the "essence" of being. Eiko Ikegami states: "External appearance, as signified by a person's choice of costume, hairstyle, cosmetics, and other decorative accessories, can function as a critical means of expressing as well as classifying a person's categorical identity; in other words, it becomes a powerful human 'identity kit.'"⁶⁹ One's body itself, including the usage of it, is already, of course, one's identity kit. Even the act of walking illustrates this. In terms of human locomotion, theater director and critic Takechi Tetsuji (1912–1988) proposes that from the mid-Edo era onward, there were at least two types of limb combination. While those engaged in physical labor such as agriculture employed a walking style called the *nanba* gait, in which the right leg and the right hand moved forward at the same time, city dwellers walked with the right leg and the left hand moving forward simultaneously.⁷⁰ In Edo-era Japan, people would certainly be judged by their decorations, locomotion, and elocution. This is no wonder, as the master discourse in the society of those days dictated that how you appear *is* who you are.⁷¹

Appearance and existence are thus interchangeable in this paradigm, but the *onnagata*'s training of the body as that which equals what exists inside went beyond creating the socially approved identity kit. Here, it is helpful to acknowledge the Buddhist notion of "mind and body as one entity" (*shinshin ichinyo*). This concept is of great moment in the context of the aforementioned cultivation. The word "cultivation" refers to physical training for the purpose of mastering artistic techniques to the extent that the practitioner's body completely internalizes the techniques as second nature. The praxis of cultivation is prevalent in what are subsumed under the name of Japanese traditional culture: performing arts, martial arts, and so forth. Yuasa Yasuo states that cultivation was adopted as a training method and theorized as such first by poets in the twelfth century and then by theater practitioners.[72] Zeami is said to have introduced cultivation to theater.

Cultivation consists of two phases: repeated somatic training (such as in posture and movements) and internalization of the particular technique as second nature. Importantly, the significance of the physical training is not for the physical technique per se. This point, though somewhat effaced in such bodily activities as martial arts and performing arts, is of great moment, for it is reminiscent of the Buddhist origins of cultivation, in which "cultivation" refers to the path to *prajñā*, intuitive insight or wisdom, and the path consists of self-regulation and meditation.[73] For instance, Fujiwara no Teika (1162–1241) states in his poetry treatise *Each Month Exegesis* (Maigetsushō) that posture is very important when one composes a poem.[74] The logic of cultivation presupposes that, states Yuasa, "*The way the body exists controls the way the mind exists.*"[75]

Furthermore, cultivation is theorized as that which internalizes second nature. Thomas P. Kasulis summarizes Yuasa's points: "Gradually, . . . the posture becomes natural or second nature. It is *second* nature because the mind has entered into the dark consciousness and given it a form; it is an acquired naturalness."[76] Accordingly, cultivation seeks the way of making what is quasi-immediate out of what is mediated. If, by scrutinizing language, psychoanalysis discovers that pure and perfect immediacy is illusion, then cultivation creates a shortcut to such illusionary immediacy by repeated training of a body. The two phenomena are uncannily related: that perfect immediacy is impossible and that quasi-immediacy can be created out of what is mediated. If language is a means of revealing the shortcut that results in the illusionary reality of immediacy, then repeated physical training (cultivation) is the method for creating, strengthening, and thus shortening the shortcut.

Just as imitation and repetition are critical in the creation of *gei*-related knowledge in the regime of esotericism, in the regime of cultivation, too, imitation and repetition play important roles in the process of acquiring and internalizing *gei*. Furthermore, faithful imitation of an object (e.g., *onnagata*'s faithful imitation of actual women) and the attainment of what they think is the perfect essence (in this case, ideal femininity) are by no means mutually exclusive. They are, in fact, one. This is because, according to the principle of cultivation, *onnagata*'s sheer imitation of women's movements leads them to femininity in the spiritual sense if the imitated movements are repeated often enough.

A logic that internalizes the concept of cultivation presupposes that what appears (externally) creates what exists (internally) and that both should be identical to each other in the ideal state.[77] It is for this reason that such texts as "The Words of Ayame" and "The Secret Transmissions of an *Onnagata*" diligently regulate *onnagata*'s physical expression of womanly sentiments.[78] This is because the expressions create the mentality, and not the other way around. Furthermore, the texts presume that the most skilled of actors fuse the two—expressions and mentality—such that no gap is perceived, and indeed, such that no gap even exists.

This idea also appears in other types of Edo texts, beyond the realm of theater, especially those that purport to tell women how to behave. For instance, "The Words of Ayame" and *Greater Learning for Women* share a similar approach to ideal femininity. The two texts detail attire, posture, daily conduct, and attitude so that the putative student can attain femininity as second nature.[79]

Another phenomenon related to this fusion of externality and internality was the conception of ideal femininity as independent of a woman's body. This is evident in, for example, *Greater Learning for Women*. The text holds that natural women embody cursed characteristics and hence need education in order to *acquire* ideal femininity. Here, constructionism and essentialism are complicit in creating ideal womanhood.[80] The text regulates women's attire (sections 12 and 14), chores (sections 10 and 17), and posture (sections 10 and 17) so that the woman can acquire good spirit (section 2), which saves her for her entire life (section 19).[81] This echoes cultivation's attention to physical imitation as that which creates one's mental attributes. Femininity here is second nature to women, as it is to *onnagata*. They should both acquire it through cultivation.

Furthermore, biological maternity is given a peculiar meaning. In eighteenth-century Japan, the preservation of *ie*, the stem-family household, amounted to *ie*'s raison d'être.[82] In addition, there already existed in society the Buddhist cosmology that "ontogeny recapitulates ontology."[83] Transmigration from the death of one being to the birth of another symbolizes the universe, which technically could imply that biological motherhood would be of highest importance in femininity, and thus non-reproductive people, regardless of their sex, would be excluded from constructing femininity. This did not occur in eighteenth-century Japan. According to Wakita Haruko, what happened instead was a phenomenon summarized by the phrase "the belly [womb] is that which is borrowed" (*hara wa karimono*),[84] which signifies the shifting importance of the womb as a vehicle to the fetus as a rider. The womb might have been sanctified, but it stood alone in this paradigm and in turn never sanctified the woman's body in its entirety.[85] *Greater Learning for Women* endorses this point, listing seven female vices that cause divorce: disobedience, infertility, amorousness, jealousy, particular disease, talkativeness, and a habit of stealing. Among these fatal vices, only infertility is redeemable: "However, if the woman remains righteous, behaves herself, and keeps off jealousy, then rather than leaving the *ie*, she should raise a child [or children] with the same surname. Or if her husband's concubine has a child [or children], then the wife does not have to leave."[86] The other side of this "redemption" is that the concubine, the biological mother of an heir of the *ie*, is not guaranteed the status of a mother of the *ie*'s progeny. She cannot climb the social ladder only by giving birth to a child, even when the child is an heir. There can hardly exist a *uterus ex machina* that changes the situation magically. This status of biological maternity opens the possibility that non-reproductive people may represent ideal femininity. In this paradigm, the body of an *onnagata* amounts to the ideal site for projecting femininity, because femininity can be constructed without involving biological women, the alleged matrix of essential vice.

• • •

The concept of an ideal femininity that allows its dislocation or liberty from a woman's body is critical in several ways. Had it not been for this concept, *onnagata* could not have established their art as the performance of womanliness, theorized their gender performance as interchangeable with women's femininity performance, and thereby consolidated the *onnagata* traditions. Early-twentieth-century Japan would later see a counteroperation to ground womanhood in the physical body of women. Ayako Kano examines this phenomenon in the modern restoration of actresses:

Women are to nature as *onnagata* are to art. Both feminist arguments in favor of actresses and misogynist arguments against actresses share this basic assumption.

This essentialist and expressive understanding of gender was a modern one, in contrast to the theatrical and performative understanding of gender exemplified in *kabuki*. Eventually the pro-actress faction overwhelmed the anti-actress faction, yet the victory was an ambivalent one. It confirmed the definition of womanhood as an essence naturally grounded in a woman's body, a definition that would also justify the reduction of woman to *nothing but* her body.[87]

Such an essentialist understanding enabled women's *victory*, to perform in public, which they had officially been prohibited to do since 1629, but it also meant that they were *doomed* to femininity, no longer *gei*-ish second-nature womanhood acquired through training but essential femininity as a built-in fate. Just as Kano sees both the positive and negative impacts of this modern restoration of actresses, one recognizes both the positive and negative impacts of the separation of ideal femininity from a woman's body that made possible *onnagata* artistry.

This severance is also congruous to the divorce between sex identity and gender identity, which was taken for granted by both *wakashu* and *onnagata*, albeit in different ways. This reminds us how far they have come. The trajectory from the female-role players of *wakashu kabuki* to the *onnagata* of kabuki was radical yet insidious because *onnagata* virtually built on the theoretical negation of what they relied on in practice. *Onnagata* denied *wakashu*'s defining characteristics, including the latter's source of beauty (namely, transience), whence came the need for acquiring a new, prolonged gender that they were to perform and reify. They found it in the constative femininity of real women and acquired it by the methodology of imitation.

Their prescription for femininity illustrates the intriguing implications and functions of imitation. Imitation was an act by which eighteenth-century virtuoso *onnagata* participated in the construction of femininity, secured their knowledge, and achieved the femininity of perfection as second nature. Imitation was also a means by which *onnagata* and women—all the doers of femininity—circulated it and hence revealed the porosity of the putative category of women. Imitation was thus an elusive act that not only helped construct "femininity" but also nullified the boundary of "women," the alleged matrix of femininity.[88] In this regard, *onnagata* were engaged in an ambivalent enterprise. On the one hand, their doing femininity effectively demonstrated the contingent and porous nature of such a category as "woman." On the other hand, as shown in the treatises, they conceptualized femininity in a way that could anticipate the impending gender economy in which femininity would be considered monolithic and fixed. What is more, they presented this version of femininity, their version, in powerful constative rhetoric.

For women, imitation was materialized as they followed *onnagata* fashions. Women and *onnagata* circulated femininity via tangible and visible markers (e.g., clothing), materializing the master discourse that how you look is who you are. Borrowing Butler's parlance, one could say that *onnagata* are to women *not* as copy is to original, but, rather, as copy is to copy.[89]

In *onnagata* artistry, the concept of imitation was related to evaluation based on the criterion of verisimilitude in everyday life. These together resulted in the phenomenon of *"onnagata* who pass." Many remarks in kabuki literature show that *onnagata* were critically acclaimed when they could pass as women offstage, suggesting that the principal mission of *onnagata* was to successfully impersonate women.[90] Indeed, an *onnagata* would be praised if he claimed to be suffering from gynecological disorders precisely because such a claim attested to his successful performance onstage.[91] When ill, an *onnagata* would be praised if he could perceive and explain his condition—whether headache or nausea—as the result of a gynecological disorder. It is not necessarily that his body needed to show symptoms specific to a gynecological disorder.[92] In fact, the phrase "suffering from gynecological disorders" was used as the epithet for skillful *onnagata* from the eighteenth to the late nineteenth century,[93] although, as Taganojō wittily puts it, "try that today, and you'd get a punch."[94]

When and why one would start being punched is germane to a new definition of *onnagata* artistry in the next era of *onnagata* history. Compatibility between women and *onnagata* in the kabuki discourse lasted until the early twentieth century. For example, when the *onnagata* Arashi Rikō visited a certain restaurant around 1875, although Rikō was only a customer, he offered to help out. An anecdote published in 1910 praises him for having passed as a maid in everyone's eyes.[95] Also in 1910, Ichikawa Monnosuke VI (1862–1914) recollected a compliment he received upon going to a public bath some time earlier. He felt as if he "was seeing stars," he recalled, when he was told, "That's the wrong way, ma'am," as he headed toward the men's bath.[96] (The wording "I felt as if I was seeing stars" might well portend the impending punch.) Another renowned *onnagata*, Iwai Hanshirō VIII (1829–1882), was described in a 1920 text as being able to "completely pass as a woman, even when wearing just lingerie."[97] And the two top *onnagata* in the first half of the twentieth century, Baikō and Nakamura Utaemon V (1865–1940), similarly stated that married *onnagata* came to resemble their wives.[98]

I am not suggesting that if we should see these historical *onnagata* today, onstage or off, we would consider them realistic. What matters most here is not so much performance as reception: how the performance of *onnagata* was received, perceived, and evaluated at that time by their contemporaries. (One needs to keep in mind that, metaphorically, the representational apparatus by which spectators make sense of performance is usually if not always naturalized to the eyes of the spectators in the said system. Theirs is invisible to them and ours to us, and it would be remiss, or even arrogant, for one to ignore the presence of such on one's part only because one can take it for granted.) Also, theoretically, this does not negate the constructed nature of *onnagata* femininity, or of any gender for that matter. It is just that this type of constructionism is not the constitutive other of essentialism: constructionism and essentialism here are not in the relation of *différance*. Rather, what kabuki literature until the early twentieth century suggests is a concept of gender that is theorized in the intertwined operation of constructionist and essentialist discourses, which are not mutually exclusive in the first place. The anecdotes about passing *onnagata* simply indicate compatibility between women and *onnagata* in the discourse of kabuki that makes possible such an operation.

In addition, what matters here is not whether or not these anecdotes are true but the fact that, until just a century ago, *onnagata* artistry was measured by the criterion of verisimilitude in everyday life. Whether the actor could pass as a woman in places crowded with women, such as restaurants and bathhouses, was considered crucial to evaluating an actor's achievement as an *onnagata*. Of course, if *onnagata* had been totally successful in passing as women, the anecdotes would not have come into existence, much less been preserved. One might say that *onnagata* artistry lay in the slippery gap between "persuasive imitation" and "total passing as the object of imitation," or in the renowned concept of playwright Chikamatsu that theoretical *gei* resides in the ambiguous space between the real and the false.[99] What is, then, natural or real *to* us?

PART III

Marginalized Centers

Bodies and Personnel

> [One day, when I was a boy, I was wandering around a corridor of a playhouse. I happened to peep at actors who were getting undressed.] Just when I noticed that some had breasts, I was caught by a staff member, who said, "Keep it to yourself, OK? If people know they're women, tickets won't sell. They're men, all right?"
>
> —*ENTERTAINMENT ILLUSTRATED*, July 1912,
> letter from a reader, "Sukina Haiyū no Sukina Gei," 188

CHAPTER 6

Naturally Disciplined

Moving Real on Procrustean Beds

IN the Edo era, the uppermost principle for *onnagata* was "to impersonate women successfully,"[1] and their performance was critically acclaimed when they plausibly looked like women. As the founder and tutelary deity of *onnagata*,[2] Ayame was said to have "reproduce[d] the figure [of the woman] intact,"[3] or even to have been "a woman intact."[4] Leiter remarks that "realism was at the core of [the] art."[5]

In the context of Japanese theater traditions, there is a far more dubious relationship between the "natural" and the "artificial" than it might seem. At first glance, this might appear similar to Chikamatsu's notion that theatrical *gei* lies in the ambiguous space between the real and the false.[6] If we are to interpret this ambiguous border as an extraneous space adjacent to what is real, then any *gei* cannot project anything intact because, by definition, *gei* becomes possible only after cultivation. (*Gei* is post-cultivation second nature, differentiated from Kantian genius.) If that were the case, the femininity that *onnagata* like Ayame performed could not theoretically represent a "woman intact." By the same token, moreover, since women in the Edo era evinced *gei*-ish womanliness, they could not be "women intact" either.

This chapter explores the interconnections among bodies, realities, and re/presentations in kabuki by exploring both how human locomotion (in this case, gait) can transform culturally and a kabuki acting technique called "puppet-gesture" (*ningyōburi*). This chapter somehow defies the strategic priority of *how* over *what*; nevertheless, this *what*—gait—is still within the realm of *how* in that it is about how people walk. Although gait as examined here is not limited to femininity or women's way of walking, both Ayame and Sakata Tōjūrō IV (b. 1931) are famous for their *onnagata* acting, and Tōjūrō associates his great success in *onnagata* movements to muscle memory learned through gait training.[7] The polyphony of gender and locomotion is a strong reminder of how insecurely and conditionally it is that our own bodies are made to operate and function. Kabuki provides us with a stimulating and useful context for this topic.

DETOUR OR SHORTCUT:
NOH LESSONS FOR KABUKI GRAMMAR

In "The Words of Ayame," Ayame recollects trying to take lessons in noh when he was young:

> My master at that time was a shamisen player, so he told me to practice the instrument well. [The master] also told me to seek noh instruction from Sir Gorozaemon [who was skilled in noh], taking advantage of the fact that he was my patron. Accordingly, I asked him several times, but he never consented, saying that I should devote myself to the "gesture and acting" [*shiuchi*] of *onnagata*. [He said that] until you receive recognition, nothing else is necessary. If you adhere to noh, it will divert your attention from the main thing [kabuki and *onnagata*]. In addition, if you learn noh in a halfhearted way, that would be bad for the theater [kabuki]. This is because [with noh lessons,] one's gesture and acting will become slippery [*nurari*], and one would also be inclined to do noh-like dance. When you master the kabuki dance and still want to try noh at that time, that would be fine. So he said, and he did not give me lessons in noh. [Section 18][8]

Ayame attributes his successful career as a kabuki actor to the fact that he followed this advice and dedicated himself to kabuki training.

In stark contrast, Tōjūrō IV, one of the major actors working today, went through intense training in noh in his youth *before* accomplishing kabuki training, *in order to* establish the foundations of his kabuki performance.[9]

Considering his successful career as a kabuki actor, noh training was far from detrimental to kabuki acting and in fact helped him accomplish kabuki training. Moreover, Tōjūrō is not the only successful kabuki actor who has taken lessons in noh. Nakamura Kanzaburō XVIII (1955–2012) similarly recounts that the noh lessons he took in his childhood were important in establishing the foundations of his kabuki acting.[10]

This divergence cannot be reduced to Tōjūrō's and Ayame's idiosyncratic preferences, as the case of Kanzaburō effectively rules out such a possibility. Likewise, while this is certainly due in large part to the fact that Tōjūrō and Ayame are separated by two and a half centuries, even that point does not necessarily explain the difference in their approach to noh training. Sadoshima Chōgorō I (1700–1757) and Ayame were approximately contemporaries and likewise active in the same region (the Kyoto and Osaka areas). In contrast to Ayame's skeptical attitude toward noh, Chōgorō states: "For one thing, when performing an opus that requires *ōkuchi* [a type of noh costume], you must dance as if you were performing noh and not break the distinctive quality. It is no good [to dance it] in the casual manner."[11] According to Gunji, those like Chōgorō, and not Ayame, were more typical of the time:

> Through the Genroku period [1688–1704], noh was actively absorbed [into kabuki dance], which must have resulted from the fact that kabuki deeply adopted the taste of the newly risen townspeople, who were the patrons of kabuki.
>
> A story about Yoshizawa Ayame, the leading *onnagata* in the Genroku period, in which he tried to learn noh from his patron but was reproached instead, was rather an exceptional case. There were many [opposite] examples of an *onnagata* who was good at noh dance disappearing in [the ups and downs of] a vogue.[12]

For Ayame, noh was something extra, which he could learn after mastering kabuki acting if he so wished, whereas noh helped Tōjūrō acquire something more fundamental to kabuki acting. This incongruity is significant, as it serves as an example of how human locomotion can transform culturally.

Noh theater consists of what Zeami calls the two basic arts, dancing and chanting,[13] and it happens that Ayame's and Tōjūrō's anecdotes are about dancing, not chanting. When declining Ayame's request for noh lessons, Gorozaemon explains the reasons, which include "if you learn noh in a halfhearted way, that would be bad for the theater [kabuki]. This is because [with noh lessons,] one's gesture and acting will become slippery."[14] In contrast, Tōjūrō's mentor Takechi sent him to several maestros for training in fundamentals, including Toyotake Yamashiro-no Shōjō (1878–1967), a legendary *gidayū* chanter of the puppet theater, for voice training, and noh actor Sakurama Michio (1897–1983), for training in noh dance (*shimai*).[15] Unlike Ayame, Tōjūrō says that he was sent to the teachers precisely because he lacked the foundations of kabuki acting.[16]

It is widely understood that kabuki dance and *gidayū* chanting[17] are the two most significant prerequisites for kabuki acting. Accordingly, the puppet theater's importance for kabuki does not stop at the fact that it is a vital "authentic tradition" (*honmon*), because, just as kabuki dance creates one's body, *gidayū* elocution creates one's voice.[18] *Gidayū* elocution is important for the basics of kabuki elocution due to kabuki's close connection with the puppet theater. If lessons in dance create a body suitable for kabuki movements (beyond dance pieces), so lessons in *gidayū* create a voice suitable for kabuki elocution (beyond pieces adapted from bunraku). Training in dance and *gidayū* implants kabuki grammar in an actor's body, including the vocal cords. Accordingly, Tōjūrō's *gidayū* voice training was to be expected. How does noh dance fit in this context? Furthermore, why do Ayame's and Tōjūrō's accounts differ so clearly?

Is it about the slippery gesture and acting, which "The Words of Ayame" associates with noh training taken before one accomplishes kabuki training? Is it that the slippery body was not appreciated in Ayame's circles but was thought of highly by Tōjūrō's? This slippery feature probably contributes comparatively little, if it does at all, to the said disparity in the anecdotes of Ayame and Tōjūrō. Considering the following words of Tōjūrō, a greater issue seems to lie in something else, namely, gait: "[The first day of my lesson,] Master Sakurama told me to walk along the edge of tatami mats [i.e., a straight line on the floor]. . . . I was doing what was called sliding steps [*suriashi*] in noh. . . . I walked back and forth along the border for several hours, and he dismissed the session. The next session was also just about sliding steps. This lasted for a half year."[19] After the six-month lesson dedicated to sliding steps alone, Sakurama told Tōjūrō that he had achieved what Takechi had asked the noh actor to teach: to walk properly.[20] The emphasis on gait is further highlighted by the absence of noh dance in the training program: "At that time, I felt ashamed that I hadn't learned anything [i.e., any noh dance] despite the fact that I had studied under noh master Sakurama Michio for [as long as] six months, so I asked him to teach me *shimai* [noh dance without costume]. He granted my request and taught me [a piece called] *Takasago*, but I don't remember the contents of it."[21] Theater director Suzuki Tadashi (b. 1939) points out, "The basis of performance onstage resides in the way in which the feet and legs are used," and "noh is often said to be the art of walking."[22]

Tōjūrō himself later realized the weight of this gait training, for it let him retain the figure of an *onnagata* even when running onstage.[23] Tōjūrō's lessons in noh were meant to establish what Suzuki calls "the basis of performance onstage." Kanzaburō's noh lessons in childhood were uncannily similar to Tōjūrō's:

> Speaking of the way of walking, the other day, there was something I was very happy about. I was playing the role of Yoshitsune in *Funa-Benkei* at the Kabuki-za Theater. [And I was praised] that the movements of my feet were beautiful....
>
> The reason why I was so happy to be complimented on walking was because I have bad memories about it from my childhood....
>
> [Among the various kinds of training curriculum set by my father was the manner of walking.] The late noh master Nanjō Hideo... let me see him walk and said, "Walk this way." But you can't walk that way so easily....
>
> I would walk quietly, and [he would say,] "Once more." I would walk reluctantly, and [he would say,] "Once more." I would walk tiredly, and [he would say,] "Once more." That sounded like the voice of a devil.[24]

Such attention to gait, not to mention exclusive emphasis on it, is totally absent from the accounts of noh lessons in "The Words of Ayame," in which noh lessons mean nothing other than noh dance lessons.

Arguably, the significance of walking goes far beyond the realm of stage performance. In biometrics, a hot field especially with the increasing emphasis on homeland security in the post-9/11 era, researchers have recently considered the possibility of using gait as a biometric.[25] Biometrics identify humans based on intrinsic physiological or behavioral features (e.g., fingerprints and signatures), and the researchers' attention to gait suggests that this biometric is considered essential to that extent. It is also noteworthy that the approach to gait in such a field as biometrics is reminiscent of the debates over gender. Gait and gender are related, at least partially, to how we do things with bodies, and both are certainly about acts that matter.

Thus, the performative principle is applicable to both (i.e., a repetitious doing creates a being), because gait in biometrics, no matter how dynamic, is a certain being to be identified. Far from static, such beings are always being rewritten and amended, as has been exposed by gender studies and as has been empirically proved by Tōjūrō. For him, gait training helped establish the foundations of kabuki acting, so that he could run as an *onnagata*. This might well be another component of the basic grammar of kabuki. What was it, then, that constituted kabuki grammar in terms of gait?

Edo-era actors, such as Ayame, must have had "something" internalized in their body usage when they walked, with or without noh training (which makes noh training an extra as opposed to part of the basics). In contrast, contemporary actors had to take an extra step to internalize this "something," and that was noh training as far as Tōjūrō was concerned. Even if it were detrimental to make one's body movements slippery with noh training, the advantage to acquiring this "something" must have been greater than any downside. My proposition is that this "something" is the *nanba* (also *nanban*) gait, or, more precisely, the body usage concomitant with it. If human locomotion—especially unconscious movements such as gait—is a palpable example of what comes naturally to most of us, what this chapter highlights is the dubious nature of such a perception, which indicates the ambiguous demarcation of natural and artificial for our bodies.

NANBA WALKING: A GAIT OF THE OTHER, THE EXTRAORDINARY, OR THE UNIVERSAL

The *nanba* gait is a style of walking in which each hand and leg move in unison—that is, "when the right leg moves forward, the right hand moves forward at the same time."[26] This parallel gait, associated with locomotion in agriculture, is said to have been a major way of walking in premodern Japan. It is usually posited vis-à-vis the predominant modern-style gait in which the opposite limbs move in unison (diagonally). Generally speaking, *nanba* movements have disappeared from daily life in Japan but are preserved in such realms as martial arts and premodern theaters, where it is employed in all traditional performing arts established in premodern Japan (noh, *kyōgen*, bunraku, kabuki, etc.). Tomie Hahn, an ethnologist and a practitioner of *nihon buyō* (a type of Japanese dance closely associated with kabuki) gives the following detailed description of the basic movements of the shoulders in *nihon buyō*: "The shoulders press downward with every step a dancer takes. Each (vertical) half of the body is coordinated such that, for example, when the left foot moves forward, the left shoulder simultaneously moves downward."[27] Although Hahn does not mention the word "*nanba*," her accounts coincide with *nanba*-related body movements as a whole.

Nanba is not confined to these stage performances but also appears in folk performance traditions. Extant examples recorded in films include *kōwaka* dance (a medieval dance genre) still performed in the city of Setaka, Fukuoka prefecture;[28] *kagura* dance (an ancient dance of offering) in Mount Hayachine, Iwate prefecture;[29] and Awa dance (a *bon* festival dance) in Tokushima prefecture.[30] *Bon* is the annual festival for the dead, a good site for keeping folk performance traditions alive, and Awa dance is an example of many such *bon* festival dances. In his 1894 monograph, Lafcadio Hearn (also known as Koizumi Yakumo) (1850–1904) wrote of a *bon* festival dance he had seen in a place he called "Kami-Ichi," which most probably was Uwaichi, Tottori prefecture, and the description implies *nanba* movements: "All together glide the right foot forward one pace, without lifting the sandal from the ground, and extend both hands to the right, with a strange floating motion and a smiling, mysterious obeisance. Then the right foot is drawn back, with a repetition of the waving of hands and the mysterious bow. Then all advance the left foot and repeat the previous movements, half-turning to the left."[31]

Nanba is said to illustrate the strong tie between Japanese premodern performance and agriculture. (For instance, when one holds a hoe, it is most likely that the right foot and the right hand move forward together.) Takechi is one of the earliest thinkers who introduced *nanba* into critical writings, and he defines "the posture of *nanba*" as "the posture determined by the principle of body motions that satisfy the demand of such [physical] labor of production" (e.g., agriculture and mining).[32] In this regard, it was not coincidence at all that he made his protégé Tōjūrō learn noh walking, which is strongly associated with *nanba*.

To be precise, *nanba* is not equal to the sliding steps that Tōjūrō and Kanzaburō learned. Sliding steps are a refined and specialized gait, the use of which is associated with *nanba*. The walking method of sliding steps is highly sophisticated, with one's lower body completely controlled and stabilized and the upper body simply placed and liberated. As illustrated in the anecdotes about Tōjūrō and Kanzaburō, this requires exhaustive training and intense kinesthetics, and it has been treated as a skill of great importance in such traditions as noh and martial arts. For example, around the sixteenth century, the Konparus and Yagyūs—major households of noh and swordsmanship respectively—are said to have exchanged information about it as highly valued, top-secret knowledge.[33] While the origins of sliding steps are unknown, dance critic Ashihara Eiryō (1907–1981), another pioneer thinker paying attention to *nanba*, proposes that it is relatively a recent method of walking, as it requires a smooth floor and appropriate *tabi*-socks.[34] Since one's arms hardly move with sliding steps, *nanba* and sliding steps are not interchangeable, but the use of the body (especially of the torso) is the same. While the *nanba* gait is associated with the seemingly "naturally" constructed locomotion used by many people in premodern Japan, the walking method of sliding steps is a heightened way of controlling one's gait and posture derived from the body usage constructed through *nanba*.

Recently, *nanba* has become a trendy topic in popular discourse in Japan. Many trade books on *nanba* have been published since the early 2000s, including *Nanba Running*, *A Theory on the Body of Nanba*, *Miraculous Body Revolution by "Nanba Walking,"* and *Remodeling the Body by "Nanba Walking."*[35] Magazines and blogs have also provided sites for popular discourse on *nanba*. One person who has played a major role in popularizing *nanba* is martial arts practitioner Kōno Yoshinori (b. 1949).[36] Intriguingly, the adoption of the *nanba* method, initially advocated by martial arts practitioners such as Kōno, by modern athletes was vital to the *nanba* boom. For instance, the success of Suetsugu Shingo, who won a bronze medal in a 2003 international competition, was attributed to a particular body usage related to *nanba*.[37] Likewise, the Tōhō High School basketball team improved its record significantly after incorporating *nanba* into its training. Two of the books mentioned above were written by a coach of the team, Kaneda Nobuo, with his colleagues: *Nanba Running* and *A Theory on the Body of Nanba*.

This transmission from martial arts to modern sports helps emphasize what is intriguing and alarming about the popular discourse on *nanba*, which forms a kind of Möbius strip, constantly flipping over the two facets of universalism and particularism. The following is a summary of typical narratives introducing *nanba*: It is taken for granted that the way we walk today, in which arms and legs are paired diagonally, is natural and rational, and the swinging of limbs made possible by diagonal body motions is said to be the source of power and speed. The recent international success of athletes such as Suetsugu, however, has demonstrated that the traditional Japanese walking style, *nanba*, is more efficient and thus scientifically superior.

In fact, some international sports stars (e.g., Michael Jordan and Chinese long-distance runner Sun Yingjie) use their bodies in a similar way, which attests to the rational advantage provided by *nanba*. *Nanba* is still used in such practices as sliding steps in noh, swordsmanship, and sumo wrestling. The typical *nanba*-related narratives, summarized here, conclude that the Japanese had long walked in this traditional way until the beginning of the Meiji era and claim that it is necessary to revalue the true merit of their cultural heritage.

As shown in the preceding summary, narratives on *nanba* are often elusive in that *nanba* is considered to be simultaneously of universal merit (scientific efficiency) and of particular merit (cultural heritage specific to Japan). In addition, the latter type of merit conceals another pair, universalism (the assumption that "all Japanese should be capable of *nanba*") and particularism ("the Japanese are specifically capable of it"). It demands our attention that the popular narrative on *nanba* falls into the category of "the theory of Japaneseness" (*nihonjinron*), the infamous narrative that claims Japanese uniqueness in an essentialist manner.[38] Due to its eye-catching quality, *nanba* is, among other things in premodern Japan, fair game for the theory of Japaneseness. To the same extent, moreover, *nanba* is also fair game for Orientalism,[39] candidly displaying the intimate relation between Orientalism and reverse Orientalism, such as the theory of Japaneseness.

Orientalist and reverse Orientalist discussions on *nanba* hinder our effective understanding of *nanba*, for they treat *nanba* and sliding steps as if they were of equal value and claim that both are characteristics of Japanese culture, thus implicitly available to all Japanese (whatever the term "Japanese" might mean). As mentioned, however, sliding steps require arduous discipline and are reserved for those who have mastered the formidable technique. Furthermore, if *nanba* can be verified as scientifically superior in terms of human locomotion, it would be necessary to examine whether it occurs sparsely worldwide as is said. Both points have already been problematized in several disciplines. As for scientific superiority, sports scientist and orthopedist Watarai Kōji, while paying attention to its cultural aspects,[40] mainly analyzes how a body operates in *nanba* from the viewpoint of sports sciences and concludes, "Takechi [rescued *nanba* from the stigma] that it was wrong. Kōno [Yoshinori] states that it is a secret of martial arts. My opinion is to accept *nanba* as one way of using [our bodies], without [charging it with too much cultural meaning]. It is one form [way] of connecting the motions of the spine and the limbs, [which is part of body motions]."[41]

As for its worldwide distribution, Kōno Ryōsen introduces various examples of *nanba* that broadly appear in dance performances, martial arts, and religious ceremonies in Asian cultures.[42] After conducting comparative study of Japanese and Chinese scroll paintings, X. Jie Yang has found *nanba* in both.[43] Kōno Yoshinori himself, the martial arts practitioner who ignited the *nanba* boom, also mentions many types of martial arts, Japanese and otherwise.[44] It is also noteworthy that, when explaining various body usages in premodern Japanese martial arts, Kōno Yoshinori focused almost exclusively on what he claimed to be the natural advantages and not cultural specificities; at one event held in the United States, he frequently used volunteers from the audience to prove his point: According to him, when a human body is used in the way refined by martial arts practitioners, the body, regardless of its cultural background, demonstrates its power most effectively.[45] Ashihara further specifies that *nanba* appears universally in body movements when people use power in an extreme way: the shot put, fencing, *naginata*-swordsmanship, ballet, and so on.[46] This observation accords with that of Watarai, who lists fencing, karate, and kendo swordsmanship.[47] Ashihara also points out that remarks about this type of gait can be found beyond the Japanese discourse as well.[48] Even though Japanese culture does not have a monopoly on *nanba*, it does not alter the significance of what *nanba* might entail, be it the said physical merit that allows extreme power or the meaning of its purported disappearance in modern Japan.

MODERN CONVERSION OF THE BODY: A GAIT, A TORSO, AND SOMATIC GRAMMAR

One significant observation made of *nanba* is that its extinction in Japan was germane to how modernity took shape in Japan—that is, *nanba* had long been embedded in the default posture of the majority of Japanese engaged in agriculture. According to this narrative, this changed in the Meiji era, when the new government needed soldiers who could move more efficiently as a group and thus introduced the Western style of walking into military training and school education. Unlike the Edo shogunate, the fledgling Meiji government adopted Westernization and modernization as its state policy, and the social transformations thus engendered were rapid and far-reaching, ranging from coiffure codes to legal systems and to epistemological grids by which people made sense of things. Modernity thus changed the cultural milieu of Japan quite drastically in the late nineteenth and early twentieth centuries, and Karatani proposes that countless kinds of inversion (*tentō*) happened in a somewhat Foucauldian manner.[49] Theater did not escape this total change,[50] but in terms of gait, school education was the realm in which its effects were immediately verifiable.

According to Murohoshi Ryugo, who examines documents about physical education at elementary schools between 1872 and 1886, various gymnastic exercises were recommended in manuals for primary teachers, such as *Handbook for Primary Teachers, Supplement* (1874): exercises to help straighten legs while walking, raise one's knees while running, and keep one's balance while standing on one leg.[51] These motions are "the opposite extremes of those of *nanba*."[52] For instance, the exercises to help keep one's balance while standing on one leg are designed to create a central pivot inside the body,[53] whereas in *nanba*, there is "no pivot or fulcrum inside one's body"[54] or two "axes, left and right."[55] The educational policy in the early Meiji era tried to amend people's daily body movements based on *nanba*,[56] and the goal of such training went beyond "the amendment of individual students' posture and gait," as it also meant to "train them to march in step in a military fashion."[57] Ultimately, states Takechi, the Meiji government aimed to create a modern military for its colonialist purposes, and the ex-samurai population was too small for that. Disappointed that its soldiers, mostly farmers, could not move in unison, the government found it necessary to train people who could march in step, which required a drastic change in locomotion.[58] Miura Masashi summarizes this process as follows: "The Japanese lost *nanba* and instead acquired [the way in which they] rhythmically marched in step. . . . It is obvious that [body usage] was modernized."[59]

To be exact, the "modernization of the body" involves locomotion of the body in its entirety, but, as demonstrated by Murohoshi's study, gait was certainly part and parcel of it. The conversion in question, however, seems a bit more complicated than presented in the narratives introduced thus far. For example, we can still observe an interesting mixture of new and old, as depicted in the film *Ran* (1985). Kyōami, a jester in service to a samurai lord, at one time teases the aged lord by singing, "Let the castle be taken, let the paddy fields be taken." As he sings, the jester dances ad lib in *nanba*. Immediately afterward, however, the actor dashes off in non-*nanba* gait as the lord becomes angry with Kyōami.[60] My reading is that the actor playing Kyōami, Pītā (Ikehata Shinnosuke) (b. 1952), followed the premodern common sense of dancing in *nanba*, or followed the choreography based on the premodern common sense, but he ran in non-*nanba*, because his own naturalized locomotion was not that of *nanba*. (Ikehata, the son of a dance-school head, has taken lessons in Japanese dance since infancy.) *Nanba* was something that many people might have done with little conscious effort in premodern Japan, as they must have internalized it as second nature. (This is not to say that *nanba* was essentially natural at that time.) This motion, however, no longer comes so easily for many people in contemporary Japan.

The mixture of new and old locomotion in the film suggests that the bodies of contemporary performers of premodern Japanese theater (Japanese dance, kabuki, etc.) are subject to two different kinds of naturalness. This does not mean that the two types of naturalness are internalized (naturalized) to an equal extent by all the performers in the said category, but it is at least certain that they are engaged in two different types of training in their quest to acquire the two types of locomotion. One is in school education (i.e., the gymnastic exercises) to make their bodies capable of marching in step, and the other is in their professional training, namely, cultivation, which teaches them to dance in *nanba*. The significance of this difference is not limited to limb combinations. As is obvious from the initial purpose set by the government, the training introduced in modern education can be understood as a Foucauldian discipline, as that which creates docile bodies. In contrast, cultivation operates in a different economy, in which religious, artistic, and martial practitioners pursue the perfection of their minds by training their bodies. A premise of great moment behind it is the Buddhist idea that *"the way the body exists controls the way the mind exists."*[61] Somewhat analogous to the positionalities of multilingual speakers, the bodies of contemporary actors engaged in traditional Japanese performing arts are the locus of multiple systems, separate kinds of locomotion, and differentiated philosophies. They are required to internalize diverse codes of locomotion through different kinds of training and discipline. (Many a kabuki actor in modern times is said to have expressed the opinion that compulsory nine-year education is an obstacle to cultivation, and considering the above point, it is not merely stealing time that they want to reserve for cultivation but is also destructive to what the cultivation aims to create.)

Kabuki actors in modern times live in this cultural milieu, and a 1975 production of *The Village School* (Terakoya) in Tokyo similarly shows an interesting mixture. When a titled retainer called Genba exits, he walks majestically in the *nanba* gait, but the minor retainers following him do not.[62] One possibility lies in choreography, as Genba himself enters with a non-*nanba* gait.⁶³ Another possibility lies in training. The actor who performed Genba was Ichikawa Yaozō IX (1906–1987), who must have learned kabuki dance more thoroughly than those who performed the other minor retainers, as kabuki circles have been extremely rank-conscious. *Nanba* is thus still used in Japanese performance, but contemporary actors are not necessarily trained in it, and the Meiji-conversion explanation persuasively fits this reading.

A few more issues further complicate understanding. For example, despite its recent popularity, *nanba* has not yet been fully explored, and there is no consensus as to the etymology of the term. One theory says that it comes from another established term, "*nanban*" (southern barbarians), which broadly signified southeastern Asia and southern Europe in Edo-era Japan.⁶⁴ Another says it derives from Nanba, the name of a place in Osaka. Another proposal is that it originates from a certain kind of shoes worn in paddy fields.⁶⁵ Regardless of its etymology, the very existence of the word "*nanba*" indicates that this style of walking was a marked form as opposed to an unmarked form. Given this markedness, it is far-fetched to consider *nanba* a default. One intriguing counterexample comes from Yoshimura Yūki (1923–1998), former head of the Yoshimura dance school and the father of Ikehata, who is quoted as saying that the meaning of the term is the opposite in the Kyoto and Osaka regions, where the Yoshimura school is based: the word "*nanba*" indicates that the limbs are paired diagonally, whereas moving the right hand and leg together (and the left hand and leg together) is the normal way.⁶⁶ However, this alone is not substantial enough to deny the markedness of what is usually known as *nanba* (i.e., the parallel gait), and the issue requires further investigation.

Furthermore, theater critic Oka Onitarō (1872–1943) left a remark that ambiguously concurs with and simultaneously contradicts the Meiji inversion narrative. The following remark from *The Secret of Gidayū Chanting* (Gidayū hiketsu) (1903) might seem to bear out the alleged drastic change that took place in the Meiji era: "The timing-pause-interval [*ma*] [of *gidayū* chanting] is like the steps of people when they walk, . . . [and] the rhythm [*hyōshi*] is like the hands that they swing while walking. . . . If the timing and rhythm [of *gidayū* chanting] are snarled, it is as if the right hand moves forward when the right leg moves forward. . . . Modulation [*yokuyō*] and speed [*kankyū*] have a natural logic [*shizen no ri*]; accordingly, to know the nature leads one to know the mystery [of the art]."⁶⁷ Here, the motion of *nanba* is used to illustrate a snarl (*motsure*). The unstated assumption is that the right hand moves forward when the left leg moves forward according to natural logic. Certainly, when put in the context of the Meiji transformations, this remark would appear representative of the new understanding of gait made possible after the change. The wording "natural logic" seems to be especially in line with the cultural milieu at that time, when Japanese society was experiencing the hasty formation of natural scientific discourses (e.g., biology and sexology).

In a different yet equally reasonable context, namely, the tradition of *gidayū* chanting, the text signifies almost the opposite. The puppet theater, like kabuki theater, was so popular in the Edo era that quite a few how-to books on *gidayū* chanting were published for dilettantes. They, too, explain rhythm and intervals of chanting with the analogy of gait. *The Secret Transmissions on Jōruri, Exegesis, the Edo Version* (Edo-ban jōruri hiden shō) (1782) reads: "Rhythm [*hyōshi*] is just like the hands that one swings following [the movements of] the legs. When the right leg moves forward, the left hand moves forward, and when the left leg moves forward, the right hand moves forward. This is the principle of *yin* and *yang*."[68] The two texts are uncannily similar, the only exception being that the Edo text says "the principle of *yin* and *yang*" while the modern critic uses the term "natural logic," but these are virtually the same in the sense that they are made responsible for the "naturalness" of respective examples and thus the legitimacy of each instruction.[69] This cluster of examples alone cannot prove that what these texts claim as "the principle of *yin* and *yang*" was the default in Edo-era Japan either. On the contrary, it might well suggest the presence of attention to the issues of gait or, even, the very possibility of markedness. Suffice it to say, however, that such words would have been impossible if human locomotion in Edo-era Japan had been monolithically based on the *nanba* gait.

How should we understand these seemingly contradictory phenomena? In the late nineteenth century, the Meiji government introduced the "Western" style of walking into school education, which corrected the way in which the majority of people walked at that time. However, both the markedness of the term "*nanba*" and the presence of Edo-era texts on *gidayū* chanting strongly indicate that *nanba* was in fact minor in Japanese society even before the Meiji era. Especially when it comes to the pairing of diagonal limbs, the manner of walking described in the *gidayū* texts as natural (in accordance with "the principle of *yin* and *yang*") is the same as the "modern"-style gait. This seems to be an impasse. Here, Takechi in effect proposes adding one more factor each to the limb combinations (diagonal and parallel) and times (premodern and modern): a torso to the former and a transitional phase to the latter.

As for the shift from *nanba* to non-*nanba*, Takechi considers that it happened gradually. Recall that he defines *nanba* in relation to body motions that satisfy the demands of the physical labor of production.[70] This idea of associating *nanba* with physical energy echoes Ashihara's notion that *nanba* appears in body motions when power is used in an extreme way.[71] Accordingly, Takechi assumes that urbanization in Edo-era Japan resulted in the emergence of people who were not engaged in such energy-consuming motions, nor could they obtain a diet of high caloric value, and this caused *nanba* to disappear gradually.[72] This cognizance is perceptive, although the exact moment when this change occurred is not certain, and Takechi himself engages in much speculation (e.g., the latter half of the Edo era;[73] from the mid–Edo era onward;[74] around the Hōreki [1751–64], Tenmei [1781–89], and/or Kansei [1789–1801] periods).[75]

Takechi's proposal drastically changes the meaning of the Meiji shift, fundamentally nullifying the validity of the popular narrative on *nanba* that aligns with the theory of Japaneseness. There is no X day of transition that can be specified. It is also impossible to posit the "Japanese" as a single entity in charge of the purported *nanba* culture. If urbanization helped people give up the *nanba* gait, then a shift not only in terms of time but also in diversity among the populace should be taken into consideration, as Takechi's point is applicable only to city dwellers and the like. Certainly, Takechi pays attention to the fact that the puppet theater, the matrix of *gidayū* music, is based in Osaka, an urban environment known as a city of merchants.[76] While such diversity no doubt hinders the attempt to consider *nanba* a Japanese cultural feature, it certainly bears out the the claim that the Meiji government needed to train its incoherent subjects into some kind of uniformity. Takeshi's proposal thus supports neither the homogenous description of the Japanese nor the clear-cut shift from traditional *nanba* to a Westernized gait in modern Japan; accordingly, his theory is not necessarily as convenient for the popular discourse as has been thought. Takechi and Ashihara are arguably the two most important critical thinkers on *nanba* to date, and while Ashihara tends to escape attention—or tends to be ignored, presumably due to his "universalist" claim—Takechi is heavily cited not only in scholarly writings but also in popular narratives. It is therefore intriguing that ideas such as this one, which contradicts the straightforward and reverse-Orientalist description of *nanba*, are hardly acknowledged, especially in the latter.

Furthermore, that leaves a formidable question: what of the body was, then, corrected by Meiji education? If *nanba* users were already in the minority in Meiji Japan, why did pupils need to exercise to straighten their legs, raise their knees, and keep their balance while standing on one leg? In fact, some thinkers cited above describe *nanba* as the combination of legs and hands (the right leg and the right hand simultaneously move forward) but add an intriguing disclaimer that the movement of hands is secondary.[77] Referring to a woodblock print by Suzuki Harunobu (ca. 1725–1770), Takechi states:

> Some female characters in his work clearly display the posture of *nanba*, while some others evince energy-saving patterns [of gait]. We need to pay attention to the following, however. Even in those cases [i.e., energy-saving non-*nanba* gait], in which the right leg is put forward and the left hand looks to be put forward, the right shoulder is downward. That the right shoulder is downward means that the right shoulder is being put forward, which indicates that the right side of the body is moving forward along with the right leg. Fundamentally, the posture of *nanba* is here preserved [in this non-*nanba* gait].[78]

What had changed in the mid-Edo era, before the introduction of Meiji discipline, was the combination of the limbs alone (from parallel to diagonal), while the usage of the torso remained the same.

Figuratively, according to martial art practitioner Kōno Yoshinori, the primary significance of his theory resides in "the system of body usage in which one does not twist one's body and does not create a pivot-fulcrum inside one's body.... This is based on what is called the '*nanba* gait,' the gait for the Japanese in the past."[79] This forms a contrast to the Meiji exercises, which were meant to create "a central pivot inside one's body" and hence to "keep one's balance with one leg."[80]

The ultimate significance of *nanba* in premodern Japan thus resides not in the combination of limbs itself but in the torso that is not twisted. This is in line with what is expected in sliding steps, in which one's arms hardly move and the lower body is totally controlled and stabilized. Kabuki performance also demonstrates such. In the aforementioned production *The Village School*, Nakamura Ganjirō II (1902–1983), the father of Tōjūrō, runs in a most impressive manner. Performing the role of a mother who sacrifices her son, Ganjirō runs out from the *hanamichi*-rampway, displaying what has been defined as the ideal kinesthetics for *onnagata*: running with knees together and shoulder blades nearly touching. Moreover, his upper body barely moves or bends.[81] Kōno Yoshinori claims that the body usage related to *nanba* enables the elderly to perform better than the young.[82] Since the septuagenarian kabuki actor does not move his arms at all, one hesitates to call it *nanba*, but the holistic motions Ganjirō displays are in accordance with what the martial-art practitioner describes as "the body usage related to *nanba*."

Given this, the dichotomized model of inversion from *nanba* gait to non-*nanba* gait, as per the limb combination (diagonal versus parallel), does not explain what happened to people's locomotion in Japan. Historically, there was one more critical mode in this conversion, in which the limbs are non-*nanba*, but the usage of the torso remains the same as in *nanba*. We may extrapolate from these that what was really denied and corrected in the Meiji era was not so much the gait alone as the management of the torso and, by extension, the holistic usage of one's body.

NANBA, PUPPET-GESTURE, AND GENDER:
BODIES, REALITIES, AND RE/PRESENTATIONS

Unlike Edo-era Ayame, Tōjūrō had to go through intense training in noh to acquire a body with a torso that did not twist during motions. That controlled and liberated body able to walk in sliding steps eventually helped Tōjūrō run onstage while retaining the figure of an *onnagata* (just like his father). In contrast, Ayame had already materialized this type of body without such conscious training.

This does not mean that *nanba* or the body usage related to it was essentially natural to Ayame and those like him, or that Ayame's contemporaries were equipped with such bodies without undergoing any training whatsoever. A handy analogy here might be the typical acquisition process of one's "first" language. Just like *gei*—acquired artistic technique implanted into one's body via repeated, longtime, physical cultivation—language and locomotion alike are acquired through training, consciously or otherwise. The analogy of language and locomotion also suggests that multiple differentiated codes of "naturalness" can theoretically coexist in human bodies, as illustrated in *Ran* and *The Village School*, although it does not mean that the several types of naturalness are always internalized and naturalized to exactly the same degree.

It is helpful here to revisit an earlier remark: biometrics approaches gait in a way similar to the way in which gender has been debated and conceptualized. For the polyphony of gait and gender effectively emphasizes how precariously and contingently our own bodies are made to operate and function. In addition, the versatility of naturalness (i.e., the possibility of multiple codes of naturalness) also signifies the usefulness of the juxtaposition of gender and locomotion. Is it not a similar manner—and a similar logic for that matter—that makes possible a person who reifies two genders (e.g., *wakashu* and *onnagata*) as well as a person who moves in both the *nanba* and the non-*nanba* gait? Is it not in a similar manner and by a similar logic that people acquire, internalize, and naturalize gender and locomotion alike? Such amendable and versatile naturalness indicates the highly insecure and flexible nature of naturalness. Furthermore, if femininity was circulated in Edo-era Japan as the citation and imitation of elocution, locomotion, and decorations (i.e., voice, accents, posture, gesture, movements, attire, and ornaments), and if not only such "external" elements as attire and ornaments but also such bodily elements as locomotion can be amended, then one should recognize that gendering takes place in a liberating and liberated site, or, depending on the perspective, a dauntingly insecure, borderless, and porous system in and by which one must enact well-ordered gender. That gender is precarious in theory and binding in practice reflects this phenomenon.

Japanese theater offers another intriguing illustration of this insidious facet of naturalness. Kabuki theater—along with its related performing arts such as dance—has a technique called puppet-gesture. It indicates specific choreography in which a human performer moves as if he or she were a bunraku puppet. Puppet-gesture tends to be used by women characters in a short sequence, usually at the climax of a piece. The technique is demanding, and the puppet-gesture technique is more important for *onnagata* acting than for male-role acting, although it is not limited to the former.[83] When beginning the sequence, the actor-dancer suddenly becomes a puppet, falling into complete silence, erasing facial expression and muting footsteps. As is done in the puppet theater using real puppets, the lines of the character that this kabuki actor is playing are spoken by a *gidayū* chanter accompanied by a shamisen player. The actor's body, from head to toe, is manipulated by other actors playing the roles of puppeteers, and footsteps are supplied by one of the puppeteers stamping the floor.

Pine, Bamboo, and Plum: Snow at Dawn (Shōchikubai: Yuki no akebono), an 1856 kabuki piece by Mokuami, frequently uses puppet-gesture when the character Oshichi beats a fire-alarm drum in a desperate attempt to save her lover. She is aware that issuing a false fire alarm is a crime subject to capital punishment, and this intensifies the situation. Gunji explains how the sequence is suitable for puppet-gesture choreography:

> Oshichi . . . appears, barefoot, chasing after [Kichisaburō to convey critical information that will save him], but the gate is already firmly locked. Knowing that his death is impending [without the information], she faints in the snow but comes to herself soon afterward. From this moment onward, it will be puppet-gesture. In a sense, it can be interpreted as the illusion that Oshichi sees after she fainted. Finally driven into a frenzy, she rushes up to the lookout and beats the drum, and everything during this process is done with stiff, inanimate actions reminiscent of a puppet. This has an effect as if it were accumulated by [filmic?] cuts, which [makes Oshichi] evince sexual appeal and grief all the more. It thereby gives audiences a heightened impression, along with the purity of the beauty and the rhythm of a human body separated from the body [itself].[84]

It demands our attention that Gunji proposes such an interesting idea as "the rhythm of a human body separated from the body." Is it something close to what Chikamatsu proposes in his theory that *gei* resides in the ambiguous border between the false and the real?

Arguably, Gunji's description is one of the most favorable views of puppet-gesture, which somehow entails a certain stigma that it is not considered legitimate for kabuki acting. Two top *onnagata* in the early twentieth century, Utaemon V and Baikō VI, spoke of it as follows. Utaemon states:

> Some people do puppet-gesture in the "Back Garden" scene [of *The Twenty-four Paragons of Filial Piety in This Country* (Honchō nijūshikō)]. [This choreography] is said to have been introduced to [the role of Princess Yaegaki in this scene], because humans cannot keep up the scene, just as with Princess Yuki and Princess Kiyo [in other plays]. I've heard that the late [Nakamura] Jakuemon [III] [1875–1927] even went so far as to take the part of a puppeteer and train himself that way. On the whole, however, it's not the right path [*hondō*] for kabuki to produce this kind of [serious and important?] play with puppet-gesture acting. I hope that the youngsters will understand this point well,

and those who can move should avoid that kind of path and go [straight] to the right path.[85]

Unlike Utaemon, Baikō used this technique but nevertheless has similar sentiments:

> For [full-fledged] skillful actors, it is reasonable to play [a role] as a human, and not . . . with puppet-gesture. But if an actor is still green or is trying to become popular, since [he is] not yet fully skillful, this technique . . . has been used as a kind of "irregular spectacle" [*keren*] so that he can amuse the audiences. Of course, it requires technique to do it, but when it comes to the right path as an actor, this is a cowardly way. I believe it's the appropriate way [*matomo na ikikata*] to express characteristics as a human.[86]

As Gunji, Utaemon, and Baikō show, puppet-gesture is received affirmatively as well as negatively, although it is highly doubtful that such an aloof, or even snobbish attitude toward it has been a majority opinion throughout kabuki history.[87] In general, the history of kabuki, far from being monolithic, is full of vicissitudes; in particular, Utaemon's generation went through the process of transforming kabuki into a decent, classical theater appropriate for a modern nation. Given kabuki's checkered history, any one actor could hardly be representative of all kabuki actors, and those like Utaemon are especially unqualified.[88]

This stigma might, or might not, be related to the technical aspects of puppet-gesture, which are certainly germane to the problem of naturalness, the immediate reason for our interest in puppet-gesture. Takechi bluntly states, "the puppet-gesture in *odori* dance is to imitate a poor puppet [and/or puppetry]."[89] Tōjūrō's explanation is more eloquent:

> In the "Back Garden" scene [in *The Twenty-four Paragons of Filial Piety in This Country*], I play [the role of Princess Yaegaki] with puppet-gesture. . . . I think that it enables the strong taste of kabuki plays [adapted from] the puppet theater. . . . In fact, when I played this role for the first time at the National Theater, I had learned the form of Princess Yaegaki from bunraku puppeteer Yoshida Bunjaku, my bosom friend these fifty years. The scales dropped from my eyes when I heard him say, "Puppet-gesture should be done poorly; otherwise, it wouldn't become puppetlike." I heard that this was what Bunjaku's master, the late Yoshida Bungorō, a maestro puppeteer of *onnagata* puppets, used to say.

Certainly, if one does it too well, then the movements become less puppetlike. But one shouldn't move poorly on purpose, so the balance is difficult.[90]

The tacit presupposition here is that bunraku puppets are capable of resembling humans, provided they are operated by expert puppeteers. Only with this premise is it possible to say that imitating puppets too well would make the gesture not puppetlike (but presumably humanlike). Yoshida Bunjaku, the puppeteer quoted in Tōjūrō's narrative, endorses this reading.[91] It now appears that puppet-gesture intends not so much to seek the ambiguous border between the false and the real as to *heighten* that border, making it *not* ambiguous. Whether blurring or heightening it, however, it would be too hasty to assign the "false" to puppets and the "real" to humans categorically.

The unstated premise about the potential of bunraku puppets (to become the "real" themselves) is further proved valid by another dancing technique related to bunraku: "puppet-body" (*ningyōmi*). Takechi defines it as follows: "On the level of conceptualization, the puppet-gesture of *odori* dance is to imitate a poor puppet [and/or puppetry], but the puppet-body of *mai* dance seems to be trying to become a proficient puppet [and/or puppetry]."[92] There are two kinds of relationship in this paradigm: between humans and puppets, and between plausible resemblance (represented here by the puppet-body) and implausible resemblance (represented here by puppet-gesture). It is not that *only* puppets are assigned artificiality, nor are they *always* assigned artificiality.

Such a dichotomy of plausible and implausible resemblance—somewhat reminiscent of *onnagata* who pass—is not reserved for "puppet-body" and "puppet-gesture." Ōnishi Shigetaka, a bunraku-theater critic, also states in a 1948 encyclopedia that when kabuki completely digests bunraku dramaturgy, as in the acting technique called *kudoki*, bunraku dramaturgy merges into kabuki dramaturgy so well that it does not signify any deviation from kabuki norms, whereas puppet-gesture highlights the disparity between humans and puppets. Just like Takechi and Utaemon, Ōnishi is skeptical about puppet-gesture and states that it results from "unnatural, perverted direction" (*fushizen na hentai-teki na enshutsu*).[93] One might say that puppet-gesture is too eccentric even for the eccentric kabuki theater; more important, it is highly suggestive that Ōnishi chose the words "unnatural" and "perverted" to refer to puppet-gesture, as these are typical terms used to discredit *onnagata* in the context of modern debates on *onnagata* versus actresses.

Takechi mentions that two dance schools in the Osaka and Kyoto regions, the Yoshimura school and the Inoue school, have skillfully and naturally incorporated the gestures of bunraku puppets into human locomotion.[94] Indeed, the Inoue school is characterized by dance movements adopted from bunraku-puppet theater.[95]

According to the Inoue school's own explanation, a "dichotomy" of plausible and implausible resemblance seems difficult to posit, and so does a dichotomy of felicitous puppet-body and infelicitous puppet-gesture. Inoue Yachiyo IV (1905–2004), the fourth *iemoto*, explains the school's use of bunraku-puppet theater, using the word "puppet-gesture":

> Puppet-gesture is what one performs by imitating the gesture of a puppet, that is, humans conversely imitate puppets. Initially, bunraku puppetry as well as other puppetry must have begun by aiming at how closely [puppets] could approach humans. As the puppetry developed, however, the amusement of people conversely imitating puppets must have been introduced into *mai* dance.
>
> However closely they approach humans, puppets have a stiffness that humans, flesh and blood, don't have. Because of that stiffness, there is cuteness of puppets in any [puppet] play, no matter how scary the play is. I think that's one of the attractive points about puppet plays.
>
> One could say that the puppet-gesture of the Inoue school is what was transformed from this very charm of puppets, that is, being stiff and innocent, to *mai* dance of humans.[96]

The puppet-gesture described here highlights the border between the false and the real. Attention to the border is further emphasized in the following principle of puppet-gesture usage:

> Puppet-gesture is used a lot in female roles, . . . and it is strangely so little used in male roles. . . .
>
> The reason for that is, as we can see in bunraku, that the procedure of gesture is very detailed [*te ga komakai*] for *onnagata* puppets, so when it is adopted in *mai* dance, its features are easily expressed. This is also because the cuteness and innocence of a puppet are more visible in *onnagata* puppets [than male-role puppets].
>
> Another reason is that when [a puppet-theater piece] is made into a *mai* piece, if all the characters in it, such as Omiwa, Motome, and Princess Tachi-

bana [in *The Travel Dance of Love at the Matrimonial Mountain* (Imoseyama koi no michiyuki)], were performed with puppet-gesture, the technique itself would not be highlighted and would lose its effect. So puppet-gesture is concentrated in Omiwa, which seems to be the most appropriate role [of the three] for puppet-gesture in terms of [its] character and appearance.[97]

Puppet-gesture is concentrated in female roles for many reasons. First, the original choreography of bunraku is more detailed for female-role puppets, which emphasizes the effectiveness of puppet-gesture. Second, the appearance of a female-role puppet is cuter and more innocent than that of a male-role puppet, which is also suitable for puppet-gesture. Finally, using this technique with a single character most enhances its effectiveness. Here, again, puppet-gesture heightens the border between humans and puppets and makes it *not* ambiguous.

No matter how tempting, it would be misleading to assign the "false" to puppets and the "real" to humans, and it is not that *only* puppets are assigned the "false," nor are they *always* assigned it. The reason for that is related to the following proposal by Takechi:

> The *mai* dance of the Inoue school is based on *nanba*. *Nanba* is the posture of labor, and it tells us that [theirs] is the dance born at the site of production. Dance in the Edo [region] was also based on *nanba* until about the time of the Shigayama school, and afterward, it became the energy-saving posture of daily life. This resulted from the fact that the creative energy of Japanese dance decreased as time went by.
>
> In order to avoid being affected by such a decline in energy, the predecessors of the Inoue school were always conscious of returning to the traditional arts. Yachiyo II sought a model in bunraku puppets, and Yachiyo III in noh. The current [*iemoto*] Yachiyo IV has also been influenced by *kyōgen* actor Zenchiku Yagorō.[98]

In this sense, it is of additional importance that the Inoue school uses puppet-gesture both explicitly and implicitly.[99] In the latter case, the "false" or "artificial" movements of puppets are seamlessly integrated into the "real" movements of humans, and, according to Takechi, such is a means of retaining the "original," "natural" locomotion of people in premodern Japan. In this regard, the movements of bunraku puppets are playing a role here, at least partially, similar to that of Tōjūrō's lessons in noh sliding steps. In the localized context of premodern Japanese theater in modern Japan, the devious and dubious nature of "naturalness" is thus exposed by such technical features as the *nanba* gait and puppet-gesture. Most intriguingly, both show similarities with gender to one extent or another. Just as *wakashu* and *onnagata* managed to materialize multiple types of gender, premodern theater practitioners in modern times utilize multiple types of locomotion. What is more, according to Takechi, naturalness is retroactively amendable. It is possible to retain, or regain, naturalness that was lost, as the Inoue school has been doing via puppet-gesture: "Japanese dance needs to go back to the *productive posture* once again, modeling [itself] after the *gei* of Yachiyo [IV], who is the virtuoso of established reputation as the pinnacle of Japanese dance. That is to say, from its [present-day] *consumptive posture*."[100] In a sense, this is what Tōjūrō did with the noh lessons. Then, what about the naturalness of gender?

Another point of interest here is that the Inoue dance school was established by Inoue Sato (1767–1854), a woman who had been teaching dances to ladies-in-waiting at the residence of the Konoes, an aristocratic family in Kyoto. At the age of thirty-one, she retired and became the first *iemoto* of the Inoue dance school. (The school would be a female-only school of *mai* dance until 1950.)[101] The name of successive *iemoto*, Yachiyo (Eight Thousand Years), was given to Sato by her employer-patron upon her retirement in appreciation for Sato's service and to lament her departure.[102] The school prospered, and in 1872, two generations later, Inoue Yachiyo III (1838–1938/1939)[103] produced a public dance performance. Referring to this event, Takechi states:

> Since the women's kabuki ban in 1629, it had not been possible for women to perform on the public stage.... After that, female stage artists managed only to go to the women's quarters at the shogunate and at samurai mansions as well as the royal court and give lessons in dance or perform kabuki as "theater-masters" [*okyōgenshi*]. Many of them also became dance teachers in town or geisha and thereby transmitted the traditions of Japanese music and Japanese dance. This is a fact of great moment that we cannot overlook, and thanks to their efforts, much traditional *gei* has [survived] until today. This, however, was inconspicuous, hidden work in society. For 250 years, it had not been [possible for them] to perform in public, for example, at playhouses, and be connected with the public.[104]

In hindsight, Sato transformed herself from a woman artist engaged in "inconspicuous, hidden work" to the founder of a successful dance school. Collectively, the successive *iemoto* of the Inoue school managed to transform the school from one engaged in hidden work to one engaged in public performance. In a sense, the Inoue school is one of the most successful examples not only of adopting puppet-gesture but also of keeping up with the times.

CHAPTER 7

Female Onnagata in the Porous Labyrinth

The Enunciated Femininity and the Enunciating Masculinity

TODAY, the word *"onnagata"* almost automatically refers to male actors playing women's roles. While denoting the role to be performed (i.e., woman), the term *"onnagata"* inevitably entails connotations regarding the one who performs: male identity, maleness, masculinity, and so on. The concept of the term *"onnagata"* is ostentatiously composed of the enunciated femininity and the enunciating masculinity. The concept of *onnagata* thus seems doomed to carry something male-ish about it, but the enunciating masculinity is not directly connected with a male body in and of itself.[1] After such connotations became fixated, women fulfilling the duty of *onnagata* apparently had little impact on the signifying power. During the Meiji era, women-actors performed kabuki in public, and thus the existence of female *onnagata* is a historical fact. They were performing a specific type of femininity established by their male predecessors in the Edo era, thereby making themselves "honorary men," succumbing to the master discourse on femininity through the excessive rendering of it.[2]

It is not even accurate to associate this enunciating masculinity in *onna-*

gata art with men, as it might well be norms in disguise. The notion that norms are represented by men, or that the gender of norms is always already masculine, is certainly too clichéd, but an analysis of female *onnagata* still helps us perceive how such a cliché becomes vividly alive—and formidably so—in actuality. Female *onnagata* were situated at a paradoxical intersection of male and female, feminine and masculine, nature and nurture, and old and new, none of which existed a priori. From the vantage point of this intersection, we can see how each of these qualities was defined, understood, and naturalized. It is a case in point of how norms are being created and at the same time the process of such creation is being effaced. Female *onnagata* thus provide convoluted materials with which to contemplate the economy and logic of femininity and, by extension, those of gendering.

MISE-EN-SCÈNE: WOMEN KABUKI ACTORS

Female *onnagata* in the Meiji era were located in an interesting landscape, one in which they were critically acclaimed when passing as men onstage. Complications arose because alongside female *onnagata* who were indistinguishable from men there were male *onnagata* who were passing as women offstage. If the highest compliment for female *onnagata* was comparison with their male peers, the equivalent for male *onnagata* was still identification with women in society. In the preceding Edo era, there were numerous anecdotes of "*onnagata* who pass." Although Taganojō, born in 1887, made a hilarious remark that such a claim as "gynecological disorders" by male *onnagata* would invite a "punch," the tradition lingered even as late as through the early twentieth century. Baikō, who was older than Tanonojō by less than two decades, left an anecdote about being mistaken for a geisha.[3] Both *onnagata* belonged to the troupe led by Kikugorō, Baikō's brother, and were immersed in a similar ethos. Moreover, Baikō, along with Utaemon, was one of the two top *onnagata* in the early twentieth century, and thus belonged to the generation that was carving out a new type of *onnagata* suitable for the new era.

Female *onnagata* came into existence in this particular locus where the Edo and Meiji eras adjoined. Women kabuki actors returned to the public stage after the collapse of Edo shogunate. Their existence, therefore, was a modern product, and yet the performance of female *onnagata* was based on a premodern economy, in both theory and practice. They were Edo-era women living in the Meiji era, and they performed in the new Meiji era in accordance with an Edo system destined to be abolished for the sake of a new system.

Also, women kabuki actors did not emerge in a historical vacuum. Although marginalized and almost invisible in kabuki historiography, women kabuki performers did eventually remerge in two forms after women's kabuki was terminated by the female performer ban in 1629: first as theater-masters, who had come into being by the latter half of the eighteenth century, and second, as their offspring, women-actors.

Theater-masters were hired by wealthy samurai patrons, who could not easily go to such vulgar places as playhouses due to their social status, and many of whom were further bound by regulations forbidding them to receive male visitors at their residences. Theater-masters staged well-known kabuki plays for these patrons at their mansions. For instance, according to *Party Diary* (Enyū nikki), a diary kept by Yanagisawa Nobutoki (1724–1792) from 1773 to 1785, theater-masters had come into existence by the time of Nobutoki. According to *Party Diary*, Nobutoki made theater-masters stage three kabuki plays on the twenty-fifth day of the ninth month of 1775.[4] Though little is known about theater-masters, they are known to have relied on the existing forms and plays of the mainstream kabuki theater. Their major—if not sole—raison d'être was to substitute for "real" kabuki actors for their patrons, who could not go to the playhouses. According to Mitamura Engyo, their performance was described as "transferring" (*utsusu*) kabuki from the three big theaters in Edo.[5] While the virtual theatergoing discussed earlier was an inexpensive alternative that enabled people to enjoy kabuki through other media (e.g., publications), patronizing theater-masters was no doubt the most lavish alternative.

The vocational ancestors of theater-masters were not necessarily all women, however, nor were they a minority of kabuki actors from the very outset. In her work on "parlor-kabuki" (*zashiki kabuki*), Hayashi Kimiko states: "The way in which parlor-kabuki [was produced] changed as time went by, but the audiences for parlor-kabuki remained as [one type of] kabuki fan, which eventually resulted in the birth of theater-masters [*okyōgenshi*], a new [type of actor who] carried kabuki."[6] The term "parlor-kabuki" comes from the fact that it was performed mainly in a parlor at a residence and not in a playhouse, although some enthusiastic patrons built private stages similar to that of a playhouse, equipped with box seats, a *hanamichi*-rampway, or even an entrance specifically for guests called a mouse-gate.[7] Such entertainment was provided mostly, but not only, at daimyo residences in Edo in order to entertain guests of honor as well as their own household members.[8] Hayashi defines the former as "hospitality" and the latter as "amusement."[9] Takei Kyōzō situates parlor-kabuki in a broader map of kabuki:

> Kabuki studies have been mainly about productions at playhouses in theater districts. We can say this as the study of [a specific] theater that was appreciated by a well-off populace in urban areas, especially Kyoto, Osaka, and Edo. Recently, [other small theaters in towns as well as in rural areas, or at temples and shrines, etc.] have received attention. It has become clear that kabuki was appreciated by [people of] broad classes.
>
> It is still mostly unknown, however, that parlor-theater [*zashiki shibai*] was greatly appreciated in urban areas, especially Edo, among the upper classes. Parlor-theater was frequently produced at the Edo residences of daimyo.... In order to have a complete picture of theater [in the Edo era], is it not necessary to investigate [both] the actual productions for the top tier [and the small theaters] appreciated by middle- and lower-class people?[10]

Therefore, parlor-theater, parlor-kabuki included, existed outside playhouses in Edo-era Japan as "another kabuki"[11] for those who, because of their social status, could not go to such "evil places" as theater districts. Historically, though, it is most certainly arguable that parlor-theater performance, and not productions at major playhouses, should be considered traditionally mainstream, because entertainment arts in the medieval period had mostly been based on patronage. Kabuki productions in theater districts (based on box office) deviated from this traditionally authentic site.[12]

Given parlor-theater's historically legitimate origin, it is no wonder that many actors engaged in it initially were major enough to be included in actor-critique booklets. Suzuki Hiroko states that this phenomenon of major actors moonlighting in parlor-theater was alive in the Kanbun era (1661–73) but nearly disappeared after the Genroku era.[13] One reason certainly lay in the shogunate's constant surveillance and regulations, which included a prohibition on actors visiting samurai residences.[14] Takei observes that a record from the Hiroshima domain has a trace of deletion of the names of two *wakashu* actors in a kabuki-related article on the sixth day of the fourth month of 1674. From this, he concludes that there must have been no reservations about noh-theater productions at samurai residences, *jōruri* productions were safe but not commendable, and kabuki productions, especially those involving *wakashu* actors, were somehow improper for daimyo.[15] Anxiety on the part of both daimyo and kabuki-circles parties was certainly not groundless, especially after the 1714 incident, which involved the actor Ikushima and the high-ranking female official Ejima and resulted in massive punishment for both parties. Parlor-theater did not disappear, however. Hence, there emerged many new types of performers who worked in parlor-theater: (1) minor actors who could not make actor-critique booklets, (2) unemployed actors who had no annual contract with any troupe at a given moment, (3) theater staff other than actors (e.g., musicians and choreographers), (4) actors who had retired from their positions at big theaters and were now townspeople, and (5) those townspeople whom Hayashi regards as "pretenders."[16] These various new types of performers were engaged in parlor-theater, and sometimes they even formed a troupe solely for the purpose of performing parlor-theater.[17]

The concrete contributions of parlor-theater performers to the birth of theater-masters, female professional kabuki actors, are not yet clear.[18] We do not know exactly how women began participating in this activity, but it at least must have been related to the following. As mentioned, parlor-theater productions happened for two reasons, as hospitality for guests, who were sometimes accompanied by their wives, and as in-house entertainment mainly for the mothers or wives of daimyo.[19] When these women were present, a separate room surrounded by bamboo blinds (*misu*) was prepared.[20] This practice of dividing the space was not limited to the case of male actors, as it was also done for theater-masters, according to Kumehachi, a disciple of one of the very last theater-masters.[21] Kumehachi further describes an occasion when she was attending her master: toward the end of the Edo era, "famous theater-masters with patron households were . . . all women of about forty years of age, and needless to say, no man could go into [the patrons' residences]. . . . Including those in charge of music and those in charge of wigs, all the members [of a troupe were] female, with no exception."[22]

Norizuki Toshihiko considers that theater-masters emerged from two groups, women related to kabuki circles and dance teachers in towns. As an example of the first group, he mentions Sato. Sato (later Iyo, Sana, and finally Osan) appears in the aforementioned *Party Diary*, and her adoptive father, Nakamura Denjirō II (d. 1781), and husband, Nakamura Nakazō I (1736–1790), were both kabuki actor-dancers.[23] This seems to parallel the situations of female members of kabuki families in other periods. For example, after *shinpa* theater came into being in the late nineteenth century, some daughters born to notable kabuki families joined it.²⁴ Now that *shinpa* is past its prime, few kabuki daughters go to shinpa these days, but quite a few seek to establish acting careers in the film industry, Takarazuka theater, and other types of contemporary theater.²⁵

Theater-masters performed kabuki for their patrons until the end of the Edo era. In addition to her master, Bandō Mitsue, Kumehachi gives several names of theater-masters who were well known toward the end of the Edo period: Matsumoto Umekichi, Mizuki Kasen, and Nakamura Toraji.²⁶ Due to the collapse of the shogunate and the samurai class that led to the Meiji Restoration, however, theater-masters lost their wealthy patrons and were left with a choice between giving up acting or "sneaking" into the periphery of the male kabuki world. Those who thus came to perform on the public kabuki stage were called "women-actors." Some played in male kabuki troupes, while many ended up forming "all-female kabuki troupes" (*onna shibai*), just as theater-masters had done. What used to be invisible in the days of theater-masters became visible in the days of women-actors, although theater-masters patronized in a closed community and women-actors commodified in a theater market were not identical.

ICHIKAWA KUMEHACHI I:
A WOMAN KABUKI ACTOR PAR EXCELLENCE

The time of women-actors and their troupes was extremely short. When Kumehachi died in 1913, she was referred to as "the very last" (*shingari*) of the women-actors,²⁷ but she was in fact one of the earliest, being a former apprentice to a theater-master. Nakamura Kasen (1889–1942) was probably the last documented woman-actor, but by about 1910, women-actors and their troupes were considered to be on the wane.²⁸ There are few scholarly analyses as to why the era of women-actors was of such limited duration. Kamiyama Akira's work is an exception, as he proposes this question "in relation to the process by which kabuki gradually obtained legitimacy as that which was 'traditional, classical theater.'"²⁹

Kumehachi was an exemplary woman-actor whose life span coincided with the duration of women-actors as a group.³⁰ She was an exceptional actor, and thus, arguably, she was not representative of women-actors as a whole. Yet an analysis of Kumehachi's case can illustrate the situation of women-actors, precisely because Kumehachi was an unusually successful woman-actor who managed to internalize kabuki.

Kumehachi started her dance training at the age of seven.[31] When she was twelve, she became a licensed dance master, taking the name Bandō Keihachi. She had initially been a pupil of dance teacher Bandō Miehachi and had at some point been referred to one of the most famed theater-masters of the time, Mitsue, who was under the patronage of three samurai households (the Kagas, Sanukis, and Akis).[32] "In general, theater-masters were uncompromising," says Kumehachi, "and my master [Mitsue] was one of the most demanding and accepted only six or seven disciples."[33] Kumehachi intended to become a theater-master herself, following in Mitsue's footsteps. When Kumehachi was eighteen (ca. 1863), however, Mitsue lost her patrons. As Kumehachi expressed it, "Our vocation [okyōgen] disappeared."[34]

Kumehachi saw her career as a theater-master terminated in the middle of her apprenticeship. She had no chance to perform onstage with Mitsue, except in such subordinate roles as a lady-in-waiting and a stage assistant, nor could she achieve her dream of winning "one patron household or so."[35] When she was about twenty-three years old (ca. 1868), Kumehachi—along with other unemployed theater-masters—began hoping to shift the venue of her performance from private mansions, which were in practice no longer available, to public playhouses, and thus to change from a theater-master to a woman-actor. A proud—if unemployed—theater-master, Mitsue found her young disciple's intentions disgraceful but had no effective reason to stop her.[36] Thus, it was decided that Kumehachi would return the name Bandō Keihachi to Mitsue and was referred to Hanshirō, a renowned *kabuki onnagata* who was frequently described as an *onnagata* who could pass as a woman.[37] He accepted her as a disciple and in November 1873 granted her an Iwai name, Iwai Kumehachi, which included the character *kume*, an important character for the Iwais.[38]

Iwai Kumehachi became extremely popular, performing both men's and women's roles. She was critically acclaimed by such highly respected writers as kabuki critic Kōdō Tokuchi (1843–1913) and Chinese-classics scholar Yoda Gakkai (1833–1909). She eventually came to be dubbed "Onna Danshū." This must have occurred after 1878, because "Danshū" was one of the haiku pen names that Ichikawa Danjūrō IX (1838–1903) used after performing the role of Saigō (Nanshū) Takamori in 1878. "Danjūrō" is one of the most important kabuki stage names, and Danjūrō IX dominated the kabuki world of his time. "Onna Danshū" can thus be translated literally as "Woman Danjūrō."[39] Therefore, Kumehachi seems to have established her *gei* as a kabuki actor, as well as her fame, by the late 1870s.

It is common practice in kabuki to liken an actor to another, more established actor. Like Kumehachi, Bandō Matasaburō (1855–1906) also received a Danjūrō-derived nickname, Nisen Danshū (Two-Dollar Danjūrō), for he was performing at cheap small theaters such as the Ryūsei-za Theater, where a ticket cost as little as two *sen*. What seems to testify to Kumehachi's achievement is the different treatment these two Danjūrō namesakes received. In 1899, Matasaburō had the honor of performing at the Kabuki-za Theater, one of the highest-ranking theaters and a place where Danjūrō often performed. Danjūrō was furious at this "invasion" of a top-notch playhouse by an actor of lower-status and was quoted as saying that the playhouse should scrape off the surface of the stage on which Matasaburō had set foot.[40] In comparison, Kumehachi's reputation was so high that, allegedly persuaded by Fukuchi Ōchi (1841–1906), the brains of kabuki circles, Danjūrō made her his disciple sometime in summer 1888 and granted her an Ichikawa name, Ichikawa Masunojō, along with its *yagō*, Naritaya.[41] Ironically, she had already become so distinguished as Iwai Kumehachi that audiences kept calling her "Kumehachi," so yet another name change followed, this time to "Ichikawa Kumehachi." She has been known by this name ever since, with the exception of some time after performing in 1890 without permission in *The Subscription Scroll* (Kanjinchō) (1840), an heirloom opus by Namiki Gohei III (1790–1855) that belonged to the main household of the Ichikawas. Danjūrō pardoned her and re-granted the name in 1897.[42] While unable to use the name because of this incident, as well as when working in other theatrical genres (e.g., *shinpa* theater), she also used the name Morizumi Gekka. Morizumi was her own last name; Gekka, "moon-flower," came from a poem that the Chinese-classics scholar composed for her. However, her specialty was kabuki, and Kumehachi was known first and foremost as a kabuki actor.[43]

ONNAGATA ACTING OF A FEMALE ONNAGATA:
TRULY FEMININE, INDISTINGUISHABLE FROM A MAN

Some *onnagata* perform only women's roles; others perform men's roles as well. Kumehachi is said to have excelled in both. Her *onnagata* performance was generally highly praised, but she was especially excellent when it came to dance, period pieces, and puppet-gesture.[44] These correspond to the skills she says she practiced while studying under Mitsue.[45] *A Maiden at Dōjōji* (Kyōganoko musume Dōjōji), a dance piece regarded as the most difficult and important opus for *onnagata*, is frequently mentioned as her specialty, as are the roles of Princess Yaegaki in *The Twenty-four Paragons of Filial Piety in This Country*, a character that has been regarded, presumably since the early nineteenth century, as one of the three most important princesses in costume plays, and Masaoka in *Precious Eaglewood and Hagi in the Previous Generation* (Meiboku sendaihagi), a major period piece.⁴⁶

The following remark from *A Metropolis in the East* (Tōyō daitokai) (1898), by Ishibashi Ningetsu and Maeda Shozan, is representative of how Kumehachi's performance of these roles was received by her contemporaries: "Resembling Danjūrō in the style of *gei*, Ichikawa Kumehachi is skillful at dancing. Once she is onstage, nobody can tell that she is not a man. When she plays such roles as Princess Yaegaki or [Hanako in] *Dōjōji*, however, she immediately transforms herself into a blooming beauty or a graceful, virtuous princess. It is impossible to realize that she is nearly sixty years old [*sic*]."⁴⁷ At the same time, there were people who took her performance negatively precisely because she was like a man. Playwright Mayama Seika (1878–1948) admits that "Kumehachi and the like are skillful, but it just seems to me the imitation of men's way of doing it."⁴⁸

> *Onnagata* had long been trying to become women.... Women are women by themselves. Why on earth do they need to imitate *onnagata*, who are made up from unnaturalness [*muri kara shiageta*]? Women just need to display their own features naturally. Kumehachi once said that ..., as a woman, she thinks as if she were a man when playing as an *onnagata*. What [she] says proves my point from the opposite direction. Only because she models herself after women performed by *onnagata*, does she need to become a man once. If she tries to perform women themselves, there is no need to do such an unreasonable thing [*muri*].⁴⁹

Seika's idea that "women are women themselves" is directly related to a new concept of femininity, that natural femininity is grounded in women's bodies, which came to be predominant in modern Japan, as Kano's analysis in the context of the debate over the "actress question"⁵⁰ demonstrates.

However, in the context of kabuki reviews, the positive remarks from *A Metropolis in the East* are more representative of the time, and two pieces of information in it deserve attention: (1) nobody can tell that she is not a man, and (2) her *onnagata* performance perfectly reifies the female character she is playing. Yet it would stretch the point if we assumed that

Kumehachi might have appeared to be a man when playing men's roles and a woman when playing women's roles, because *A Metropolis in the East* does not mention Kumehachi's performance of men's roles. Rather, the word "man" in the comment "nobody can tell that she is not a man" in effect signifies the norm, so that the statement should be understood to mean that nobody can tell that she deviates from the authentic norm. The 1898 book uses the word "man" because the standards of kabuki artistry had been presented by male actors, and it is in this sense that the remark is a compliment. This fashion of praising female performers did not disappear after the era of woman-actors. In 1975, for example, Ichiyama Nasorō, a female dancer, was described in a similar way when performing a man's part.[51] It is noteworthy, however, that Kumehachi was so described when performing not only men's but also women's roles.[52] In this paradigm, a category of "non-man" would therefore connote not so much "anti-man" (dichotomy) as "lesser man" (spectrum).[53]

The logic of the above quotation is thus twofold. Kumehachi has acquired an authentic kabuki body, which is default masculine; her *onnagata* performance is perfect according to the established criteria of kabuki. Kumehachi herself makes remarks that correspond to this reading: "You see, I've a thin physique, so I do *onnagata* more [than male roles],"[54] but "in my childhood, I learned lots of dance pieces in male-roles,"[55] and "experiences in dancing the male-part were beneficial for my cultivation."[56] Furthermore, according to Morizumi Kikuko, Kumehachi's adopted daughter, when Kumehachi was asked to give lessons in *onnagata* acting to actresses, she insisted that male-role acting was important for the proper cultivation of *onnagata* acting for actresses.[57]

At first glance, her reasoning for this claim seems simply a matter of balance alone, as she states in her instructions on *onnagata* acting for women: "Especially when [we female *onnagata*] are performing among male actors, it's just the right temperature if [we] do the *onnagata* role as if it were a male role. If [we] join men as an intact woman as is, [our] *gei* becomes small and unglamorous."[58] What remains a hiatus here is more visible in another article of hers, which shows that the issue cannot be reduced to the matter of balance: "You might think that it's easy for women-actors to do *onnagata*, but it's not that easy. Certainly, the body is a woman's body, so it might not require much effort to become a woman anew, but onstage, a woman *as is* would become small. *Especially* when one is performing among male actors, the balance would be bad [among performers] unless she plays the role of a woman, thinking that she is a man."⁵⁹ The defect of the female performer's *gei* being small is present even when she is not performing among men, unless she acts as if she were a man. Women's *onnagata* acting cannot be perfect unless it accords with the established criteria of *onnagata*, which are by default masculine-based. Indistinguishable from a man, Kumehachi has achieved this.

This reading is also in line with reviews that characterize Kumehachi as a traditional, good old kabuki actor reminiscent of kabuki in the Edo era, such as this one published in 1912: "Danzō's voice was low but powerful, and so were the lines Kumehachi spoke. Especially when Kumehachi appeared from a gate . . . I felt as if I had been facing an actor from the bygone past who was just emerging vividly from a woodblock print."⁶⁰ The woodblock print flourished in the Edo era, and kabuki actors were popular subjects. It thus here signifies "kabuki in the past." Kabuki itself was then termed "old theater" (*kyūgeki*) vis-à-vis new theatrical genres that emerged at that time (especially as opposed to "new theater" [*shingeki*]). Even in the old theater, Kumehachi's acting belonged to the party of "old among olds, extremely old," as she herself described it.⁶¹ Such admiration of the past entails the risk of becoming obsolete. As Tamura Toshiko (1884–1945) writes, "The death of old actor Ichikawa Kumehachi [was taken by theater circles today as] a natural incident . . . in the sense that what should disappear disappeared."⁶² In any case, we can say without fear of contradiction that Kumehachi was trained in the old, legitimate fashion of the kabuki theater and that her acting, including her *onnagata* performance, was regarded as authentic in accordance with kabuki traditions.

Kumehachi's reputation for authentic *gei*—not only attractive but also true to the mainstream tradition of kabuki—is significant in the context of Japanese arts, as it indicates that women-actors were not considered newcomers differentiated from the men actors who preceded and coexisted with them. More important, theater practitioners—or *gei* practitioners in general—had established in premodern Japan the notion that creativity and traditionality should be closely connected in exercising *gei*.⁶³

Kumehachi's reputation also neatly echoes her accounts on training in the fundamentals. She frequently mentioned that dance, *gidayū* chanting, and painting are the basis of *gei*. Among them, dance and *gidayū* chanting are indispensable, she says, and lessons in painting not only help actors select colors for their costumes but also provide them with a sense of both overall theatrical balance onstage and appropriate posture.⁶⁴ Painting does not seem to be construed as a must by the majority of kabuki actors, but it is certainly not unique to Kumehachi. Danjūrō also painted, and so did Utaemon.⁶⁵ Unlike painting, dance and *gidayū* chanting are widely understood to be prerequisites for kabuki acting. Lessons in dance create a body suitable for kabuki movements (especially so for *onnagata*),⁶⁶ and lessons in *gidayū* create a voice suitable for kabuki elocution.⁶⁷

The significance of *gidayū* chanting in the context of women-actors, especially female *onnagata*, is complex. *Gidayū* is situated in a broader realm of Japanese *gei* established in premodern Japan, something generically called "traditional Japanese arts" today. In it, the notion of faithfully following one's master has long been considered critical to the mastery of knowledge, *gei* included, although in modern Japan this concept came to be underrated in accordance with the relegation of the concept of copy vis-à-vis original.⁶⁸ Unlike *onnagata*, *gidayū* chanters are by definition "generalists," covering a wide range of characters, from young girls to old men. *Gidayū* chanting must cross over any imaginable borders for the human voice in Edo-era Japan, and yet the basis of such a crossing over is, by default, a masculine voice. These conditions confine female practitioners of *gidayū* chanting in a bundle of double binds, whether women kabuki actors learning *gidayū* or female *gidayū* chanters.⁶⁹ Overall, the double binds will no doubt be déjà vu for any reader interested in women's history, feminist history, and so on; simultaneously, this particular case demonstrates that female masculinity, which is largely sexualized in the context of gender theory (by definition, Western theory), is not in a binding relationship with sexuality, at least on the level of theory.⁷⁰

In the paradigm that *gei* practitioners are expected to master *gei* by imitating predecessors and that artistic traditions have been monopolized by male practitioners, imitating male predecessors is for female *gei* practitioners the only way of obtaining legitimacy, authenticity, and membership in the tradition in question (e.g., *gidayū* circles and kabuki circles). This is not simply a matter of maneuvering for position in a community. Rather, it points directly to an important aspect of artistry in premodern Japan. In this context, creativity has been theorized in deep relation to traditionality, in which the concept of "authentic traditions" has been of uppermost importance. Creativity is valued when incorporated with authentic traditions, which represent legitimacy and authenticity. According to noh dramatist-theorist Zeami, considered a central figure not only for noh artistry theory alone but also for performance theory of Japanese theater, "Even when you study bygone things and admire a novelty, do not distort the traditions."[71] Theatrical performances are evaluated in terms of this basic idea:

> Now, there should be excellent, average, and mediocre noh performances. A play must be called excellent when it has an authentic source [*honzetsu*], novelty, Grace, and something interesting. It should be taken as a first-rate performance if such a play is well performed and successfully received. It should be taken as a second-rate performance if one well performs an opus that is not good but proper, in accordance with its source, and the performance is successfully received. It should be taken as a third-rate performance if one skillfully and diligently performs a false play [*ese* noh] with no authentic source.[72]

The matter of compatibility between creativity and traditionality is not limited to the level of play scripts or performances but is applicable to actors' bodies as well. While a play internalizes traditions with authentic sources, the body of an actor internalizes traditions with the fundamental molds (*katagi*, lit., a "woodcut" and an "exemplary model"): "There will be no life of noh if one is inattentive to the fundamental molds of one's own school. He would be a weak, unreliable player. Only after one ultimately masters the fundamental molds of one's own school can one know various other ways."[73] In this way, *gei* is a site where creative activities and traditions meet. Ultimately, this unification means that *gei* practitioners aim to incorporate traditions into their present-time creative activities. Sometimes their ultimate goal is also that they will be incorporated into the traditions, changing their status from the subject of enunciation (consecutive mentors of a school) to the subject of the enunciated (the origins of the teachings).[74]

In this paradigm, if a female practitioner of *gidayū* chanting chooses not to imitate male predecessors, by not anchoring her *gei* to a masculine voice, it means, in effect, that she relinquishes the possibility—no matter how small—that she will be able to operate in the established economy. Indeed, the playwright Seika recommended that female *onnagata* go their own way without imitating male *onnagata*,[75] and a similar opinion was voiced by a male *gidayū* chanter, Takemoto Tosatayū VI (1863–1941). Tosatayū, who had female disciples, was quoted as saying that female *gidayū* chanters should chant in a feminine way, without imitating male chanters.[76] Seika's and Tosatayū's recommendations present a fatal dilemma for female practitioners in traditional arts, especially when such recommendations come from the party of male practitioners who are faithfully observing such principles themselves. If a tradition (a long-standing community dedicated to a specific *gei*) maintains the artistic standards as masculine, and if female practitioners are encouraged to go their own way, the practical result is to exclude the latter from the mainstream tradition, confining them to a separate branch, a euphemism for a second-rate periphery. Yet, of course, remaining in the mainstream does not automatically save the female practitioner from the cul-de-sac, as it means that she has made critical errors in two ways: defying her superiors and rejecting society's definition of femininity, to which it no doubt wishes to keep assigning her.

In the final analysis, however, it is those women who did not go their own way who eventually received recognition in a tradition. For example, female *gidayū* chanter Takemoto Tosahiro (1897–1992), a disciple of Tosatayū's, was critically acclaimed in accordance with the norms in her field and became the first female *gidayū* chanter designated as a Living National Treasure (Ningen Kokuhō) in 1982. Mizuno Yūko offers an important analysis of Tosahiro's success, as materialized by the decoration, because she deliberately chose not to adopt a feminine manner of *gidayū*, which was once a new vogue. Tosahiro followed the mainstream (read "masculine") style of performance. Mizuno lucidly summarizes as follows:

> Depending on the perspective, the [feminine manner of *gidayū*] represented the birth of a new genre in the realm of *gidayū* created by men.... Women *gidayū* did not develop it, however, as it was constantly abused as collapsed *gei*, something that cannot be called *gidayū*.... If audiences [truly appreciated and supported] the [feminine manner of *gidayū*], it would have been able to remain. They did not support it in public, though. This was because, should they have done so, they would have been regarded as the ones who had no taste in *gei*.[77]

Against Tosatayū's admonition that female *gidayū* chanters should chant in a feminine manner, Tosahiro chose to imitate men. Certainly, her voice in recorded performances is indistinguishable from those of male chanters.[78] Some might be tempted to categorize Tosahiro and Kumehachi as shameless honorary men. Indeed, they remained trapped in "the master's way of seeing."[79] Their historical position is further complicated by the fact that, in practice, their choice could have well been the best possible option, given the above-mentioned milieu. In theory, their excessively masculinized rendering of stereotyped femininity displays "historical constructs" of women.[80]

Female performers taking lessons in *gidayū* chanting, accordingly, inevitably indicates that their *gei* will come to entail a certain masculine element, which is also applicable to *onnagata* artistry. As a result, she may receive the "compliment" that "nobody can tell she is not a man once she is onstage." In a 1961 review of an all-female Takarazuka production of *gidayū kabuki* (kabuki pieces adapted from bunraku), Kitagishi Yūkichi writes of male-role actor Kamiyo Nishiki (1917–1989): "Kamiyo Nishiki's [elocution] was splendid, [suitable for] a *jōruri* period piece. Such [excellent] intonation, pause, and low tone of voice made me forget that it was kabuki performed by women."[81] Kamiyo is praised in the same manner as is Kumehachi. The two female actors have at least two things in common: training in *gidayū* and experience in male-role acting.

Yet their success in kabuki should not be reduced to their experience in male-role acting alone. At first glance, Watanabe Tamotsu seems to suggest that

> Ichikawa Kumehachi even impressed Danjūrō IX.... Initially, Kumehachi was a male-role actor, sharing a range of *gei* similar to Danjūrō's. The photographs of *Dōjōji* [she left], for example, show us that she follows the process of becoming a man who then disguises himself as a woman. In this sense, [the pictures] demonstrate an amazing [approach to the woman's role in *Dōjōji*], which is one not of actresses but of *onnagata*....
>
> There is another kabuki performed by women, that is, the *gidayū-kabuki* study group of Takarazuka theater.... Kamiyo Nishiki attracted people's attention, and she was initially a male-role actor in Takarazuka. In this sense, she has the same structure of *gei* as that of Ichikawa Kumehachi. For kabuki productions, her structure of *gei* as a male-role actor was certainly useful.
>
> Attempts to use actresses in kabuki have been made several times in the last seventy-seven years [since 1886]. Most of them ended up failures, however. Ichikawa Kumehachi and Kamiyo Nishiki were exceptions, as they had a unique structure of *gei*. This fact implies one thing to us, that is to say, the exceptional cases of success were [limited to] actresses who had skill in disguising themselves as men. Those actresses who failed did not have such skill.[82]

While acknowledging the significance of male-role acting, focusing on it alone would miss the point. The training in *gidayū* chanting is already a formidable vehicle for acquiring masculine elements in *gei*, whether for men or women, and whether for male-role players or female-role players (regardless of their offstage gender). This does not offset the significance of the male-role acting Kumehachi and Kamiyo did; it is certainly likely that their masculine *gei* was made possible by, and further fostered by, the combination of the two. Having said that, the following review of another production of *gidayū kabuki* by Takarazuka, a few years after the one introduced above, emphasizes the important role of *gidayū* lessons for women's performance of kabuki in general (beyond such an actor as Kamiyo):

> Even if it's not a pure kabuki piece, such a period piece as *Date Masamune* was performed by a mixture of kabuki actors and actresses, with no awkward impression. This fact was interesting, as it supports the possibility of actresses participating in the genre of kabuki.
>
> Among the actresses [in *Date Masamune*], five out of [six, except for Yamada Isuzu,] were either current or former Takarazuka stars, and one of the reasons they managed to blend in with the kabuki stage was that Takarazuka theater does the *gidayū-kabuki* study group every year, inviting kabuki actors and a woman *gidayū* chanter as mentors.
>
> Even though she did not perform this time, the likes of Kamiyo Nishiki would be able to dance in classical kabuki.[83]

The only non-Takarazuka actor mentioned here is Yamada Isuzu (1917–2012), the daughter of an *onnagata* of *shinpa* theater, Yamada Kusuo (1879–1948), but she also took lessons in *gidayū*.[84] She also participated in genuine kabuki troupes numerous times,[85] and theater reviews indicate that she could have become another Kumehachi. While she was too late for the era of women-actors, Yamada was indeed another female *onnagata* in her own right.

It is in this context that one should read Kumehachi's training in *gidayū*. It is well documented that Kumehachi's voice was "low but powerful."[86] When recalling her performance of Princess Yaegaki on 2 March 1890, playwright Okamoto Kidō (1872–1939) described it as "bereft of feminine traits" and "low."[87] Although Kidō did not find it attractive that Kumehachi's voice had lost its feminine traits, this description accords with *gidayū* elocution norms. Moreover, because of the masculine feature of *gidayū* explained above, Kumehachi's unfeminine voice should not be understood solely on the grounds that she was also playing male roles, as Kidō claims.[88] It is more fundamentally related to her training in *gidayū*. In the words of Taganojō, "Well grounded in *gidayū*, Kumehachi's elocution was so sonorous that men would have been put to shame."[89] In short, Kumehachi studied a well-established, mainstream method of kabuki training, and her reputation indicates that her acting matched the standards of kabuki artistry.

Two *onnagata* techniques—the use of shoulder blades (*kaigarabone*) and "eye raising" (*metsuri*)—further illustrate the accord between Kumehachi's acting and what had been established as *onnagata* artistry. These techniques are usually considered necessary when the male bodies of *onnagata* successfully present femininity. However, Kumehachi's acting also required these techniques, which suggests a far more complicated picture than one based on the popular notion that *onnagata* techniques are a vehicle for creating artistic femininity that is available only to the bodies of male *onnagata*. First, in order to make their shoulders look slender, *onnagata* would pull their elbows behind their backs and try to bring the shoulder blades together[90] (at the same time, they would walk with their knees together, holding a piece of paper between them).[91] When Mori Ritsuko (1890–1961), an actress who also did kabuki plays, learned the role of Princess Yaegaki from Kumehachi, Kumehachi told her that "both shoulder blades should be attached together when it comes to princesses."[92] Second, to raise the corners of their eyes and make them almond-shaped, like the eyes of women in woodblock prints of the Edo era, *onnagata* would use a long, narrow strip of cloth known as *metsuri*.[93] Just as with the shoulder-blade technique, this eye-raising is physically painful,[94] but it is considered necessary for the creation of a feminine face. One of Kumehachi's journal articles contains eleven photographs of her: three at home, three in men's roles, and five in women's roles. It is obvious that she is using *metsuri* in the five *onnagata* pictures.[95]

In the realm of literary texts, Kumehachi also appears quite typical, as if she were just another male *onnagata* in mainstream kabuki circles. As far as kabuki is concerned, accounts-on-*gei* literature is classified into detailed explanations of a specific role and the training the actor has received, which usually overlaps with his or her life story. A single text can discuss just one or both of these topics. The former is usually a meticulous description of a given role (e.g., Princess Yaegaki), explaining the concrete tasks and movements of the part, mental preparation for it, music and props that are used, and so forth. The latter involves the actor speaking more generally on her or his specialty and the training required for it. Sometimes, the actor specifies a topic, such as *onnagata* technique. Because of the significance attached to training in *gei* acquisition, the accounts on training are easily interchangeable with narratives on artistry. Whatever the topic, the actor usually refers extensively to his or her predecessors and contemporaries, illustrating the points at hand with anecdotes. Kumehachi left behind several texts that, taken together, cover all the topics mentioned above. Sometimes she describes her training under Mitsue's guidance, or records what Danjūrō told her; at other times, she focuses on *onnagata* artistry, explaining its nuts and bolts or zeroing in on a specific role (e.g., Masaoka in *Precious Eaglewood and Hagi in the Previous Generation*) and detailing how to cooperate with a *gidayū* chanter in this scene or that or how to divide lines while doing the movements.[96]

It is noteworthy that Kumehachi's accounts on *onnagata* training and artistry in general, the role of Masaoka, and so forth, do not differ from those produced by male *onnagata*. This is not to say that her specific points on Masaoka are identical to those made by other *onnagata* who played that role.[97] Rather, in terms of structure, her accounts-on-*gei* are in line with those of other (male) *onnagata*. In her "Instructions for *Onnagata*" (Onnagata no kokoroe), for example, Kumehachi gives pointers for *onnagata* performance in the same manner as that of her male counterparts. It is rather difficult to tell from the text itself that this work was not produced by a male *onnagata*. At one point, she does say, "You might think that women are better at the roles of women," then immediately negates it, with "but that's not the case."[98] This is virtually the only place where this text deviates from other *onnagata* instructions produced by male *onnagata*. Moreover, even this sentence is ambiguous: does Kumehachi mean that "you might think that women are better [than men] at the roles of women," or that "you might think that women are better at the roles of women [than the roles of men]"? This is a moot point, however, since she negates the possibility of both even as she poses it.

Not only does she speak in her own accounts-on-*gei*, but Kumehachi is also cited in those of others. This is of great significance because it incorporates the person cited into a tradition. Kitamura Rokurō (1871–1961), a renowned *onnagata* of *shinpa* theater, is quite vocal about his admiration for Kumehachi, recalling that he imitated Kumehachi extensively: "What I did for the first day of the production was . . . everything that I admired of Kumehachi, movements, elocution, everything. . . . When I played at the Minato-za Theater, I asked Wakahachi, a disciple of Kumehachi's, to do the makeup of my face [so that I looked like her]. On the stage, of course, I walked like Kumehachi."[99]

As explained earlier, in terms of power politics, *shinpa* constituted the periphery of the kabuki establishment, but Kumehachi's influence did not remain in such a marginal realm as *shinpa* ("marginal" only as seen from a center). In 1927, Sawamura Gennosuke IV (1859–1936), a kabuki *onnagata* famous for his performance of dashing women's roles, explained the role of Otomi of *Scandalous Comb in the World of Love Affairs* (Yowanasake ukina no yokogushi; 1853) by Segawa Jokō III (1806–1881): "[When I first performed it,] I went to Kumehachi, . . . because I heard that Kumehachi knew it well. . . . So my Otomi is what I learned from Kumehachi. . . . As for the makeup scene of Otomi [in which Otomi applies makeup onstage], Kumehachi taught me what maestro Kikujirō II did. . . . [I failed in it, but] I want to put it in the record because it is the *kata* ['form' or 'pattern'] of maestro Kikujirō."[100] Gennosuke goes on to state that he and Kumehachi agreed that Baikō would be the most suitable *onnagata* to take over the choreography of Onoe Kikujirō II (1814–1875) in Otomi's makeup scene, and if he does, this *kata* would be passed down safely to later generations.[101] In fact, Baikō did later perform this *kata*, according to Taganojō, who was trained by Gennosuke in his youth and later joined the troupe of Kikugorō, Baikō's brother, to which Baikō belonged.[102] In short, the transmission of Otomi's makeup scene involved not only Kikujirō, Kumehachi, and Gennosuke but Baikō as well. It has now become one of the major *kata* performed in the said scene. In this sense, Gennosuke's prophecy certainly came true.

This is remarkable because kabuki circles have been highly rank-conscious. The rank of an actor would be determined by various types of rank (e.g., not only those of venues, as mentioned before, but also those of stage names and of actors with whom they collaborate). The history of kabuki artistry and dramaturgy consists of traditions transmitted through high-ranking actors. Kikujirō, Gennosuke, and Taganojō were all major *onnagata*; moreover, Baikō was a prime *onnagata* in the early twentieth century. Gennosuke's tribute to Kumehachi quoted above is from *Night Stories by Seigaku* (Seigaku Yawa), which was originally a series published in a journal. It is extremely interesting that when the original journal articles were later turned into a monograph, the part about Gennosuke and Kumehachi preferring that Baikō carry on Kikujirō's *kata* was omitted.[103] Even Kumehachi's coaching of Gennosuke may have been perceived as impertinent by some readers; if so, her pondering on Baikō as the one to carry on Kikujirō's choreography of Otomi's makeup scene would have been beyond the pale for them. This omission contributed to Kumehachi's marginalization in, or even eradication from, the discourse on kabuki after her day. In the landscape of the early twentieth century, however, Kumehachi is located well inside the *onnagata* tradition, even if not at the center, which Utaemon and Baikō occupy.[104]

Of note here is that Baikō was major from the very beginning of his career, whereas Gennosuke and Taganojō started their careers at small theaters and became major in due course. Taganojō explains that a certain prejudice associated with such a past tends to linger, as he knows both from his own experience and from what he had heard from Gennosuke.[105] Gennosuke and Taganojō praise Kumehachi quite openly—compared to other actors who started out major—and this candidness might partially be due to their small-theater background. In addition, considering Gennosuke's background as such, it is also most likely that his pondering on Baikō as the candidate for taking over Kikujirō's choreography was already an annoyance for rank-conscious people.

Gennosuke and Taganojō were not the only advocates of Kumehachi in mainstream kabuki circles. Nakamura Sōjūrō (1835–1889), one of the key figures in kabuki in the Kyoto and Osaka regions of his time, who was also active in theater reform movements, left a telling anecdote:

> In July of the last year [1888], he performed Shigenoi [of *Beloved Wife and Multicolored Reins* (Koi nyōbō somewake tazuna)] at the Kado-za Theater [in Osaka]. It was a huge success through all ages. Connoisseurs wondered whose *kata* it was, as Sōjūrō performed the role using the new *kata*.... Nobody figured it out. A certain person asked him whether it was his own innovation or somebody else's *kata*. He answered that it was a *kata*. [The inquirer] further asked whose *kata* it was, listing names of maestros of the past. Sōjūrō answered that it was Kumehachi's *kata*. The inquirer was appalled at this, saying, "Isn't Kumehachi a woman-actor in Tokyo? Isn't it a shame for [such a big-name actor as] Suehiroya [Sōjūrō] to follow the way in which a woman-actor had done it?" Sōjūrō is said to have replied, "Nay, and this is not just about Kumehachi. If there is a good *kata*, I will take it even if it comes from an actor at a small theater. All actors are my masters."[106]

This anecdote is quite illustrative of Kumehachi's complicated position in the kabuki establishment. Kumehachi was indeed involved in kabuki circles, as epitomized in her role transmitting *kata* to Gennosuke and Sōjūrō, but there was also a tendency to minimize her influence, or even her existence, as epitomized in the editing of *Night Stories by Seigaku* or in the skeptical attitude of the inquirer in the story of Sōjūrō.

Aside from the issue of ranking in kabuki circles, there is another issue, that is, the possibility that Kumehachi was considered a formidable invader of the theater market and the theater establishment. In comparison, her master Mitsue has been mentioned in the discourse of kabuki much more simply and tenderly. When she lost her patrons, Mitsue did not become a woman-actor and ended up being a proud former theater-master. As far as the establishment was concerned, she presented no threat, whereas Kumehachi invaded the men's world of kabuki as a woman-actor.[107]

A letter from a reader of the theater journal *Entertainment Illustrated* magazine (Engei gahō), published in 1912, is germane here. The reader recollects wandering around a corridor in a playhouse as a boy. He ended up peeping at actors who were getting undressed. Just when he noticed that some had breasts, a man in a uniform of the troupe caught him and said, "Keep it to yourself, OK? If people know they're women, tickets won't sell. They're men, all right?"[108] It is hardly possible to obliterate this type of anecdote from theater journals around that time.[109] Furthermore, similar reminiscences can be found in actors' accounts-on-*gei*.[110] This raises the intriguing question of what might have happened had Kumehachi never become famous. Would she have continued to pass as a man, as a young, jobless Kumehachi most likely did?[111] If Kumehachi had not become famous, there would have been no news photographs of her posing at home, no interviews detailing her life as a former theater-master, and so forth. In the journal articles published after she died, Kumehachi appears quietly, as though she were a high-ranking, but not top-notch, normal (male) kabuki actor in the Meiji era. Some articles record a rumor that an impostor using the stage name Kumehachi II has appeared; in some, "Ichikawa Kumehachi I" is listed in tables (*banzuke*) of "maestros of the recent past."[112]

We have thus far seen how Kumehachi's acting fit within the mainstream kabuki artistry of her day and was, indeed, perceived as such. We should keep in mind, however, that although the actor Kumehachi was functioning as a "normal" constituent of the kabuki economy, that does not necessarily mean that she was receiving her fair share from the system. Even though Danjūrō recognized Kumehachi's talent and accepted her as his disciple, he is said to have lamented, "Kumehachi would have made a good match for me if only she were a man."[113] Alleged remarks like this were widely circulated.[114] Kumehachi's kabuki performance made her contemporaries believe that she had the capacity to equal Danjūrō, yet she was effectively barred from achieving the same heights as a male, such as costarring in a play with Danjūrō. As theater critic Mishima Sōsen (1876–1934) put it: "She had the misfortune not to be born as a man. If Kumehachi had been a man, her performance would have made her a superstar like Danjūrō, if a little bit smaller."[115] Moreover, no matter how authentic Kumehachi's *onnagata* acting was, the very definition of *onnagata*—according to which such authenticity was evaluated—was about to change.

FEMALE ONNAGATA IN THE POROUS LABYRINTH OF FEMININITY CONSTRUCTION: THE DISCIPLINED, ACCLAIMED, AND ABJECTED

Thus far such words as "mainstream," "traditions," "established," and "default" have been used statically, for the sake of clarity. The fact is, however, that kabuki came to a crisis in the late nineteenth century and needed to redefine itself in order to survive the cultural upheaval that accompanied the Meiji Restoration. The fledgling Meiji government's policy of Westernization and modernization was far-reaching, and "theater was one of the most conspicuous sites for the new government to display Japan's legitimacy as an advanced nation."[116] As the eccentric, deviant, and queer theater of the people, kabuki was far from appropriate for this politically charged mission, which necessitated legitimizing kabuki. This could well have been a daunting task for kabuki, but it was its only chance for social survival (unless, perhaps, it went totally underground). Ironically, it was also a rare chance for kabuki to upgrade its social status, as noh theater was in too dire a situation after losing its samurai patrons (as were the theater-masters). The entire phenomenon of kabuki reforms is beyond the scope of this book, but, roughly speaking, there were theoretically three options for legitimizing kabuki: modernizing, Westernizing, or traditionalizing. The first two options were tried out, but to no avail. *Western Kabuki: Strange Drifting Tale* (Hyōryū kidan seiyō kabuki), of 1879, by Mokuami, and *The Rising-Sun Flag's Consecutive Victories on the Seas and Land* (Kairiku renshō asahhi no mihata), of 1894, by Fukuchi, among others, were box-office failures. Accordingly, "kabuki as a whole hurried to make itself over as a classical [theater]" at the turn of the century.[117]

The process of making itself over as a classical, traditional theater did not simply mean preserving kabuki as an antiquity. "Traditional kabuki" needed a new definition that could help it survive in this time of modernization and Westernization, and "traditional *onnagata*" required a new definition that could survive amid a society experiencing the hasty formation of natural scientific discourses (e.g., biology and sexology). Although the status of *onnagata* as the cultural icon of kabuki is secure today, this has not been a given throughout the history of kabuki. In the late nineteenth and early twentieth centuries, *onnagata* had to fight for their raison d'être vis-à-vis emerging actresses.

Although the new actresses performed new types of theater and not kabuki, their highly publicized emergence was intimidating for *onnagata*. Hanayagi Shōtarō (1894–1965), a renowned *shinpa*-theater *onnagata* and disciple of Kitamura, recalled that he lost confidence in his vocation after seeing Matsui Sumako (1886–1919), one of the most famous pioneer actresses.[118] Hanayagi's nervousness about Matsui provides a telling contrast to his master's optimistic admiration for Kumehachi. While Kitamura had buoyantly respected a female performer of his time, Hanayagi, only a few decades junior to him, felt threatened by his contemporary female performer. In 1909, Baikō voiced anxiety similar to that of Hanayagi when he was asked whether he wanted to join a delegation for an exhibition in London: "I would love to go to London. . . . But I have heard that actresses are valued in foreign countries, so *onnagata* like myself might be excluded even if we want to go."[119]

Such apprehensions were not groundless. Theater journals such as *Kabuki* and *Entertainment Illustrated* magazine published debates around this time that questioned the comparative validity of actresses and *onnagata*.[120] Analyzing the debates in terms of the modern concept of femininity epitomized by actresses such as Matsui, Kano states that there were pro-actress, anti-actress, and eclectic groups, all of which shared the idea of "align[ing] women with what they are 'essentially,' 'physically,' and 'naturally,'" which was "set against the male *onnagata*'s 'patterns,' his 'art,' or 'artifice.'"[121] She demonstrates that such an essentialist understanding of gender (natural femininity grounded in women's bodies) was a modern concept made possible at that time due to the confluence of scientific discourse and Japan's position in global politics. It is little wonder that Baikō and other male *onnagata* were threatened by the new actresses, whose bodies were (considered) the matrix of natural femininity and whom the pro-actress group supported.

Does this mean that *onnagata*'s artistic-artificial femininity was discovered to be inferior to the newly conceptualized natural femininity of women? One participant in the debates seems to suggest this by asserting, "No matter how skillful an *onnagata* might be, it is unbearable to line him up with an actual woman. It goes without saying that a real woman is more womanly [than *onnagata* are]."[122] However, this idea of *onnagata*'s artistic femininity as detached from natural femininity, whether seen positively or negatively, was not in line with the logic of femininity construction seen in premodern kabuki, according to which an excellent *onnagata* had to pass as a woman in everyday life. It was certainly bearable, contrary to the assertion cited above, to place him next to an actual woman at, for example, restaurants and bathhouses. Rather, the important differentiation was made between excellent and mediocre *onnagata*—and by no means between women and *onnagata* en masse—whether or not it was unbearable to line them up with actual women.

Given this, it should be clear that the raison d'être of *onnagata* at the beginning of the twentieth century was not threatened by any inferiority in artistic-artificial femininity. Rather, the threat lay in the very fact that *onnagata* artistry, as theorized by *onnagata* themselves, presupposed compatibility between women and *onnagata* as the doers of femininity. In this scheme, the femininity-construction mechanism not only consciously built on the performative but also operated insidiously in both essentialist and constructionist discourses, as illustrated by two extreme cases of acclaimed *onnagata*: Hanshirō, who looks like nothing other than a woman, and Kumehachi, who looks like nothing other than a man. *Onnagata* might surely have been superior performers of femininity, but not the exclusive ones. In the late Meiji, however, when the return of actresses was strongly associated with new, scientific discourses that grounded natural femininity in women's bodies alone, *onnagata* could no longer brag about their ability to suffer from gynecological disorders, a stage that they reached through *onnagata* training. When the concept of natural femininity in women's bodies was discovered as the constitutive other of the artistic-artificial femininity constituted in men's performance, the concept of artistic femininity was simultaneously discovered as that which was not natural femininity. This was the moment when the dichotomy of natural femininity and artistic femininity came into being in this context. In this moment, a new definition of *onnagata* as the exclusive doers of artistic femininity emerged, independent of women themselves. Independent though they were, modern *onnagata* were defined in line with modern actresses in the sense that they were both regarded as scientifically controlled by their natural sexes.

Onnagata gradually but successfully materialized this in the ensuing few decades. Intriguingly, women slowly stopped evaluating male *onnagata*'s performance of women's roles and instead began admiring their presentation of the (alleged) artistic essence of femininity. The lessons in feminine appearance that *onnagata* gave to women readers, and not fellow *onnagata*, in theater journals and other publications in the early and mid-twentieth century should be understood not so much in the context of Edo-era precept-literature traditions (e.g., *Greater Learning for Women*) as in the context of this redefinition of *onnagata* artistry. Nevertheless, there will be some lingering elements of the bygone past.

In the last section, we saw that Kumehachi could operate as a normative member of the kabuki economy. We now see that the economy in question was being rewritten at that very moment. Denied the logic of their femininity construction, *onnagata* could no longer rely on "imitation" as the basic concept of their construction of femininity, on their "compatibility" with women in everyday life as one of the criteria of their artistry, or on the fundamental premise of *gei*, namely, arduous training (a doing) would make a body that could suffer from gynecological disorders (a being).[123] Performative versatility, suited for a porous labyrinth of gendering and made possible by cultivation, was now at stake. As the constitutive other of the natural femininity of actresses and, by extension, women in general, *onnagata*'s artistic femininity now had to be the exclusive property of male *onnagata*. A concomitant was the establishment of a new approach to knowledge in modern Japan that granted a privileged status to "originality," which inevitably meant the relegation of its constitutive other, "imitation." Given the inferior attribution of imitation, it is little wonder that *onnagata*'s femininity, which was about to be categorized as artistic femininity, could no longer afford to be associated with imitation. To all intents and purposes, male *onnagata* could no longer afford to coexist with female *onnagata*.

Female *onnagata* who could embody the latter type of femininity—through rigorous training in dance, *gidayū* elocution, shoulder-blade usage, and other techniques such as eye raising—were an epistemological oxymoron in this new landscape. They were simply misfits.[124] They belonged neither to the category of natural femininity nor to that of artistic femininity. As far as advocates of the natural femininity of women were concerned, female *onnagata* might have been considered traitors of a sort, since they had obtained the status of "honorary men" by obeying the master discourse. By the same token, advocates of the superior artistic femininity of male *onnagata* would likely have had an even more drastic reaction, for female *onnagata* threatened the very validity of the definition of male, artistic *onnagata* in and of itself. Thus the more skillful female *onnagata* were, the more dangerous they became. (In this threat lies a possible junction that divides female *onnagata*, whose demise we are witnessing, and female *gidayū* chanters, who still exist today.) Furthermore, even though it is now thought that *onnagata* movements require male bodies,[125] this understanding emerged only through the modern redefinition of *onnagata* artistry, and female *onnagata* (at least disciplined ones like Kumehachi and, later, Yamada) were empirical proof to the contrary. Thus the fact that male *onnagata* have mostly defined the kinesics of "feminine" in kabuki[126] does not mean that only men can do it. The raison d'être of male *onnagata* can only be secured, however, if female *onnagata* are abjected.[127]

The existence of women-actors on the stage was short-lived. In a world saturated with the idea that *onnagata*'s artistic femininity could be achieved only by male *onnagata*, we are made to believe that women-actors were onstage for only a few decades because they did not measure up to the job. The example of Kumehachi suggests, however, that women-actors were abjected precisely because they could do the job, and because their ability was not in line with the gender regulation of the new, modern definition of *onnagata* artistry and, by extension, with that of Japanese society as a whole. The porous nature of gender-construction theorization, which helped the likes of Kumehachi gain acceptance in the tradition of *onnagata*, was now denied by the new gender regulation. In addition, the impending elimination of actors' mobility between big theaters and small theaters (and the eventual disappearance of small theaters) would degrade the environment for women-actors. Likewise, the imminent change in the definitions of "hereditary succession," which used to be broadly defined but gradually converged at the idea of bloodline, also helped close the crevices. Together, these changes drastically rewrote the map. As playwright Takeshiba Kisui (1847–1923), a disciple of Mokuami, recalled in 1920, "Theater totally changed within the past forty or fifty years, . . . and *onnagata* changed most drastically."[128] What disappeared from the stage were male *onnagata* who could suffer from gynecological disorders and female *onnagata* who were indistinguishable from men. It may not be coincidence that Hanshirō, Kumehachi's penultimate master, was among the last male *onnagata* of premodern times and that Kumehachi herself was among the last women-actors.

The greatest irony for the likes of Kumehachi was that the very same societal change that had made women-actors possible economically was destined to deny the existence of its own protégées epistemologically.

Changes in society deprived theater-masters of their vocation and thus thrust some of them, as women-actors, into kabuki circles. These changes, while certainly rapid and drastic, also entailed an insidious theoretical break in terms of cognitive practice (e.g., how to understand gender). It took several decades for this epistemological discontinuity to materialize in kabuki, but when it did so, it reified as the rejection of women-actors within the kabuki economy for the sake of new definitions of kabuki and of *onnagata*. If the societal change in Meiji Japan was responsible for both the birth and the demise of Meiji women-actors, then the extinction of these women-actors was merely a delayed reification of this discontinuity. Tamura would describe it as "a natural incident... in the sense that what should disappear disappeared."[129] They were brought to the public stage by social conditions specific to the premodern/modern shift. In that sense, women-actors were literally *modern* female kabuki actors, and yet they were paradoxically bound by *premodern* concepts. They were Edo women living in the Meiji era; Meiji transformations simultaneously resulted in the advent of women-actors *in practice* and yet destined their wane *in a theoretical sense*. The duration of Kumehachi's career, and by extension that of Meiji women-actors, fell into the time lag of the discontinuity, or, one may say, into the grace period of their fate. An epistemological inversion took a long time in this case, much longer than a Michel Foucault—and a Karatani Kōjin for that matter—would assume, but far shorter than the women-actors themselves no doubt hoped.

PART IV

Origins of Onnagata

Modern Reformation

> I heard of a small troupe led by one Danzaburō, a disciple of Danjūrō VIII. . . . I badly wanted to become an actor, so I cut off my hair, made it into [a masculine style], and joined the troupe.
>
> —ICHIKAWA KUMEHACHI I, "Gigei no Hanashi" (82–83)

CHAPTER 8

Toward Contemporary Onnagata

Art in Their Blood

For male *onnagata*, the existence of female *onnagata* in and of itself was already a consummate victory. Male *onnagata* had gained the reputation of representing femininity that is ideal enough to be imitated by female performers. Their triumph did not stop there. When modernity dramatically changed the cultural and epistemological milieu of late-nineteenth- and early-twentieth-century Japan, there came into being a notion that biologically correct women should naturally perform women onstage. Despite the cul-de-sac, male *onnagata* managed to survive, by successfully being deployed in a newly established dichotomy of "the natural femininity of actresses" versus "the artistic-artificial femininity of male *onnagata*," with female *onnagata* unable to secure their lot in these modern categories. The key lies in blood.

LABYRINTH CLOSED? PARALLELED FATES
OF ADOPTED SONS AND ANCIEN ONNAGATA

Onnagata went through radical changes in modern times, and Utaemon V, born in 1865, was instrumental in determining a new *onnagata* definition, reifying the discontinuity of premodern and modern *onnagata*. Not only was he the prime *onnagata* of his time, but he also reached the apex of kabuki circles after Danjūrō's demise in 1903, and it was unprecedented in the men's world of kabuki for an *onnagata* to hold a position of leadership.[1] The traditionally observed inferior status of not only females but also male *onnagata* helps highlight the fact that the very reasoning that makes it possible to assign such inferior status to some people in this community is associated with gender and not sex. It is thus not so much male-centric as masculinity-centric. If Utaemon managed to neutralize the inferior status of *onnagata*, that must have reflected not only his individual "political competence"[2] but also the fact that *onnagata* had just lost compatibility with women, a highly valued characteristic expected of premodern *onnagata*, such as Hanshirō, who could pass as a woman even when wearing only lingerie.

The phrase "from Hanshirō to Utaemon" is itself handy shorthand for a shift from premodern to modern *onnagata*, and their respective images at that time—domestic Hanshirō and politically ambitious Utaemon—effectively dramatize the transposition. The two *onnagata* also had an interesting could-have-been connection. Utaemon was not born into a kabuki family but was adopted by Nakamura Shikan IV (ca. 1830–1899), who played both men's and women's roles. Before that, though, the boy was initially brought to Hanshirō as a potential son-to-be: "[When my father passed away in 1874, I was introduced to Iwai Hanshirō for adoption.] I thought, no way can I go to that 'Big Forehead,' who looks like a woman. . . . In this way, I ended up being adopted by Shikan in 1875."[3]

It is quite suggestive that the boy who would later initiate a new era of *onnagata* had intuitively denied the *ancien*-taste *onnagata* representative of the preceding era. It is not that the boy rejected the maestro *despite* his forte; on the contrary, the very characteristic of Hanshirō, for which he had been critically acclaimed before, was now intuitively and categorically rejected by the enfant terrible. Although Utaemon later did indeed use Hanshirō's *kata* ("form" or "pattern" of acting),[4] here we can retrospectively witness a decisive juncture dividing premodern and modern *onnagata*. At the beginning of modern times, the artistry of *onnagata* ended up being defined categorically as artistic property reserved exclusively for male *onnagata*. Femininity enacted by *onnagata* was now understood distinctively as the artistic, artificial, and theatrical performance of male actors, which was isolated from the daily femininity of "genuine women" (*hontō no onna*),[5] borrowing the wording of distinguished *onnagata* Utaemon VI, the second son and heir of Utaemon V, who also led kabuki circles in his own time.

Not everything about Utaemon was new and modern, however. The praxis of adoption, by which Utaemon ended up becoming a kabuki actor in the first place, was a well-established and long-lasting custom in Japan. It is also noteworthy that another prime *onnagata* at that time, Baikō VI, was likewise an adopted son of Onoe Kikugorō V (1844–1904). "Gender" and "adoption" are related in a theoretical sense, as will be discussed shortly. Furthermore, they also operated in tandem in this historical setting. Kabuki families have long institutionalized the practice of adoption for the sake of hereditary art, which was also common in many family businesses in Japan.

Especially in premodern times, many *ie* with family businesses made broad use of adoption. When there was no capable heir by blood, adoption was a vital expedient for transmitting *ie* in order to guarantee the prosperity of *ie* and its multigenerational enterprise. (In other words, even if there was a child or children by birth, should they be unable to prove their capability for the family business, adoption was still a possibility.) Kathleen S. Uno sums up an *ie* as less a biological community than a corporation,[6] and in that sense, preservation was *ie*'s raison d'être. In kabuki-related literature, one frequently encounters the phrase "art of the family" (*ie-no-gei*; lit., "acquired artistic technique [*gei*] of the stem-family household [*ie*]"), which implies that specific artistic styles, particular choreography, performance theory, and the like have been established, perfected, and transmitted from generation to generation in the said family. More often than not, such transmission has been secured not so much by blood-family members as by disciplined and determined devotees of the specific art of the family, and adoption was for a long time an indispensable praxis for this operation. While neither the concept of the art of the family nor the praxis of adoption was unique to kabuki circles,[7] quite a few famous kabuki families have actively utilized adoption until quite recently for the sake of the art of the family. Even many so-called born princes (*onzōshi* in popular discourse)[8] of major kabuki households today would find that their grandfathers or great-grandfathers had been adopted not only from other—usually minor—kabuki families but also from families not associated with the theater at all. When it comes to bloodline, therefore, quite a few kabuki princes today can trace their biological ancestors only two or three generations back in their respective kabuki households. Artistically, however, they might well be a fifteenth-generation heir of a renowned kabuki family, whose successive members have collectively devoted themselves to the art of the family.

The meaning of hereditary succession has gradually changed, however, as it has converged at the idea of bloodline. Consequently, the term "hereditary succession" has in effect become the synonym for "bloodline succession" in contemporary Japan, and these two terms are now used nearly interchangeably. Kabuki circles are not an exception to this transition, and as Ōzasa Yoshio states, kabuki society has now become much more ancestry oriented as defined by blood than it used to be.[9] The adoption praxis has not ceased completely, and there still exist today several major kabuki actors who were adopted from both within and beyond kabuki circles. For example, Tamasaburō, arguably the most acclaimed *onnagata* today, designated a Living National Treasure in 2012, was born into a non-kabuki family and was accepted as a disciple and subsequently as an adopted son by a major kabuki actor, Morita Kan'ya XIV (1907–1975). The same is also true for one of the most popular actors in the younger generation, Kataoka Ainosuke VI (b. 1972): first he was accepted as a disciple of Nizaemon and subsequently as an adopted son of Kataoka Hidetarō II (b. 1941), Nizaemon's son.[10] They are, however, definitely in the minority among their peers, who are most likely privileged born princes of big-name kabuki households. This is in stark contrast to the situation of kabuki actors a few generations before them, in which so many top actors were adopted sons: for instance, Ichimura Uzaemon XV (1874–1945) of non-kabuki lineage; Nakamura Kanzaburō XVII (1909–1988) from another kabuki family; Ichikawa Danjūrō XI (1909–1965), the son of Kōshirō VII, himself born into a non-kabuki family; and, as mentioned, Utaemon V and Baikō VI. The case of Uzaemon in particular is illustrative of the previous regime, as he is said to have been born to the illegitimate daughter of a samurai and a French American, but in this regime, what mattered more than genes was his legitimate status as the adopted son of Ichimura Uzaemon XIV (1847–1893) and the training he received as such.

What made this shift possible, along with what it generated simultaneously, was a bundle of various issues. Probably most significant epistemologically among them concerned the idea of the natural, which many scholars across disciplines and geographic areas have noted in relation to modernity. In modernity, scientific knowledge has played a significant role in evaluating, prioritizing, and authorizing a wide range of information and knowledge, epistemological cosmologies included. In this sense, modernity itself is already a considerable factor when one discusses anything related to gender, due to its obsessive tendency to *polarize* things and *scientifize* matters (i.e., *make* something scientific, including a possibility of disguise). It is one powerful way by which modernity naturalizes various *cultural* phenomena.

The previous regime maintained nature and second nature in an intimate (even interchangeable) relationship; in turn, nature in modernity formed a polarized relationship with that which was not nature.

Japanese theater offers one illustrative example in a concept discussed in Kano's analysis of the emergence of modern actresses: natural femininity physically grounded in women's actual bodies.[11] Here, the Natural is being made the sole reason for the Social and the Cultural, whereas it had previously been thought that the latter operated in its own right before modern times. Femininity performed by trained theater performers (e.g., *onnagata*, male and female alike) fell into the category of second nature in premodern times and into that of non-natural in modern times. Therefore, from premodern to modern times, the cognitive locus of this specific femininity shifted from a certain place intimate with that which housed naturals to another place that was the extreme opposite to the Natural. It was, accordingly, also the time when the dichotomy of natural femininity and artificial femininity was conceptualized, established, and naturalized (i.e., made invisible).

If it was the moment when gender came to be understood exclusively via natural components of our bodies, it was also the time when people began focus on bloodline alone for family heredity. Here, gender and lineage are akin in a theoretical sense. Given this, it is no wonder that their respective shifts (toward a focus on the Natural) happened simultaneously in the context of modern Japan. Such an epistemological transition was thus germane to the changing attitude toward the praxis of adoption, as it brought with it the idea that biological children were *incomparably* preferable to adopted children, because they were considered capable of carrying on family traditions—such as the family business, the art of the family, and the like—due precisely to their DNA.

Yet the picture was much more complicated than an instant victory of the Natural over the Cultural. Most major actors start their kabuki training and careers as privileged birth sons of big kabuki households,[12] but it would be absurd to divide what they came to embody into the effect of training and of genes. Moreover, the absence of any ancestral blood in their veins did not prevent a Tamasaburō and an Ainosuke from emerging. Cultivation, an established shortcut to second nature, is a key concept in this cultural context. If modern scholars find it necessary or useful to discuss lineage in terms of blood percentages as such, that unwittingly reveals an obsession with the biological (read natural) *on the part of scholarship*.[13] In addition, Tamasaburō, Ainosuke, and other adopted kabuki bigwigs have not found it necessary to hide the fact that they are adopted sons. What underlines these two different attitudes toward the practice of adoption is twofold: (1) the presence—or absence—of semi-unconditional trust in the natural qualification that biological offspring putatively share *through* physical connection with their ancestors and (2) lingering cultivation values. While its theoretical impact was drastic and irreversible, the tide of the Natural in practice manifested itself gradually here, entailing a residue from the previous regime. The bloodline was not the sole defining feature in the paradigm in kabuki circles (and beyond) in premodern episteme, but in modern times it came to dominate—not monopolize—those who had been subject to the regime of cultivation, including kabuki circles. Cultivation used to be universal in premodern Japanese culture, but in modern times it became a rare feature specific to limited arenas. For those involved in family traditions, such as the art of the family, the ability to carry over their *gei* is the ultimate asset. Arguably, here again, the Natural (e.g., DNA) is being made responsible for such an asset, that is, the Social and the Cultural.

Biological offspring are to adoptees as women (e.g., actresses) are to *onnagata*. The latter group, adoptee-descendants and *onnagata*, had been epistemologically equivalent, supported or legitimated by premodern systems, while the former group, biological descendants and women (e.g., actresses), found powerful advocates in the modern natural sciences and their idea of things that are natural. Women and male *onnagata* were not mutually exclusive ahistorically, and neither were biological and adopted descendants. Rather, they *became* mutually exclusive upon the advent of a specific modern valorization of the Natural. Before that, there was no clear boundary between them, let alone the absolute binary polarizing them, at least epistemologically. Just like male *onnagata* who managed to obtain bodies capable of suffering from gynecological disorders, adopted sons can hope to attain a stage at which they mentally as well as physically resemble their ancestors, be it individually or collectively. (One might resemble, for example, a certain individual in the household; one might carry a certain aura that many members of the family tree, past and present, evince.) They had a means by which they could identify themselves with those with whom they did not share natural, scientifized (i.e., *made* scientific) traits.

The key here lies in the performative mechanism of *gei* training, that is, cultivation. In order to achieve artistic techniques as a quasi-intuitive and semi-direct part of an individual practitioner's body, cultivation has to be long-lasting (usually for a lifetime), repetitive, physical, and industrial. It is a performative operation because it creates a *being* out of a repetitious *doing*. Quasi-immediacy (second nature) is created out of what is mediated (concrete, repetitious training of one's body). By definition, both *onnagata* and adopted sons in kabuki families are to engage in cultivation defined as such. According to the logic of cultivation, the practitioner will certainly become a woman-as-is in the case of *onnagata* and a faithful and talented successor or descendant for the household in the case of adoptees.

It is in this sense that an adopted son of a kabuki household can hope to resemble his ancestor in his looks, elocution, locomotion, and so on, which often materialize in literature related to kabuki (e.g., theater reviews, interviews, etc.). "Art" (culture) here is never the constitutive other of "genes" (nature), but, rather, the two are conceptualized as interwoven. "Genes" and "art" exist together, and not in causal or opposite relationships, which creates a substantial contrast to the modern dichotomy of the artistry of *onnagata* and the natural bodies of actresses that were considered the exclusive matrix of femininity.[14] It is this logic of cultivation that was overwhelmed, if not totally overruled, by the modern superiority of the Natural. With Western, modern natural sciences and their infiltration into the epistemological grids, by which people made sense of things, the general concept of biological offspring gained a status that is not merely quantitatively preferable to that of adoptee-descendants (A is relatively better than B) but, more important, qualitatively unique beyond comparison (A is the *one and only*). If we regard females as scientifically verifiable women, then biological offspring can be considered scientifically traceable descendants, and this makes them unique and natural entities in their own right.

Given this change in attitude toward what is presupposed to be scientifically natural, the aforementioned anecdote about Utaemon V is extremely intriguing. In the boy's denial of *ancien onnagata* lay an impending shift from the premodern fusion of the natural and the cultural. The anecdote is, though, clearly the product of an era when the practice of adoption was still taken for granted. Furthermore, things are also highly elusive in terms of the emergent new definition of *onnagata* artistry that is odds with the previous expectation (passing as a woman). Utaemon V himself left seemingly contradictory remarks such as that married *onnagata* would usually come to resemble their wives and that he had adopted the *kata* of Hanshirō.[15]

One more element remains to be added to this picture: the demise of small kabuki theaters and the closure of actors' mobility between first-class big theaters and second-class small ones. The two issues are intricately related because the disappearance of second-class small theaters meant that actors were no longer able to move between first-rate and second-rate playhouses. In addition, kabuki is highly rank-conscious, and the rank of a venue where an actor performs is indicative of his or her own rank and status as an actor. Thus, the closure of mobility between first-rate and second-rate playhouses fixed an actor's status in the kabuki-actor hierarchy. The *onnagata* Taganojō started his acting career at a top-tier small theater (i.e., the upper edge of the second-rate zone in the kabuki world). He witnessed the situation of small theaters during his youth:

> [Between big theaters and small theaters,] there were also mid-theaters [*chū-shibai*], . . . where big-name actors didn't hesitate to play. They rarely worked at small theaters, . . . [but in some exceptional cases, they did. There was a variety of small theaters.] The special one was the Miyato-za Theater, where many good actors played all right, but [. . . on the other hand] you'd always hear "Don't go to Kaisei-za and Ryūsei-za," 'cause they were special in a different way, a bad way. [Once you worked there, you'd have no hope whatsoever, of going up to a big theater.] Bandō Matasaburō performed there. People called him "Two-Dollar Danjūrō," 'cause he looked like [Danjūrō]. He really was a skillful actor, you see, but people looked down on him.[16]

Taganojō's career illustrates upward mobility, as he was then recruited by a troupe led by Kikugorō VI, a top actor whose name is still used to refer to his time period (the Kiku-Kichi era). Taganojō was designated a Living National Treasure in 1968, which was unprecedented—even unthinkable—for an actor with a small-theater background. Arguably, he was the last renowned kabuki actor whose career illustrated kabuki actors' mobility from small-theater to mainstream kabuki circles. Just as with adopted sons and *ancien onnagata*, small theaters as a venue for kabuki, and, moreover, as that which was interchangeable with mainstream kabuki, were about to face difficulties.

That particular time was such a consolidating moment, as one's status was in the process of being fixated according to a new economy. Two phenomena reified this transition: (1) the establishment of the irreconcilable demarcation between biological and adopted sons in the management of a family business and (2) the modern re/discovery of the mutually exclusive nature of the biological and the disciplined performers of femininity, women and *onnagata*. For actors in the midst of this consolidation process, the fact that the locations of their activity were transformed into a monolithic site helped foster such a fixation all the more.

ORIGINS OF ONNAGATA AS WE KNOW THEM TODAY: THE DEPLOYMENT OF POLARITIES

Several modern polarities were concomitant with the transition from premodern to modern *onnagata*. The new categorical demarcation of artificial and natural simultaneously made possible and was made possible by the Natural. It also had the theoretical capability of nullifying the performative premise of cultivation, which was to maintain nature and second nature in an intimate relationship. In practice, the theoretical capability was only partially realized in the sense that the regime of cultivation was not eradicated, but it nevertheless brought a great shift, as the cultivation paradigm lost its universal status in society and ended up being allowed to survive in a very specific realm (e.g., traditional theater, martial arts, etc.). The modern fate of premodern *onnagata*—*onnagata* who could pass as women in society—must be understood with this premise. Due to the respected status of acquired second nature, this premise hardly found it necessary to distinguish natural gender and artificial gender in an absolute manner. Whereas nature and second nature had been closely related to each other, the Natural and the nonnatural (artificial) were now polarized, forming a new dichotomy of natural and disciplined entities.

The dichotomy of artificial gender and natural gender is one manifestation of what can be called modern binarisms. Far from unique in modernity, the cognitive tendency to dichotomize is omnipresent, but *how* and *on what grounds* things are deployed in a binary system differ spatially, temporally, and epistemologically. The artificial/natural gender dichotomy was among the dualisms realized in Japanese society in modern times, and it is critical to understand how *onnagata* were involved in the perception of gender at that time. Another related dichotomy—that of male and female—also pertained to the subject matter, and both of these pairs operated in tandem in helping foster the transformation of the artistry of *onnagata* and its reception.

By no means does it indicate the absence of the male/female binary in Japanese society before that. Not only did differentiation between the two sexes exist, but the way in which people perceived other sexes (e.g., intersex) was also based on the binary of the two sexes. It was not *the* ultimate index that bisected people in premodern Japan, however. The male/female distinction had been of lesser social importance than class differences in premodern times, and this affected womanhood, as did occupation and age grades, as that which categorized humans.[17] The sex-gender binary in premodern Japan was *simply* one parameter *among* many dividers for classifying humans. In this sense, the doomed dualism of masculinity and femininity, which in practice is unflinchingly binding in modern times, is, in theory, unsubstantiated. At the beginning of modern times, though, the rigid two-sex binary system became a certain meta-imperative, surpassing distinctions based on these other markers. The male/female binary was upgraded in modern times as a meta-criterion for bisecting people, and modern *onnagata* ended up performing femininity in this context.

Here, male versus female and artificial gender versus natural gender were two types of scientifized binarisms firmly materialized in modern Japan. Added to those was a certain demarcation between constructionism and essentialism. As they were reified, *onnagata* were facing the formidable task of justifying their performance of femininity by altering not merely the performance itself but, more importantly, its perception. In the previous regime, the performative versatility of cultivation had opened up the possibility of cross-gendering human enterprises. In that premodern regime, *onnagata*'s performance of femininity aimed at second nature, which formed an intimate relationship with nature; in turn, in modern times, it aimed at the Artistic, which now formed a polarity with the scientifized Natural. This was where the Foucauldian birth of *onnagata* was made possible, the origins of *onnagata* as we know them today.

A concise epithet particular to modern *onnagata* is "even more womanly than women," which is still frequently used in reference to, for example, Tamasaburō. In several ways, this manner of predicating their alleged essence is revealing as to what turned out to be new and unprecedented about modern *onnagata* and modern conceptions of gender performance. On the level of language, the subject of such description (that is, prescription in disguise) cannot be women, because, logically speaking, only non-A can be *more something than* A. It is also noteworthy that, when this expression is used, the signified concept is a broad, *abstract* idea of femininity and not a concrete woman of any sort. When Tamasaburō is praised with this phrase, he is not being compared to any actual woman in particular, but such a compliment assumes an idealized, generic reification of femininity that his performance is said to realize. If premodern counterparts aimed at becoming excellent doers *among* many doers of femininity, most of whom were women, then modern *onnagata* are to be understood as *transcendent* doers of femininity in isolation—that is, *onnagata* are *insiders* in the former paradigm and *outsiders* in the latter. If modern *onnagata* are even more womanly than women in an *abstract* way, then, their premodern predecessors tried to master the art so that they could pass as *concrete* women even offstage. For if one is to *pass* in everyday life (e.g., in restaurants and bathhouses), the role to be performed should be a specific persona and never a generalized, idealized concept such as the "essence of feminine beauty"—a typical compliment for modern *onnagata*. There must have existed a certain channel through which an abstract concept of femininity came to be an issue of significance at the onset of modern times.

Further importance lies in the dual tasks of modern *onnagata*'s gender performance: they should perform femininity independently of actual women and make it apparent that their sex is categorically non-female, namely, male. Although non-female is interchangeable with male in the dominant social discourse, both in theory and in practice, non-female and male are not equivalent. A more rigorous way of phrasing it is as follows: non-female and male are not equivalent *in practice*, while *in theory* they are sometimes likely to be *made* equivalent. What is critical about saying of *onnagata*'s sex being male is that, except for very limited exceptions, people have no way of verifying sex directly by, for instance, genitalia, to say nothing of chromosomes. Only by reading gender performances do people *assume* (and are made to believe) that they know the sex of most people around them. Then it is not so much the combination of "sex and gender" as that of "gender and gender" that matters for modern *onnagata*. They are expected to excel in performing two types of gender: femininity defined as ideal, artificial, and nonexistent in reality, on the one hand, and unquestioned, unspecified masculinity (a certain definition of which is tacitly assumed), on the other.

Natural femininity was conceptualized as the property of females alone, and *onnagata* came to assume the responsibility of performing what are considered natural masculinity on the one hand (in order to verify his sex being male) and artistic femininity on the other (in order to secure their raison d'être against women who monopolize alleged natural femininity). What underlay new *onnagata* were several modern dichotomies (male/female and Natural/artificial), which in turn were made possible at the cost of that which could not be deployed neatly in a binary system. The abjecteds and obliterateds include (1) male *onnagata* who could pass as women, (2) female *onnagata* indistinguishable from male *onnagata*,[18] (3) the relativity of gender distinctions, and (4) the relativity of the weight of gender.

Many modern male *onnagata* themselves have indeed claimed artistic femininity as their exclusive property. Nakamura Shikan VII (1928–2011), one of the major *onnagata* of his time, is firm regarding this point: "If women performed women's roles [in kabuki, *onnagata*'s] charms would disappear, I think. Lately, they have come to have really good figures of nice proportions, but the voice is a woman's voice no matter what, isn't it? If it comes to that, in the case of [male] *onnagata*, it wouldn't be attractive at all if they spoke in a woman's voice itself. If *onnagata* can invoke the glamour that women don't have, charms that women don't have, then that can be called a success."[19] His uncle Utaemon VI likewise states in an interview: "*Onnagata* should not become genuine women [*hontō no onna*. . . . The way in which *onnagata*] make up for the part and carry themselves [*funsō konashi*] shouldn't approach those of women in actuality [*genjitsu no onna*]."[20] Indeed, the interviewer praises Utaemon, saying that his "casual demeanor [during the interview] made her sense 'woman' much more than women would do," reminding us of the typical epithet "even more womanly than women."[21]

The evaluation of *onnagata* changed in exactly the same manner. Among premodern *onnagata*, Hanshirō had a high reputation as the last *onnagata* in a true sense. Mastering the criterion of *onnagata* who pass, Hanshirō was described by Kisui as capable of passing as a woman even when wearing only lingerie.[22] Likewise, Gennosuke, himself a renowned *onnagata* and Taganojō's teacher, considers Hanshirō an exemplary genuine *onnagata* of a sort that no longer existed after him: *onnagata* who are right-minded and sensible as *onnagata*, who would become a woman, leaving his shoes turned inward even when taking them off in a hurry.[23] The 1920 article by Kisui refers to "forty or fifty years" ago as the time when premodern *onnagata* still existed. In turn, Gennosuke, in an interview probably conducted in 1934, states that the good old way lasted until about 1881 or 1882. From these statements, one may infer that the time when premodern *onnagata* still existed was the 1870s through the early 1880s.

Both Kisui and Gennosuke regard plausibility offstage as the defining criterion for *onnagata*'s arts onstage and, based on that, conclude that Hanshirō was the last *onnagata*. In stark contrast, Baikō VI, four decades younger than Hanshirō, was commemorated as follows: "One thing that I cannot forget is that, [despite the fact that Baikō was an *onnagata*, he] did not say anything selfish in a womanly manner [*joseiteki na wagamama*] or effeminate [*memeshī*]. Even on this point alone, I, as a person who has known many actors, cannot help missing him."[24] Here, approximation to women is no longer seen positively in the discourse of *onnagata*. Moreover, considering that Baikō still had a lingering *ancien-régime* anecdote about being mistaken for a geisha,[25] this transitional point held the demarcation not only of the two genders *onnagata* were required to play (femininity and masculinity) but also of body (form) and mind (contents), the ultimate interdict in the previous epistemological economy.

One more phase remained for *onnagata* to pass through. Some younger-generation actors appear to be much more audacious than Shikan and Utaemon in asserting that artistic femininity is their sole property. For example, Ichikawa Ennosuke IV (b. 1975) and Ichikawa Shun'en II (b. 1970) both declare that they are the model of femininity that women should hope to imitate. Ennosuke states he would always say "none" when asked what element of women he takes as his cue; rather, he says, he would like women to learn from him and his fellow *onnagata*.[26] Ennosuke then explains that not only is it physically impossible for women [to do *onnagata* acting], but the mindset of an *onnagata* is stressful. Likewise, Ichikawa Shun'en states: "There are so many kinds of [feminine] techniques hidden in kabuki that women can steal and use. If you see kabuki from that kind of perspective, it'll be another different way of appreciating [kabuki] you can benefit from."[27] This not only reconfirms male actors' assertion that *onnagata*-femininity is their exclusive property. It also recognizes the recurrent theme of *onnagata* as the paragons of femininity, and yet its significance differs between premodern and modern contexts.

Furthermore, aside from self-appointed paragons like Ennosuke and Shun'en, the phenomenon itself is valid on the whole, onstage and off. In 2008, Tamasaburō appeared in commercials for a cosmetics company, telling women how to be beautiful.[28] Three years later, he delivered the keynote speech at an event promoting healthy lifestyles for menopausal women. His talk was about "eternal female beauty" (*eien no joseibi*), and one can safely assume that the audiences were mostly middle-aged women.[29] As for onstage femininity, some well-known female actors collaborate in reinforcing the formidable reputation of male *onnagata* as the irreplaceable performers of artistic femininity. Two such instances are film and stage actor Sugimura Haruko (1906–1997), famous for her roles in films directed by Naruse Mikio and Ozu Yasujirō, and *shinpa*-theater actor Namino Kuriko (b. 1945), the daughter of Kanzaburō XVII. Her father is said to have spoken very highly of Namino as an actor, saying that she "would have made a great kabuki actor" if she were a man,[30] yet Namino repeatedly states that she is no match for her younger brother Kanzaburō XVIII: "[When I performed with him doing *onnagata*,] I truly felt that actresses can't stand comparison with *onnagata*. . . . When he's playing a man's role, no problem at all. . . . But when my brother does an *onnagata*, it's impossible [for me to match]."[31] Equally illustrative are Sugimura's repeated compliments to *onnagata*: "There are lots of things I've learned from *onnagata*. [. . . Male *onnagata*] are better [than actresses]."[32]

In this way, modern *onnagata* gradually but firmly secured their latest cultural position as artists who are even more womanly than women and as the authority on artistic femininity. Regarding the establishment of this cultural status, Mizuochi Kiyoshi notes Tōjūrō's spectacular rise to the stardom in 1953, the then Nakamura Senjaku II, associating it with its historical setting:

> Back then, it was still called the postwar era. What had been predominant in prewar times was denied one after another, and anything new was praised excessively. Kabuki was no exception to that. With its plots based on loyalty and [sacrifice as] a substitute, kabuki was regarded as the uppermost militaristic theater and thus was denied by new intellectuals. [The predicament] was solved by the existence of excellent *gei* by virtuoso actors such as Kikugorō, Kichiemon, Enjaku, and Baigyoku, but they passed away one by one, and kabuki was facing a crisis that we cannot believe today. Especially, *onnagata* were the target of criticism by reform parties. In a democratic society where the equality of the sexes is realized, why are *onnagata* necessary? Actresses can do the job. In a nutshell, this is what people loudly shouted.
>
> Senjaku's Ohatsu [the role that made the *onnagata* Senjaku a star] emerged during such a time.
>
> Aside from acting the role of Ohatsu, Senjaku was also made to bear another role.
>
> The role in question was to prove the necessity of *onnagata*. What is more, the role was to prove it in an explicitly popular way to the masses. The success of Ohatsu resulted in a phenomenon called the Senjaku boom, and those young

women who created the boom hailed Senjaku, saying, "Senjaku-san's *onnagata* are more beautiful than women."[33]

In the history of modern kabuki from the Meiji era to date, the period encompassed by World War II and the subsequent U.S. occupation is significant, as it brought other drastic changes to kabuki as a whole, although there is no enough space to explore them in detail.[34] No matter how drastic, the early-twentieth-century changes did not fixate kabuki once and for all. Debates over the necessity of *onnagata* recurred from time to time, for example, the mid-1950s debate between two theater critics, Takechi and Tobe Ginsaku.[35] Mizuochi indicates that, around the time when Tamasaburō, born in 1950, came of age, Japan had already reached a social consensus about kabuki as a source of pride.[36] *Onnagata* also enjoyed the same upward shift.

For a complete image of modern *onnagata*, a few more phenomena remain to take into account. However much like counterevidence they might appear, they instead complicate and enrich our understanding of modern *onnagata*. Although there was a drastic shift from the expectations of premodern *onnagata* (insider doers of femininity comparable to women) to the expectations of modern *onnagata* (outsider doers of femininity transcending women), the performance methodology for approximating the womanliness of women did not disappear from the *onnagata*'s physical lexicon so easily. For instance, Ichikawa Shōchō II (1886–1940) was an extremely popular *onnagata* of the new regime, and yet his reputation was made possible by his "naturally womanly" appearance, which caused people to coin the phrase "a woman like Shōchō" (*Shōchō no yōna onna*).[37] He came to be so popular that this epithet eventually became a compliment for women. One would be remiss to regard him as an *ancien onnagata* who had outlived his time. Shōchō was, after all, a product of the twentieth century and performed in *shingeki* as well.[38] Rather than finding him analogous to Hanshirō,[39] we should see in him another type of new *onnagata*, one in accord with the new logic who can nevertheless pass as a woman "naturally." Baikō VI is another example. As one of the two earliest modern *onnagata* of importance, Baikō was complimented as not effeminate,[40] and yet he was also said to have passed as a geisha.[41] Utaemon VI defines *onnagata* and "women in actuality" as mutually exclusive,[42] but his father, Utaemon V, once expressed his wish to train his son to do men's roles as well, for the youngster's motions had become womanly due to his *onnagata* experiences, and this was not suitable for actors in a new age.[43]

In a similar way, Taganojō laughs away typical premodern kudos for premodern *onnagata* passing as women,⁴⁴ but theater critic Andō Tsuruo (1908–1969) said in an interview with him that Taganojō too looked like a woman in a bathhouse: "Having a bath together here at Shima [spa] like this, seen from the back, you're nothing but a granny. Haven't you heard that? When you're naked, washing your body, that back view, I mean."⁴⁵ Taganojō agreed, citing a maid's remark: "A maid gave a laugh, you see. 'Sir, you're like a woman when you turn backward' (laughter)."⁴⁶ In short, even after epistemological grids were altered and the cultivation regime lost its universal status in Japanese society at large, an approximation of the womanliness of women remained in the *onnagata*'s physical lexicon.⁴⁷ To be precise, the value of the cultivation regime did not totally disappear in modern Japan. Rather, it lost its status as a universal cultural norm in Japanese culture and became a rare characteristic specific to limited realms in modern Japan.

Another piece of counterevidence that deepens and sharpens our understanding of modern *onnagata* lies in their own accounts of their art in relation to women. As mentioned, Utaemon V ended up adopting the *kata* (form) of Hanshirō, whom he had so strongly rejected as someone who looked like a woman. Utaemon also admitted that he was mistaken in assuming that the performers in a certain review he had seen were male until he was told that they were in fact female.⁴⁸ In a very subtle manner, he does not totally dismiss compatibility between premodern and modern *onnagata* and between male and female performers. In the previous regime, Kumehachi, a famous female kabuki actor, was highly valued by male actors including Gennosuke, Taganojō, and Sōjūrō. Through these male actors who did not hesitate to recognize the merit of her performance, Kumehachi managed to participate in the transmission of *kata*, although her involvement in such traditions has been more or less erased from kabuki historiography.⁴⁹ Most intriguingly, male kabuki actors expressing such a view did not cease to exist. Arashi Yoshisaburō V (1907–1977) speaks of Nakamura Tokiko, a disciple of Nakamura Karoku III (1849–1919): "Another actor I can't forget from my days at the Miyato-za Theater is woman-actor Nakamura Tokiko, a very skillful one, indeed. [. . . I played with her at some point . . .] . She did both female roles and [male roles . . .]. From [what I know] of her acting, I cannot agree with the theory that says 'actresses cannot do *onnagata*'s plays.'"⁵⁰

The era of "women-actors" (i.e., professionally trained female kabuki actors), whom Yoshisaburō mentions, ended in the early twentieth century. Tamasaburō was thus born too late to witness women-actors as such, but he too has left subtle and informative remarks. In one interview he states that he had been seeing the world with the eyes of a man, with which he had been doing *onnagata*. He continues, however, to explicate the womanliness his acting is said to enact and mentions some female actors who he thinks are using the same mechanism of performance, that is, presenting femininity as a work of art (*sakuhin*): Greta Garbo (1905–1990), Marlene Dietrich (1901–1992), Takehara Han (1903–1998), and Sugimura. The said mechanism is possible only for those who have "unique talent" (*dokutoku no sainō*), he says, but he does not mention a male body as a prerequisite for it.[51] For master practitioners, it is not so much the sex of a body as talent, training, and dedication to the art that matter for acting. There remain many gray zones in which many kinds of dichotomies proposed in modern times can hardly be neatly demarcated. Even Utaemon VI, extremely skeptical about the possibility of women performers as *onnagata*, states that the role of Asaji in the 1957 film *Throne of Blood* (Kumonosu-jō), directed by Kurosawa Akira, can be performed by *onnagata*,[52] unwittingly implying the existence of roles that both male *onnagata* and female actors can perform.

The idea of a Foucauldian birth has proved a useful—if not unconditionally applicable—way to understand the history of *onnagata* artistry. A certain shift in a Foucauldian manner, or inversion if you will, has happened quite dramatically from time to time, but it almost always entails a certain residue from a previous economy. In the case of Edo-era *onnagata* who established *onnagata* artistry (e.g., Ayame and Kikunojō), such a residue was reified as the contradiction of their relying on their predecessors' praxes while theoretically negating their principles of transience. In the case of women-actors at the beginning of modern times, we saw the remains of the day in their grace period, during which they managed to participate in the mainstream kabuki enterprise. Exactly in the same way, a modern transformation of *onnagata* artistry that Utaemon V uncannily forecasted in 1874 as a young boy turned out to be drastic and absolute in theory but elusive and confusing in practice.

Albeit in a nuanced manner, however, things have definitely changed. The intimacy between nature and second nature in the premodern episteme has been replaced by the polarized relationship between the Artificial and the scientifized Natural in modern times. Second nature was highly respected in the former, and the Natural valorized in the latter. It is in this sense that one must also recognize the birth of the demarcation of constructionism and essentialism and that of body (form-exterior) and mind (contents-interior). In this paradigm, *onnagata* have performed femininity as second nature in premodern times and as the Artificial in modern times. Drastic changes in the artistry of *onnagata* and notions of their performance of femininity were the result of this epistemological shift. Given this, it is no wonder that male *onnagata* successfully assumed the authority of artistic femininity in modern Japan.

Epilogue

The Journey Continues

WITH an outlook reminiscent of his father's attitude toward premodern *onnagata*, Utaemon VI was consistently dismissive of any possibility that female performers could act as *onnagata*. He was not known for elucidating his famed *onnagata* acting in words, but he was adamant on the point that *onnagata* have nothing to do with actual women.[1] For him, the respective matrices of *onnagata*-femininity and female-femininity were mutually exclusive. Given this, his remark about Asaji, the wife of a samurai in the 1957 Kurosawa film *Throne of Blood* is suggestive, as it recognizes in the role of Asaji a space that male *onnagata* and female performers could theoretically share.[2] Upon seeing the film, he thought that *onnagata* could well play the role that a female actor played in film.

This is telling, as Asaji was performed by Yamada, who in fact played kabuki as *onnagata*. The daughter of a *shinpa*-theater *onnagata*, Yamada actually performed women's roles in kabuki alongside major kabuki actors, including Utaemon VI and his "rival" *onnagata* Baikō VII, as well as male-role players Onoe Shōroku II (1913–1989) and Matsumoto Kōshirō VIII (1910–1982). And her acting was considered in line with kabuki economy. In July 1968, she played with Kōshirō's two sons—Kōshirō IX (b. 1942) and Nakamura Kichiemon II (b. 1944)—in *Yaji and Kita's Walking Tour on the Tōkaidō Highway* (Yaji Kita Tōkaidōchū hiza-kurige), of 1802–14, by Jippensha Ikku (1765–1831). Theater critic Fujita Hiroshi states: "Also in this production, Isuzu had considerable presence as the leading *onnagata* (*tate-oyama*) of kabuki domestic pieces (*sewa-kyōgen*)."³ It is thus never absurd that she said, "There can't be any other actress who joined kabuki troupes as frequently as I did. It is something that I'm proud of, a little bit."⁴

Despite that, Yamada is primarily thought of as a film actor today, well known to international audiences for her starring roles under such auteur directors as Mizoguchi Kenji, Naruse, and Kurosawa.⁵ Obituaries published in 2012 reflect this public knowledge, with hardly any mention of her kabuki career. Even so, Yamada's own account of her performance *in film*—namely the role of Asaji—cannot conceal the proximity of theatrical practices in traditional settings and what we are made to think of a film star such as Yamada. Explaining a certain scene in which Asaji endlessly washes her hands, believing that her hands are covered with blood, Yamada says that Kurosawa asked her "if it's possible to put gold dust into the pupils in order to make my eyes gold-colored, like those in a noh mask."⁶ With no material available to insert safely into her eyes at that time, she tried her best by rehearsing many times; the outcome is astonishing, and images from this scene have been well circulated.⁷ Even in film, Yamada shows—and Utaemon VI affirms—that male *onnagata* and female actors can be in an intimate relationship in terms of acting styles.⁸ As a cultural medium, film might have a wider impact on society today, but even so, it seems far-fetched to ignore such an obvious connection between her screen and stage acting. It might well be, however, necessary to neglect her kabuki achievement *precisely because* it was astonishing. This echoes the marginalization of Kumehachi in kabuki historiography.

The historical era of women-actors was of limited duration, ending approximately in the 1910s. When Yamada, born in 1917, came of age, therefore, that era was already gone, but considering her kabuki career and her acting style, which was congruous with kabuki norms, it is quite possible to regard Yamada as an artistic successor to them. The performance of female *onnagata*, such as Kumehachi, was acclaimed as indistinguishable from that of male *onnagata*; Yamada performed kabuki in a way that was reminiscent of the historical women-actors. As previously mentioned, kabuki faced a few more drastic changes during World War II and the ensuing U.S. occupation. Postwar confusion brought flexibility to kabuki circles, followed by Tōhō Company's attempt to launch a kabuki enterprise. The kabuki industry came to be monopolized by Shōchiku Company in modern times, and Tōhō first challenged the monopoly in the early twentieth century. While this attempt ended after only about a few years, Tōhō restarted it in the mid-1950s and continued through the early 1980s.[9] The aforementioned 1968 production, for which Yamada is praised as having presence as kabuki's leading *onnagata*, was a Tōhō-kabuki production. Yamada performed women's roles from kabuki plays both in Tōhō-kabuki productions and beyond. She performed with major actors, including Baikō VII and Utaemon VI, both Living National Treasures and considered the two greatest *onnagata* of their time. Utaemon especially—dubbed *jotei* (empress in her own right) by some—dominated kabuki circles. Yamada was, thus, not quietly situated in a niche, such as amateur kabuki circles, which explains her pride. "It is something that I'm proud of, a little bit."[10] In Yamada, a female *onnagata* was resurrected.

Theater reviews and recorded performances confirm that Yamada's acting was much closer to an *onnagata* style than we might have been made to believe. Enomoto was irritated when critics "commended" Yamada by calling her a "woman-actor" rather than an "actress."[11] It is critical to keep in mind that women-actors used the same acting techniques as male kabuki actors and that the highest compliment for female *onnagata* was to be compared favorably to their male counterparts. This type of compliment for female actors presupposes and stabilizes a certain hierarchy of the performance of femininity based on the sex of actors (male over female). Behind this manner of praising female actors was obvious sexism, which Enomoto found pathological, but he did not disagree that Yamada had characteristics close to those of women-actors, nor did he dismiss such characteristics. He wrote *Woman-Actor* (Onna yakusha), a biographical play about Kumehachi, and Yamada played the title role in its premiere in January 1979 at the Teikoku Theater, Tokyo. In the play, Yamada performed major roles that Kumehachi had played, not only *onnagata* roles but men's roles as well. Through her acting techniques and performance styles, Yamada reminded critics of historical female kabuki actors.

It was not just theater critics who took this view. In his obituary of Yamada published on 10 July 2012, Kichiemon recalled performing with her both in film and onstage, using that very word: "[Yamada] carried an atmosphere [of] woman-actor."[12] This is not a coincidence, given a putative utterance of Taganojō, who taught kabuki to Yamada: "Hey, Yamada has come to resemble me, hasn't she?"[13] In the ethos of what Hahn correctly calls "the art of following,"[14] this is the highest compliment that a disciple could ever dream of obtaining. Yamada also took lessons in kabuki from other actors, such as Nakamura Matagorō II (1914–2009).

Despite all these accomplishments, Yamada's stage career in kabuki has been belittled tremendously. For instance, obituaries summarizing her career hardly mention it,[15] and it seems more likely than not that her involvement in kabuki is about to be extirpated from history. One cannot be surprised, after seeing that Kumehachi's contribution to mainstream kabuki was skillfully erased, and yet, both cases of erasure hinder us from effectively understanding *onnagata* artistry, their construction and performance of femininity, and, by extension, gender. Some might think that women kabuki actors in mainstream kabuki were just made possible by a historical coincidence. Certainly it was just that. It was also a historical coincidence, however, by which they were dismissed. They were abjected for the sake of a normative system, and not because of women's limitations as such, whether physical, mental, or artistic, which James R. Brandon correctly calls "unsubstantiated myths."[16] Or, one might recall, "The Master's Tools Will Never Dismantle the Master's House."[17]

It might be technically possible to minimize Yamada's achievement by questioning whether or not we can regard such plays as Tōhō-kabuki and kabuki plays newly written in modern times as genuine kabuki, as these are the two major clusters of plays Yamada actively performed. In response to such skepticism, one must remember that kabuki has been expanding its repertoire continuously. One telling example from its recent history lies in *No Sleeve Wet upon Showering America* (Furu Amerika ni sode wa nurasaji) by Ariyoshi Sawako (1931–1984). Sugimura played the title role in its premiere in 1972; afterward, the play was also presented by the *shinpa*-theater troupe. Having played the title role in *shinpa* on many occasions, Tamasaburō successfully presented it as a kabuki play in December 2007 at the Kabuki-za Theater, Tokyo.[18] It is hardly possible to pinpoint the definition of kabuki theater, and as such, it is unreasonable to exclude from kabuki Tōhō-kabuki, new plays written in modern times, or successful female actors such as Kumehachi and Yamada, or, for that matter, many others like them who must have surely existed but abjected.

Kabuki has shown us a checkered labyrinth of gendering, in which femininity has been performed, defined, claimed, conceptualized, naturalized, and so on, and which, no less important, will not lead us to any absolute conclusion. As of this writing, the latest definition of *onnagata* artistry seems solid and secure, but readers must have grasped that everything has been—and thus will remain—contingent. Simultaneously, one cannot afford to overlook that there have always been something and somebody that are made to pay the price to make it possible to form, sustain, and naturalize a system, be it an economy of androgynous aesthetics, that of paragons of womanhood, a meta-dichotomy of male/female, or a binary of Artificial/Natural, just to name a few. In this sense, the labyrinth that *onnagata* let us peep into is just one instance of countless labyrinths of gendering that people have been wandering through in many societies, past and present. The labyrinth *onnagata* have shown us reminds us that labyrinths under the name of "gender" can be formidable in practice at any given moment and often quite violently compulsive, and yet, in theory, they are so elusive, precarious, and contingent. That is to say, in theory, a labyrinth of gendering can never delineate the boundary of its corridors conclusively ("femininity" in the present case), when countless doers of femininity have been constantly involved in constructing its porous and ever amendable labyrinth. It might not be amorphous, but it is ever changing. We cannot even be sure what the matrix of femininity is in the first place. Allegedly, it is considered "women" in many societies today, but then how can we define "women"? Yet one can hardly escape from the labyrinth itself; a gender system is, in practice, formidably unflinching and unforgiving.

In the immediate past, that is, the time of the modern reformation of *onnagata* artistry, male *onnagata* who could pass as women and female *onnagata* indistinguishable from male *onnagata* were made to disappear in order to secure a new definition of *onnagata* artistry and thereby make possible the origins of *onnagata* as we know them today. As of now, the definition seems firmly secured, that is to say, artistic femininity, which is exclusive property of male *onnagata*, is on the kabuki stage. Even more womanly than women, *onnagata* are the authority of artistic femininity in that sense. It is extremely ironic to associate *onnagata* artistry so resolutely with male actors alone, given that their art is, both in theory and in practice, made possible by the very presupposition of "femininity [being] separable from women's anatomical sex."[19]

Also lost in the modern reformation of *onnagata* were the relativity of gender distinctions and the relativity of the weight of gender. As for the relativity of the weight of gender, Tamasaburō and Zeami have made insightful statements. Detailing noh acting, Zeami once explained that the roles of women of high status were more difficult to perform than those of women of lower status.[20] This simply reconfirms that class differences carried more weight than gender distinction in premodern times. Likewise, Tamasaburō indicates race and ethnicity as intriguing concepts in a manner somehow congenial to that of Zeami speaking of class. He made a telling remark when recollecting his experience playing the role of Nastasya in *Nasutāsha/Nastazja*. He says that he "insisted [to the Polish director Wajda] that I wasn't confident in playing a European woman in Europe."[21] In the context of this interview, his words somehow imply that assuming a European was his bigger concern, compared to playing a woman in and of itself. Readers will also recall another international collaborative project Tamasaburō was engaged. That is, he participated in *kunqu* productions of *The Peony Pavilion* with Chinese actors, in which he spoke and sang in Chinese. These collaborations inevitably entail many acts of crossing (not only gender but also language, race and ethnicity, performance grammar, and so on), thereby reminding us of the very *relativity* of the weight of gender.

In this case in point of the relativity of gender, or, also in the recent resurrection of a female *onnagata* for that matter, one can see how dynamically the current artistry of onnagata is still related to its history. Considering a history of "gender" as we have seen above, we may well be witnessing an impending anticlimax of "modern gender" in this paradigm. A few paragraphs earlier, I hinted that things might not change soon; but here, I recognize a certain herald of changes. This ambiguity invokes a clichéd but ever cogent notion of "gender" as precarious and binding at the same time.

NOTES

PREFACE

1   Needless to say, this does not assign any meta-capability in critical thinking to gender studies. History tells us that almost any cluster of knowledge has its own issues, as it has been part of endless unfortunate cases: thus, technically, some devoted mothers can be complicit in racist movements, those who are against racism can be sexist, acute feminists can be ignorant about colonial power structures, incisive thinkers on class issues can be indifferent to gender discrimination in their own households, those who are involved in environmental issues can be insensitive to their own domestic animals, devoted activists in women's right movements can cooperate with those involved in war crimes, and so on, and so forth.

INTRODUCTION

1   Considering this "flower" status—beautiful yet inferior—it is no wonder that women characters on the kabuki stage are frequently, if not exclusively, engaged in "what women appear to do most often in realistic theater," that is, "getting raped, going crazy, and, of course, dying" (Hart, "Introduction," 5). Lynda Hart's remark, while from a different context, is nevertheless relevant to kabuki. And when those miserable women destined to be raped, driven mad, and murdered are actually killed in kabuki, the action unfolds inch by inch. Murder scenes in kabuki are usually choreographed in an extremely slow tempo, with countless insertions of *mie*-pose by both the murderer and the victim, be they men or women.

Mie is a pose, accompanied by sharp sound effects from *tsuke* (hardwood clappers [*ki*] beat on a wooden board), in which the actor rhythmically and gradually fixes his gaze, facial expression, and posture and sustains this tableau for a while. Typical pieces of background music used in murder scenes are uncannily leisurely, peaceful, and sometimes even jovial, with titles such as "jizō-sutra" (*jizōkyō*), "dew and silver grass" (*tsuyu-wa-obana*), "evening-to-wait" (*matsuyoi*), "your-sleeve" (*omae-no-sode*), and "kasai-music" (*kasai-aikata*). Together, the music and the movements of the pose prolong the victim's dying moment.

It has frequently been pointed out that that kabuki highly aestheticizes violence (see, e.g., "Beautiful Cruelty," in Leiter, *Frozen Moments*; and "The Beauty of Torture," in Mezur, *Beautiful Boys*). Of course, the aestheticization of violence is not specific to kabuki; for the aestheticization of violence in the context of media studies and American culture, see Bruder, *Aestheticizing Violence*.

2 Said, *Orientalism*, quoting Marx, *The Eighteenth Brumaire of Louis Bonaparte*.
3 Ernst, *Kabuki Theatre*, 195. No source provided.
4 Barlow, "Femininity," 388.
5 Jennifer Robertson states: "During the Tokugawa period (and beyond), the paragons of female-likeness were *onnagata*: male Kabuki actors who performed 'female' roles, sometimes offstage as well as on" ("Shingaku Woman," 90).
6 Kano, *Acting Like a Woman*.
7 Enomoto, "Onnagata Engi," 258. The female actor thus praised is Yamada Isuzu (1917–2012), arguably the latest woman-actor and female *onnagata*.
8 Pola, *Utsukushii*.
9 Bandō Tamasaburō, "Eien."
10 Robertson, "Shingaku Woman," 90.
11 Ibid. Shingaku (Heart learning) was a movement in the Edo period directed toward the moral education of the people.
12 The basic mechanism of this dramaturgy, and by extension that of identity creation, is by no means specific to kabuki but accords with broader traditions in Japanese arts that incorporate various *hon* (original) elements in their creative activities (discussed in further detail in Maki Isaka, *Secrecy*, 45–72). Within these parameters, each tradition differs on *how* specifically to combine *hon* features with novelty, and kabuki presents one dramatic example in the sense that it retains contradictory impulses instead of seeking what might be called middle ground. Precisely speaking, the significance of authentic traditions—and thus the proportion of authentic traditions to *kabuku*—varies depending on regions and time period.

Primary authentic traditions for kabuki are noh and *kyōgen* of medieval times (*hongyō*). Unlike noh, which consists of dancing and chanting, *kyōgen* relies on gesture and dialogue. In addition, the puppet theater (later known as bunraku) also plays the same role (authentic traditions) for kabuki, in which case the term "*honmon*" is used, rather than "*hongyō*." Bunraku is another theater of the common people that emerged roughly simultaneously with kabuki, and both theaters have been in a close relationship on many levels, from drama texts to elocution.
13 Postlewait and Davis, "Theatricality," 4–5.
14 Kano, *Acting Like a Woman*, 4.
15 In the context of Western theater, Sue-Ellen Case states: "As a result of the suppression of real women, the culture invented its own representation of the gender, and it was this fictional 'Woman' who appeared on stage, in the myths and in the plastic arts, representing the patriarchal values attached to the gender while sup-

pressing the experiences, stories, feelings and fantasies of actual women. . . . Within theatre practice, the clearest illustration of this division is in the tradition of the all-male stage. . . . This practice reveals the fictionality of the patriarchy's representation of the gender" (*Feminism*, 7).

16 Robertson, "Gender-Bending," 53.
17 For Takarazuka, see Robertson, *Takarazuka*.
18 For reasons mentioned here (specialties and age limits), I assume that one of the most promising—and indeed necessary—comparative studies is that of *onnagata* and *nandan* in Chinese theater and that such studies should involve experts in each subject. From the perspective of the Chinese counterparts, Min Tian mentions *onnagata* ("Male *Dan*," 78–97). For kabuki's viewpoint, see Toita, "Kyōgeki no Hana," 56–64. Siyuan Liu expanded the target of comparative analysis to the modern Chinese genre *huaju* (spoken drama) and *shinpa* theater in Japan (*Performing Hybridity*). Born in the late nineteenth century, *shinpa* (new faction or school) ended up being congenial to kabuki and has used *onnagata* as well. While scholarly analyses are relatively scant, theater practitioners themselves have long been engaged in cross-cultural networking. For instance, Tamasaburō recently collaborated with a *kunqu* troupe in both Japan (Kyoto, 2008) and China (Beijing and Suzhou, 2008 and 2009), and this kind of activity started several generations before him. For the related topic of *onnagata* in film, see, e.g., Fujiki, "Canonising Sexual Image."
19 Zeami, *Shikadō*, 112–13.
20 Kinjinsai, *Kokon Yakusha Rongo Sakigake*, 483.
21 Atsumi et al., "Onoe Baikō Tsuioku," 63 (this part was written by Matsumoto Kōshirō VII).
22 In her analysis of *onnagata*, Katherine Mezur proposes that "a male sexed body beneath" is the key to "the onnagata fiction of female-likeness" (*Beautiful Boys*, 25, 259). I agree that the male identity of *onnagata* has carried weight, but for different reasons.
23 See, e.g., Fausto-Sterling, "Five Sexes, Revisited," 19–23.
24 For example, women can be associated not only with nature vis-à-vis culture, as in many societies, but also with culture vis-à-vis nature, as during the Victorian Age. It is imperative to keep in mind, however, that this theoretical "slipperiness" does not negate the fact that gender in practice can be extremely binding. For instance, Ueno Chizuko states that in terms of division of labor between the sexes, "'fighting' is an act that men monopolize in any society" (*Kafuchōsei*, 198–99). (This statement was made some time ago and no doubt appears rather naive, especially after Abu Ghraib.) Consequently, whenever using words such as "typical," "ideal," and the like, I mean that they are bracketed by an invisible remark: "so it is said." Behind those words are social norms that define what is typical, ideal, and so forth.
25 Incidentally, this is related to a problem that some Japanese feminists saw in Japanese Buddhism, that is to say, a correlation between "open-minded gender understanding" and "extremely binding gender praxes." See, e.g., Minamoto Junko, "Buddhism," 87–115.

[168] NOTES TO INTRODUCTION

26   See, e.g., Butler, *Gender Trouble*; Butler, "Imitation," 13–31.
27   One may want to see in this instance an operation somewhat analogous to what Tania Modleski explains as the principle of reverse: "'mimesis,' or mimicry, is a time-honored tactic among oppressed groups, who often appear to acquiesce in the oppressor's ideas about it, thus producing a double meaning: the same language or act simultaneously confirms the oppressor's stereotypes of the oppressed and offers a dissenting and empowering view for those in the know" ("Feminism," 129). For the limitations—and indeed potential jeopardy—of the principle of reverse as a "political and representational strategy," Hart states that "while it effects a kind of subversive catharsis for the oppressed group, it reifies the dominant constructions of members of that group" ("Identity," 125).
28   That the term *"chi no michi"* (gynecological disorders) was used in a compliment for actors is an exceedingly twisted phenomenon. To begin with, it is obviously a discursive violence offensive to patients with gynecological diseases. Needless to say, this phenomenon is not specific to kabuki or to Japan, as the tendency toward charging a disease with cultural meanings—whether romanticizing, stigmatizing, valorizing, and so on—is omnipresent, regardless of (or, more frequently, against) the interests of patients. The discursive use and abuse of diseases and the sick, especially in relation to gender, has been an important subject for critical analyses, as, for example, in Mary K. DeShazer's book *Fractured Borders*. Furthermore, in a cultural milieu in which the analogy to "woman" almost always entails negative connotations, it is highly perverse to use a word signifying the illness (a negatively defined state) of females (a negatively defined being) in a compliment. Here, the double negative creates a positive, that is, men projecting femininity.
29   See Yoshida Setsuko, *Edo Kabuki Hōrei Shūsei*; *Zoku Edo Kabuki Hōrei Shūsei*; *Edo Kabuki Hōrei Shūsei Nenpyō*.
30   Since this entertainment is attributed to a woman called Okuni, whose details are mostly unknown, it is also called "Okuni kabuki" or *yūjo kabuki* (female entertainers' [prostitutes'] kabuki).
31   The end date of *yarō kabuki* is hard to pinpoint. Takei Kyōzō thinks it lasted from the 1650s through the 1670s (*Wakashu Kabuki*, 3). Kabuki as a theatrical art (e.g., its dramaturgy and acting methodology) is considered to have attained perfection with *Genroku kabuki*, which began a short time before the Genroku era (1688–1704) for which it was named. "*Yarō kabuki*" is the term used to indicate what had come before the perfection of *Genroku kabuki*.
32   Scott, *Kabuki Theatre*, 169.
33   Pronko, *Theatre*, 196.
34   Mezur, *Beautiful Boys*, 7.
35   For example, Mezur states: "Although there may have been some imitation of female characteristics by some kabuki onnagata in the early *yarō* (adult fellow) [sic] kabuki of eighteenth century, onnagata gender roles are not limited to the imitation or representation of women, the female body, or the ideal Woman as defined within a bipolar gender system" (*Beautiful Boys*, 7). She specifies the *onnagata* in question as "Yoshizawa Ayame I (1673–1729) and other early onnagata,

whose records and notes allude to their 'imitation' of women" (255). I concur with her in seeing aspects of imitation in Ayame and the other *onnagata* in the establishment period but differ in the following two points. It is anachronistic to place Ayame in *yarō kabuki* (see n. 31), and the imitation aspects of Ayame and those who adopted similar methods established the artistry of *onnagata*.

36 The term "paragons of womanhood" was inspired by Robertson's "the paragons of female-likeness" ("Shingaku Woman," 90), although "female-likeness" and "womanhood" are not identical. Robertson defines the former as follows: "In Tokugawa times as now, the suffix *-rashisa* indicated approximation to an ideal mode or model of existence (*kata*)" (89). In turn, "womanhood" here suggests a broader concept in order to signify attributions associated with those who are called "women."

37 For this point, see also Maki Isaka, *Secrecy*.

38 Or, even with such a modifier, one still recognizes the limitations of one book. As Hart writes, "No homage is paid here to an imaginary canon; no illusions are held that one book can contain the field of feminist performance" ("Introduction," 3).

39 I focus particularly on those actors who managed to be engaged, to a certain extent, in mainstream kabuki in order to analyze a system at work effectively. They were the ones who—for the very reason that they were in close contact with the mainstream—put themselves in the risky position of being vulnerable to elimination. Women kabuki actors have existed in other cultural loci as well. Loren Edelson's book *Danjūrō's Girls*, a study of women kabuki actors in modern times, is an important addition to the latter topic, discussing the Ichikawa Girls' Kabuki Troupe.

40 For a discussion of one of the most important, Ichikawa Kumehachi I, see Edelson, "Female Danjūrō"; Edelson, *Danjūrō's Girls*, 20–25. In addition, James R. Brandon, exceptionally in the existing kabuki studies, describes as "unsubstantiated myths" the popular notion that "only a male actor can suggest the essence of a woman, only a man possesses the physical strength to wear a heavy wig and multiple kimono, and so on" ("Reflections," 122).

41 Hart, "Introduction: Performing Feminism," 4.

42 I am borrowing Hart's parlance from her analysis of American contemporary feminist performance art: "Finley uses parody and travesty, excessive rendering of the stereotypes, in an effort to swell the models to their limits and explode them" ("Motherhood," 130).

1. GENESES OF A MAZE

1 *Kabuki Hyōbanki Shūsei*, vol. 5, 38; vol. 3, 200. These are taken from actor-critique booklets published in the third month of 1712 and the third month of 1702, respectively. Actor-critique booklets (*yakusha hyōbanki*) were a popular genre of periodicals published regularly from the mid-seventeenth century throughout the Edo era, sometimes several issues in the same month. Whether the contents of actor-critique booklets can be called "theater reviews" due to their strong focus on actors

alone is open to discussion, but that does not affect their incomparable value in kabuki studies. In addition, as Fujita Hiroshi puts it, the tendency to focus on actors is still valid in contemporary kabuki-theater reviews ("Kabuki-shi no Keifu," 196.) Each issue of actor-critique booklets has its own title; for example, *Actors' Dancing Fans* (Yakusha mai-ōgi) was published in the fourth month of 1704. The present book uses the name of the genre for the sake of clarity.

2   See, e.g., Hishikawa, *Kokon Yakusha Monogatari*, 3. See also Takei, "Onnagata no So" 288–98.

3   An actor-critique booklet issued in the first month of 1720 contrasts its contemporary *onnagata* performance with that at the beginning of the *onnagata* tradition "in the time of Ukon [Genzaemon]" (*Kabuki Hyōbanki Shūsei*, vol. 7, 493–94). Another issue, published in the first month of 1723, lists him immediately after women's kabuki: "After women's kabuki ceased, the one who was called Ukon Genzaemon . . ." (vol. 8, 307).

4   Ihara Toshirō, *Kabuki Nenpyō*, 59. As for the exact year of the performance in question, held at the Ichimura-za Theater in Edo, accounts vary. See Takeuchi, "Ukon Genzaemon," 56. For Genzaemon's career, see also Takei, "Onnagata no So," 288–98; Sekine, *Tōto Gekijō Enkakushiryō*, 492–97. Ihara Toshirō's *Kabuki Nenpyō*, the eight-volume chronological table on kabuki from 1559 to 1907, cites extensive primary sources including unpublished texts.

5   Takeuchi, "Ukon Genzaemon," 65.

6   We know from historical documents that similar bans were repeatedly issued. See Takei, *Wakashu Kabuki*, 5; Ihara Toshirō, *Kabuki Nenpyō*, 24, 49, 55, 63–66; Hattori, "Seiritsuki no Kabuki," 30–32. See also the following by Yoshida Setsuko: *Edo Kabuki Hōrei Shūsei*; *Zoku Edo Kabuki Hōrei Shūsei*; *Edo Kabuki Hōrei Shūsei Nenpyō*.

7   Only with this understanding can we really appreciate that the presence of the remaining female players did not threaten *onnagata*.

8   Takei, *Wakashu Kabuki*, 4.

9   This probably explains the following observation the scholarship has made. In terms of their performance typology, women's kabuki and *wakashu kabuki* were isolated (Takei, *Wakashu Kabuki*, 4; Gunji, *Kabuki no Katachi*, 201). Indeed, if young boys and women were engaged in kabuki (i.e., song, dance, and "prostitution") simultaneously and women's kabuki overshadowed *wakashu kabuki* in terms of popularity, this inequality implies more difference than similarity in their entertainment and art. After all, *wakashu kabuki* remained a minor genre until the female performer ban.

10 Ihara Toshirō, *Kabuki Nenpyō*, 49. See also Kawatake Shigetoshi, *Nihon Engeki Zenshi*, 268. See also the following by Yoshida Setsuko: *Edo Kabuki Hōrei Shūsei*, 24–25; *Zoku Edo Kabuki Hōrei Shūsei*, 17; *Edo Kabuki Hōrei Shūsei Nenpyō*, 12.

11 Ihara Toshirō, *Kabuki Nenpyō* 64; see also 63–65. See also Yoshida Setsuko, *Edo Kabuki Hōrei Shūsei*, 40; *Edo Kabuki Hōrei Shūsei Nenpyō*, 18.

12 To avoid confusion, I have thus far used the term "*onnagata*" for kabuki only and called their predecessors in *wakashu kabuki* "female-role players." Historical

documents record, however, that this term was in use before the *wakashu-kabuki* ban, in 1638 and 1648 (Ihara Toshirō, *Kabuki Nenpyō*, 53, 59). This also supports the continuity between *wakashu kabuki* and kabuki.

13 Ihara Toshirō, *Kabuki Nenpyō* 59, 73, 86, 127.
14 Takei, *Wakashu Kabuki*, 4–6; Gunji, *Kabuki no Katachi*, 201.
15 Gunji, *Kabuki no Katachi*, 207.
16 This continuity helps explain why kabuki virtually remained queer until the late nineteenth century, when it transformed contemporary and queer into traditional and classic. For the transformation, see Kano, *Acting Like a Woman*, 85–119; Ōzasa, *Nihon Gendai Engekishi*, 31–32, 53; Kawatake Shigetoshi, *Nihon Engeki Zenshi*, 855–57.
17 Donald H. Shively states, "Homosexual practices had become extremely prevalent during the military campaigns of the fifteenth and sixteenth centuries and were also common in Buddhist monasteries. During the seventeenth century some of the shogun and feudal lords exercised their preference for beautiful youths" ("Social Environment," 9).
18 Schalow, "Introduction," 27.
19 Ibid.
20 Ibid., 27–28. It is extremely intriguing to think about this phenomenon in relation to another popular understanding at the time that the "heterosexual" marriage was aimed at the preservation of *ie*, the stem-family household, and seems intended to preserve human bodies (reproductive marriage), while the *wakashu-nenja* relationship preserved samurai manhood (spiritual marriage). Incidentally, "same-sex sexuality" in this discursive context refers almost exclusively to that of males. Practices of male-male relationships have another term, *nanshoku* (male eros), the antonym of which is *joshoku* (female eros). *Joshoku* indicates practices of male-female relationships and not female-female relationships. These neatly symmetrical terms unwittingly reveal that the doer, if not the subject in a modern sense, of sexual practices is expected to be always male. Figuratively, Ihara Saikaku's *The Great Mirror of Male Eros* begins with a section titled "Competition between Two Types of Eros" (Iro wa futatsu no monoarasoi), which compares male-male and male-female relationships (*Nanshoku Ōkagami*, 25).
21 Schalow, "Introduction," 29.
22 Irigaray, "Commodities," 193; emphasis in original. Irigaray uses the term "homosexuality" to indicate what we now usually think of as homosociality: something on which "the economy as a whole is based" (192). The *wakashu-nenja* relationship helps emphasize that homosexuality and homosociality are in effect closely associated.
23 Ihara Saikaku, *Nanshoku Ōkagami*, 45, 53–54, 72–73, 118–19. In an earlier work, I stated, "The concept that regards 'violence as manly' is an issue to investigate in relation to masculinity" ("Gender," 276). Shortly afterward, the abuse of prisoners at Abu Ghraib in Iraq reminded us that violence is by no means foreign to women, but a question still remains as to why violence is to be conceptualized in association with masculinity, whether it is male masculinity or female masculinity.

See Halberstam, "Contradictions," 238–40; Halberstam, *Female Masculinity*; Takemura, "Violence-Invested (non) Desire," 65–71. From another perspective, "femininity," Hart states that when women are engaged in atrocities, "the patriarchal prescription for women as non-violent is challenged by their act" and that, following Jeffner Allen, "this definition is essential to the maintenance of heterosexual ideology.... The male-defined monolithic category *Woman* is exclusive of violence—to be a woman means to be a person incapable of violence" ("'They Don't Even Look Like Maids,'" 136–37; emphasis in original). Hart examines the important theme of femininity in relation to violence in *Fatal Women* and "Killing Representation."

24 Ihara Saikaku, *Nanshoku Ōkagami*, 50.
25 Michel Foucault states, "The sodomite had been a temporary aberration; the homosexual was now a species" (*History of Sexuality*, 43). This remark can be applied with care to *wakashu* as well. The Way of *wakashu* was not even an aberration, since the stage of *wakashu* was regarded as a significant developmental and, importantly, transient phase for males. Otherwise, it would have been extremely difficult for *Hidden behind the Leaves* (Hagakure), a treatise on samurai norms by Yamamoto Tsunetomo (1659–1721), to praise the Way of *wakashu* and the preservation of the *ie* simultaneously. The text was dictated by Tashiro Tsuramoto, a junior samurai who was also Tsunetomo's peer (Yamamoto and Tashiro, *Hagakure*, 263–65).
26 Ihara Saikaku, *Nanshoku Ōkagami*, 270–71.
27 Ibid., 270–71.
28 Ibid., 271.
29 Imao, *Henshin no Shisō*, 146. While strongly suggesting a different nature for *futanarihira*, Imao retains the traditional scholarship's interpretation of the surrogate nature of *futanarihira*: "The body of *futanarihira* is to the end a body for male homosexual intercourse. Their charm is that of *wakashu*. Theirs are not women's bodies, nor women's charm. They are merely the surrogate bodies and charm of women" (*Yakusha Banashi Hyōchū*, 232).
30 *Kabuki Hyōbanki Shūsei*, vol. 7, 493–94.
31 Imao, *Henshin no Shisō*, 145.
32 Hurst, *Armed Martial Arts*, 53–81.
33 Nakarai, *Bokuyō Kyōka Shūi*, 351. I have not been able to confirm the identity of Mannosuke in kabuki historiography. Possibilities include Shimada Mannosuke (Sunaga, "Futanarihira no Keifu," 209), Murayama Mannosuke (Kawatake Toshio, "Kabuki," 105), Yamamoto Mannosuke, who is described in the actor-critique booklet of the fourth month of 1660 as having a "fine face, but... artistic technique is not good" and in the fifth month of 1663 as "dull, needless to say," and Yamazaki Mannosuke, described in the fifth month of 1662 as "vivid lip like a red flower, bright eyes like a cotton rose, and his dance is skillful. The nose is not so good" (*Kabuki Hyōbanki Shūsei*, vol. 1, 21, 39, 61, 54). It is possible that the Mannosuke in the poem was too early a person to be documented in kabuki publications, was not inside kabuki circles, or was not inside enough to be included in those publications.

34 Hishikawa, *Kokon Yakusha Monogatari*, 3.
35 Sunaga, "Futanarihira no Keifu," 209–10.
36 Ihara Saikaku, *Nanshoku Ōkagami*, 50.
37 Imao, *Henshin no Shisō*, 146; see also Hattori, *Kabuki Seiritsu no Kenkyū*.
38 This may appear to echo some recent results of academic sexology studies in North America: that the actual incidence of intersex is much higher than we are led to believe (Fausto-Sterling, "Five Sexes, Revisited," 19–20); that intersexuality had been considered in the context of sex-as-continuum until fairly recently, when it was replaced by the notion of sex-as-dichotomy. To be precise, the spectrum in question was based on, in the words of Thomas Laqueur, a one-sex model in which "women were essentially men" and "men and women were arrayed according to their degree of metaphysical perfection" (*Making Sex*, 4–5). In this paradigm, the more perfect, the more masculine, and vice versa. Notice that the recent outcome of sexology introduced here is not particularly Japan related.
39 For that matter, the English term "intersexuality" also builds on a dualistic understanding (Fausto-Sterling, "Five Sexes, Revisited" 19).
40 According to *Nihon Kokugo Daijiten*, vol. 17, 408.
41 We may not dismiss, however, the possibility that some *futanarihira* might have been intersex due to the higher-than-believed occurrence, although I cannot locate any data regarding the exact incidence of intersex in seventeenth-century Japan.
42 "When they stripped off this [uncanny] person's clothes secretly, there [they found] both the roots of male and female. This is that which is *futanari*" (*Yamai no Sōshi*, 82–83).
43 Or by virtue of a phallus? It is noteworthy that, in ukiyo-e, the woodblock prints that flourished in Japan from the seventeenth to the nineteenth century, "distinguishing the boys from the girls requires a little practice" (Lane, *Images*, 52). With faces and figures that are almost identical, the coiffures, clothing, and language (titles of works, poetry, names, or the like) are often the only clues by which to distinguish male from female. Lane also demonstrates, however, that many ukiyo-e went through "restoration" before reaching the modern market, and "restoration" often means the concealment of genitalia ("Shunga," 36–40). He shows that recovered ukiyo-e, including works depicting boys and girls who appear to be identical twins, reveal the girls displaying their sexual organs and the boys theirs, which are ostentatiously huge and unmistakably male (ibid.). Viewers at the time must not have needed "practice" to tell the girls from the boys, and we may even see here the extreme "genitaliaism" that totally reduces gender to sexual organs. This implies a category, or categories, of "beautiful boys" whose sex was categorically considered male, as symbolized by the gigantic genitalia, yet whose gender was left "androgynous," as indicated by faces and figures identical to those of the girls.
44 *Yamai no Sōshi*, 83. *Eboshi* were also used by *shirabyōshi*, cross-dressing female entertainers.
45 Terajima, *Wakan Sansai Zue*, 177.
46 Minamoto no Shitagō, *Shohon Shūsei Wamyō Ruijūshō*, 48, 565.
47 Ōki, *Ochibashū*, 488.

48 Fausto-Sterling, "Five Sexes, Revisited" 19.
49 See Modleski's "principle of reverse" ("Feminism," 129) and Hart's criticism of it ("Identity," 125–26).
50 The term "sex identity" is used only for the sake of analysis; it is a narrower notion than sexual identity. This term is used for the sake of convenience when discussing the identity of male, female, etc., without involving too much of vast and multilayered issues encompassed in sexual identity as a whole.

2. DENIAL OF TRANSIENCE

1 *Kabuki Hyōbanki Shūsei*, vol. 7, 493–94. For similar remarks, see also ibid., vol. 8, 307, 441–42.
2 In retrospect, a certain shift in the meaning of the term *"onnagata,"* be it literal or connotative, is visible in this transformation—that is to say, from "those in charge of women's roles" to the "paragons of womanhood." There are several accounts as to the exact meaning of the *kata* (*gata*) part of the term. Robertson thinks that it means "exemplary models ... to approximate" ("Gender-Bending," 53). There is another explanation of the term *"onnagata,"* which pays attention to the typology of kabuki personae, such as *dōkegata* (*kata* of the clown) and *oyajigata* (*kata* of the old). In the latter context, *onnagata* means those in charge of women['s roles]. See, e.g., Torigoe, "Kinsei Engeki no Shisō," 39. The latter theory is valid in its attention to etymology, whereas the former is effective in grasping the gist of what *onnagata* became after this transformation. The characters used for the word *"onnagata"* have also shifted, albeit gradually, from those meaning "woman-direction" to those meaning "woman-form," although both ways of writing the term coexist at almost any given moment. For example, the characters meaning "woman-form" are used predominantly today, but the other—namely, "woman-direction"—still exists in some specific cases, such as idioms established with the specific character, titles of literary works, and writers' preferences. Likewise, *oyama* is another, and older, way of pronouncing the term, and the relationship between *oyama* and *onnagata* is analogous to that between "woman-direction" and "woman-form"—that is, the term *"onnagata"* is prevailingly used today except for idioms (e.g., *tate-oyama* [leading *onnagata*]), references to historical documents, and personal preferences. I would like to take this opportunity to express my thanks to Ying Zhang for taking the trouble to use both "woman-direction" and "woman-form" when translating my article into Chinese ("Dui bei mofang zhe de mofang," 253–91).
3 Ihara Saikaku, *Nanshoku Ōkagami*, 178–79.
4 Ibid., 234.
5 Ibid., 249.
6 Fukuoka, "Ayamegusa," 322.
7 Accounts vary. See, e.g., Imao, *Yakusha Banashi Hyōchū*, 286.
8 *Jibun no hana* and *makoto no hana*, respectively (Zeami, *Fūshikaden*). Noh dramatist Zeami is regarded as the central figure in performance theory on Japanese theater, which he recorded in numerous secret treatises. While the most authentic copies of

his treatises had long been kept in his family and troupe, so-called pirated editions were circulating at least since the late sixteenth century, which no doubt contributed to his influence on Japanese performance theory. Nakamura Yasuo states that notions in Zeami's treatises were absorbed by other artistic treatises through a certain pirated edition, not only by noh practitioners but also by *kyōgen* actors and chanters of the puppet theater ("Kaisetsu," 800). For details on this phenomenon, see Maki Isaka, *Secrecy*, 37, 69, 91–92, 98, 166–67. For the paradox of well-known secret treatises in the context of *gei*, see ibid., 73–99. The introduction to "The Words of Ayame" itself begins by saying that it is secret (Fukuoka, "Ayamegusa," 317).

9 Shively, "Social Environment," 9.

3. PRESCRIPTION FOR FEMININITY

1 Fukuoka, "Ayamegusa," 320.
2 Yamamoto Jirō, "Ayamegusa," 31.
3 Both *The Actors' Analects* and *The Pioneering Analects from Past and Present Actors* are anthologies, written and compiled by writers other than Ayame or Kikunojō, and their bibliographies require an annotation. "Ayamegusa" had already printed in its entirety, but with a slightly different title ("Ayamekusa"), as an appendix in another book in 1771 (Fukuoka, "Ayamekusa," 194–98), and Doi Jun'ichi states that this version was the oldest as a published monograph and that its printing blocks were used with slight modifications by *The Actors' Analects* (ibid., 136). Gunji Masakatsu states that the appearance of the partial contents of "Ayamegusa" as well as advertisements in earlier documents indicates the circulation of far earlier copies ("Kaisetsu," 297–98, 301–3). For example, *The Complete Book of Actors through All Ages, the New Edition* (Shinsen kokon yakusha taizen), first published in 1750, lists "Ayamegusa" in the "works cited" section (Hachimonji and Hachimonji, *Shinsen Kokon Yakusha Taizen*, 8). Per convention, the present book uses *The Actors' Analects* version (Fukuoka, "Ayamegusa," 317–26). For an English-language translation of "The Words of Ayame," see Fukuoka, "Words of Ayame," 49–66.
4 "The Secret Transmissions of an *Onnagata*" had long been considered lost, and the only available version was the citation in Ihara Toshirō, *Nihon Engekishi*, 677–78. Later research has shown, however, that the text was included in *The Pioneering Analects from Past and Present Actors* (Imao, "'Onnagata Hiden,'" 52–57). The contents of "The Secret Transmissions of an *Onnagata*" appear in the anthology without a title (Kinjinsai, *Kokon Yakusha Rongo Sakigake*, 482–83). Imao assumes that the title is most likely to have been chosen by Ihara himself ("'Onnagata Hiden,'" 53). For a discussion of the epistemological connotations of this title, see Maki Isaka, *Secrecy*, 73–74. The present book follows the convention of treating it as an independent text and calling it "The Secret Transmissions of an *Onnagata*" but uses the version in *The Pioneering Analects from Past and Present Actors* (Kinjinsai, *Kokon Yakusha Rongo Sakigake*, 482–83).
5 Gunji, *Kabuki no Katachi*, 230–31. See also Imao, "'Onnagata Hiden,'" 54; Uehara, "Onnagata Geidan Tsunagi-kō," 50–53.

6   Fukuoka, "Ayamegusa," 326. For the sake of convenience, I assign a section number to each clause of both "The Words of Ayame" and "The Secret Transmissions of an *Onnagata*." The original texts do not have section numbers but introduce each clause with the phrase "For one thing."
7   Kinjinsai, *Kokon Yakusha Rongo Sakigake*, 483.
8   Hachimonji and Hachimonji, *Shinsen Kokon Yakusha Taizen*, 51.
9   *Kabuki Hyōbanki Shūsei*, vol. 7, 193–94.
10 Ibid., 419, 590–91. The phrase "the three cities" (*sanganotsu*) refers in this context to Edo, Kyoto, and Osaka.
11 Ibid., 510–11.
12 Ibid., 671–72.
13 Fukuoka, "Ayamegusa," 320. Needless to say, one's theory and practice do not necessarily coincide all the time. As for "The Words of Ayame" and Ayame's own acting career and reputation as described in such documents as actor-critique booklets, Inoue Nobuko observes that Ayame was not necessarily highly acclaimed in roles on which he meticulously expounded in the treatise (i.e., a high-ranking courtesan) and made a reputation for himself with his performance in roles that he is reluctant to discuss (i.e., samurai women) ("Shodai Yoshizawa Ayame," 300–314; "Yoshizawa Ayame," 249–60). Reluctant though he might have been, Ayame does discuss the roles of samurai women on several occasions, which will be discussed in detail.
14 *Kabuki Hyōbanki Shūsei*, vol. 8, 191–92. Nachi is a religious place renowned for Nachi Falls, and Kōya is another famous religious place. See also ibid., 378, 509, 534, 609. The quoted review appears in the section "Yoshizawa Gonshichi," the name Ayame used as a male-role actor. Ayame says that the name Gonshichi is a nickname for Gorozaemon, his patron, which he took to commemorate advice Gorozaemon had given him that he considered instrumental in his success as a kabuki actor (Fukuoka, "Ayamegusa," 322).
15 *Kabuki Hyōbanki Shūsei*, vol. 8, 378, 509, 534, 609.
16 Nakarai, *Bokuyō Kyōka Shūi*, 351.
17 Fukuoka, "Ayamegusa," 320. This quotation comes not from Ayame's words but from an annotation in which Fukuoka interprets what Ayame had said.
18 Ihara Saikaku, *Nanshoku Ōkagami*, 50.
19 Kinjinsai, *Kokon Yakusha Rongo Sakigake*, 483.
20 Ihara Saikaku, *Nanshoku Ōkagami*, 25–29.
21 This shift to "surrogate female eros in a surrogate setting" seems somewhat congenial to, if not coincident with, what Case asserts in a different context, that men playing women's roles signifies an element of female impersonation that is "the patriarchy's representation of the gender" (*Feminism*, 7). This also helps revisit debates on the butch-femme aesthetic in feminisms (see Case, "Toward a Butch-Femme Aesthetic," 282–99; Hart, "Identity," 119–37; Jackson, "Theatricality's Proper Objects," 186–213). It also concerns, in one way or another, female masculinity.
22 Kinjinsai, *Kokon Yakusha Rongo Sakigake*, 483.
23 Fukuoka, "Ayamegusa," 320.

24 Ibid., 320.
25 Takahashi Hiroko states: "If a certain idea that a successful *onnagata* should remain an *onnagata* for his entire life was established after Ayame's male-role acting, his bold attempt means to carry great weight for the history of *onnagata* artistry development" ("Shosei Yoshizawa Ayame ni okeru Tachiyaku no Gei," 32).
26 Gunji, *Kabuki no Katachi*, 230–31; Imao, "'Onnagata Hiden,'" 54; Uehara, "Onnagata Geidan Tsunagi-kō," 50–53.
27 Kinjinsai, *Kokon Yakusha Rongo Sakigake*, 482–83.
28 The introductory section says that it contains thirty clauses (Fukuoka, "Ayamegusa," 317) but has only twenty-nine clauses. It is interpreted in annotations as follows: "It is in fact twenty-nine clauses. It probably means 'approximately thirty clauses'" (Fukuoka, "Ayamegusa," ed. Gunji, 317); "This total includes the introduction" (Fukuoka, "Words of Ayame," ed. Dunn and Torigoe, 49). Imao states that "The Words of Ayame" could well have contained "more than thirty items," some clauses of which could have been lost before 1771 when it was included as "Ayamekusa" in *The Overview and Details of Actors, the New Edition* (Shinkoku yakusha kōmoku) (*Yakusha Banashi Hyōchū*, 177). While Imao's theory is important, for the sake of convenience, the numbering system in the present book is based on Gunji's first theory and refers to sections 1 through 29.
29 Imao, "'Onnagata Hiden,'" 54.
30 Fukuoka, "Ayamegusa," 318–21, 323–24, 326.
31 Ibid., 317–20, 324.
32 For more details on the mechanism and logic of this operation, see Maki Isaka, *Secrecy*, 45–63.
33 Fukuoka, "Ayamegusa," 319.
34 Ibid., 317. For a prescription derived from this, see ibid., 319 (section 7). Incidentally, Gunji points out in an annotation on "The Words of Ayame" that section 1 is uncannily similar to a remark in a monograph on the puppet theater published in 1756 (Fukuoka, "Ayamegusa," ed. Gunji, 422–23). In the remark in question, Ichiraku states: "Chikugo-no-jō replies as follows. First, one must chant with a deep understanding about speech-like patterns [*kotoba*] of high-ranking courtesans. If you chant it in an unconcerned way [*betabeta*], it will sound spineless [*dajaku*] and thus vulgar. You ought to think about words that are naive [*atome mo naku*] and soft and tender [*bonjaku to yawaraka*]. As long as you manage to chant this, then you can easily chant all other things. This is because the one who chants is originally [*ganrai*] a man, so that he possesses something stern and sharp [*kitto shitaru koto*] from birth [*mumaretsuki ni*]" (*Chikuhō Koji*, 27).

Gunji presumes that either of the two texts cited the other or, alternatively, Hachimonji Jishō, the editor of *The Actors' Analects*, added his own ideas. Such a phenomenon that similar remarks appear in several treatises across fields is not unfamiliar in the realm of artistic treatises in Japan, and more importantly, it is not considered "fatal" in this context as we would think today, as originality and creativity are not identical to each other in this realm involved in *gei* transmissions. Rather, creativity and traditionality should be compatible. For this phenomenon and its epistemological implications, see Maki Isaka, *Secrecy* 45–63, especially 56.

35 Fukuoka, "Ayamegusa," 318–19. This somehow concerns theories of female masculinity. Within the frame of Takarazuka theater and popular culture in contemporary Japan, Nakamura and Matsuo state that female masculinity in the said context is not necessarily sexualized, as is its counterpart in the West, where "one of the greatest tragedies of post-Freudian society in the United States is the sexualization of all human relationships from mother-infant onwards" ("Female Masculinity," 61). Likewise, in the context of *onnagata* traditions, female masculinity seems directly related to class, much more so than to sexuality as in the Western context. The matter concerns female *onnagata*.

36 Fukuoka, "Ayamegusa," 323–24. Regarding the phrase "go up in the world," Uehara Teruo proposes an alternative reading that means to urinate in the standing position ("Geidan," 39). In terms of sentence structure, both interpretations are technically possible. Charles J. Dunn and Torigoe Bunzō translate it as "make his way in the profession" (Fukuoka, "Words of Ayame," ed. Dunn and Torigoe, 62). Imao's annotation is "become a full-fledged *onnagata*" (*Yakusha Banashi Hyōchū*, 322). Having considered the context of this clause as well as the text in its entirety (e.g., whether a text that praises hesitation in eating as a virtue dares to describe excretion), I have followed Imao's as well as Dunn and Torigoe's interpretations and do not adopt Uehara's theory without further evidence, although there might be room for discussion. For one thing, attention to concrete and physical things is of great moment for the text as well as for artistic theory in premodern Japan. For another, Miyao Shigeo records that a certain folding screen depicts an *onnagata* urinating in the seated position in his dressing room; although Miyao does not specify the work in question, he implies that it is an Edo-era piece (*Edo no Onnagata Haiyū to sono Kōi*, 106). Another possibility is that it was a double entendre to be read as both. It is quite common rhetoric for Japanese literary works to allude second meanings (e.g., the pivot word in poetry).

37 See, e.g., Mezur, *Beautiful Boys*, 259; Senelick, *Changing Room*, 89.

38 Fukuoka, "Ayamegusa," 319–21.

39 Ibid., 319–20. In another context, Philip Auslander analyzes the non-comical quality attributed to women in terms of the act of exercising power ("Brought to You," 316–25).

40 Kinjinsai, *Kokon Yakusha Rongo Sakigake*, 482.

41 Mezur, *Beautiful Boys*, 26. Mezur at one point states: "there may have been some imitation of female characteristics by some kabuki onnagata in the early *yarō* (adult fellow) kabuki of eighteenth century [sic]" (7), whom she specifies as "Yoshizawa Ayame I (1673–1729) and other early onnagata" (255). Later, after citing Benito Ortolani's remark on "The Words of Ayame" ("From Ayame derive the codification of the teaching and the practice of extending the impersonation of a woman to the actor's private life, in an effort to achieve true realism on the stage" [*Japanese Theatre*, 181]), she states otherwise: "Perhaps instead of impersonation or realism, Ayame I practiced a hyperreal theatricality, which referenced the appearances,

customs, and manners of female-likeness" (94). She also describes "Ayame I's onnagata gender role image" as "neither female nor male" (89). For her discussion on Ayame and "The Words of Ayame," see ibid., 88–98; on Kikunojō and "The Secret Transmissions of an *Onnagata*," see ibid., 98–105.

42   Mezur, *Beautiful Boys*, 259. Mezur also states, "Perhaps we should cease to argue that women are not capable of acting the male-created feminine ideal" (259), and presents the above proposal instead. Whether it is about "[acting?] ability" or a "male sexed body" with "the presence of male sexual organs" (25), her theory belongs to a party that regards the *onnagata*'s performance of femininity as foreign to the gender performance of women.

43   Ernst, *Kabuki Theatre*, 195.

44   Ibid., 195.

45   I consulted the following texts: Fukuoka, "Ayamegusa"; Fukuoka, "Words of Ayame"; Fukuoka, "Ayamekusa"; and Imao, *Yakusha Banashi Hyōchū*.

46   Mezur, *Beautiful Boys*, 5, 26–27; Buruma, *Japanese Mirror*, 116.

47   It would be not only impractical but also somewhat unfair, however, to expect a work outside a particular field to check original texts in the field thoroughly. That said, arguably, one of the most visible examples is Garber, *Vested Interests*, 245. Other examples include works on Russian male ballet and traditional Chinese theater: see Senelick, *Changing Room*, 89; Scholl, "Queer Performance," 309; Tian, "Male *Dan*," 87; Tian, *Mei Lanfang*, 47.

48   Tian's "Male *Dan*" first mentions "The Words of Ayame," an English-language translation by Dunn and Torigoe, and follows with the said quotation from Ernst's work (86–87).

49   See, e.g., Brandon, "Reflections," 122–25; Leiter, *Frozen Moments*, 147–56.

50   Barthes, *Empire*, 53.

51   Case, *Feminism*, 7.

52   For the "male gaze," see Mulvey, "Visual Pleasure," 11.

53   Linguistics first paid attention to the concept of performativity, especially its illocutionary aspect; illocution is to utter something *in* which a speaker does things, such as "to pronounce" (Austin, *How to Do Things*, 101–3). Just as with a pure constative statement, a perfect illocutionary speech act, *in* which the speaker retains final control over what he or she utters as well as its consequence, was found unlikely, and another element of the performative, that is, perlocution, came to demand our attention. A perlocutionary speech act is an act *by* which we do things with words, and the consequences do not remain *in* the utterance. Although we should not take for granted a clear-cut distinction between illocutionary and perlocutionary acts (Benhabib, "Epistemologies," 128), it is the latter that emphasizes the theoretical acuteness of performativity, that is, a *doing* creates a *being*. Again, theoretical incapability does not necessarily mean that nonexistent practices and illusionary concepts—whether a constative statement or an illocutionary speech act—can operate in our lives.

54   Robertson, "Shingaku Woman," 89.

55   Wakita Haruko states: "I think that the class difference is greater than the male-

female difference in premodern society, and that only within an equal class does the male-female difference emerge explicitly. Only when equality among the four classes [samurai, farmers, artisans, merchants (by extension, 'all the people')] is established after a fashion in modern society is the difference between male and female perceived strongly" (*Chūsei ni Ikiru Onna-tachi*, 242).

56 Fukuoka, "Ayamegusa," 317–20; Kinjinsai, *Kokon Yakusha Rongo Sakigake*, 482.
57 Fukuoka, "Ayamegusa," 317.
58 Imao, *Henshin no Shisō*, 144–45. See also Imao's another wording, *onna no genten* (the starting point of women), to explain the high-ranking courtesan's femininity in section 1 of "The Words of Ayame" (*Yakusha Banashi Hyōchū*, 186).
59 Leiter, "From Gay to *Gei*," 217.
60 See, e.g., Inoue, "Shodai Yoshizawa Ayame," 304, 306; Hattori, "Ayamegusa," 29; Tobe, "Shosei Yoshizawa Ayame," 16.
61 Kawatake Toshio, "Ayame no Kyo to Jitsu," 46. Hattori Yukio's reading is similar to Kawatake's, although, by inserting the role (onstage), his point becomes somewhat vague: "[Ayame brought up the case of a high-ranking courtesan's role because it] is the most difficult to perform for young *onnagata*. This is because this role requires one to represent *the* abstract beauty as substance, that is, a 'woman' in and of itself as a 'non-man,' which *onnagata* as men do not have" ("Waka-oyama," 111).
62 Kawatake Toshio, "'Onnagata' no Kiseki," 29.
63 "Dominant cultural ideology appears in representation as naturalized and seemingly nonideological" (Dolan, *Feminist Spectator*, 41).
64 Fukuoka, "Ayamegusa," 317–18.
65 Incidentally, by seeing a herald of the modern episteme, which materialized in the late nineteenth century in Japan, here I am closer to Laqueur than to Foucault. The concept of episteme explains how human perception is governed by a grid of knowledge fields. According to Foucault, plural types of episteme are mutually exclusive by definition, so that a society at any given moment resides in a single episteme. There remains, though, room for argument over whether plural types of episteme really cannot coexist under any circumstances. Utilizing the Foucauldian concept of episteme, Laqueur at one point states: "Here I differ from Foucault, who would see one *episteme* decisively, once and for all, replacing another" (*Making Sex*, 21).
66 Zeami, *Fūshikaden*, 20. Noh theater, before its establishment as a "high art," fell into a category analogous to that of kabuki in the Edo era. At its inception, in the fourteenth century, what would later be known as noh (lit., "talent" or "arts") was sometimes derogatorily referred to as an "activity of beggars," and the enthusiasm of social elites for such a "vulgar" entertainment was considered by some aristocrats a manifestation of the "world that is now *kabuki*" (Kitagawa, *Zeami*, 31). The word "kabuki" here is a common noun referring to anything eccentric, deviant, queer, and the like.
67 Zeami, *Fūshikaden*, 21.
68 An actor's proximity to the reality to be represented is an omnipresent issue that many theater practitioners have dealt with, among them, Konstantin Stanislavski (1863–1938).

69 Satō Yuki, "Bandō Tamasaburō Intabyū," no page nos.; *Nasutāsha/Nastazja*. I am not suggesting that the factor of "race" or "ethnicity" did not exist in Japanese theater before modern times. Chinese characters appear in noh, bunraku, and kabuki plays, that is, all major theatrical genres established in premodern Japan. Zeami himself mentions "Karagoto" (China things) but says that resemblance does not matter (*Fūshikaden*, 26–27). This clearly differs from Tamasaburō's case here as well as Zeami's own cases of high-ranking men or women. Tamasaburō would later realize what he says here as a formidable combination of language, gender, and ethnicity when he collaborated with a *kunqu* troupe. In *The Peony Pavilion* (Mudanting; *Botantei* in Japanese) (Kyoto, Japan: 2008; Beijing and Suzhou, China: 2008 and 2009), he performed with Chinese actors and sang and spoke in Chinese.

70 Although Tamasaburō does not use any word that explicitly suggests the balance among the Japanese and Polish actors, his juxtaposition of languages and of actors implies this element. In fact, this is similar to the balance between male actors and actresses that was furiously debated when female actors officially came back to the Japanese stage in modern times. For the debates, see Kano, *Acting Like a Woman*, 16–24.

71 On the juxtaposition of modernity's obsessive dualism-ism with *gei* practitioners' will to incorporate them, see Maki Isaka, *Secrecy* 138.

72 Kinjinsai, *Kokon Yakusha Rongo Sakigake*, 482.

73 Fukuoka, "Ayamegusa," 318.

74 Ibid., 318.

75 Ibid., 318.

76 Ibid., 320.

77 Masaki, "Shodai Yoshizawa Ayame no 'Soko ni Urei no Omoiire,'" 80–96. Incidentally, samurai women is a type of *kabuki* role (*yakugara*) that is not for all females in the samurai class but for those who are good at martial arts, loyal, and courageous. While Masaki's discussion is specifically about samurai-women roles, the instructions in "The Words of Ayame" are about women in the samurai class in general. The gist of his instructions, however, points to what is expected of actors playing samurai-women roles.

78 Ibid., 91. Satō Chino further examines how Ayame's proposal was inherited, with some radical changes, by later *onnagata*, focusing on Kikunojō in a particular play ("Kakikae," 69–82).

79 Takahashi Hiroko, "Shosei Yoshizawa Ayame ni okeru Tachiyaku no Gei," 28–43.

80 Inoue, "Shodai Yoshizawa Ayame," 300–314; Inoue, "Yoshizawa Ayame," 249–60.

81 Inoue, "Yoshizawa Ayame," 260.

82 Fukuoka, "Ayamegusa," 319.

83 Ibid., 318–19.

84 *Kabuki Hyōbanki Shūsei*, vol. 3, 548.

85 Cf. Butler, *Gender Trouble*; Butler, *Excitable Speech*.

86 *The Book of Disease* recounts that a certain person's appearance made people feel ill at ease because this person looked like a man and a woman. The Peeping Tom in the picture is laughing cheerfully. In contrast, the accompanying narrative

reveals that, thus "diagnosed" as intersex, the mystery was solved in the sense that the person's sex and gender corresponded to each other: "people felt o[b] otsukana[g]ari [hazy, uncertain, dubious, ill at ease]" (*Yamai no Sōshi*, 82–83, 175). The striking contrast formed by the two kinds of media—pictorial and literary texts—is noteworthy.

87   Robertson, "The 'Magic If,'" 50.
88   LaFleur, *Buddhism*, 47.
89   Fukuoka, "Ayamegusa," 319, 321, 323–24.
90   Hachimonji and Hachimonji, *Shinsen Kokon Yakusha Taizen*, 25, 49–50, 53.
91   Taking the *onnagata*'s transformation as superimposition is actually in line with a long-standing understanding of kabuki acting in general. In what Hattori calls a "doubling change," an acting person first transforms himself into the actor, which is already a role in its own right, and next into the role itself. Importantly, "this is not a simple metamorphosis (*tanjun na henshin*)," because the first transformation should not be effaced (*Kabuki no Kōzō*, 53, see also 54–56).
92   Roughly speaking, representation is a form of expression that effaces its mediated nature: what *looks* immediate and thus realistic. In turn, presentation is a form of expression that openly recognizes its mediated nature. For those concepts in the context of Japanese literature, see Fowler, *Rhetoric*, 28–42.

4. CANONIZATION

1   Hattori, "Waka-oyama," 113.
2   Yamamoto Jirō, "Ayamegusa," 31.
3   Canonization no doubt entails uneasy issues for many authors, as the act of enunciation (e.g., writing) is visibly central to it. As Hart effectively frames it, "To represent it unproblematized is to construct it" ("Canonizing Lesbians?" 280); the "it" in the quotation refers to the probability of gender being read as an inherent property of bodies, and this probability is the defining logic of *Modern American Drama*, the anthology that includes Hart's essay. Here I am borrowing the structure of logic and not the specific referent itself. Certainly, "The Words of Ayame" and "The Secret Transmissions of an *Onnagata*" are indispensable to an analysis of *onnagata* in terms of gender, not only because the two texts contain notions informative of gender theorization but also because—precisely because—those notions have been instrumental in defining *onnagata* artistry and ideas about femininity. Yet that alone should not automatically justify my complicity in reinforcing canonization. This is because canonization inevitably operates on the principle of exclusion ("Canons, by definition, must set certain limits; they must be formulated as this, but not this. They are thus inherently exclusionary" [Hart, "Canonizing Lesbians?" 279]). In other words, despite my statement that whether or not a text was righteously canonized is an aporia, such a statement would be nearly a disclaimer should it be presented alone, with no further investigation. To put it precisely, a text is canonized based on a vested interest in a system, in the disguise of righteousness, and at the cost of other texts that are eliminated. Need-

less to say, kabuki discourse is no exception. Female *onnagata* would be eradicated from it in the early twentieth century, and there is no guarantee that her eighteenth-century predecessors did not face a similar fate. (This is a classic cliché of evidence, which is capable of proving presence but not absence.) What is really necessary here is recognition that a text like "The Words of Ayame" is canonical as such and attention to *how* it has been canonized.

4   It is literally impractical, even meaningless, to list works that fall into this category. Almost every secondary source I have used comments on Ayame and "The Words of Ayame," and many also mention Kikunojō and/or "The Secret Transmissions of an *Onnagata*." For more on their acting careers, based on such documents as actor-critique booklets, see Takahashi Hiroko, "Shosei Yoshizawa Ayame Nenpu" 53–63; Satō Chino, "Ganso Segawa Kikunojō Shukkin Nenpu" 163–87. Satō Chino gives an account of Ayame's life ("Yakusha no Ikishini," 180–88) as well as an analysis of Kikunojō's acting ("Ganso Segawa Kikunojō no Geifū," 41–55). Tobe Ginsaku provides a detailed list of *onnagata*'s role types and explains each with various accounts-on-*gei*, beginning with "Ayame I through Today's Utaemon VI" ("Onnagata," 138–60). Outside the confines of the theater, Takahashi Noriko studies Kikunojō's influence on picture books ("Kurohon Aohon to Segawa Kikunojō," 33–48); although about a phenomenon not limited to the theater proper, her work is of great moment as the kabuki industry and publication culture were deeply interconnected.

5   The table of contents of *The Pioneering Analects from Past and Present Actors* reads "Transmissions from the Late Segawa Kikunojō Concerning the Dance and Realistic Arts of *Onnagata*" (Ko Segawa Kikunojō shosagoto jigei onnagata no den), but the text does not carry a title (Kinjinsai, *Kokon Yakusha Rongo Sakigake*, 467, 482–83). The anthology simply includes the ten items by Kikunojō in the section titled "Narratives on *Gei* by Actors in the Past" (Kojin yakusha gei-banashi), which contains accounts by thirteen actors (ibid., 479–91).

6   Ihara Toshirō, *Nihon Engekishi*, 677.

7   Imao, "'Onnagata Hiden'" 53.

8   Figuratively, "The Secret Transmissions of an *Onnagata*" has been, and still is, frequently paired with "The Words of Ayame" in kabuki studies. This is especially intriguing when it comes to those works written in the Japanese language. More often than not, they faithfully use the title probably chosen by Ihara, as written in Ihara's original Chinese characters: "woman-direction." This is interesting especially because another Chinese character for *kata* is usually used for the term "*onnagata*": "woman-form." Therefore, in works written in Japanese, one would typically see *onnagata* as "woman-form" in the main text and "woman-direction" in the title of "The Secret Transmissions of an *Onnagata*." In its table of contents, *The Pioneering Analects from Past and Present Actors* uses "woman-form" when referring to the part attributed to Kikunojō (Kinjinsai, *Kokon Yakusha Rongo Sakigake*, 467]. In short, regardless of the circumstances under which it became a canon, "The Secret Transmissions of an *Onnagata*" is treated, in exactly the form introduced by Ihara, as a significant *onnagata* treatise in kabuki studies.

9   Kagayama, "Kyō no Geidan," 200.
10 Nakamura and Tobe, Gendai o Ikiru 'Ayamegusa,'" 33–34.
11 Yamakawa, "Onoe Taganojō Intabyū," 233.
12 Onoe Baikō VI, Onnagata no Koto, 16, 70–71, 97, 118–19.
13 Ibid., 119. This anecdote appears in Kinjinsai, Kokon Yakusha Rongo Sakigake, 483.
14 Hachimonji and Hachimonji, Shinsen Kokon Yakusha Taizen, 51; emphasis added.
15 Kinjinsai, Kokon Yakusha Rongo Sakigake, 468, 469, 474, 475.
16 Ibid., 473–74; emphasis added. Furisode (lit., "swinging sleeve") is clothing for adolescence. It was originally for both girls and boys before their initiation into adulthood but became a girls-only item.
17 Ibid., 482–83.
18 Banritei, Yakusha Meibutsu Sode Nikki, 256; emphasis added.
19 Hattori proposes that the author of this book did not see Ayame's performance—because Ayame was too early in terms of time and too far away in terms of location—and had no chance to read "The Words of Ayame," which was published slightly earlier than The Famous-Product Journal, Actors' Sleeves ("Waka-oyama," 109, 110).
20 Fukuoka, "Ayamegusa," 319.

5. FEMININITY IN CIRCULATION

1   Shikitei, Sanshibai Kakusha Hyōbanki, 479–529. The term "three theaters" (sanshibai, also sanza) refers to three big theaters in the city of Edo: the Nakamura-za, Ichimura-za, and Morita-za Theaters (or their substitutes, e.g., the Kawarasaki-za Theater, depending on the time). All three major cites—Edo, Kyoto, and Osaka—had licensed theaters known as "big theaters" (ōshibai), which were also considered the highest-ranking theaters. The original four big theaters in Edo were reduced to three after the Ejima-Ikushima incident in 1714. Actor Ikushima Shingorō (1671–1743) is said to have had an affair with Ejima (1681–1741), one of the highest-ranking female officials in the service of the shogun's mother. When the affair was exposed, it resulted in not only exile for Ejima and Ikushima but also blanket punishment for all parties concerned, ranging from banishment to capital punishment, and the complete closure of kabuki playhouses for a while. A number of regulations ensued, another example, along with the female performer ban in 1629 and the wakashu ban in 1652, of the shogunate exercising its overwhelming power over kabuki. The effects must have been overarching, far beyond the number of playhouses. Takahashi Hiroko states, for example, that Ayame was performing in Edo at that time and presumes that this must have made him cautious about post-performance activities ("Shosei Yoshizawa Ayame ni okeru Tachiyaku no Gei," 37).
2   Osanai, "Tsukiji Shōgekijō to Watakushi," 43. Osanai's definition of audiences is in line with his overall conceptualization of the new type of theater he established with his peers (namely, shingeki [lit., "new theater"]), as he defined it as that which is not kabuki (also kyūgeki [old theater]) ("Tsukiji Shōgekijō wa Nani no Tameni Sonzai Suruka," 48–49). For a discussion of how Osanai dealt with kabuki, see Maki Isaka, Secrecy, 101–36; Maki Isaka, "Osanai Kaoru's Dilemma," 119–33.

3   In general, *yagō* refers to the name of a merchant's shop. Kabuki actors came to have *yagō* presumably in the late seventeenth century, and it became a must for them in the early eighteenth century; see "Yagō," by Kawatake Shigetoshi, in Engeki Hakubutsukan, *Engeki Hyakka Daijiten*, vol. 5, 435. Just as with merchants' *yagō*, there are various histories on actors' *yagō*, such as ancestors' hometowns, names of shops that actors ran as second businesses, or commemoration of epochal events in families. For example, Ayame decided on Tachibanaya as his *yagō*, in honor of his patron Tachibanaya Gorozaemon, for he was grateful for useful advice that Gorozaemon had given to him (Fukuoka, "Ayamegusa," 322). Not only do *yagō* function as pet names that audiences would shout as compliments to individual actors, but in due course *yagō*, along with family names, have also come to connect kabuki families and function as an index of *gei* traditions (e.g., the acting fashion of Naritaya, etc.).

4   Féral, "Theatricality," 96.
5   Hattori, *Kabuki no Genkyō*, 386.
6   Most notably, Hattori, *Ōinaru Koya*.
7   Hattori and Ichinoseki, *Ehon Yume no Edo Kabuki*.
8   Hattori, *Kabuki no Genkyō*, 388.
9   Hattori and Ichinoseki, *Ehon Yume no Edo Kabuki*, no pg. nos.
10   The Kanamaru-za Theater (formerly Konpira Ōshibai) was built in 1835, modeled after a big theater in Osaka. Kotohira, a famous site of pilgrimage, was very active in hosting kabuki productions next to the three major cities of Edo, Kyoto, and Osaka. The structure of this theater is documented in detail (see, e.g., Leiter, *Frozen Moments*, 231–56; *Kenchiku Mappu*). The building had not been used for a long time, but it was restored due to a long-term effort by people in Kotohira (and beyond). Kabuki has been produced at Kanamaru-za on a regular basis since 1985; it also appears in films as a stand-in for the aforementioned Nakamura-za Theater (*Ashura-jō; Sharaku*). See also Hattori, *Kabuki no Genkyō*, 388–89; Hattori and Kawazoe, "Kabuki Gekijō Kenkyū no Kako to Genzai," 12–15.
11   Hattori and Kawazoe, "Kabuki Gekijō Kenkyū no Kako to Genzai," 23–25.
12   A kabuki stage started from its initial adaptation of a noh stage (a square performing space 3 *ken* by 3 *ken* in size (3 *ken* equal approximately 19.39 feet) but kept increasing its size, reflecting the need for a more space for seats resulting from kabuki's popularity as well as the need for more space onstage resulting from kabuki dramaturgy (increasingly spectacular choreography and complicated stage settings). According to Yuichirō Takahashi, the stage expanded from its initial 3 *ken* to 5 *ken* in 1688, and to 6.5 *ken* in 1725, which "remained more or less the same for about 150 years," that is, for the rest of the Edo period; it further increased after that, and the present-day Kabuki-za in Tokyo, has a stage 13 *ken* wide ("*Kabuki Goes Official*," 139). As for expansion in modern times, Hattori offers slightly different figures: 12 *ken* (Kabuki-za built in 1889), 11.5 *ken* (Ichimura-za built in 1892), 13 *ken* (Hongō-za built in 1912), 15 *ken* (rebuilt Kabuki-za), and 12 *ken* (the present-day National Theater) (Hattori and Kawazoe, "Kabuki Gekijō Kenkyū no Kako to Genzai," 24). Incidentally, after Hattori and Kawazoe's paper was published

in 2007, the Kabuki-za Theater went through another rebuilding, and the latest Kabuki-za Theater was built in 2013.

Even after stages began to be enlarged, scripts still begin with the traditional phrase "main stage of three ken" (*hon-butai san-gen*). See, e.g., *Sukeroku, the Flower of Edo* (Sukeroku yukari no Edo-zakura), *Arrowhead* (Yanone), and *Saint Narukami* (Narukami), first performed in 1713, 1729, and 1742 respectively (*Sukeroku*, 61; *Yanone*, 52; *Narukami*, 194). The continued use of the popular phrase must be an example of kabuki paying homage to noh, one of its important predecessors: authentic traditions.

13 Hattori and Kawazoe, "Kabuki Gekijō Kenkyū no Kako to Genzai," 24.
14 *Hachijō Kadensho*, 513.
15 Hattori, *Ōinaru Koya*, 107–21.
16 Ibid.
17 Hattori, *Edo Kabuki no Bi-ishiki*, 215–38.
18 Kimura, *Gekijō Ikkan Mushimegane*, 311.
19 Chikamatsu serves as an epitome of kabuki's deep relationship with the puppet theater, having written for both kabuki and the puppet theater. More importantly, plays written for the puppet theater have become important repertoires for kabuki, which actively adapted them. These constitute a vital category of kabuki plays, namely, *maruhon-mono* (also *gidayū kyōgen*).
20 Gunji, "Kaisetsu," 20.
21 Gondō, "Gaisetsu 1," 3. Today, many kabuki scripts are available in English translations. See, for example, *Kabuki Plays on Stage*, edited by James R. Brandon and Samuel L. Leiter, a five-volume series published by the University of Hawai'i Press in 2004.
22 This triplet is a modified version extracted from Gondō Yoshikazu's five categories of textual materials for kabuki studies: (1) drama texts [scripts]; (2) actor-critique booklets; (3) playbills, chronicles, and chronological tables; (4) theater-books; and (5) laws and ordinances ("Gaisetsu 1," 2). Notice that the five categories include all the textual materials for kabuki studies, whereas the three-category classification covers publications available to Edo-era theater lovers and relevant to their kabuki experience. Also note that the definition of "theater-book" (*gekisho*) is not strict. Gondō defines it as those books on kabuki produced in the Edo era that are not scripts, actor-critique booklets, chronicles, and the like (ibid., 5). Accordingly, it is theoretically possible that a book about kabuki history can be regarded as a theater-book and as a chronicle, depending on the criteria in operation.
23 See, e.g., Takahashi Noriko, "Kurohon Aohon to Segawa Kikunojō," 33–48; Schalow, "Figures," 59–69.
24 The rental library business was active in the Edo era, supported by the popularity of reading, including among the common people (Nagatomo, "Edo," 99–109). Rental libraries were also instrumental in maintaining the popularity of reading (Nagatomo, "Hon'ya," 83–94), and such theater-related publications as actor-critique booklets and theater-books were among the items they handled (ibid., 85).

As for the difficulty of determining the number of copies of published books, see Munemasa, "Meiji Shoki no Tosho Shuppan Busū," 119–23.
25 Matsumiya, *Edo Kabuki to Kōkoku*.
26 Kimura, *Gekijō Ikkan Mushimegane*, 311.
27 The incident was the Ejima-Ikushima incident.
28 Whereas most of the current kabuki theaters (except for such theaters as Kanamaru-za) are equipped with chairs, playhouses in the past used the *masu* system. A *masu* is a box seat with no chairs, and its capacity is far more flexible than a cluster of individual chairs. Another factor is the custom of *oikomi* (chase-in). When a play was a hit, audiences were squeezed into cheaper box seats.
29 Hattori and Kawazoe, "Kabuki Gekijō Kenkyū no Kako to Genzai," 21. Elsewhere, Hattori mentions the figure of one thousand as all-inclusive, including not only the audience but also actors and staff (Hattori and Ichinoseki, *Ehon Yume no Edo Kabuki*, no pg. nos.).
30 It must have been especially so after the Ejima-Ikushima incident in 1714.
31 The interaction was not limited to kabuki and the "surrogate" mediums by which people enjoyed it; each "surrogate" medium affected the others. Honda Yasuo examines how an entertainment such as voice mimicry (i.e., one type of "surrogate" kabuki medium) influenced prose literature as well ("Kaiwa-tai no Sharebon no Seiritsu ni tsuite no Shiron," 51–63).
32 Hachimonji, *Yakusha Zensho*, 199–241.
33 Kimura, *Gekijō Ikkan Mushimegane*, 311. For the phenomenon of publications involved in the popularity of kabuki, see also Gerstle, "Culture of Play," 188–216.
34 Ōzasa, *Nihon Gendai Engekishi*, 18.
35 *Onna Daigaku*, 531–33.
36 Namura, *Onna Chōhōki*, 20.
37 Hachimonji, *Yakusha Zensho*, 229. For this phenomenon, see also Yoshikawa, "Kabuki-geki," 80; Yoshikawa, "Genroku-ki," 183.
38 Kinjinsai, *Kokon Yakusha Rongo Sakigake*, 483.
39 Ibid., 483. See Mulvey, "Visual Pleasure," 6–18, for "male gaze" and "to-be-looked-at-ness."
40 Kinjinsai, *Kokon Yakusha Rongo Sakigake*, 483.
41 Robertson, "Shingaku Woman," 90.
42 Butler, "Imitation," 22.
43 Butler, *Gender Trouble*, 31; emphasis in original.
44 Barthes, *Image*, 142–48.
45 Rose, *Authors and Owners*, 142.
46 See, e.g., Zeami, *Fūshikaden*, 14, 37, 46.
47 For further details, see Maki Isaka, *Secrecy*, 45–63.
48 It does not directly mean, however, that esotericism and modernity can be demarcated clearly. For esotericism's ambiguous relationship to modernity, see ibid., 101–36.
49 In this sense, it does not seem to be coincidence that these popular books of kabuki

leave much room for the voices and movements of particular actors for the sake of virtual theatergoing. Certainly, it is mainly by voice and bodily movement that an actor, or any person for that matter, passes. For instance, in her *Fires in the Mirror*, Anna Deavere Smith performs across such categories as race, gender, age, nationality, and class, and what she changes from one role to another consists of vocal tone, language, costume, props, and movement. Here, the way physical things exist controls the way identities exist. For an analysis of voice and movement in modern Japanese theater, see Kano, *Acting Like a Woman*, 219–30.

50 Kinjinsai, *Kokon Yakusha Rongo Sakigake*, 482.
51 Fukuoka, "Ayamegusa," 317, 319–21.
52 Kinjinsai, *Kokon Yakusha Rongo Sakigake*, 482.
53 Fukuoka, "Ayamegusa," 320.
54 Ibid., 323.
55 Ibid., 319.
56 Ibid., 320.
57 Kinjinsai, *Kokon Yakusha Rongo Sakigake*, 483.
58 Ibid., 489. This passage is excerpted from "The Fifty Transmissions of the Flower and the Fruit" (Kajitsu gojū sōden), a section that contains instructions left by Ichikawa Danjūrō II (1688–1759) and Sawamura Sōjūrō I (1685–1756).
59 It might well be questionable to categorize dying as everyday life. The decision to do so results from my reading of Ayame's definition of "the usual state" (*tsune*) as things offstage as opposed to things onstage, and I classify dying as the former.
60 Nakamura and Tobe, "Gendai o Ikiru 'Ayamegusa,'" 33–34.
61 *Kabuki Hyōbanki Shūsei*, vol. 3, 548; from an issue published in the fourth month of 1704.
62 *Kabuki Hyōbanki Shūsei, Dai-2-ki*, vol. 3, 55; from an issue published in the first month of 1746.
63 Importantly, it is by no means effective to consider that each concept (*onna* and *onnagata*) is monolithic and that the interaction between them is lineal. Such a model of interaction would be much too simple even if bilateral. Rather, it is that this interaction occurs among multiple concepts of *onnagata* and equally multiple concepts of *onna*, and that such an interaction continues to create new definitions of *onna* and *onnagata*. Given this, in order to understand the phenomenon at hand effectively, one should phrase it as follows: the circulation of femininity *among*—and not *between*—*onnagata* and women. For the sake of convenience, I omitted the preposition "among," but the multiplicity of this phenomenon should be kept in mind.
64 Tamiya, "Zoku 'Nijinshū,'" 349.
65 Kaneko, "Nijinshū," 345. It is noteworthy that both the words of Kuhei and "The Fifty Transmissions of the Flower and the Fruit" (introduced in n. 58) show great similarities to the two canonized texts "The Words of Ayame" and "The Secret Transmissions of an *Onnagata*." On the one hand, it demonstrates how popular these ideas were; on the other hand, it also implies that such texts as the words of

Kuhei and "The Fifty Transmissions of the Flower and the Fruit" would have been canonized if, like "The Secret Transmissions of an *Onnagata*," they had been lucky enough to be introduced in the same manner by the renowned philologist.

66 Yuasa, *Shintairon*, 101; emphasis in original.
67 For further details, see Maki Isaka, *Secrecy*, 63–72.
68 I use the words "exterior" and "interior" only for the sake of clarity and for analytical purposes and not to endorse the idea of a clear boundary between the two. Rather, such a boundary in and of itself is being questioned here. An internal identity can be differentiated from external appearances only historically and not naturally: a historical product of modernity. (Equally, it is no wonder that Osanai later attempted to separate the interior from the exterior in his new-theater projects. For further details, see Maki Isaka, "Osanai Kaoru's Dilemma," 128.) *Onnagata* discourse in the Edo period is not located in modern episteme.
69 Ikegami, *Bonds of Civility*, 245.
70 Takechi, *Kabuki I*, 168–72.
71 This is also an example of a situation in which an analysis of *onnagata* can construct a fruitful dialogue with American feminist thinking. Peggy Phelan states: "The Eastern dance forms represented at the congress [the September 1986 International School for Theatre Anthropology Congress]—Balinese dance-drama, Indian *kathakali* and *odissi*, Japanese *kabuki*, and Chinese opera—proved to be the most disturbingly interesting. These Eastern theatrical roles are essentially mythic and, as Roland Barthes has remarked, myth 'organizes a world which is without contradiction because it is without depth. . . .' Such classical female roles played by men or women do not, by definition and design, penetrate the 'identity' of any female; they are surface representations whose appeal exists precisely *as* surface" ("Feminist Theory," 109; emphasis in original). Phelan's attention to the importance of surface is acute, at least in the context of Japanese kabuki. What I would like to modify here is that, in the said paradigm, the identity of female as such is located precisely on the surface, and not somewhere deep down or within the alleged depths. In this sense, the significance of surface is highly epistemological. Accordingly, while Phelan states that "'reading' them depends not on plausibility or coherence but rather upon immediate recognition of the comic artifice *and* reverent idealization of the form which organizes the image the dancer projects" (109; emphasis in original), plausibility in fact amounts to a critical factor of *onnagata* artistry, whether reading it or writing it. It is not to say that the surface ahistorically retains such epistemological significance in Japan; on the contrary, there would later be demarcation between interior and exterior.
72 Yuasa, *Shintairon*, 124–25.
73 Ibid., 116–17.
74 Fujiwara no Teika, *Maigetsushō*, 131, 137–38. It is worth noting, from the viewpoint of esotericism, that Teika emphasizes that he heard the teachings from his father, Fujiwara no Shunzei (1114–1204), according to the principle explained above as hearsay dynamics.

75   Yuasa, *Shintairon*, 153; emphasis in original. This understanding can demonstrate both similarities to and differences from postmodern theorizations of bodies and languages. As for an analysis of the postmodern "assertion that discourse constitutes its object, or that there is no outside of language," see Kirby, *Telling Flesh*, 149.

76   Kasulis, "Editor's Introduction," 6; emphasis in original.

77   Tadano Makuzu (1763–1825), one of the rare female writers of the Edo era, proposed intriguing and important counterevidence regarding the exteriority-interiority fusion. Bettina Gramlich-Oka states, "Makuzu's gender definition extends to what *lies beneath the visible*" (*Thinking Like a Man*, 186; emphasis added). Makuzu unambiguously asserts this point: "Even though an *onnagata* in the theater has a woman's appearance, since he has a man's body, in his heart he harbors abusive feelings toward women. As he performs he thus in fact takes pleasure in what should be a pitiable scene. I finally came to realize that is why he performs in ways that appeal to the men in his audience. Women, on the other hand, take no pleasure in a villain's capturing a beautiful young woman and doing with her what he wishes" (Tadano, "Solitary Thoughts," pt. 1, 25).

78   It is because of the externality-internality fusion clearly demonstrated by both texts that I foreground their similarities. As for the disparity, my remarks have been made in passing (e.g., difference in rhetoric of laconic versus narrative, difference in focus on technical versus mental, etc.). One more incongruity deserves special attention, but even in the said distinction, the two texts nevertheless share a similar understanding in terms of the externality-internality fusion. This discrepancy is related to the acting careers of the two actors. As mentioned, Kikunojō was somewhat luckier in representing the principle of perpetuity than Ayame was, because the former was praised for his youthful, beautiful appearance until his death while the latter struggled, which resulted in his switching to male-role acting. In kabuki studies, this gap in their stage lives is sometimes made to explain a change in *onnagata* artistry that possibly took place in the two decades between the actors. Gunji states: "[That Ayame attempted to become a male-role actor despite his own words] is nothing other than a mystery, but I think that it was partially because of the times. That is to say, back then, it was still expected that, as one aged, an actor frequently changed the type of roles he performed.

"Another reason I can think of is that the duration of *onnagata* role types was prolonged during the time of Segawa Kikunojō I due to the change of *onnagata* costume and dramaturgy. . . . It was only with Segawa Kikunojō that *onnagata* technique became stable enough to make possible a sixty-year-old *onnagata* wearing long-sleeve kimono [reserved for youth]" (*Kabuki no Katachi*, 229–30).

Taguchi Akiko also holds an understanding similar to that of Gunji: "It was the time of Segawa Kikunojō I, who was born some twenty years after Ayame, when *onnagata* became *onnagata* as we know them today. That is to say, *onnagata* apply deformation [as their expressing methodology] to the women they perform" (*Edo-jidai no Kabuki Yakusha*, 147).

Not only do these kabuki scholars differentiate Ayame and Kikunojō, but they also relate the discontinuity to the differences between the two kinds of *onnagata* theories enunciated in the two texts. In fact, the two scholars conclude that the essence of Ayame's performance lies in a realistic sketch (*shajitsu*) of women, whereas Kikunojō's is a constructed form (*kata*) that signifies Woman and seeks a theoretical explanation from the two treatises (Gunji, *Kabuki no Katachi* 230–31; Taguchi, *Edo-jidai no Kabuki Yakusha*, 147–49). Put another way, they see the transition of *onnagata* artistry from the imitation of women to the construction of artistic and artificial femininity in the two *onnagata* and their texts.

While the attention to *kata* in "The Secret Transmissions of an *Onnagata*" is significant, my questions are as follows. To begin with, if the two texts had presented fundamentally separate points and the newer one had become the status quo for *onnagata* tradition, then "The Secret Transmissions of an *Onnagata*," and not "The Words of Ayame," would have been treated by later *onnagata* as the single most important treatise on *onnagata* artistry. That did not happen, however. More important, precisely due to the externality-internality fusion, realistic sketches and forms cannot be distinguished clearly, not to mention put in the relation of *différance*. In other words, while I agree with the observations made by the kabuki scholars that "The Words of Ayame" aims at "realistic sketches" while "The Secret Transmissions of an *Onnagata*" seeks "forms," I consider them two *slightly different* tactics for the sake of the same strategy, which is to present womanliness as that which merges the exterior and the interior.

79   *Onna Daigaku*, 202–5. For a comprehensive analysis of etiquette books in the Edo era, see Ikegami, *Bonds of Civility*, 324–59.
80   The question of whether constructionism and constructivism can be effectively differentiated in this particular context requires further analysis.
81   *Onna Daigaku*, 202–5.
82   Uno, "Women," 17–41; Minamoto Ryōen, *Tokugawa Shisō Shōshi*, 98–100.
83   Sanford, "Wind, Waters, Stupas, Mandalas" 24.
84   Wakita, "Kankō ni Atatte," 3.
85   An *ie* in this context is, therefore, not so much a biological community as a corporation. See Uno, "Women," 23.
86   *Onna Daigaku*, 202.
87   Kano, *Acting Like a Woman*, 23–24; emphasis in original.
88   Regarding the aforementioned objection to the exteriority-interiority fusion proposed by Makuzu, Gramlich-Oka offers an insightful observation: "In particular when we consider the prevalent notion in medical discourse that gender did not depend on biological sex, it was not unfeasible for the *onnagata* to be defined within the category of woman. For that reason, perhaps, Makuzu's view of the *onnagata* was a direct critique of this perception. Since, by her account, she had seen two of the leading *onnagata* (Segawa Kikunojō II and Nakamura Noshio) up close at her father's home, we can assume that Makuzu had the opportunity to observe them carefully. I can only conjecture about whether, when Makuzu eradicated and simply rejected the idea that the *onnagata* could ever be a 'woman,' her view represented the fear that the *onnagata* undermined the already ambiguous and

fluctuating category of woman, which she sought to clarify unconditionally. Perhaps seen in a context in which the gendered notions of woman, feminineness, and femaleness were vague and changeable, Makuzu's categorization of the two sexes might explain the rigid essentialism that tried to refute what she saw as the elusiveness of gender" (*Thinking Like a Man*, 187).

89   Cf. "gay is to straight *not* as copy is to original, but, rather, as copy is to copy" (Butler, *Gender Trouble*, 31; emphasis in original).

90   "Onnagata wa daiichi onna ni narisumashi" (Hachimonji and Hachimonji, *Shinsen Kokon Yakusha Taizen*, 69).

91   "Sareba butai mo hon no onna to mieshi to nari" (ibid., 70). Here Sawamura Kodenji I (b. 1665) is described as follows: "In the fourth month of 1683, [a group including Kodenji went on for an excursion to a temple. On their way back,] Kodenji said, it seems like I'm having gynecological disorders [*chi no michi*], as I'm being swayed on a palanquin all day long. Gen'emon, a male-role actor, laughed at this, saying, even if you are an *onnagata*, what nonsense for a man to have gynecological disorders. Saikaku intervened, however. Since [he has memorized] women's language well, he just describes a headache as gynecological disorders, which must demonstrate his daily etiquette. It is commendable for *onnagata* if they use women's language even for trivial things. [In this manner, Saikaku] is said to have acclaimed [Kodenji]. Accordingly, [Kodenji] is said to have looked like a real woman onstage as well" (ibid.).

92   This problem should not be totally explained away as rhetoric, however. Cultivation was a significant means of *internalizing* second nature in one's body. In addition, as Minamoto Junko explains, a Buddhist concept called "metamorphosis into male" (*henjō nanshi*) presupposes transformation on the level of the body, "the idea that a woman could not become a buddha without first being reborn in a male body" ("Buddhism," 88).

93   Such an idea, or, more precisely, a logic that made possible such an idea, was not necessarily isolated. Robertson states: "Shingaku rhetoricians . . . sought to fuse sex and gender. . . . Sex was perceived as subordinate to gender" ("Shingaku Woman," 90). Needless to say, Shingaku (Heart learning) did not aim to create male *onnagata* who could suffer from gynecological disorders. Aim and intention aside, however, on the level of the logic that the discourses presuppose, *onnagata* introduced here are more in line with the examples Robertson analyzes than with present-day *onnagata*, whose artistry is understood as the exclusive property of male *onnagata*.

94   Yamakawa, "Onoe Taganojō Intabyū," 233.

95   Ihara et al., "Gekidankai 3," 74.

96   Ichikawa Monnosuke, "Ichikawa Monnosuke Jiden," 134.

97   Takeshiba, "Meiji Shonen no Onnagata,"36.

98   Onoe Baikō VI, *Onnagata no Koto*, 99; Isaka Baisetsu, "Godaime Utaemon no Kaikyūdan Jō," 102. Nakamura Utaemon VI, the son of Utaemon V, stands by this point: "When my mother did the *marumage* hairdo, she looked exactly like my

father [in the role of] Lady Tamate" ("Watashi no Rirekisho," 343). Although the son describes his mother as looking like his father, considering the father's own words, as well as the multilateral citation discussed earlier, we cannot know whether she resembled him or he resembled her.

99   Hozumi Ikan recorded Chikamatsu's words as follows: "That which is *gei* resides in the ambiguous border (*hiniku*) between what is real (*jitsu*) and what is false (*kyo*)" ("Chikamatsu no Gensetsu," 358). This notion is called "*kyojitsu hiniku no kan*" or "*kyojitsu hiniku kan ron*" (the theory of an ambiguous border between the false and the real) and is frequently cited in the realm of Japanese theater (Shuzui and Ōkubo, "Kaisetsu," 16).

6. NATURALLY DISCIPLINED

1   Hachimonji and Hachimonji, *Shinsen Kokon Yakusha Taizen*, 69.
2   See, e.g., *Kabuki Hyōbanki Shūsei*, vol. 5, 38, and vol. 3, 200.
3   "Sonomama no sugata" (*Kabuki Hyōbanki Shūsei*, vol. 3, 548).
4   "Sonomama no onna" (ibid, 316).
5   Leiter, *Frozen Moments*, 154.
6   Hozumi, "Chikamatsu no Gensetsu," 358.
7   Sakata, *Sakata Tōjūrō*, 49.
8   Fukuoka, "Ayamegusa," 322. This section, the second-longest section in the treatise, recounts how Ayame benefited from Gorozaemon's patronage. The wealthy landed samurai provided not only pecuniary sponsorship but also intellectual support that was instrumental for Ayame's success as an actor. Ayame was especially grateful for the advice regarding noh, and he took his patron's nickname, Gonshichi, which he certainly used when he was a male-role actor in 1721 and 1722. Ayame's *yagō* (shop name), Tachibanaya, also expresses the debt of gratitude he owed to this patron.
9   Sakata, *Sakata Tōjūrō*, 48–49.
10 Nakamura Kankurō, *Nakamuraya Sandai Yakusha no Seishun*, 182–83.
11 Renchibō, "Sadoshima Nikki," 376.
12 Gunji, "Kabuki Buyō," 51.
13 Zeami, *Shikadō*, 112.
14 Fukuoka, "Ayamegusa," 322.
15 Sakata, *Sakata Tōjūrō*, 47–51. Takechi was born into a millionaire-merchant household, and he and his father exhausted their wealth protecting practitioners of traditional arts in wartime, who were all much obliged to them. Accordingly, Takechi managed to make an unusually luxurious arrangement for the schooling of his protégés.
16 Ibid., 47–51.
17 *Gidayū* is a musical genre subsumed under *jōruri*. It is named after Takemoto Gidayū (1651–1714), a famous chanter in the history of the puppet theater. A *gidayū* chanter, accompanied by a shamisen player, recites all the puppets' lines and pro-

vides a descriptive narration as well. To be precise, the puppets' lines and the narration are not strictly demarcated. For an analysis of this phenomenon, see Sakai, *Voices*, 140–76.

18 *Onnagata* Nakamura Shikaku II (1900–1981) states: "The cultivation for elocution of kabuki actors has depended on *jōruri* training. This is because in *jōruri*, a single chanter will do everything, from scenes and weather to all the people from every single class, so one can learn [all of those]. This was the basic education [in elocution for kabuki actors]" ("Kabuki Haiyū no Hassei Shugyō," 12).

19 Sakata, *Sakata Tōjūrō*, 48. To be precise, we do not know whether or not Tōjūrō's body movement was made slippery compared to a hypothetical body that would not have gone through such training, so, theoretically speaking, we cannot totally erase—or ascertain—the possibility of slippery gestures.

20 Ibid., 48.

21 Ibid., 48–49.

22 Suzuki Tadashi, "Ashi no Bunpō," 64.

23 Tōjūrō gives a concrete example of the role of Ohatsu in *Double Suicide at Sonezaki* (Sonezaki shinjū) (1703) by Chikamatsu, the performance that brought him a great success as an *onnagata*. He associates his ability to run swiftly in the role of Ohatsu, taking her lover's hand while retaining the figure of an *onnagata*, with the said gait training of his youth: "Such memories of the body [of the training] came to have an effect [on me] in later performances" (Sakata, *Sakata Tōjūrō*, 49).

24 Nakamura Kankurō, *Nakamuraya Sandai Yakusha no Seishun*, 181–83.

25 Nixon, Tan, and Chellappa, *Human Identification*, 2.

26 Takechi, *Kabuki I*, 168.

27 Hahn, *Sensational Knowledge*, 64–65.

28 Nihon Geijutsu Bunka Shinkōkai, "Kōwakamai."

29 *Hayachine no Fu*.

30 Watarai, "'Nanba' Aruki o Kangaeru," pt. 2, 68–69.

31 Hearn, *Glimpses*, 133.

32 Takechi, *Kabuki I*, 173.

33 Watanabe Ichirō, "Heihō Densho Keisei ni tsuite no Ichi-shiron," 655, 659.

34 Ashihara, "Mitsugorō," 91–93.

35 Yano, Kaneda, and Oda, *Nanba Bashiri*; Yano et al., *Nanba no Shintairon*; Gakushū, *Kakumei*; Gakushū, *Kaizō*.

36 See, e.g., Kōno and Maeda, *Ken no Shisō*, 27–44.

37 Oriyama, *Suetsugu Shingo Takano Susumu Eikō eno Josō*, 144–49.

38 "The theory of Japaneseness" tends to be certain self-appointed Orientalism (also known as reverse Orientalism) and performs feats of simultaneously *presupposing* and *inducing* the uniqueness of the Japanese (see Maki Isaka, *Secrecy*, 10). Sakai Naoki points out that it is the narrative excusing the Japanese for not becoming Westerners because they are uniquely Japanese ("Joron," 20). As for reverse Orientalism, Kano lucidly defines it as "an internalization of the Orientalist paradigm by the Orientalized" ("Toward a Critique," 522; see also 539–43). In the case of *nanba*, the excuse is visibly devious: the Japanese learned how to walk in the Meiji

era, but in fact, what they had done before was unique and superior. While the comprehensive explanation of the theory of Japaneseness is beyond the scope of this book, it performs feats of presupposing the uniqueness of the Japanese while inducing it at the same time at the cost of intellectual vulnerability. The constant shift between universalist and particularist narratives, unwitting or otherwise, is one of such "intellectually slippery" methods deployed in the theory of Japaneseness (see Maki Isaka, *Secrecy*, 10–11).

39 For example, it appeared in an episode of the sitcom *Scrubs*, in which a resident wearing kabuki makeup walks in the *nanba* gait, and audiences are expected to be amused by the weirdness of kabuki as represented by these two features, makeup and *nanba*.

40 Watarai, "'Nanba' Aruki o Kangaeru," pt. 1, 69–72.

41 Ibid., pt. 2, 72. *Nanba* is also studied in the realm of high technology. The High Technology Research Center at the Saitama Institute of Technology created a robot called Genbe (also Genbei), which does the *nanba* movements. As Robertson discusses, high technology is not independent of cultural values: "I argue that new bio- and robot technologies are being deployed to reify old or 'traditional' values" ("Robo Sapiens Japanicus," 369). For the robot Genbe, see, e.g., Kawazoe, "Mechanism of Robustness," 241–42.

42 Kōno Ryōsen, "Butō, Bujutsu, Shūkyō Girei," 202–28.

43 Yang, "'Nanba Aruki,'" 176–82. This study was supported by a fellowship from the Japan Foundation in the fiscal year 2007, which is indicative of the presence of academic attention to *nanba* (182).

44 Kōno and Mitsuoka, *Bugaku Tankyū*.

45 Kōno and Kōno, *Unfamiliar Japanese Martial Arts*. To be precise, Kōno Yoshinori did not mention the term *"nanba"* when explaining various specific body techniques; it was obvious, however, that the basic posture he maintained and the basic posture each technique is based on require *nanba*.

46 Ashihara, "Nanban," 64–75.

47 Watarai, "'Nanba' Aruki o Kangaeru," pt. 2, 68.

48 Ashihara, "Nanban," 66–67. Ashihara gives an example of French scientist and chronophotographer Étienne-Jules Marey (1830–1904), who mentions this type of locomotion in passing: "One sometimes sees on a Greek vase a group of runners in the most curious positions. . . . On the Greek vase the arm and leg belonging to the same side are represented as moving in the same directions. Now, was this style of running . . . really practiced on the ancient race-course? or is it a mistake on the part of the decorator of the vase? This is a question we are unable to answer. . . . It is certainly a question worth considering" (*Movement*, 171).

49 Karatani, *Nihon Kindai Bungaku no Kigen*.

50 For a discussion of this change in the context of modern Japanese theater, see Maki Isaka, "Osanai Kaoru's Dilemma," 119–33.

51 Murohoshi, "Meiji Ikō no Wōkingu Kyōiku," 64–65.

52 Ibid., 64.

53 Ibid., 65.

54 Kōno and Maeda, *Ken no Shisō*, 29.
55 Murohoshi, "Meiji Ikō no Wōkingu Kyōiku," 65.
56 Ibid., 66.
57 Ibid., 64.
58 Takechi, *Dentō Ronkō*, 74–79.
59 Miura, *Shintai no Zerodo*, 138. For a good summary of the scholarly discussion on *nanba*, see Hayamizu, "Nanba Aruki-kō"; for discussion on *nanba* in kabuki studies, see Ōya, "'Nanba' Genryū-kō."
60 Ran.
61 Yuasa, *Shintairon*, 153; emphasis in original.
62 *Terakoya*.
63 Ibid.
64 Ashihara, "Nanban," 64–65.
65 Watarai, "'Nanba' Aruki o Kangaeru," pt. 1, 72. For the *nanba* shoes, see Ushioda, *Mono to Ningen no Bunkashi*, 58–67, 91–92, 233. Ushioda proposes that the name of the shoes comes from *nae* (young rice plant) (60).
66 Quoted in Hirano, *Nihon Buyō Nyūmon*, 79.
67 Oka, *Gidayū Hiketsu*, 87.
68 Nakayama, *Edo-ban Jōruri Hiden Shō*, 227.
69 Nearly identical remarks also appear in other *gidayū*-chanting handbooks. See, e.g., *Hanakenuki* (also known as *Ongyoku Hanakenuki*) (1797) (Taihei, *Hanakenuki*, 241); *Chikuhō Sōben Shō* (1807) (Katayama Rinrokken, *Chikuhō Sōben Shō*, 248). In addition, Takechi cites a text called *The Secret Opuses of Jōruri, Supplement* (Zōho jōruri hikyoku shō) (1757) as the only text that includes this sentence: "If the right leg moves forward, the left hand moves forward" (Takechi and Tomioka, *Dentō Geijutsu towa Nani Nanoka*, 211). For the text in question, see the supplement section of *The Secret Opuses of Jōruri, Exegesis* (Jōruri hikyoku shō) by Takemoto Harima-no-Jō (*Jōruri Hikyoku Shō*, 28). As mentioned above, though, there are several texts besides this text that include similar remarks.
70 Takechi, *Kabuki I*, 173.
71 Ashihara, "Nanban," 64–75.
72 Takechi, *Kabuki I*, 170; Takechi, *Bunraku*, 467.
73 Takechi, *Bunraku*, 467.
74 Takechi, *Kabuki I*, 169.
75 Takechi states: "In a sense, kabuki had already lost its raison d'être in the Tenpō era [1830–44]. In my opinion, that is. Since that time, there has been no creative energy. . . . [This is] because *nanba* disappeared as urbanization progressed. So kabuki became an urban art, and amid that [process of urbanization], it lost the expressive power of *nanba* and its own raison d'être. It was until approximately the Tenmei era [1781–89] that something *nanba*-ish was still vividly alive in kabuki" (Takechi and Tomioka, *Dentō Geijutsu towa Nani Nanoka*, 210–12).
76 Ibid., 211.
77 See, e.g., Miura, *Shintai no Zerodo*, 134; Hayamizu, "Nanba Aruki-kō," 21–22.

78 Takechi, *Kabuki I*, 172. Unfortunately, Takechi does not specify the woodblock print to which he refers. Cf. Hahn, *Sensational Knowledge*, 64–65.
79 Kōno and Maeda, *Ken no Shisō*, 29.
80 Murohoshi, "Meiji Ikō no Wōkingu Kyōiku," 64–65.
81 *Terakoya*.
82 Kōno and Maeda, *Ken no Shisō*, 31.
83 Onoe Baikō VI states: "Among *onnagata*'s technique is 'puppet-gesture'" (*Onnagata no Koto*, 112). In bunraku, most of the puppets except for the minor ones are maneuvered by three puppeteers, with the main puppeteer moving the head and the right hand, the second one the left hand, and the third one the feet. The method of three puppeteers using a puppet was invented in 1734 and has been in use ever since.
84 Gunji, *Odori no Bigaku*, 205.
85 Nakamura Utaemon [V], "Geidan," 55. The quotation is from "Night Stories by Kaigyoku" (Geidan Kaigyoku yawa), accounts-on-*gei* by Nakamura Utaemon V, dictated to Abe Yutaka, a series published by *Entertainment Illustrated* magazine (Engei gahō) from October 1933 through April 1941. Kaigyoku is one of Utaemon V's haiku pen names. "Night Stories by Kaigyoku" was later published as a monograph, *The Kata of Kabuki* (Kabuki no Kata), edited by Abe, and is considered an important accounts-on-*gei* book by Utaemon V (Tokyo: Bunkoku Shobō, 1950; rpt., Tokyo: Tōkyō Gakufū Shoin, 1959). Incidentally, I have not yet finalized the reading of the phrase "those who can move should avoid" puppet-gesture (*ugokeru hito wa sonna michi o yukazu ni*). One strong possibility is that since puppet-gesture requires heightened kinesthetics, Utaemon might have been warning those who are physically capable of doing it *not* to be tempted to do so.
86 Onoe Baikō VI, *Onnagata no Koto*, 113. Although himself a practitioner of puppet-gesture, Baikō endorses Utaemon's "accusation" in concrete terms: "[We] often do puppet-gesture. Puppets can show off the beauty of the form, doing gestures humans cannot do, with the idea that the puppets must resemble humans. But when humans become puppets, . . . there is hardly any reason to look good. But, for example, in the role of Princess Yuki in *Kinkakuji Temple*, one would need to keep up the scene alone, completely tied up [with string]. You would not be able to do that without considerable skill, but if you do puppet-gesture, that'll work. Say, for example, sitting down at the edge of a well. Even if you can't do it as a princess, you can do it as a puppet.

"Of course, Mr. Itō Seiu would say that it's possible to show off [your skill] even if you're tied up, but as far as we are concerned, puppet-gesture can let you cheat (*ocha o nigosu*), so we are using it" (*Ume no Shitakaze*, 210).
87 Utaemon V's ancestor Nakamura Utaemon III (1778–1838), though not related by blood, is recorded as skilled at puppet-gesture and came into vogue with that skill (Sawai, "Sansei Nakamura Utaemon no 'Ningyōburi,'" 15–34).
88 Sawai Manami studies another actor who played a significant role in assuring the position of kabuki in modern Japan, Ichikawa Danjūrō IX (1838–1903), and con-

cludes that, despite his well-known contempt for puppet-gesture, he was well trained in the technique ("Kyūsei Ichikawa Danjūrō to 'Ningyōburi,'" 156–61).

89   Kawaguchi, Yoshimura, and Takechi, "Mai no Gijutsu," 147. Although this article was published under the three names, the ideas in it can be considered Takechi's for the following reasons. The text was reprinted in another book of his, with a note appearing at the end: "Upon hearing the accounts-on-*gei* of Kawaguchi Hideko, the *iemoto* of the Kawaguchi dance school, and Yoshimura Yūki, the *iemoto* of the Yoshimura dance school, I added my ideas, systematized them, and published this piece" (Takechi, "Mai no Gijutsu," 113–34.) Another work of Takechi's also contains this piece and treats it as his own work (*Bunraku*, 458–71). Only the first version contains photographs of dance sequences by Kawaguchi and Yoshimura, which are highly illustrative of the text. *Iemoto* (stem-family head) is the institutionalized head of a school dedicated to a specific *gei*, and many schools of dance, tea ceremony, and the like, tend to operate in the *iemoto* system, a hierarchical and hereditary institution for a specific *gei*. For *iemoto*, see also Maki Isaka, *Secrecy*.

90   Sakata and Kameoka, *Yume*, 32–33.

91   "In 1999, when Ganjirō-san [Tōjūrō] played [the role of] Princess Yaegaki using puppet-gesture, in the 'Back Garden' scene, . . . I told him that if he does puppet-gesture too well, [he] wouldn't look like a puppet. This is what my master[, the late Yoshida Bungorō,] always said. He would say, 'The poorer, the better.' Ganjirō-san grasped the true meaning quickly and performed wonderfully" (ibid., 34–35). Yoshida Bungorō III (1869–1962) left his own accounts-on-*gei*, in which I cannot locate the alleged remark to which Tōjūrō and Bunjaku refer. This is not unexpected, as his accounts-on-*gei* are about bunraku puppetry and not about kabuki's adoption of it (see Yoshida Bungorō, *Bungorō Geidan*).

92   Kawaguchi, Yoshimura, and Takechi, "Mai no Gijutsu," 147. In contrast, Gunji's definition of "puppet-body" does not assign a specifically positive attribution to it, which is not surprising considering his already positive view of "puppet-gesture": "Also, . . . there are some pieces in which dancers become puppet-body. The puppet in this case is either a mechanical puppet [*karakuri ningyō*] or a puppet on a float [*dashi ningyō*]" (*Odori no Bigaku*, 205).

The distinction between *odori* dance and *mai* dance is highly complicated, and there is no clear-cut boundary. Figuratively, another term for dance, *buyō* (not to be confused with *butō*) is written with the characters for *mai* and *odori*. Takechi himself states: "It is often said that Japanese dance [*nihon buyō*] contains two types, *mai* and *odori*, but when it comes to the difference between them, the fact is that we can hardly answer that question" ("Mai no Gijutsu," 129). He relates *mai* to the motion of circling and *odori* to that of jumping but then continues: "In actuality, it is easy to find the influence of *mai* in *odori*, and sometimes *mai* contains the elements of *odori* as well" (129). Gunji also associates *odori* with jumping and *mai* with circling (*Odori no Bigaku*, 128). Inoue Yachiyo IV (1905–2004), a former *iemoto* of the Inoue school (a school specializing in *mai*), offers a slightly different explanation: "If *odori* is vibrant and curvilinear (*yakudō-teki de kyokusen-teki*), *mai* is static and linear (*sei-teki de chokusen-teki*)" (Katayama Keijirō, *Inoue Yachiyo*

Geiwa, 60). Gunji further states that *odori* is unconscious (*muishiki*) and thus difficult to connect with language, whereas *mai* is ritualistic, artificial, and conscious, which enabled it to become *monomane* (mimicry, role-playing) and to be connected with literature and storytelling (*Odori no Bigaku*, 129).

93   Ōnishi, "Kudoki, Ningyōburi," 69.
94   Kawaguchi, Yoshimura, and Takechi, "Mai no Gijutsu," 147.
95   Endō, *Sansei Inoue Yachiyo*, 210–13; Okada, "Inoue-ryū to Ningyō Jōruri," 81–93. The Inoue school is also characterized by its use of noh theater (see, e.g., Katayama Hiromichi, "Kyōmai Inoue-ryū no Hongyō-mono," 8–10). It is said that Inoue Yachiyo II (1790–1868), the second *iemoto* of the school, actively adopted noh and *bunraku* elements (Endō, *Sansei Inoue Yachiyo*, 211–13; Katayama Keijirō, *Inoue Yachiyo Geiwa*, 206; Katayama Keijirō, "Kyōmai Inoue-ryū no Nagare," 180–83). There are several accounts of Yachiyo II's life dates: for 1795–1868, see Okada, "Inoue-ryū to Ningyō Jōruri," 81; for 1781–1868, see Kyōto Shinbun Henshūkyoku, *Kyōmai*, 49. The latter book is a revised reprint of Inoue Yachiyo IV's autobiography, which was published as a series in the newspaper *Kyōto Shinbun*.
96   Katayama Keijirō, *Inoue Yachiyo Geiwa*, 206–7.
97   Ibid., 208–9.
98   Takechi, *Dentō to Danzetsu*, 288. Yachiyo II is said to have studied noh seriously (Endō, *Sansei Inoue Yachiyo*, 211–13; Katayama Keijirō, *Inoue Yachiyo Geiwa*, 206; Katayama Keijirō, "Kyōmai Inoue-ryū no Nagare," 180–83). Yachiyo III married noh actor Katayama Kurōemon VI. Their grandson, noh actor Katayama Kurōemon VIII (also known as Katayama Hiromichi), married a disciple of Yachiyo III, later Yachiyo IV. Noh actor Katayama Keijirō is the son of Kurōemon VIII and Yachiyo IV and the uncle of Yachiyo V, the current head of the school.
99   Katayama Keijirō, *Inoue Yachiyo Geiwa*, 210. Explicit examples are called "*gidayū-things*" (*gidayū-mono*).
100 Takechi, *Dentō to Danzetsu*, 288; emphasis added.
101 Inoue Yachiyo IV says that the school declined requests from male dancers who hoped to learn the Inoue dance until 1950, when she began teaching several kabuki actors—including Tōjūrō—upon Takechi's request. She explains her reason for breaking an important rule as follows: "We had an argument at that time as well, but I decided to break our longtime tradition because that was a pure project that Mr. Takechi was doing for the sake of the reconstruction of theater, spending his own money" (Kyōto Shinbun Henshūkyoku, *Kyōmai*, 53–54).
102 Ibid., 47.
103 For the life dates 1838–1939, see Katayama Keijirō, "Kyōmai Inoue-ryū no Nagare," 183; for 1838–1938, see Okada, "Inoue-ryū to Ningyō Jōruri," 81.
104 Takechi, *Buyō no Gei*, 267.

7. FEMALE ONNAGATA IN THE POROUS LABYRINTH

1   Cf. Mezur: "A performative onnagata gender role is a fiction of female-likeness based on a male 'body beneath.' In other words, the performer is actually a Japa-

nese man (with male genitalia) underneath the onnagata stylized acts" ("Beautiful Boys," 7).

2. Here, I am borrowing Hart's parlance, which is set in a different context, American contemporary feminist performance art: "Madonna has already succumbed to the master discourse on femininity through the excessive rendering of the maternal" ("Motherhood," 124). Needless to say, the term "honorary man" is bracketed here, which Enomoto finds pathological in the given context, that is, modern Japanese theater ("Onnagata Engi," 258).

3. Mishima, "Baikō Katsugare no Hanashi," 59.
4. Yanagisawa, *Enyū Nikki*, 162–63.
5. Mitamura, *Ryūei Saigo no Okyōgenshi*, 122.
6. Hayashi, "Daimyō," 226.
7. Ibid., 221, 224, 225. A *hanamichi*-rampway runs from the stage through the auditorium. A mouse-gate (*nezumi-kido*) is a small entrance in the theater for audiences.
8. Suzuki Hiroko, "Genroku Kabuki," 104. Daimyo is a privileged samurai status with an allowance of 10,000 *koku* or more. (A *koku* is a unit of cubic measure, used to measure a domain that generates rice equivalent to the number of *koku* indicated.) Daimyo were obligated to maintain residences in Edo, where they had to stay on a regular basis and retain their wives and offspring.
9. Hayashi, "Daimyō," 214.
10. Takei, *Wakashu Kabuki*, 309. The primary sources for parlor-theater are considerably different from those for kabuki in theater districts and consist mainly of (1) patrons' diaries, such as Nobutoki's *Party Diary*, and (2) records of domains that used the services of parlor-theater, including three by Shuzui, "Tottori," "Zoku Tottori," and "Zoku Zoku," or other records; see Takei, *Wakashu Kabuki*, 310–18.
11. Hayashi, "Daimyō," 226. A note on terminology: Historically, the term "*zashiki-kyōgen*" (parlor-theater) had been used; Takei states that he coined the term "*zashiki-shibai*" (parlor-kabuki) from the historically used phrase "*zashiki-kyōgen*," which appears in a record of the Hirosaki domain (*Wakashu Kabuki*, 332). Hayashi agrees that it accurately describes the entertainment arts in question; she employs a narrower word, "*zashiki-kabuki*," for occasions when kabuki was part of the performance ("Daimyō," 216). Both "*zashiki-shibai*" and "*zashiki-kabuki*" are translated here as "parlor-kabuki" for the sake of clarity. Other types of theater were also used, such as *jōruri*. Primary sources other than domain records, such as theater-books, also use the phrase "*zashiki-kyōgen*"; for example, in a section titled "Rural Theater" (Inaka Shibai no Koto), *The Complete Book of Actors through All Ages, the New Edition* reads as follows: "Especially in Edo, there is a troupe called Kanryaku-za [Simple Theater]. It will cost much more to hire a true theater [*hon-shibai*] for parlor-theater. So [Kanryaku-za] is hired instead and made to perform as the entertainment for guests" (Hachimonji and Hachimonji, *Shinsen Kokon Yakusha Taizen*, 17).
12. Takei, *Wakashu Kabuki*, 333.
13. Suzuki Hiroko, "Kyōhō-ki Edo Kabuki," 24.

14 Hayashi, "Yashikikata," 219–23.
15 Takei, *Wakashu Kabuki*, 313. The names were deleted by pasting a piece of paper over them, but Takei managed to read the names through the paper. Takei extrapolates from this that some domain records do not contain information on parlor-theater even if it was produced (312–13).
16 Suzuki Hiroko, "Kyōhō-ki Edo Kabuki," 28, 30, 36; Suzuki Hiroko, "Genroku Kabuki," 110; Hayashi, "Yashikikata," 223–26.
17 Takei, *Wakashu Kabuki*, 309; Suzuki Hiroko, "Kyōhō-ki Edo Kabuki," 36, 40.
18 Hayashi, "Daimyō," 225.
19 Ibid., 214, 213; Takei, *Wakashu Kabuki*, 312–13.
20 Hayashi, "Daimyō," 221.
21 Ichikawa Kumehachi, "Gigei no Hanashi," 109.
22 Ichikawa Kumehachi, "Meika Shinsōroku," 108.
23 Norizuki, "Okyōgenshi to Iu Edo no Joyū," 11–16. Sato appears in Yanagisawa, *Enyū Nikki*, 162–63.
24 For example, Ichikawa Suisen III (1917–1978) was the granddaughter of Danjūrō IX; Mizutani Yaeko II (b. 1939) is the daughter of Morita Kan'ya XIV (1907–1975); and Namino Kuriko (b. 1945) is the daughter of Nakamura Kanzaburō XVII (1909–1988). *Shinpa* emerged as a new type of theater but ended up being congenial to kabuki theater. In short, *shinpa* plays were kabuki-oriented but performed by new people. In terms of dramaturgy and acting methodology, *shinpa* belonged to the kabuki establishment, and in terms of power politics, *shinpa* constituted the periphery of the establishment. Due to its congruous relationship with kabuki, *shinpa* helps highlight the destiny of female members of kabuki families, which is epitomized by the following phrase from a tribute to Suisen: "Suisen, who would have probably been Ichikawa Danjūrō XI, if she had been born male" (Agi, "Ichikawa Suisen o Itamu," 114). Likewise, Kanzaburō is said to have spoken of his daughter as follows: "If she were a man, Kuriko would have made a great kabuki actor" (Komatsu, *Kanzaburō, Araburu*, 141). To all intents and purposes, *shinpa* functioned as the constitutive outside, that is, the exterior necessary to assure the interior, and the transference of women from kabuki to *shinpa* was a telling phenomenon.
25 While it is outside the topic of the present chapter, "kabuki daughters who perform" contrast with another cluster of kabuki daughters: those who marry kabuki actors. In the Edo era, states Taguchi, "for the wives of kabuki actors, there were some geisha, the daughters of merchants, and the like, but the majority of them were nevertheless related to kabuki circles, especially actors' daughters and sisters" (*Edo-jidai no Kabuki Yakusha*, 164). The difference between the two groups is intriguing, especially for kabuki in modern times, because it helps explain what Ueno has named "the power of the Empress Dowager": "In patrilineal society, there is no other way for women to survive than becoming 'the mother of a son.' It is women's wisdom and strategy for their survival in patriarchy that they dominate their sons and become 'mothers of an heir.' I call this 'mother's power' 'the power of the Empress Dowager.' Only because they have hope to attain the position [with] the 'power of the Empress Dowager' at the end of their lives do women become

complicit in patriarchy" ("Orientarizumu," 123). Arguably, this applies more to kabuki circles today than to those of the Edo era, for, as Ōzasa Yoshio suggests, kabuki society has now become ancestry oriented, defined by blood, much more than it used to be (*Nihon Gendai Engekishi*, 335–40). Related to this phenomenon are the meaning of biological maternity and the meaning of Nature. The following words by Namino Yoshie, the wife of Kanzaburō XVIII and the mother of his two sons, appear to evince a certain serenity of an Empress Dowager that offsets the chagrin of a kabuki daughter:

"'I was born as the second daughter of kabuki actor Nakamura Shikan VII. Everybody, including my mother, not to mention my father, must have been hoping, "definitely a son, this time for sure," but I was born betraying their expectations.

"'What? Another girl?'

"'What a pity.'

"'My condolences.'

"'Don't get disappointed.'

"These were the first greetings of those who came to congratulate. Some even could not make [it to the home or hospital] and returned home, so I heard.

"Even [people not interested in] feminism or women's lib will surely think, 'That's too bad,' but in the kabuki world, where only after a boy is born [could you hear] 'Congratulations,' there is nothing you can do about it if you're greeted with condolences when a girl is born" (*Sannin Momotarō*, 13–14).

The three Momotarōs in the book title signify her husband and her two sons, all of whom played the role of Momotarō for their respective stage debuts.

26 Ichikawa Kumehachi, "Meika Shinsōroku," 108. Mitsue was a disciple of Bandō Mitsugorō III (also known as Eiki Mitsugorō, Eiki-no Mitsugorō) (1773–1831), a major male kabuki actor.

27 Takenoya et al., "Ichikawa Kumehachi Tsuiokuroku," 140 (this part was written by [Oka] Onitarō).

28 Kamiyama, "Kumehachi no Zanzō," 18–20.

29 Ibid., 17–18.

30 For mention of Kumehachi in English-language works, see Brandon, "Kabuki and Shakespeare," 24, 28, 48; Kano, *Acting Like a Woman*, 32, 69, 169, 239; Mezur, *Beautiful Boys*, 117; Levy, *Sirens*, 246–47; Edelson, *Danjūrō's Girls*, 7–8, 12, 17, 20–25, 31–36, 40, 42, 84, 87, 107, 111–12, 163, 186–87, 189; Edelson, "Female Danjūrō," 69–98. As for Japanese-language texts, there are quite a few theater reviews, interviews, and the like produced in Kumehachi's time; later texts do not so much analyze as introduce those primary sources, except for Kamiyama, "Kumehachi no Zanzō," 17–23. I am in total agreement with the following remark by Brandon: "Kumehachi's career is fascinating and deserves further attention" ("Kabuki and Shakespeare," 48).

31 Ichikawa Kumehachi, "Gigei no Hanashi," 79. When calculating her age, Kumehachi most probably uses the traditional East Asian age-counting method.

32 Depending on the manner of their association with the employer or patron, there

were two types of theater-masters: (1) employed theater-masters (*oyashiki-zuki*), who would routinely offer relatively light entertainment with no stage costumes and the like; (2) theater-masters under patronage (*okakae* or *odeiri*), who would offer full-scale entertainment on special occasions (Ichikawa Kumehachi, "Meika Shinsōroku," 107, 109–10, 112). Mitsue was the second type of theater-master. Mitsue's reputation can be conjectured from the fact that the photograph of her costume was included in a monograph on kabuki costume, and according to its authors, the costume was owned by the Tokyo National Museum at the time of publication: Sōma and Torii, *Kabuki*, 8. Kabuki actor Bandō Mitsugorō VIII (1906–1975) and Takechi also speak of Mitsue as a formidable *gei* practitioner, whom Mitsugorō's father, Mitsugorō VII (1882–1961), had known (Bandō and Takechi, *Gei Jūya*, 32–33).

33 Ichikawa Kumehachi, "Meika Shinsōroku," 108.

34 Ibid., 113. As for her biography, accounts vary, especially regarding her birth date. I have thus far located five possible dates of birth: (1) the third month of 1834, (2) the fifth month of 1834, (3) 1835, (4) the twenty-eighth day of the eleventh month of 1844, and (5) the twenty-eighth day of the eleventh month of 1846. Intriguingly, even her own accounts are not consistent. As of this writing, my conclusions are that she was most likely born in 1846 and that this phenomenon seems not so much a result of sheer confusion or sloppy treatment of dates as a symptom of something critical. First, it tells us that the attribution of maturity—rather than youth—carried a positive implication for women performers in this context. Second, this confusion strongly suggests that Kumehachi ended up being a "misfit," both in terms of gender and of time, for a new era of modern Japan and modern kabuki.

This book follows the theory that she was born on the twenty-eighth day of the eleventh month of 1846. The year 1834 was predominantly cited as the year of birth in her time (see, e.g., Sugiura, *Joyū Kagami*, 81; Iguchi, *Joyū Kagami*, 84). A newspaper article puts 1835 as the birth year (Sokō, "Kumehachi Ichiza no Wakatake-za o Miru," 3). See also Karasuyakko, "Onna Yakusha to Joyū," 152, which describes Kumehachi as "one year or two—or three at the very most—shy of eighty," apparently based on the theory that she was born in 1834 or 1835. Likewise, Ishibashi and Maeda describe her as "nearly sixty years old" (*Tōyō Daitokai*, 189), indicating roughly the late 1830s as her year of birth. When she passed away in July 1913, however, two other possibilities—1844 and 1846—began to be circulated, although many publications kept mentioning the year 1834 as another possibility (e.g., Takenoya et al., "Ichikawa Kumehachi Tsuiokuroku," 154; Takeshiba et al., "Ikeru Joyū Kumehachi," 78–79).

But in an article published in 1907, Kumehachi says, "I'm seventy-four this year" ("Meika Shinsōroku," 115), apparently supporting a birth year of 1834. In another article in the same year, she contradicts herself, saying, "I've been performing up to now, and I'm an aged granny over sixty" ("Gigei no Hanashi," 79), suggesting a birth year of either 1844 or 1846.

The date seems to have been settled as 1846, as epitomized by the entry in the standard encyclopedia of Japanese theater; see "Ichikawa Kumehachi," written by

Kokubu Tamotsu, in *Engeki*, vol. 1, 166. Shinoda Masayuki, however, accepts 1844 as the date but does not specify the reason ("Kenkyū Happyō Yōshi," 98).

Certainly, the events narrated by Kumehachi here would have been considerably puzzling had she been born in 1834 or 1835, which would make 1851 or 1852 the year in which Mitsue lost her patrons. It would also make 1856 or 1857 the year in which Kumehachi tried to shift her career from theater-master to woman-actor. In sum, both 1834 and 1835 can hardly be possible, 1844 remains within the range of possibility, and 1846 seems most likely.

35 Ichikawa Kumehachi, "Meika Shinsōroku," 110, 113.

36 Ichikawa Kumehachi, "Gigei no Hanashi," 83. Mitsue's view reflects their reality (i.e., within the hierarchy that positions theater-masters' performance as higher than that of actors playing at big theaters in town). This view is inconsistent with today's understanding of kabuki, which marginalizes theater-masters.

37 A 1920 work reads: "Most *onnagata* [forty or fifty years ago] were to all intents and purposes women, onstage, at home, in dressing rooms, anywhere. . . . [Among them,] Hanshirō was the most impressive. . . . People still talk about him, but, my, you can't see such a beautiful *onnagata* since he passed away. . . . He could completely pass as a woman, even when wearing just lingerie. . . . [When I visited him at home, he would always dress like a woman], and he surely looked like nothing other than a woman" (Takeshiba, "Meiji Shonen no Onnagata," 36).

38 Takeshiba et al., "Ikeru Joyū Kumehachi," 78 (this part was written by Suzuki Shunpo). Mitsue referred Kumehachi to Hanshirō by virtue of the same *yagō* (shop name) to which the Bandōs and the Iwais belonged, Yamatoya (Ichikawa Kumehachi, "Gigei no Hanashi," 83). Kabuki families are connected by family names and *yagō*.

39 Due to the complex usage of the word "*onna*" in the discourse of kabuki, we should be careful not to reduce the character for "woman" in Kumehachi's names—*me* in "Kumehachi" (nine-woman-eight) and *onna* in "Onna Danshū" (Woman Danjūrō)—to the fact that she was a woman. The name Kumehachi was originally written differently. *Hachi* was the same character, "eight," but *kume* was a pseudo-Chinese character that combined "long" and "rice," and an important character for Iwai names. There was no "woman" in the original "Kumehachi," and since she came into vogue with this name, there were still residual uses of the old form as well as a mixture of the old and new forms in journals and books even after the characters were changed. "Woman" (*me*) here does not carry primary importance in terms of the sex of the actor. The same *me* character is used in kabuki (male) names as well (e.g., Omezō and Metora). Also, Kumehachi's nickname, Onna Danshū, blends into the discourse of kabuki so nicely that it does not seem to signify any deviation from the norm. The custom of addressing male *onnagata* as "Onna Such and Such" is not absent in the kabuki discourse. Ichikawa Shōchō II (1886–1940), a prominent *onnagata* known for his delicate appearance, was dubbed "Onna Takashimaya" after his *yagō*, Takashimaya. The "Onna" in "Onna Takashimaya" indicated that he was an *onnagata* and not a woman performer. Given this, there is a hypothetical but logical possibility that Kumehachi would have been dubbed "Onna Danshū" even if she had been a male *onnagata*.

40 Onoe, Fujiura, and Hakii, "Seigaku Yawa to Yonsei Gennosuke," 81. Kabuki circles have traditionally been extremely rank conscious, and the ranking of playhouses is one significant factor for ranking actors. Accordingly, actors have been careful about where they perform. While the Kabuki-za Theater was in the top tier of big theaters (ōshibai), the Ryūsei-za Theater was at the bottom of the small theaters (koshibai). Although there was mobility up to a certain point (that is, it was possible for an actor to transfer from a small-theater troupe to a big-theater troupe), such mobility was limited. In addition, it was possible only until the early twentieth century. Taganojō, who also performed with Matasaburō at a top-tier small theater, states: "People called him Two-Dollar Danshū, 'cause he looked like [Danjūrō]. He really was a skillful actor, you see, although people looked down on him [because he performed at the Ryūsei-za Theater]" (Onoe and Andō, "Onoe Taganojō Geidan," pt. 2, 145).

41 Danjūrō was quoted as saying in a newspaper article, 11 July 1888, that he had admitted Iwai Kumehachi ("Onna Haiyū," 3). According to Shinoda, it took several months from admission as a disciple (June 1888) to the name-taking ceremony of Ichikawa Masunojō I (September 1888), during which time she also used another name, Ichikawa Keishū ("Kenkyū Happyō Yōshi," 98). Shinoda further states that several incorrect names based on false reports circulated in newspapers (ibid., 100).

It is impressive that Kumehachi managed to have such prominent masters as Mitsue, Hanshirō, and Danjūrō, but a strong connection to kabuki circles had never been out of the ordinary. Master-disciple relationships and family ties illustrate the association between the kabuki establishment and female kabuki actors (both theater-masters and women-actors). As noted above (n. 26), her master, Mitsue, was a disciple of a major kabuki actor, Mitsugorō. Other examples include, in the case of women-actors, Matsumoto Kinshi, who was Matsumoto Kinshō's disciple; Bandō Noshio, the daughter of Bandō Shūchō II and the wife of Shūchō III; Ichikawa Rikinosuke, who was Ichikawa Gonjūrō's disciple; and Bandō Tamasaburō III, the daughter of Morita Kan'ya XII, the great grandfather of the present Tamasaburō (Tamasaburō V).

42 Shinoda, "Kenkyū Happyō Yōshi," 98.

43 Takenoya et al., "Ichikawa Kumehachi Tsuiokuroku," 138–55; Takeshiba et al., "Ikeru Joyū Kumehachi," 73–79; Sugiura, Joyū Kagami, 81; Iguchi, Joyū Kagami, 84–86.

44 Takenoya et al., "Ichikawa Kumehachi Tsuiokuroku," 139, 141–42, 150–51, 154–55; Takeshiba et al., "Ikeru Joyū Kumehachi," 74–75.

45 Ichikawa Kumehachi, "Gigei no Hanashi," 82; Ichikawa Kumehachi, "Meika Shinsōroku," 108, 112, 115–16.

46 See, e.g., Karasuyakko, "Onna Yakusha to Joyū," 151–54.

47 Ishibashi and Maeda, Tōyō Daitokai, 189.

48 Mayama, "Onnagata," 53.

49 Mayama, "Engeki," 35.

50 Kano, Acting Like a Woman, 16–24.

51 Tobe, "Kichō," 52.

52 As for Kumehachi's performance of men's roles, see, e.g., Ide, "Fukagawa no Onna Shibai," 118–20. See also Bungo no Kami, "Fukagawa-za," 164–65: "[She looked really aged last month], but seeing this *Kezori*, one would dismiss such an impression. . . . Kumehachi presented a magnificent appearance and spoke her lines skillfully. . . . When she stood on the gunwale in the final scene, it was extraordinary; it is by no means possible to think that she is a woman."
53 This is congenial to Laqueur's proposal of a one-sex model: "men and women were arrayed according to their degree of metaphysical perfection" (*Making Sex*, 4–5).
54 Ichikawa Kumehachi, "Meika Shinsōroku," 112.
55 Ichikawa Kumehachi, "Gigei no Hanashi," 83.
56 Ichikawa Kumehachi, "Meika Shinsōroku," 113.
57 Obana, "Joyū Rekihōroku," 28.
58 Ichikawa Kumehachi, "Onnagata," 113.
59 Ichikawa Kumehachi, "Gigei no Hanashi," 85; emphasis added.
60 Karasuyakko, "Onna Yakusha to Joyū," 153.
61 Ichikawa Kumehachi, "Meika Shinsōroku," 116.
62 Takenoya et al. 145, "Ichikawa Kumehachi Tsuiokuroku" (this part was written by Tamura).
63 For a more detailed discussion of this concept, see Maki Isaka, *Secrecy*, 59–61.
64 See, e.g., Ichikawa Kumehachi, "Gigei no Hanashi," 85; Takenoya et al., "Ichikawa Kumehachi Tsuiokuroku," 150 (this part was written by Morizumi Kikuko).
65 Isaka Baisetsu, "Godaime Utaemon no Kaikyūdan Jō," 109.
66 See, e.g., ibid., 101; Nakamura Utaemon V, *Kaigyoku Issekiwa*, 206.
67 See, e.g., Nakamura Shikaku, "Kabuki Haiyū no Hassei Shugyō," 12. Also, *onnagata* Onoe Baikō VII (1915–1995) states: "For *onnagata*, domestic, 'realistic' plays [*sewamono*] are more difficult than dance and the like. Dance is regulated by music. And then, for period pieces [*jidaimono*], *gidayū* helps one perform" (Onoe, Mizutani, and Kinoshita, "Zandankai," 2). In contrast, *onnagata* Nakamura Tokizō V (b. 1955) objects to the idea that *gidayū* is a prerequisite for kabuki acting, including that of *onnagata*. Explaining how he has set up training menus for his two sons, he states: "Baishi [IV, the eldest son (b. 1987)], an *onnagata*, does *kiyomoto* and *koto*-zither. Mantarō [the second son, a male-role actor (b. 1989)] is now doing noh chanting and dance, and I am thinking of adding *gidayū* [to his training menu]. *Onnagata* don't do *gidayū*, as it would deform the vocal cords" ("Jibun no Monosashi o Motsu," 45).
68 In her ethnographic work, Hahn records this notion as still valid in a Japanese dance school (Tachibana-ryū) in contemporary Japan. She calls it "the art of following," a student learning Japanese dance (*nihon buyō*) by following and imitating the teacher (*Sensational Knowledge*, 87), living proof of a tradition that negotiates the space between premodern knowledge and modern episteme.
69 Just as female actors existed in kabuki (theater-masters and women-actors), female *gidayū* performers did, and still do, exist. For detailed documentation and an insightful analysis of female *gidayū* chanters, see Mizuno, *Edo Tōkyō Musume Gidayū no Rekishi*.

70 Nakamura and Matsuo state in the context of Takarazuka theater and popular culture in contemporary Japan that female masculinity is not necessarily sexualized, making a contrast to its counterpart in the West, where "one of the greatest tragedies of post-Freudian society in the United States is the sexualization of all human relationships from mother-infant onwards" ("Female Masculinity," 61). That *gidayū* helps create masculinized *gei* for female performers also demonstrates a possible case of non-sexualized female masculinity. Hierarchy, or, by extension, class, rather than sexuality, is operating in the formation of female masculinity here.
71 Zeami, *Fūshikaden*, 14.
72 Ibid., 30. The term Zeami uses for "authentic source," "*honzetsu*," is the equivalent of "*hongyō*" and "*honmon*" in kabuki discourse. "*Honzetsu*" is used mostly in the context of noh theater and poetry composition to signify their preceding traditions.
73 Ibid., 44.
74 "The subject of the enunciated" (product of the enunciating act) is inside a product such as a text. In the context of *gei* and cultivation, the subject of the enunciated is typically those who established a school, including a mystic figure such as a deity who initially bestows teachings upon the school founder in a dream. The subject of the enunciated authorizes the knowledge. For further details on these mechanisms and logic, see Maki Isaka, *Secrecy*.
75 Mayama, "Engeki," 35; Mayama, "Onnagata," 53.
76 Bungo, "Takemoto Tosatayū," 76.
77 Mizuno, *Edo Tōkyō Musume Gidayū no Rekishi*, 289–90.
78 Performances by Tosahiro are available on CDs. One is included in A. Kimi Coaldrake's book *Women's Gidayū and the Japanese Theatre Tradition*: tracks 4 (n.d.), 7 (20 November 1982), 8 (20 November 1982), and 9 (1 September 1971). While Tosahiro sounds rather aged in tracks 4, 7, and 8, recorded when she was in her mid-eighties, track 9 was recorded a decade earlier and demonstrates her robust, masculine-based, and thus authentically *gidayū* performance, playing the roles of a young husband, a young wife, a bodhisattva, and the narrator (*The Miracle at Tsubosaka* [Tsubosaka reigenki]).
79 Hart, "Introduction: Performing Feminism," 4.
80 In the context of American contemporary feminist performance art, Hart analyzes Karen Finley's *The Theory of Total Blame* (1988), concluding that it "moves toward analysis of historical constructs that render women as always already mothers, and hence as origins of cultural horror. Here Finley uses parody and travesty, excessive rendering of the stereotypes, in an effort to swell the models to their limits and explode them" ("Motherhood," 130).
81 Kitagishi, "Takarazuka Gidayū Kabuki," 89. The term "*jōruri*" is used here interchangeably with "*gidayū*."
82 Watanabe Tamotsu, *Kabuki*, 16–17.
83 Honchi, "Kabuki to Takarazuka Joyū," 58. Utaemon VI was skeptical about the idea that *gidayū* can help female actors gain masculine *gei*: "New pieces [of kabuki]

might be performed by actresses, but when it comes to plays with *gidayū*, I think it's only *onnagata* [who can do it]" (Enoki, "Narikomaya," 82). Kataoka Gadō XIII (1910–1993), another important *onnagata* contemporary of Utaemon's, asserts the same: "[When it] entails *denden* [i.e., *gidayū*], it's impossible for actresses to do" (Enoki, "Kataoka," 106). In this interview, Gadō also remarks that "my father told us frequently that if audiences say we look like women, that's fine, but it's not good if they say we're like actresses" (106).

84 Tsuda, *Kikigaki Joyū Yamada Isuzu*, 199–200. However, Yamada explains that she learned just the gist of *gidayū* chanting and indicates that she learned the shamisen part of *gidayū* music more extensively, as her master told her that the chanting part would destroy the vocal cords and thus would not be suitable for actresses (ibid.). This is somehow reminiscent of the *onnagata* Tokizō's opinion that excludes *gidayū* from the training of *onnagata*.

85 Ibid., 143.

86 Karasuyakko, "Onna Yakusha to Joyū," 153.

87 Okamoto, *Meiji Gekidan*, 159.

88 Ibid., 159. Kidō praises the visual aspect of Kumehachi's Princess Yaegaki, which he finds superior to that of Danjūrō (160).

89 Onoe Taganojō, "Watashi no Rirekisho," 185.

90 Nakamura Utaemon V, *Kaigyoku Issekiwa*, 207.

91 The practice of holding a piece of paper would be done in training sessions and not actual performances (Isaka Baisetsu, "Godaime Utaemon no Kaikyūdan Jō," 101).

92 Kikusui, "Joyū Rekihōroku," 196.

93 Nakamura and Fujio, "Beni to Oshiroi," 163.

94 Onoe Umenosuke, *Onnagata*.

95 Ichikawa Kumehachi, "Meika Shinsōroku," no page number.

96 Ibid.; Ichikawa Kumehachi, "Gigei no Hanashi,"; Ichikawa Kumehachi, "Onnagata" 110–15; Ichikawa Kumehachi, "Ichikawa Kumehachi no Atarigei," 54–63.

97 For Utaemon V's version of Masaoka, see, e.g., Isaka Baisetsu, "Godaime Utaemon no Kaikyūdan Jō," 106–7; for Baikō VI's version, see Onoe Baikō VI, *Onnagata no Koto*, 74.

98 Ichikawa Kumehachi, "Onnagata," 113.

99 Kitamura, "Meika Shinsōroku," 70–71.

100 Sawamura, "Meiryū," 115–16. *Kata*, literary "form" or "pattern," refers to the specific acting of a choreographed pose or a series of such poses established by maestros in the past.

101 Ibid., 116.

102 Onoe, Fujiura, and Hakii, "Seigaku Yawa to Yonsei Gennosuke," 65–66. As for this particular play, I have not been able to locate further sources proving that Baikō learned the role of Otomi from Gennosuke. However, Atsumi Seitarō records that Baikō learned the role from Gennosuke in a variant play, a woman-version adaptation, *Scandalous Comb Preferred by Young Women* (Musume gonomi ukina no yokogushi) (1864), by Mokuami ("Onoe Baikō Tsuiroku," 59).

103 Sawamura, *Seigaku*, 292–93. Seigaku was one of the haiku pen names of Gennosuke.
104 Here I differ from Mezur, who states that "Kumehachi remained an outsider to the professional male kabuki world" (*Beautiful Boys*, 117).
105 Onoe and Andō, "Onoe Taganojō Geidan," pt. 4, 87, 90.
106 Aeba, "Nakamura Sōjūrō Den," 104. Reprint of a series published in *Yomiuri Shinbun* from 12 October 1889 to 17 October 1889 (per a note in the quoted article). For Sōjūrō's involvement in theater reform movements, see Kobitsu, "Nakamura Sōjūrō no Engeki Kairyō to sono Ri'nen," 45–54.
107 As for how male kabuki actors treated Mitsue, see, e.g., Bandō and Takechi, *Gei Jūya*, 32–33. For a similar tension between the establishment and newcomer theater practitioners in the context of *shingeki*, see Maki Isaka, "Osanai Kaoru's Dilemma," 119–33.
108 "Sukina Haiyū no Sukina Gei," 188. I regard this remark by the staff member as the most supportive evidence of Mezur's concept of "a male body beneath," which is a key idea of her analysis of *onnagata*. She states: "A performative onnagata gender role is a fiction of female-likeness based on a male 'body beneath.' In other words, the performer is actually a Japanese man (with male genitalia) underneath the onnagata stylized acts" (*Beautiful Boys*, 7); "The only valid reason a Japanese woman cannot play onnagata roles is because she does not have a male body beneath the kimono; therefore, the ambience of the difference between female gender acts and the male body beneath is not possible. Indeed, the presence of male sexual organs underneath the kimono is a *requirement* for kabuki onnagata performance, because the spectator must be able to imagine a male body beneath the feminine costuming" (25; emphasis in original); "women cannot enact the onnagata fiction of female-likeness because they do not have a male sexed body beneath" (259).

Technically, there are two different issues in her claim: (1) a male sexed body (with male sexual organs) constitutes a prerequisite for *onnagata* acting; (2) spectators necessitate an image of such a body when receiving an *onnagata* performance.

The staff member's anxious remark partially supports the latter point, although the image of the *onnagata* that the staff member insists on maintaining does not necessitate "male genitalia" in and of themselves. Images can stand alone, for in typical theatergoing at kabuki playhouses, audiences usually have no way of checking for the presence of "male sexual organs" underneath the kimono of *onnagata*; that does not, however, impede their appreciation of *onnagata* performances. Most of the audiences who came to see the troupe to which the staff member belonged obviously did not notice the absence of "male sexual organs" or the presence of "breasts" (except for the infantile Peeping Tom). Nor did their lack of knowledge discourage them from enjoying the performances.

There is more to this. I recognize that there can be a certain kind of thrilling pleasure on the part of an informed spectator who witnesses impostors passing as the very people whom they have disguised themselves to be. That thrilling pleasure might well be connected to the fact that this spectator knows—or *thinks* he or she knows—that these people are not the people they are pretending to be. Knowing that the woman on the stage, in front of our very eyes, is in fact a man can bring a certain thrilling pleasure. That pleasure, however, does not warrant anything other than the impostors themselves. It does not mean that those whose identities have been stolen cannot project fictitious images as much as the impostors. It is this type of feat that the idea of a male sexed body beneath as a must for *onnagata* is performing in the realm of spectatorship.

My skepticism is greater when it comes to the part of performance. I find it difficult to follow Mezur's argument in theoretical terms. She cites Judith Butler for the famed concept of gender as a performative and states, "I focus on the deconstruction of the idea of gender as a core identity or 'essence,' inseparable from female or male genitalia" (*Beautiful Boys*, 7). As long as the presence of "male sexual organs" (25) or "male genitalia" (7) is being considered a prerequisite, however, the proposal seems to be like a photographic negative in the sense that the presence and the absence are exchanged in the picture, and, borrowing Hart's parlance, albeit from a different context, it "would only reassert the binary distinction through reversal" ("Motherhood," 131). As history proves in the form of female *onnagata* like Kumehachi, a male-sexed body was not a prerequisite for *onnagata* artistry. It is certainly "a male-authorized and male body-based gender performance," as Mezur effectively states (7), but it is by no means confined within the male-sexed body as such.

109   See, e.g., the memoirs written under the pseudonym Kōkō (Kōbeni?), an unknown writer whom *Entertainment Illustrated* magazine introduces as "a certain middle-aged woman who was a disciple of Danjūrō IX about thirty years ago. She was playing minor roles such as a lady-in-waiting" ("Mukashi Gatari," pt. 1, 166–67; pt. 2, 120–21).

110   Onoe Taganojō, "Watashi no Rirekisho," 185.

111   Officially, the Metropolitan Police Department permitted theatrical productions using male and female performers in August 1891 (Ōzasa, *Nihon Gendai Engekishi*, 61). Needless to say, we already know that former theater-masters did not wait for several decades for official permission. Kumehachi describes her days after Mitsue became unemployed as follows: "I was doing nothing in particular [for a while, but I really loved theater].... And then I heard of a small troupe led by one Danzaburō, a disciple of Danjūrō VIII.... I badly wanted to become an actor, so I cut off my hair and made it into *chonmage* and joined the troupe" (Ichikawa Kumehachi, "Gigei no Hanashi," 82–83; see also Ichikawa Kumehachi, "Meika Shinsōroku," 113). *Chonmage* is a male hairstyle in premodern times, and this passage indicates that Kumehachi was cross-dressing in order to join the troupe. As for cross-dressing offstage, Robertson introduces a poignant example a half century before Kumehachi of a woman named Take who cross-dressed and styled herself as Takejirō in the 1830s: "She was arrested, punished, imprisoned, fined, and eventually exiled for, essentially, appropriating 'male' gender" ("Shingaku Woman," 92). As is obvious from the aforementioned "honorary-man" status of female *gidayū* chanters, the ambiguous reception of women "crossing over" boundaries cannot be ex-

plained too clearly, such as premodern/modern, East/West, and so forth. Beyond her/his time and space, Take/Takejirō's case is a reminder of what Hart discusses in *Fatal Women*. Also related to this phenomenon is men crossing over boundaries, which Mitsuhashi Junko discusses in *Josō to Nihonjin*, 126–59.

112   *EG* 4.2 (February 1917): 164; 8.12 (December 1921): 25; 9.5 (May 1922): 91. The first article was published without a title or the name of the author. The next two items (tables) were signed by Kondō Shōu. The existence of Kumehachi II is evidence that the stage name "Kumehachi" came to have some value in the kabuki system.

113   Takenoya et al., "Ichikawa Kumehachi Tsuiokuroku," 139. There are several variants of this purported remark of Danjūrō's, which include, "Kumehachi, dude, she left it behind inside her mother's womb" and "If only she had testicles" (Ide, "Fukagawa no Onna Shibai," 120).

114   Another example below is taken from a theater review published in a newspaper dated 23 November 1909. Also, notice that Kumehachi in this review signifies "a big theater" in Tokyo: "A rare chance in these days to enjoy the taste of a big theater from Tokyo. Especially, Kumehachi's extraordinarily skill remains the same as ever and was impressive indeed. . . . In act 3, Kumehachi finally appeared as the wife, Hasue. It is a sheer wonder that this actor is a septuagenarian granny, born in 1835 [*sic*]. Expressive eyes, plump cheeks, and smooth and detailed *gei* like streaming water, all these things are not only beautiful but skillful, which impressed me tremendously. No wonder the late Naritaya [Danjūrō IX] said, 'Kumehachi would make a good match of me, if she had testicles.' When [the wife] flees at the end, upon the death of Nureginu [and all], [Kumehachi] was extraordinary. The next piece was a dance opus, and [Kumehachi's] high-ranking courtesan was perfect, so much so that the audiences were mesmerized. After transforming [from the courtesan] into a mountain female demon, [Kumehachi] displayed [her skill] at the fighting scene, dealing with many chasers. Many must have been surprised again, thinking, that was a granny born in the Tenpō era [1830–44] [*sic*]. She also showed some new gestures and expressions, as she joined a *shinpa* troupe as well. I also appreciate [such a new attempt]. Given that such an aged actress can do this much, actresses nowadays, be tough and try your best" (Sokō, "Kumehachi Ichiza no Wakatake-za o Miru," 3).

115   Karasuyakko, "Onna Yakusha to Joyū," 152. One of the pen names Mishima used was Udo (lit., "crow [*karasu*] "fellow" [*yatsu*; *yakko*]. While this article includes the *furigana* reading of "Karasuyakko" (ibid., 152–54), I suspect it is a typo.

116   Kano, *Acting Like a Woman*, 6.

117   Ōzasa, *Nihon Gendai Engekishi*, 53.

118   Ozaki, *Joyū no Keizu*, 108–10.

119   Onoe Baikō VI, "Onnagata wa Ikitakutemo," 90. Incidentally, Tamasaburō III, a woman actor, was dispatched to the United States for an international exposition in 1904, where she passed away the following year.

120   See, e.g., *Kabuki* 96 (July 1908), 99 (October 1908), 100 (November 1908), 104 (March 1909), 111 (October 1909); *EG* 6.1 (January 1912), 6.2 (February 1912), 6.3 (March 1912).

121 Kano, *Acting Like a Woman*, 17, 22.
122 Yanagawa, "Joyū wa Ōi ni Yūbō," 46.
123 To be precise, the performative mechanism per se—a repetitious doing creating a being—remained valid for *onnagata*, but this particular prescription for "gynecological disorders" became impossible.
124 Given this new landscape, the confusion regarding Kumehachi's year of birth seems to illustrate the misfit nature of female *onnagata*. The likes of Kumehachi were, both in terms of gender and of time, a misfit. If she had been born male, as Mishima put it, Kumehachi would have been a superstar (Karasuyakko, "Onna Yakusha to Joyū," 152). If she had been born ten or twelve years earlier, and thus if her master lost her patrons when Kumehachi was twenty-eight or thirty instead of when she was a fledgling at eighteen, she would have been able to seek another career, such as a dance teacher, given her honorable educational background as a former theater-master, just as her Kyoto "sister" did (i.e., the Inoue dance school). We do not know how the various theories about her birth year came to be circulated, but it seems to be more than coincidence that Kumehachi herself seemed partially accountable for the confusion and that both the year 1834, which was predominantly cited in her time, and the year 1846, which is probably the most likely, were the year of the Horse in the twelve earthly branches (or zodiac signs). This is because the twelve earthly branches were closely tied to people's sense of "year" and, along with the ten heavenly stems, tightly connected with the calendar system in use.
125 For instance, Senelick states: "Only a man with a highly developed upper body strength can accomplish [*onnagata* movements]" (*Changing Room*, 89).
126 "Masculine anatomy determined female movements" (ibid.).
127 In this sense, the following words of Utaemon VI reverse the causality, unwittingly or otherwise: "Women-actors in the Meiji era, like Kumehachi, were extinguished. If women could do [*onnagata*], they would have been revived, but in actuality they haven't. From it [it's obvious, or, I gather] *onnagata* are impossible without men's technique" (Konishi, "'Ripōto,'" 80).
128 Takeshiba, "Meiji Shonen no Onnagata," 36.
129 This comes from Tamura's words mourning Kumehachi's death: "The death of old actor Ichikawa Kumehachi [was taken by theater circles today as] a natural incident . . . in the sense that what should disappear disappeared" (Takenoya et al., "Ichikawa Kumehachi Tsuiokuroku," 145 [this part was written by Tamura]).

8. TOWARD CONTEMPORARY ONNAGATA

The subject of part IV—*onnagata*'s changes in modern times—requires much more space than allotted in this book; accordingly, I can only highlight some theoretically critical points. The subject, especially that of female *onnagata* in contemporary kabuki, deserves full discussion in a book-length space.

1 Utaemon V's supremacy, symbolized by his ascendance to the positions of executive chairperson of technique (*kanbu gigei iinchō*) at the Kabuki-za Theater (1906)

and president of the Great Japan Association for Actors (Dai Nihon Haiyū Kyōkai), is unprecedented in kabuki history, according to Watanabe Tamotsu, that is, an *onnagata* assumed the highest position in these circles, surpassing male-role actors (*Onnagata no Unmei*, 57, 75–90). His second son and successor, *onnagata* Utaemon VI, followed a similar career path, including service as president of the Japan Association for Actors (Nihon Haiyū Kyōkai), successor to the Great Japan Association for Actors, from 1969 through 1999, and designation as a Living National Treasure in 1968.

2   Watanabe, *Onnagata no Unmei*, 85.
3   Ihara Toshirō, *Utaemon*, 17–18.
4   Utaemon used Hanshirō's *kata*, when, for example, playing the role of Princess Yaegaki (Nakamura Utaemon [V], "Geidan," 53–54).
5   Enoki, "Narikomaya," 82.
6   "The corporate nature of the *ie* shaped household priorities. Preservation of household property, occupation, name, and status in the local community were vital concerns. The fundamental goal was household continuity, not the well-being of individual members" (Uno, "Women," 23).
7   The Yagyū family is a famous example in the realm of martial arts. See Maki Isaka, *Secrecy*.
8   *Onzōshi* is a popular term widely and loosely used to refer to the sons of major families in a specific arena, kabuki circles included. Its tacit aristocratic implication comes from its origin, as it was historically a term referring to the sons of Minamoto families, whose ancestors are minor royal princes. The term "*onzōshi*" thus connoted their present privileged status as well as their imperial origins. Also noteworthy in this semiroyal treatment of kabuki-youngsters today is the fact that, before modern times, the social status of kabuki-actors was so low that they were not treated as human (Ōzasa, *Nihon Gendai Engekishi*, 18).
9   Ibid., 335–40. This remains valid in 2015.
10 Another important exception of late concerns disciples of Ichikawa Ennosuke III (b. 1939), currently Ichikawa En'ō II. The National Theater (Kokuritsu Gekijō) houses a program for educating and training youngsters (male only) with no familial ties to kabuki households who intend to become kabuki actors. Graduates of this program usually become disciples of established kabuki actors. Many would remain minor actors for good, and their activities include not just acting onstage but, more important, assisting their masters both on and off the stage; when performing, they usually play such roles as ladies-in-waiting and minor retainers. Those who became Ennosuke III's disciples are arguably the rare exceptions, because quite a few managed to become popular actors performing major roles themselves (e.g., Ichikawa Ukon, Ichikawa Shun'en, Ichikawa Emiya, and Ichikawa Emisaburō). They and Ennosuke came to form, in effect, a family in its own right. This is a highly commendable and exceptional achievement. The year 2012 witnessed a radical change in this family, however. That year, film and TV actor Kagawa Teruyuki (b. 1965), who is Ennosuke's biological son by his ex-wife, suddenly succeeded to a kabuki name of great importance in the Ichikawas: Ichikawa

Chūsha IX. The news surprised those in the know for two reasons. Kagawa had never done kabuki until then, and, echoing his exceptional attitude toward his disciples as described above, Ennosuke had previously shown no intention of accepting as his successor his biological son who had no kabuki training. It is intriguing that the direction Ennosuke has taken resembles the big movement discussed here: from adopted to biological sons. The 2012 event does not nullify the significance of Ennosuke's and his disciples' accomplishments.

11 Kano, *Acting Like a Woman*.
12 Ōzasa, *Nihon Gendai Engekishi*, 335–40.
13 See, e.g., Ogawa, *Edo Bakuhan Daimyōke Jiten*, 569 for his discussion of the Yagyūs.
14 Kano, *Acting Like a Woman*.
15 For Utaemon's use of Hanshirō's *kata*, see Nakamura Utaemon [V], "Geidan," 53–54. As for his remark on married *onnagata*'s tendency to resemble their wives, see Isaka Baisetsu, "Godaime Utaemon no Kaikyūdan Jō," 102.
16 Onoe and Andō, "Onoe Taganojō Geidan," pt. 2, 142–45. For small theaters, see also Edelson, "Playing for the Majors," 75–87.
17 See, e.g., Wakita, *Chūsei ni Ikiru Onna-tachi*, 242; Robertson, "Shingaku Woman," 89.
18 By female *onnagata* who were abjected, I mean mostly those who were engaged in mainstream kabuki and therefore put themselves in the position of being vulnerable to eradication. Women kabuki actors have also existed in other realms.
19 Kawatake Toshio, *Nihon no Koten Geinō*, 143.
20 Enoki, "Narikomaya," 82.
21 Ibid., 81. Exceptionally, Tamasaburō's opinion is more nuanced than those of these actors. On the one hand, his concept of *onnagata*'s femininity is in accordance with the modern definition (i.e., abstract femininity conceptualized by a non-female performer), but he does not exclude female performers in the final analysis. See, e.g., his interview in *The Written Face*.
22 Takeshiba, "Meiji Shonen no Onnagata," 36.
23 Gennosuke states, "There were great *onnagata* in the good old days. Like Iwai Hanshirō, there won't be anyone like him anymore. Never, you know. Even Danjūrō, *that* Danjūrō admitted Hanshirō. The difference [between the likes of him and *onnagata* nowadays] is, to begin with, he was right-minded and sensible as an *onnagata* (*oyama no kokorogake*). He spent his daily life as a woman, and he would come to regular rehearsal wearing women's [clothing], with the purple forehead cap [for *onnagata*]. And then, when we had a dress rehearsal, he would come wearing long-sleeve kimono. Can't imagine nowadays. It was like that until, say, around [1881 or 1882]-ish, I think. Are there any *onnagata* now? I think there aren't any. I know, there are actors who do *onnagata*, bunch of them, but they do men's roles, too. I think they're not *onnagata* from the bottom up, that's what I think. . . . [How to become sensible as *onnagata*?] In a word, it's just that you become a woman. Say, you rush to the room [on the stage], running all the way from the *hanamichi* rampway, and when you take off your zori or geta [at the

NOTES TO CHAPTER 8 [215]

entrance], they should be left turned inward. Nothing starts otherwise, although these are just details" (Kurosaki, *Geidan Hyakuwa*, 60–61). Kurosaki introduces Gennosuke as seventy-six years old; thus the interview must have been conducted in 1934, assuming that Kurosaki is using the traditional East Asian age-counting method.

24 Ōtani, "Baikō no Kōfū o Omou," 26–27.
25 Mishima, "Baikō Katsugare no Hanashi," 59.
26 Ennosuke IV states, "I'm often asked in interviews, like, 'What elements in women do you take your cue from?' So I always answer, 'Nothing.' What we are performing is the *sei* (sex and/or gender) of '*onnagata*,' different from [that of] actual women. Maa [the role I played recently] was well received, because I, who am a man, performed the existence that was impossible in reality. It's impossible to play it unless one's a man. Simply put, it's the charm that Umezawa Tomio [a popular *onnagata* in "mass theater" (*taishū engeki*)] gives out. It's a woman who radiates men's charms, and who's not just pliable. . . . I do both men's roles and *onnagata*, but doing *onnagata* is really tough. For we have to kill our bodies first. The movements of *onnagata* are really a burden on one's body. By and large, *onnagata* harm their knees. Women cannot do the movements of *onnagata* in kabuki, because their skeletons could not sustain them, and besides, the costumes are too heavy for them to move around in. . . . [Audiences are mostly women.] When I perform as an *onnagata*, I don't take my cue from them, but I do sometimes reconstruct the atmosphere of women in my performance. I hope many women keep coming to playhouses. And I'm happy if they take a look at how thoughtful we *onnagata* are. It requires much effort to look beautiful. I want them to learn that. Nope, I hope they'll feel it" (Ichikawa and Takahashi, "Bokutachi ga Enjiru 'Onnagata,'" 172–73).
27 Ichikawa Shun'en, *Onna Zukuri*, 15. Before this statement, Shun'en states: "When you see kabuki, I would recommend that you think 'Why is it beautiful?' and 'What in kabuki is beautiful?' Not just sigh, thinking, 'Wow, it's beautiful.'

"For kabuki is a treasure house of the aesthetic of women.

"It might be unexpected, but we *onnagata* do not aim at 'approximating women.' Isn't it unnatural if I as a man try to become a woman, no matter what?

"It's not that. It's rather that I as a man pursue the question of 'how can one appear as a woman?' By refining one's gesture, posture, and makeup. In short, this is something we do as 'technique.' . . . (14).
28 Pola, *Utsukushii*. It consists of eleven parts: (1) Nature (Shizen), (2) Yearning (Akogare), (3) Fundamentals of Beauty (Utsukushisa no kihon), (4) Maintenance of skin (Ohada no oteire), (5) For the Sake of the Expression of Female-Likeness (Josei-rashisa no hyōgen, sono tame ni), (6) What the Ultimate Beauty Is . . . (Kyūkyoku no utsukushisa towa . . .), (7) Correlation between Aging and Beauty (Nenrei to utsukushisa tono kakawari), (8) Message for All Women (Subete no josei eno messēji), (9) Making of *Beauty, toward the Interior of It* (Meikingu mūbī: *Utsukushii, no Uchigawa e*), (10) Interview with Bandō Tamasaburō (Bandō Tamasaburō-san Intabyū), and (11) Interview with Kobayashi Mao (Kobayashi Mao-san Intabyū). All of these were made available online for a limited time at the

company's official site (http://www.pola.co.jp/cmpage/index.html); the first two, "Nature" and "Yearning," were also released on TV in September 2008.

29 Bandō Tamasaburō, "Eien."
30 Komatsu, *Kanzaburō Araburu*, 141.
31 Seki, *Atarashī Kanzaburō*, 28. See also Seki, *Joyū de Arukoto*, 286. Just like their father, however, Kanzaburō XVIII himself has said that Namino "would have been a great kabuki actor if she were a man" (Nakamura Kankurō et al., *Nakamuraya Sandaiki*, 104); that she "inherited the talent [from their genius father]" (Nakamura Kankurō, *Kankurō Towazugatari*, 52). Kanzaburō XVII's oldest disciple, Nakamura Kosanza, also states that she "is identical to [Kanzaburō XVII], from her face to her character" (Nakamura Kankurō et al., *Nakamuraya Sandaiki*, 41).
32 *The Written Face*. See also Sugimura, "Usotsuki Juban," 72.
33 Mizuochi, *Kamigata Kabuki*, 239–40.
34 For this important agenda, see, e.g., Brandon, "Myth and Reality," 1–110; Leiter, *Rising from the Flames*. The importance of kabuki's repeated changes (in the beginning of modern times and during and after World War II) is complicated. It should be understood in relation to one of the most significant characteristics of kabuki in that it defines itself through two opposite kinds of impulse: toward *kabuku* (being strange, queer, crazy, etc.) and toward identifying with authentic traditions (*hongyō* and *honmon*). Accordingly, repetition does not nullify the significance of each transition. It is noteworthy, however, that the Meiji case was unprecedented, as kabuki for the first time became an authorized tradition, as symbolized by imperial inspections and new epithets, such as *kyūgeki* (old theater), vis-à-vis *shingeki* (new theater), and *kyūha* (old faction/school), vis-à-vis *shinpa* (new faction/school). Incidentally, kabuki has recently expressed its strong desire to be pop, crazy, and so on, highlighting the validity of these two modes of self-identification.
35 See, e.g., Takechi and Tobe, "Kabuki." In this debate, Takechi asserts that *onnagata* are not necessary, grounding his argument on the ability of women performers, as proved by Yorozuyo Mineko (b. 1919), a former Takarazuka-revue actor. In general, Takarazuka actors have been especially suited to kabuki acting. Takechi also made a contradictory remark elsewhere: "it wouldn't work well if one trains [actresses for kabuki]" (Takechi and Tomioka, *Dentō Geijutsu towa Nani Nanoka*, 132). Takechi is a thought-provoking thinker, whose ideas deserve an independent book-length analysis in their own right.
36 After discussing Tōjūrō (then Senjaku), Mizuochi states: "Tamasaburō [would later] receive a compliment similar [to that given to Tōjūrō], but when Tamasaburō emerged, there had already been a social consensus that kabuki was the theater that Japan was proud of. In the case of Senjaku, however, there was no such thing" (*Kamigata Kabuki*, 240).
37 Kagayama, *Shin-kabuki*, 40.
38 For Shōchō's engagement in *shingeki* and its theoretical meanings, see Maki Isaka, "Osanai Kaoru's Dilemma," 119–33; Maki Isaka, *Secrecy*, 101–36.
39 For possible counterevidence, see, e.g., Takechi's opinions. On the surface, Takechi here seems to suggest a certain possibility of relating Shōchō to premodern tradi-

tions, when explaining this trend of approximating women by using the term *"onna-gei"* (acquired artistic technique of women) vis-à-vis *"otoko-gei"* (acquired artistic technique of men). Roughly speaking, premodern *onnagata* represent *onna-gei* and modern *onnagata* represent *otoko-gei*, but a cluster of *onnagata* who perform with *onna-gei* remains (Takechi and Tobe, "Taidan," 59). This statement was made in a casual dialogue, which is not necessarily suitable for the rigorous debate that a thinker like Takechi would prefer, and this could have limited his discussion.

40 Ōtani, "Baikō no Kōfū o Omou," 26–27.

41 "It was 26 February 1887, when Baikō was still [using his previous stage name] Einosuke, a kabuki troupe of [Danjūrō, Kikugorō, Sadanji, Shikan, etc.] was honored with the inspection of His Majesty the Emperor Meiji at the mansion of the minister of foreign affairs, Mr. Inoue. Einosuke was in a dance piece, *Genroku Dance*. The next day, on the twenty-seventh, the troupe was honored with the inspection of Her Majesty the Empress Dowager Shōken. Everything went smoothly through the last piece, *Genroku Dance*. [Her Majesty returned to the palace], and everybody was relieved. Baikō was in the dressing room, still wearing the costume of the piece, when a robust officer rushed into the room. 'Hey, you, come here and pour sake,' and he grasped Baikō's hands to bring [the actor] with him. Baikō [resisted,] saying, 'I'm an actor, sir.' . . . Taking him to be a geisha, the officer had come to fetch her to make her serve at the party. Baikō [could not convince the officer that he was an actor and] finally began crying. Eventually, Baikō revealed the place where the distinction between a man and a woman is clear at a single glance, and thanks to that, the officer released him. This is still a favorite anecdote of Baikō's" (Mishima, "Baikō Katsugare no Hanashi," 59).

42 Enoki, "Narikomaya," 82.

43 Nakamura Utaemon [V], "Nakamura Utaemon Kataru," 33. Incidentally, Utaemon VI's respect for his father is well documented and is mentioned in nearly all published interviews and the like; he once said that he also liked the types of roles that Baikō VI was performing ("Seinen Haiyū Taikan," 87).

44 Yamakawa, "Onoe Taganojō Intabyū," 233.

45 Onoe and Andō, "Onoe Taganojō Geidan," pt. 6, 45.

46 Ibid., 46. The interview took place in Shima, Gunma, on 20 and 21 August 1966 (ibid., pt. 1, 158).

47 Maybe we are also seeing here a gradual separation of body (form-exterior) and mind (contents-interior) in this context, a detachment that the cultivation regime would find evidence of one's imperfect status. Successful *onnagata* nowadays, especially those known for their feminine beauty, are frequently associated with such attributes as "political" and "strong-minded." See, e.g., Kataoka and Bandō, "Hanagata Kissashitsu," 50. Such associations most certainly claim and manage to confirm their masculinity.

48 Nakamura Utaemon [V], "Zoku Kaigyoku Yawa," 64–67.

49 See, e.g., Aeba, "Nakamura Sōjūrō Den," 104; Sawamura, "Meiryū," 115–16.

50 Arashi, *Godaime Yoshisaburō Geiwa*, 37. His father, Arashi Yoshisaburō IV (1872–

1912), was the aforementioned Sōjūrō's disciple, and Yoshisaburō V himself was a disciple of Taganojō at one time. Together, this might explain his open-minded attitude toward non-"typical" kabuki actors, such as female actors. Incidentally, Karoku is the father of Kanzaburō XVII.

51   *The Written Face.*
52   Enoki, "Narikomaya," 82.

EPILOGUE

1   See, e.g., Enoki, "Narikomaya," 82; Konishi, "'Ripōto,'" 80.
2   Enoki, "Narikomaya," 82.
3   Fujita, *Henreki*, 204.
4   Tsuda, *Kikigaki Joyū Yamada Isuzu*, 143.
5   For example, Yamada appears in *Osaka Elegy* (1936) and *Sisters of the Gion* (1936) by Mizoguchi; *Tsuruhachi and Tsurujiro* (1938), *Song Lantern* (1943), and *Flowing* (1956) by Naruse; and *Throne of Blood* (1957), *The Lower Depths* (1957), and *Yojimbo* (1961) by Kurosawa.
6   Tsuda, *Kikigaki Joyū Yamada Isuzu*, 122; *Kumonosu-jō*.
7   Ibid., 122. The noh mask in question is *deigan* (muddy eyes). For an image, see Nihon Geijutsu Bunka Shinkōkai, "Deigan."
8   For another example of how Yamada's acting of the Asaji role illustrates the closeness of her acting to traditional theater, Yamada expounds on how she developed the elocution of Asaji in this scene: "I paid a visit to a mental hospital for a study, where I saw a woman patient uttering a voice like a child's. In order to evince an atmosphere of madness, I used that" (Tsuda, *Kikigaki Joyū Yamada Isuzu*, 124). This is somehow similar to Utaemon V's account of how he planned his acting of the Lady Yodo role in *Little Cuckoo and the Setting Moon at the Isolated Castle* (Hototogisu kojō no rakugetsu) for a Tokyo production in 1906 (Ihara Toshirō, *Utaemon*, 149–75). Written by Tsubouchi Shōyō (1859–1935), this work was first published in 1897. See also Watanabe Tamotsu, *Onnagata no Unmei*, 155.
9   Tōhō Company's kabuki enterprise, including its productions (usually called Tōhō-kabuki), is another topic that calls for further attention and analysis.
10 Tsuda, *Kikigaki Joyū Yamada Isuzu*, 143. Yamada also identified herself primarily as a stage actor (ibid., 126), which presents a sharp contrast to the way in which she is now being remembered: mostly, or exclusively even, as a film star.
11 Enomoto, "Onnagata Engi," 258. As is obvious from the article title, "Acting of *Onnagata* and Acting of Actresses: Pathology of the History of Japanese Modern Theater," Enomoto is opposed to this ethos that valorizes male *onnagata* at the expense of female performers. Enomoto was extremely well versed in kabuki and its related performing art *rakugo* (storytelling performed in narration and mime); he frequently worked with kabuki actors as well as with Yamada herself.
12 "Yamada Isuzu san Shikyo," 31.
13 Tsuda, *Kikigaki Joyū Yamada Isuzu*, 219. I said that this is a putative utterance, because this remark appears in Yamada's autobiography, and as of this writing, I

have not been able to locate other sources that contain this exact wording. According to Yamada, Taganojō said this to his wife. There are, however, similar remarks of Taganojō's commenting on and complimenting Yamada in other sources, including his own diary (Ōtsuki, *Ningen Kokuhō Onoe Taganojō*).

14 Hahn, *Sensational Knowledge*, 87.
15 See, for example, Lim, "Isuzu Yamada"; Bergan, "Isuzu Yamada Obituary"; Bernstein, "Isuzu Yamada"; Macy, "Isuzu Yamada"; "Yamada Isuzu san Shikyo."
16 Brandon, "Reflections," 122.
17 Lorde, *Sister Outsider*, 110–13. In addition, "In blackface, white men portrayed black men; black men portrayed white men portraying black men; and men, both black and white, became female impersonators and acted the 'wench'" (Eric Lott, quoted in Willis, "I Shop," 189–90).
18 Bandō Tamasaburō, "Kongetsu no Komento," November and December 2007; Bandō Tamasaburō, "Tamasaburō Shinema Kabuki."
19 Barlow, "Femininity," 388.
20 Zeami, *Fūshikaden*, 21.
21 Satō Yuki, "Bandō Tamasaburō Intabyū," no pg. nos; *Nasutāsha/Nastazja*.

BIBLIOGRAPHY

ABBREVIATIONS

DG   *Dentō to Gendai* (Traditions and today)
EG   *Engei Gahō* (Entertainment illustrated magazine)
IKKB   *Iwanami Kōza Kabuki Bunraku* (Iwanami lectures on kabuki and the puppet theater)
KKH   *Kabuki: Kenkyū to Hihyō* (Kabuki: Research and criticism)
NG   *Nihon no Geidan* (Accounts-on-*gei* in Japan)
NKBT   *Nihon Koten Bungaku Taikei* (Collected Japanese classical literature)
NSBSS   *Nihon Shomin Bunka Shiryō Shūsei* (Collected historical documents of Japanese popular culture)
NSSSS   *Nihon Shomin Seikatsu Shiryō Shūsei* (Collected historical documents of the lives of Japanese people)
NST   *Nihon Shisō Taikei* (Collected Japanese thought)
OKEZ   *Osanai Kaoru Engekiron Zenshū* (The complete writings on the theatrical theory of Osanai Kaoru)
TDR   *TDR/The Drama Review: The Journal of Performance Studies*
TTK   *Teihon Takechi Kabuki: Takechi Tetsuji Zenshū* (Takechi kabuki, the standard edition: The complete works of Takechi Tetsuji)

Aeba Kōson. "Nakamura Sōjūrō Den" (Biography of Nakamura Sōjūrō). *Kamigata* 74 (February 1937): 98–105.

Agi Ōsuke. "Ichikawa Suisen o Itamu" (Mourning Ichikawa Suisen). *Engekikai* 36.12 (November 1978): 114.

Arashi Yoshisaburō. *Godaime Yoshisaburō Geiwa* (Yoshisaburō V's Accounts-on-*gei*). Tokyo: Shin Nihon Shuppansha, 1981.

Ashihara Eiryō. "Mitsugorō no Ashi" (Mitsugorō's legs and feet). *Shisō* 210 (1939): 83–94.

———. "Nanban" (Nanba). *Shisō* 230 (1941): 64–75.
Ashura-jō no Hitomi (Blood gets in your eyes). Directed by Takita Yōjirō. Performed by Ichikawa Somegorō and Miyazawa Rie. Shōchiku, 2005.
Atsumi Seitarō et al. "Onoe Baikō Tsuioku" (In memory of Onoe Baikō). *EG* 28.12 (December 1934): 56–69.
Auslander, Philip. "'Brought to You by Fem-Rage': Stand-up Comedy and the Politics of Gender." In *Acting Out: Feminist Performances*, edited by Lynda Hart and Peggy Phelan, 315–36. Ann Arbor: University of Michigan Press, 1993.
Austin, J. L. *How to Do Things with Words*. Cambridge, MA: Harvard University Press, 1962.
Bandō Mitsugorō and Takechi Tetsuji. *Gei Jūya* (Ten nights for *gei*). Kyoto: Shinshindō Shuppan, 1972.
Bandō Tamasaburō. "Eien no Joseibi o Tsuikyū Shite: Watashi-ryū Kenkō-zukuri" (Quest for eternal female beauty: My way of building health). Keynote speech at Kenkō-zukuri wa Anata ga Hiroin: Midoru-eiji kara Kagayaku Sutāto (You are the heroine of building your health: The shining start from middle age), the eighteenth forum of Josei no Kenkō to Menopōzu (Women's health and menopause). Supairaru Hall, Tokyo, 5 March 2011.
———. "Kongetsu no Komento" (This month's comments). Tamasaburo Bando Official Site. November and December 2007. http://www.tamasaburo.co.jp/. Accessed 2 April 2014.
———. "Tamasaburō Shinema Kabuki *Furu Amerika ni Sode wa Nurasaji* o Kataru" (Tamasaburō speaks about cinema kabuki *No sleeve wet upon showering America*). Kabuki-bito, 30 May 2008. http://www.kabuki-bito.jp/news/2008/05/__photo_93.html. Accessed 2 April 2014.
Banritei. *Yakusha Meibutsu Sode Nikki* (The famous-product journal, actors' sleeves). Edited by Tachikawa Hiroshi. In *Kabuki*, edited by Gondō Yoshikazu, Munemasa Isoo, and Moriya Takeshi, 243–64. Vol. 6 of *NSBSS*, edited by Geinōshi Kenkyūkai. Tokyo: San'ichi Shobō, 1973.
Barlow, Tani. "Femininity." In *The Palgrave Dictionary of Transnational History*, edited by Pierre-Yves Saunier and Akira Iriye, 388–92. Basingstoke and New York: Palgrave, 2009.
Barthes, Roland. *Empire of Signs*. Translated by Richard Howard. New York: Hill and Wang, 1982.
———. *Image Music Text*. Translated by Stephen Heath. New York: Hill and Wang, 1977.
Benhabib, Seyla. "Epistemologies of Postmodernism: A Rejoinder to Jean-François Lyotard." In *Feminism/Postmodernism*, edited by Linda J. Nicholson, 107–30. New York: Routledge, 1990.

Bergan, Ronald. "Isuzu Yamada Obituary: One of the Greatest Female Stars of Japanese Cinema." *The Guardian*, 11 July 2012. http://www.theguardian.com/film/2012/jul/11/isuzu-yamada. Accessed 2 April 2014.

Bernstein, Adam. "Isuzu Yamada, 95, Acclaimed Japanese Actress." *Washington Post*, 12 July 2012. http://www.washingtonpost.com/entertainment/movies/isuzu-yamada-95-acclaimed-japanese-actress/2012/07/12/gJQAjTc5fW_story.html. Accessed 2 April 2014.

Brandon, James R. "Kabuki and Shakespeare: Balancing Yin and Yang." *TDR* 43.2 (Summer 1999): 15–53.

———. "Myth and Reality: A Story of Kabuki during American Censorship, 1945–1949." *Asian Theatre Journal* 23.1 (2006): 1–110.

———. "Reflections on the *Onnagata*." *Asian Theatre Journal* 29.1 (Spring 2012): 122–25.

Bruder, Margaret Ervin. *Aestheticizing Violence, or How to Do Things with Style*. Diss., Indiana University, 2003. Ann Arbor: UMI.

Bungo. "Takemoto Tosatayū to Jogi no Kai" (Takemoto Tosatayū and the Women's Gidayū Association). *EG* 33.8 (August 1939): 76.

Bungo no Kami. "Fukagawa-za" (The Fukagawa-za Theater). *EG* 5.9 (September 1911): 164–65.

Buruma, Ian. *A Japanese Mirror: Heroes and Villains of Japanese Culture*. London: Jonathan Cape, 1984.

Butler, Judith. *Excitable Speech: A Politics of the Performative*. New York: Routledge, 1997.

———. *Gender Trouble: Feminism and the Subversion of Identity*. New York: Routledge, 1990.

———. "Imitation and Gender Insubordination." In *Inside/Out: Lesbian Theories, Gay Theories*, edited by Diana Fuss, 13–31. New York: Routledge, 1991.

Case, Sue-Ellen. *Feminism and Theatre*. New York: Routledge, 1988.

———. "Toward a Butch-Femme Aesthetic." In *Making a Spectacle: Feminist Essays on Contemporary Women's Theatre*, edited by Lynda Hart, 282–99. Ann Arbor: University of Michigan Press, 1989.

Coaldrake, A. Kimi. *Women's Gidayū and the Japanese Theatre Tradition*. London: Routledge, 1997.

DeShazer, Mary K. *Fractured Borders: Reading Women's Cancer Literature*. Ann Arbor: University of Michigan Press, 2005.

Dolan, Jill. *The Feminist Spectator as Critic*. Ann Arbor: UMI Research Press, 1988.

Edelson, Loren. *Danjūrō's Girls: Women on the Kabuki Stage*. New York: Palgrave, 2009.

———. "The Female Danjūrō: Revisiting the Acting Career of Ichikawa Kumehachi." *Journal of Japanese Studies* 34.1 (Winter 2008): 69–98.

———. "Playing for the Majors and the Minors: Ichikawa Girls' Kabuki on the Postwar Stage." In *Rising from the Flames: The Rebirth of Theater in Occupied Japan, 1945–1952*, edited by Samuel L. Leiter, 75–87. Lanham, MD: Lexington Books, 2009.

Endō Yasuko. *Sansei Inoue Yachiyo: Kyōmai Inoue-ryū Iemoto, Gion no Onna Fudoki* (Inoue Yachiyo III: The record of a woman in Gion, *iemoto* of the Inoue school of *mai* dance in Kyoto). Tokyo: Riburopōto, 1993.

Engeki Hakubutsukan (Kawatake Shigetoshi et al.), ed. *Engeki Hyakka Daijiten* (Encyclopedia of theater). 6 vols. Tokyo: Heibonsha, 1960–62.

Enoki Sono. "Kataoka Gadō." *Engekikai* 25.3 (March 1967): 106–7.

———. "Narikomaya Shibuya no Adesugata" (Fascinating Utaemon at his residence in Shibuya). *Engekikai* 22.8 (August 1964): 80–82.

Enomoto Shigetami. "Onnagata Engi to Joyū Engi: Nihon Kindai Engekishi no Byōri" (Acting of *onnagata* and acting of actresses: Pathology of the history of Japanese modern theater). *Kokugakuin Zasshi* 85.11 (November 1984): 256–66.

Ernst, Earle. *The Kabuki Theatre*. Honolulu: University of Hawai'i Press, 1974. First published by Oxford University Press, New York, 1956.

Fausto-Sterling, Anne. "The Five Sexes, Revisited." *The Sciences*, July–August 2000: 19–23.

Féral, Josette. "Theatricality: The Specificity of Theatrical Language." Translated by Ronald P. Bermingham. *SubStance* 31.2–3 (2002): 94–108.

Foucault, Michel. *The History of Sexuality*. Vol. 1, *An Introduction*. Translated by Robert Hurley. New York: Vintage Books, 1978.

Fowler, Edward. *The Rhetoric of Confession: Shishōsetsu in Early Twentieth-Century Japanese Fiction*. Berkeley: University of California Press, 1988.

Fujiki, Hideaki. "Canonising Sexual Image, Devaluing Gender Performance: Replacing the *Onnagata* with Female Actresses in Japan's Early Cinema." In *Remapping World Cinema: Identity, Culture and Politics in Film*, edited by Stephanie Dennison and Song Hwee Lim, 147–60. London: Wallflower Press, 2006.

Fujita Hiroshi. *Henreki: Joyū Yamada Isuzu* (Wanderings: Actress Yamada Isuzu). Tokyo: Kawade Shobō Shinsha, 1998.

———. "Kabuki-shi no Keifu 1" (Genealogy of kabuki journals, part 1). *Kabuki* 2 (October 1968): 193–97.

Fujiwara no Teika. *Maigetsushō* (Each month's exegesis). Edited by Hisamatsu Sen'ichi. In *Karonshū Nōgakuronshū* (Collection of poetry theory and noh theory), edited by Hisamatsu Sen'ichi and Nishio Minoru, 125–39. Vol. 65 of *NKBT*. Tokyo: Iwanami Shoten, 1961.

Fukuoka Yagoshirō. "Ayamegusa" (The words of Ayame). In *Yakusha Banashi* (The actors' analects), edited by Hachimonji Jishō. In *Kabuki Jūhachibanshū* (Eighteen great kabuki plays), edited by Gunji Masakatsu, 317–26, 422–23. Vol. 98 of *NKBT*. Tokyo: Iwanami Shoten, 1965.

———. "Ayamekusa." In Hachimonji Jishō, *Shinkoku Yakusha Kōmoku* (Overview and details of actors, the new edition), edited by Munemasa Isoo and Doi Jun'ichi. In *Kabuki*, edited by Gondō Yoshikazu, Munemasa Isoo, and Moriya Takeshi, 194–98. Vol. 6 of *NSBSS*, edited by Geinōshi Kenkyūkai. Tokyo: San'ichi Shobō, 1973.

———. "The Words of Ayame." In Hachimonji Jishō, ed. *The Actors' Analects*. Edited and translated by Charles J. Dunn and Bunzō Torigoe. New York: Columbia University Press, 1969. 49–66.

Gakushū Kenkyūsha, ed. *"Nanba Aruki" de Kyōi no Karada Kakumei* (Miraculous body revolution by *"nanba* walking"). Tokyo: Gakushū Kenkyūsha, 2004.

———, ed. *"Nanba Aruki" de Shintai Kaizō* (Remodeling the body by *"nanba* walking"). Tokyo: Gakushū Kenkyūsha, 2005.

Garber, Marjorie. *Vested Interests: Cross-Dressing and Cultural Anxiety*. New York: Routledge, 1992.

Gerstle, C. Andrew. "The Culture of Play: Kabuki and the Production of Texts." *Oral Tradition* 20.2 (2005): 188–216.

Gondō Yoshikazu. "Gaisetsu 1: Kabuki no Kenkyū to sono Shiryō" (Overview, part 1: Research on kabuki and its materials). In *Kabuki*, edited by Gondō Yoshikazu, Munemasa Isoo, and Moriya Takeshi, 1–7. Vol. 6 of *NSBSS*, edited by Geinōshi Kenkyūkai. Tokyo: San'ichi Shobō, 1973.

Gramlich-Oka, Bettina. *Thinking Like a Man: Tadano Makuzu (1763–1825)*. Leiden: Brill, 2006.

Gunji Masakatsu. "Kabuki Buyō no Nagare" (The passage of kabuki dance). *Makuai* 10.9 (September 1955): 50–53.

———. *Kabuki no Katachi* (The form of kabuki). Vol. 2 of *Gunji Masakatsu Santeishū* (The selected works of Gunji Masakatsu). Tokyo: Hakusuisha, 1991.

———. "Kaisetsu" (Commentary). In In *Kabuki Jūhachibanshū* (Eighteen great kabuki plays), edited by Gunji Masakatsu, 13–49, 293–304. Vol. 98 of *NKBT*. Tokyo: Iwanami Shoten, 1965.

———. *Odori no Bigaku* (The aesthetics of dance). Tokyo: Engeki Shuppansha, 2000.

Hachijō Kadensho (Eight-volume book of transmission of teachings on the Flower). Edited by Nakamura Yasuo. In *Kodai Chūsei Geijutsuron* (Theory on artistry from the ancient to medieval periods), edited by Hayashiya Tatsusaburō, 511–665. Vol. 23 of *NST*. Tokyo: Iwanami Shoten, 1973.

Hachimonji Jishō. *Yakusha Zensho* (The complete book on actors). Edited by Ōshima Masakazu, Munemasa Isoo, and Takatsuki Kazuko. In *Kabuki*, edited by Gondō

Yoshikazu, Munemasa Isoo, and Moriya Takeshi, 199–241. Vol. 6 of *NSBSS*, edited by Geinōshi Kenkyūkai. Tokyo: San'ichi Shobō, 1973.

Hachimonji Kishō and Hachimonji Zuishō. *Shinsen Kokon Yakusha Taizen* (The complete book of actors through all ages, the new edition). Edited by Hirose Chisako and Horiguchi Yasuo. In *Kabuki*, edited by Gondō Yoshikazu, Munemasa Isoo, and Moriya Takeshi, 5–86. Vol. 6 of *NSBSS*, edited by Geinōshi Kenkyūkai. Tokyo: San'ichi Shobō, 1973.

Hahn, Tomie. *Sensational Knowledge: Embodying Culture through Japanese Dance*. Middletown, CT: Wesleyan University Press, 2007.

Halberstam, Judith. "The Contradictions of Female Masculinity Before and After Abu Grahib." Lecture summary reported by Junko Yoshikawa. *F-GENS: Frontiers of Gender Studies* 3 (March 2005): 238–40.

———. *Female Masculinity*. Durham, NC: Duke University Press, 1998.

Hart, Lynda. "Canonizing Lesbians?" In *Modern American Drama: The Female Canon*, edited by June Schlueter, 275–92. Rutherford, NJ: Fairleigh Dickinson University Press, 1990.

———. *Fatal Women: Lesbian Sexuality and the Mark of Aggression*. Princeton: Princeton University Press, 1994.

———. "Identity and Seduction: Lesbians in the Mainstream." In *Acting Out: Feminist Performances*, edited by Lynda Hart and Peggy Phelan, 119–37. Ann Arbor: University of Michigan Press, 1993.

———. "Introduction." In *Acting Out: Feminist Performances*, edited by Lynda Hart and Peggy Phelan, 1–12. Ann Arbor: University of Michigan Press, 1993.

———. "Introduction: Performing Feminism." In *Making a Spectacle: Feminist Essays on Contemporary Women's Theatre*, edited by Lynda Hart, 1–21. Ann Arbor: University of Michigan Press, 1989.

———. "Killing Representation: Feminism and Violence at the Limit." *Psychoanalytic Review* 84.5 (October 1997): 789–812.

———. "Motherhood According to Finley: The Theory of Total Blame." *TDR* 36.1 (Spring 1992): 124–34.

———. "'They Don't Even Look Like Maids Anymore': Wendy Kesselman's *My Sister in This House*." In *Making a Spectacle: Feminist Essays on Contemporary Women's Theatre*, edited by Lynda Hart, 131–46. Ann Arbor: University of Michigan Press, 1989.

Hattori Yukio. "Ayamegusa" (On "The Words of Ayame"). In Hakii Kōzō et al., *Gendai no Geidan* (Contemporary accounts-on-*gei*), edited by Dentō Geijutsu no Kai, 28–30. Vol. 11 of *DG*. Tokyo: Gakugei Shorin, 1970.

———. *Edo Kabuki no Bi-ishiki* (Aesthetics of kabuki in Edo). Tokyo: Heibonsha, 1996.

———. *Kabuki no Genkyō: Ji-shibai to Toshi no Shibai-goya* (Native provinces of kabuki: Village theaters and urban playhouses). Tokyo: Yoshikawa Kōbunkan, 2007.

———. *Kabuki no Kōzō: Dentō Engeki no Sōzō Seishin* (The structure of kabuki: Creative spirit of traditional theater). Tokyo: Chūōkōronsha, 1970.

———. *Kabuki Seiritsu no Kenkyū* (Study of the formation of kabuki). Tokyo: Kazama Shobō, 1968.

———. *Ōinaru Koya: Kinsei Toshi no Shukusai Kūkan* (Extraordinary playhouses: Sites of a fete in early modern urban cities). Tokyo: Heibonsha, 1986.

———. "Seiritsuki no Kabuki" (Kabuki in the formative period). In *Kabuki no Rekishi I* (History of kabuki, part 1), edited by Torigoe Bunzō, Uchiyama Mikiko, and Watanabe Tamotsu, 1–34. Vol. 2 of *IKKB*. Tokyo: Iwanami Shoten, 1997.

———. "Waka-oyama (waka-onnagata): Gei no Kakuritsu to Tenkai" (Young *onnagata*: The establishment and development of *gei*). *Kabuki* 12 (April 1971): 107–15.

Hattori Yukio (text) and Ichinoseki Kei (illustrations). *Ehon Yume no Edo Kabuki* (Picture book of dream kabuki in Edo). Tokyo: Iwanami Shoten, 2001.

Hattori Yukio and Kawazoe Yū. "Kabuki Gekijō Kenkyū no Kako to Genzai: Ōinaru Koya kara Nijūnen" (Studies of kabuki playhouses in the past and the present: Twenty years since *Extraordinary Playhouses*). *KKH* 39 (November 2007): 5–29.

Hayachine no Fu (Ode to Mount Hayachine). Directed by Haneda Sumiko. Jiyū Kōbō, 1982.

Hayamizu Sayoko. "Nanba Aruki-kō" (On *nanba* walking). *Aichi Kenritsu Daigaku Jidō-Kyōiku Gakka Ronshū* 39 (2006): 21–26.

Hayashi Kimiko. "Daimyō Yashiki ni okeru Kabuki" (Kabuki productions at daimyo residences). In *Kabuki no Rekishi I* (History of kabuki, part 1), edited by Torigoe Bunzō, Uchiyama Mikiko, and Watanabe Tamotsu, 213–27. Vol. 2 of *IKKB*. Tokyo: Iwanami Shoten, 1997.

———. "Yashikikata ni okeru Kabuki Jōen o Megutte" (About kabuki productions at samurai residences). In *Nihon Bungaku Kenkyū Taisei Kabuki, Jōruri* (Collected research papers on Japanese literature: Kabuki and *jōruri*), edited by Suwa Haruo, 214–30. Tokyo: Kokusho Kankōkai, 1993.

Hearn, Lafcadio. *Glimpses of Unfamiliar Japan*. Vol. 1. Boston: Houghton Mifflin Company, 1894.

Hirano Hidetoshi, ed. *Nihon Buyō Nyūmon* (Introduction to Japanese dance). Tokyo: Engeki Shuppansha, 2000.

Hishikawa Moronobu. *Kokon Yakusha Monogatari* (The tales of actors through all ages). In vol. 4 of *Edo Jidai Bungei Shiryō* (Documents of literary arts in the Edo period), edited by Kokusho Kankōkai, 1–14. Tokyo: Meicho Kankōkai, 1964.

Honchi Eiki. "Kabuki to Takarazuka Joyū" (Kabuki and Takarazuka actresses). *Geinō* 7.3 (March 1965): 58–59.

Honda Yasuo. "Kaiwa-tai no Sharebon no Seiritsu ni tsuite no Shiron: Niwaka to Ukiyo Monomane, Kowairo no Hatashita Yakuwari" (Essay on the formation of books of wit and fashion written in a colloquial style: Roles played by ad-lib comedy, *ukiyo* mimicry, and voice mimicry). *Kokugo to Kokubungaku* (November 1959): 51–63.

Hozumi Ikan. "Chikamatsu no Gensetsu: Naniwa Miyage Hottan Shō" (Discourse of Chikamatsu: Excerpt from the introduction to *The Souvenirs from Naniwa*). Edited by Shuzui Kenji and Ōkubo Tadakuni. In *Chikamatsu Jōrurishū Ge* (Collection of *jōruri* by Chikamatsu Monzaemon, part 2), edited by Shuzui Kenji and Ōkubo Tadakuni, 355–59, 406. Vol. 50 of *NKBT*. Tokyo: Iwanami Shoten, 1959.

Hurst, G. Cameron, III. *Armed Martial Arts of Japan: Swordsmanship and Archery*. New Haven: Yale University Press, 1998.

Ichikawa Kamejirō and Takahashi Issei. "Bokutachi ga Enjiru 'Onnagata' wa Josei nikoso Mite Hoshii" (We want women to see *onnagata* that we play). *Fujin Kōron* 1261 (November 2008): 170–73.

Ichikawa Kumehachi. "Gigei no Hanashi" (On artistic technique). *EG* 1.4 (April 1907): 79–86.

———. "Ichikawa Kumehachi no Atarigei: Menoto Masaoka" (Ichikawa Kumehachi's successful repertoire: Wet nurse Masaoka). *EG* 5.11 (November 1911): 54–63.

———. "Meika Shinsōroku 7" (True documents of distinguished masters, part 7). *EG* 1.9 (September 1907): 107–22.

———. "Onnagata no Kokoroe" (Instructions for *onnagata*). *Kabuki* 84 (April 1907): 110–15.

Ichikawa Monnosuke. "Ichikawa Monnosuke Jiden" (Autobiography of Ichikawa Monnosuke). *Kabuki* 121 (July 1910): 132–35.

Ichikawa Shun'en. *Onna Zukuri* (Creation of women). Tokyo: Tokuma Shoten, 2006.

Ichiraku. *Chikuhō Koji* (History of the Takemoto and Toyotake troupes). Edited by Marunishi Michio. In *Ningyō Jōruri* (The puppet theater), edited by Tsunoda Ichirō and Yokoyama Tadashi, 20–34. Vol. 7 of *NSBSS*. Tokyo: San'ichi Shobō, 1975.

Ide Shōu. "Fukagawa no Onna Shibai" (Woman theater at Fukagawa). *EG* 5.9 (September 1911): 118–20.

Iguchi Seiji. *Joyū Kagami* (The directory of actresses). Tokyo: Engei Gahōsha, 1912.

Ihara Saikaku. *Nanshoku Ōkagami* (The great mirror of male love). In *Teihon Saikaku Zenshū* (The complete works of Saikaku, the standard edition), by Ihara Saikaku, edited by Ehara Taizō, Teruoka Yasutaka, and Noma Kōshin. Vol. 4. Tokyo: Chūōkōronsha, 1964.

Ihara Seiseien et al. "Gekidankai 3" (Meeting on stories about theater, part 3). *Kabuki* 116 (March 1910): 66–74.

Ihara Toshirō. *Kabuki Nenpyō* (The chronological table of kabuki). Edited by Kawatake Shigetoshi and Yoshida Teruji. Vol. 1. Tokyo: Iwanami Shoten, 1956.

———. *Nihon Engekishi* (History of Japanese theater). Reprint. Tokyo: Kuresu Shuppan, 1996. First published by Waseda Daigaku Shuppanbu, Tokyo, 1904.

———, ed. *Utaemon Jiden* (Autobiography of Utaemon). Tokyo: Shūhōen Shuppanbu, 1935.

Ikegami, Eiko. *Bonds of Civility: Aesthetic Networks and the Political Origins of Japanese Culture.* Cambridge: Cambridge University Press, 2005.

Imao Tetsuya. *Henshin no Shisō: Nihon Engeki ni okeru Engi no Ronri* (Thought of metamorphoses: Logic of performance in Japanese theater). Tokyo: Hōsei Daigaku Shuppankyoku, 1970.

———. "'Onnagata Hiden' to Kikunojō no Ishiki" ("The Secret Transmissions of an *Onnagata*" and Kikunojō's consciousness). *Engekigaku* 1 (March 1959): 52–57.

———. *Yakusha Banashi Hyōchū* (Annotation to *The Actors' Analects*). Tokyo: Tamagawa Daigaku Shuppanbu, 1992.

Inoue Nobuko. "Shodai Yoshizawa Ayame no Jitsuzō: Genroku Hōei-ki o Chūshin ni" (Real image of Yoshizawa Ayame I: Mainly during the eras of Genroku and Hōei). *Joshi Seigakuin Tanki Daigaku Kiyō* 30 (March 1998): 300–314.

———. "Yoshizawa Ayame no Kō-hansei to sono Shinka: The True Value of the Art of Ayame Yoshizawa the First in the Latter Half of His Life." *Seigakuin Daigaku Ronsō* 12.2 (February 2000): 249–60.

Irigaray, Luce. "Commodities among Themselves." In *This Sex Which Is Not One*, translated by Catherine Porter, with Carolyn Burke, 192–97. Ithaca, NY: Cornell University Press, 1985.

Isaka Baisetsu. "Godaime Utaemon no Kaikyūdan Jō" (Reminiscences of Utaemon V, part 1). *Kabuki* 137 (November 1911): 100–109.

Isaka, Maki. "Box-Lunch Etiquette: Conduct Guides and Kabuki *Onnagata*." In *Manners and Mischief: Gender, Power, and Etiquette in Japan*, edited by Jan Bardsley and Laura Miller, 48–66. Berkeley: University of California Press, 2011.

———. "Dui bei mofang zhe de mofang: 'Nüxing' de shehui xingbie—qi lishixing, caoyanxing ji qi zai nüxing tezhi chuanbo zhong de canyu." Translated by Zheng Yanfang, checked by Zhang Ying. In *Nanxing yanjiu: Masculinity Studies*, Wang Zheng and Zhang Ying, editors-in-chief, 253–91. Shanghai: Shanghai Sanlian Shudian, 2012.

———. "The Gender of *Onnagata* As the Imitating Imitated: Its Historicity, Performativity, and Involvement in the Circulation of Femininity." *Positions: East Asia Cultures Critique* 10.2 (Fall 2002): 245–84.

———. "Images of *Onnagata*: Complicating the Binarisms, Unraveling the Labyrinth." In *PostGender: Gender, Sexuality and Performativity in Japanese Culture*, edited by Ayelet Zohar, 22–38. Newcastle upon Tyne: Cambridge Scholars Publishing, 2009.

———. "Osanai Kaoru's Dilemma: 'Amateurism by Professionals' in Modern Japanese Theatre." *TDR* 49.1 (Spring 2005): 119–33.

———. *Secrecy in Japanese Arts: "Secret Transmission" as a Mode of Knowledge*. New York: Palgrave, 2005.

———. "What Could Have Happened to 'Femininity' in Japanese Stagecraft: A Memorial Address to Yamada Isuzu (1917–2012)." *Positions: Asia Critique* 21.3 (Summer 2013): 755–59.

———. "Women *Onnagata* in the Porous Labyrinth of Femininity: On Ichikawa Kumehachi I." *U.S.-Japan Women's Journal* 30–31 (2006): 105–31.

Ishibashi Ningetsu and Maeda Shozan. *Tōyō Daitokai* (A metropolis in the East). Tokyo: Shun'yōdō, 1898.

Jackson, Shannon. "Theatricality's Proper Objects: Genealogies of Performance and Gender Theory." In *Theatricality*, edited by Tracy C. Davis and Thomas Postlewait, 186–213. Cambridge: Cambridge University Press, 2003.

Kabuki Hyōbanki Shūsei (Collected kabuki actor-critique booklets). Edited by Kabuki Hyōbanki Kenkyūkai. 11 vols. Tokyo: Iwanami Shoten, 1972–77.

Kabuki Hyōbanki Shūsei, Dai-2-ki (Collected kabuki actor-critique booklets, series 2). Edited by Yakusha Hyōbanki Kenkyūkai. 11 vols. Tokyo: Iwanami Shoten, 1988–95.

Kagayama Naozō. *Shin-kabuki no Sujimichi* (The trace of *shin-kabuki*). Tokyo: Mokujisha, 1967.

———, ed. "Kyō no Geidan" (Accounts-on-*gei* today). In *Kabuki Zensho* (Complete book of kabuki). Vol. 3, 159–209. Edited by Toita Yasuji. Tokyo: Tokyō Sōgensha, 1956.

Kamiyama Akira. "Kumehachi no Zanzō: Onna Yakusha to Joyū no Aida" (The after image of Kumehachi: Between women-actors and actresses). *Geinō* 34.9 (September 1992): 17–23.

Kaneko Kichizaemon. "Nijinshū" (The dust in the ears). In *Yakusha Banashi* (The actors' analects), edited by Hachimonji Jishō. In *Kabuki Jūhachibanshū* (Eighteen great kabuki plays), edited by Gunji Masakatsu, 327–45, 426–34. Vol. 98 of *NKBT*. Tokyo: Iwanami Shoten, 1965.

Kano, Ayako. *Acting Like a Woman in Modern Japan: Theater, Gender, and Nationalism*. New York: Palgrave, 2001.

———. "Toward a Critique of Transhistorical Femininity." In *Gendering Modern Japanese History*, edited by Barbara Molony and Kathleen Uno, 520–54. Cambridge, MA: Harvard University Asia Center, 2005.

Karasuyakko. "Onna Yakusha to Joyū" (Women-actors and actresses). *EG* 6.1 (January 1912): 151–54.

Karatani Kōjin. *Nihon Kindai Bungaku no Kigen* (Origins of modern Japanese literature). Tokyo: Kōdansha, 1988.

Kasulis, Thomas P. "Editor's Introduction." In *The Body: Toward an Eastern Mind-Body Theory*, by Yuasa Yasuo, 1–15. Edited by Thomas P. Kasulis, translated by Shigenori Nagatomo and Thomas P. Kasulis. New York: State University of New York Press, 1987.

Kataoka Takao and Bandō Tamasaburō. "Hanagata Kissashitsu, Sawayaka Taidan: Futari de Katarō Miryoku no Shūhen" (Café of stars, refreshing dialogue: Let us two talk about the surroundings of charm). *Engekikai: Zōkan* 41.8, special issue (July 1983): 48–61.

Katayama Hiromichi. "Kyōmai Inoue-ryū no Hongyō-mono" (*Hongyō* pieces of the Inoue school of *mai* dance in Kyoto). *Butai Tenbō* 1.5 (November 1951): 8–10.

Katayama Keijirō. *Inoue Yachiyo Geiwa* (Inoue Yachiyo's accounts-on-*gei*). Kyoto: Kawahara Shoten, 1967.

———. "Kyōmai Inoue-ryū no Nagare: Sono Tokushoku o Tadotte" (The passage of the Inoue school of *mai* dance in Kyoto: Tracing its characteristics). In Gotō Katsuichi, *Shashinshū Kyōmai Inoue-ryū* (Collection of photographs of the Inoue school of *mai* dance in Kyoto), 176–85. Kyoto: Ayumi Shobō, 1984.

Katayama Rinrokken. *Chikuhō Sōben Shō* (Takemoto Toyotake dual theories, exegesis). Edited by Inobe Kiyoshi. In *Ningyō Jōruri* (The puppet theater), edited by Tsunoda Ichirō and Yokoyama Tadashi, 243–54. Vol. 7 of *NSBSS*. Tokyo: San'ichi Shobō, 1975.

Kawaguchi Hideko, Yoshimura Yūki, and Takechi Tetsuji. "Mai no Gijutsu: Yamamura-, Yoshimura-ryū o Chūshin ni" (Technique of *mai* dance: Mainly on the Yamamura and Yoshimura schools). In Tobe Ginsaku et al., *Hōgaku Hōbu* (Japanese music and Japanese dance), edited by Dentō Geijutsu no Kai, 129–51. Vol. 6 of *DG*. Tokyo: Gakugei Shorin, 1969.

Kawatake Shigetoshi. *Nihon Engeki Zenshi* (Complete history of Japanese theater). Tokyo: Iwanami Shoten, 1959.

Kawatake Toshio. "Ayame no Kyo to Jitsu: Genroku-ki Onnagata no Kokoro to Katachi" (Fictionality and reality of Ayame: The mind and form of *onnagata* in the Genroku era). *Kabuki* 25 (July 1974): 42–49.

———. "Kabuki no Onna" (Women in kabuki). *Kabuki* 12 (April 1971): 98–106.

———. *Nihon no Koten Geinō: Meijin ni Kiku Kyūkyoku no Gei* (Classical performing arts of Japan: Ultimate *gei* as told by maestros). Kanagawa: Kamakura Shunjūsha, 2007.

———. "'Onnagata' no Kiseki" (The trajectory of "*onnagata*"). *Kabuki* 19 (January 1973): 26–34.

Kawazoe Yoshihiko. "The Mechanism of Robustness in Dynamic Waking NANBA by a Humanoid Biped Robot GENBE Based on the Distributed Control of the Physical Body in a Martial Art." *JSME Annual Meeting*, 2005.7: 241–42.

Kenchiku Mappu: Architectural Map. "Kanamaru-za (The Kanamaru-za Theater)." http://www.arch-hiroshima.net/a-map/kagawa/kanamaru.html. Accessed 21 April 2014.

Kikusui. "Joyū Rekihōroku 9: Mori Ritsuko Shōzen" (Records of visits with actresses, part 9: Mori Ritsuko, part 2). *EG* 6.7 (July 1912): 193–97.

Kimura Mokurō. *Gekijō Ikkan Mushimegane* (Theater under the microscope). Edited by Munemasa Isoo. In *Kabuki*, edited by Gondō Yoshikazu, Munemasa Isoo, and Moriya Takeshi, 309–38. Vol. 6 of *NSBSS*, edited by Geinōshi Kenkyūkai. Tokyo: San'ichi Shobō, 1973.

Kinjinsai Shin'ō. *Kokon Yakusha Rongo Sakigake* (The pioneering analects from past and present actors). Edited by Gunji Masakatsu. In *Kinsei Geidōron* (Theory on the Way of arts in the premodern period), edited by Nishiyama Matsunosuke, Watanabe Ichirō, and Gunji Masakatsu, 463–92. Vol. 61 of *NST*. Tokyo: Iwanami Shoten, 1972.

Kirby, Vicki. *Telling Flesh: The Substance of the Corporeal*. New York: Routledge, 1997.

Kitagawa Tadahiko. *Zeami*. Tokyo: Chūōkōronsha, 1972.

Kitagishi Yūkichi. "Takarazuka Gidayū Kabuki o Miru: Takarazuka Daigekijō" (Watching the Takarazuka *gidayū kabuki*, at the Takarazuka Grand Theater). *Engekikai* 19.12 (December 1961): 89.

Kitamura Rokurō. "Meika Shinsōroku 19" (True documents of distinguished masters, part 19). *EG* 2.6 (June 1908): 62–84.

Kobitsu Matsuo. "Nakamura Sōjūrō no Engeki Kairyō to sono Ri'nen" (Nakamura Sōjūrō's theater reform and his ideas). *Nihon Engeki Gakkai Kiyō* 6 (1963): 45–54.

Kōkō (Kōbeni?). "Mukashi Gatari: Wakaba no Otozure" (Memoirs: The coming of young leaves). *EG* 22.2 (February 1928): 166–67; 22.4 (April 1928): 120–21.

Komatsu Narumi. *Kanzaburō, Araburu* (Kanzaburō, being rough). Tokyo: Gentōsha, 2010.

Konishi Chizuru, ed. "'Ripōto' Magarikado ni Tatsu Onnagata" (Report: *Onnagata* at a turning point). *Engekikai* 21.7 (July 1963): 80–84.

Kōno Ryōsen. "Butō, Bujutsu, Shūkyō Girei: Geinō to Matsuri no Shintairon e" (Dance, martial arts, and religious ceremonies: Toward a theory of the body of performing arts and festivals). In *Gijutsu to Shite no Shintai* (Body as a technology), edited by Nomura Masaichi and Ichikawa Miyabi, 202–28. Vol. 1 of *Sōsho: Shintai to Bunka* (Bodies and Cultures series). Tokyo: Taishūkan Shoten, 1999.

Kōno Yoshinori and Kōno Harunori. "Unfamiliar Japanese Martial Arts from the Pre-Edo Period." Lecture and demonstration presented at Ralph Rapson Hall, Minneapolis, 28 May 2012.

Kōno Yoshinori and Maeda Hideki. *Ken no Shisō* (Thought of the swords). Tokyo: Seidosha, 2001.

Kōno Yoshinori and Mitsuoka Hidetoshi. *Bugaku Tankyū: Sono Shin o Motomete* (Investigation into the martial science: Searching for its truth). Kyoto: Tōkyūsha, 2005.

Kumonosu-jō (Throne of blood). Directed by Kurosawa Akira. Performed by Yamada Isuzu and Mifune Toshirō. Tōhō, 1957.

Kurosaki Teijirō. *Geidan Hyakuwa* (One hundred stories of accounts-on-*gei*). Tokyo: Hakubunkan, 1940.

Kyōto Shinbun Henshūkyoku, ed. *Kyōmai* (*Mai* dance in Kyoto). Kyoto: Tankōsha, 1960.

LaFleur, William R. *Buddhism: A Cultural Perspective*. Englewood Cliffs, NJ: Prentice-Hall, 1988.

Lane, Richard. *Images from the Floating World: The Japanese Print*. New York: Konecky & Konecky, 1978.

———. "Shunga: The Disappearing Act." *Geijutsu Shinchō*, June 1994: 20–27, 36–40.

Laqueur, Thomas. *Making Sex: Body and Gender from the Greeks to Freud*. Cambridge, MA: Harvard University Press, 1990.

Leiter, Samuel L. "From Gay to *Gei*: The *Onnagata* and the Creation of *Kabuki*'s Female Characters." In *A Kabuki Reader: History and Performance*, edited by Samuel L. Leiter, 211–29. Armonk, NY: M. E. Sharpe, 2002.

———. *Frozen Moments: Writings on Kabuki, 1966–2001*. Ithaca, NY: East Asia Series, Cornell University, 2002.

———, ed. *Rising from the Flames: The Rebirth of Theater in Occupied Japan, 1945–1952*. Lanham, MD: Lexington Books, 2009.

Levy, Indra. *Sirens of the Western Shore: The Westernesque Femme Fatale, Translation, and Vernacular Style in Modern Japanese Literature*. New York: Columbia University Press, 2006.

Lim, Dennis. "Isuzu Yamada, Actress Who Worked with Kurosawa, Dies at 95." *New York Times*, 15 July 2012. http://www.nytimes.com/2012/07/16/movies/isuzu-yamada-actress-who-worked-with-kurosawa-dies-at-95.html. Accessed 2 April 2014.

Liu, Siyuan. *Performing Hybridity in Colonial-Modern China*. New York: Palgrave, 2013.

Lorde, Audre. *Sister Outsider*. New York: Crossing Press, 1984.

Macy, Roger. "Isuzu Yamada: Iconic Japanese Screen Actress Who Brought a Memorable Intensity to Her Roles." *Independent*, 18 August 2012. http://www.independent.co.uk/news/obituaries/isuzu-yamada-iconic-japanese-screen-actress-who-brought-a-memorable-intensity-to-her-roles-8057318.html. Accessed 2 April 2014.

Marey, E. J. *Movement*. Translated by Eric Pritchard. London: William Heinemann, 1895.

Masaki Yumi. "Shodai Yoshizawa Ayame no 'Soko ni Urei no Omoiire'" (Yoshizawa Ayame I's meditative pose with hidden sorrow). *KKH* 17 (June 1996): 80–96.

Matsumiya Saburō. *Edo Kabuki to Kōkoku* (Advertisement and Kabuki in Edo). Tokyo: Tōhō Shobō, 1973.

Mayama Seika. "Engeki Zakkan" (My impressions of theater). *EG* 4.12 (December 1910): 32–36.

———. "Onnagata wa Nagaki Kenkyū no Kekka" (*Onnagata* is a result of longtime study). *EG* 6.1 (January 1912): 52–53.

Mezur, Katherine. *Beautiful Boys/Outlaw Bodies: Devising Kabuki Female-Likeness*. New York: Palgrave, 2005.

Minamoto Junko. "Buddhism and the Historical Construction of Sexuality in Japan." *U.S.-Japan Women's Journal: English Supplement* 5 (1993): 87–115.

Minamoto no Shitagō. *Shohon Shūsei Wamyō Ruijūshō (Ruijushō): Honbun-hen* (Collected various versions of *Classified Glossary of Japanese Denominations*: Main Texts). Edited by Kyōto Daigaku Bungakubu Kokugogaku Kokubungaku Kenkyūshitsu. Kyoto: Rinsen Shoten, 1968.

Minamoto Ryōen. *Tokugawa Shisō Shōshi* (Concise history of Tokugawa thought). Tokyo: Chūōkōronsha, 1973.

Mishima Sōsen. "Baikō Katsugare no Hanashi" (Story of Baikō when he was deceived). *EG* 26.1 (January 1932): 59.

Mitamura Engyo. *Ryūei Saigo no Okyōgenshi* (The last theater-master at the shogunate). In *Kubō-sama no Hanashi* (Stories about shoguns). In vol. 1 of *Mitamura Engyo Zenshū* (The complete works of Mitamura Engyo), 119–36. Tokyo: Chūōkōronsha, 1976.

Mitsuhashi Junko. *Josō to Nihonjin* (Cross-dressing in female clothing and the Japanese). Tokyo: Kōdansha, 2008.

Miura Masashi. *Shintai no Zerodo: Nani ga Kindai o Seiritsu Sasetaka* (Zero degrees of the body: What made modernity established?). Tokyo: Kōdansha, 1994.

Miyao Shigeo. "Edo no Onnagata Haiyū to sono Kōi" (*Onnagata* and their actions in the Edo era). *Kokubungaku Kaishaku to Kanshō* 27.1 (October 1962): 106–10.

Mizuno Yūko. *Edo Tōkyō Musume Gidayū no Rekishi* (History of girls' *gidayū* in Edo and Tokyo). Tokyo: Hōsei Daigaku Shuppankyoku, 2003.

Mizuochi Kiyoshi. *Kamigata Kabuki* (Kabuki in the Kyoto and Osaka regions). Tokyo: Tōkyō Shoseki, 1990.

Modleski, Tania. "Feminism and the Power of Interpretation: Some Critical Readings." In *Feminist Studies/Critical Studies*, edited by Teresa de Lauretis, 121–38. Bloomington: Indiana University Press, 1986.

Mulvey, Laura. "Visual Pleasure and Narrative Cinema." *Screen* 16.3 (Autumn 1975): 6–18.

Munemasa Isoo. "Meiji Shoki no Tosho Shuppan Busū: Kyōto, Nagata Chōbei-ke no

Baai" (The number of copies of books published in the early Meiji era: A case study of the Nagata Chōbei family in Kyoto). *Bungaku* (December 1981): 119–23.

Murohoshi Ryugo. "Meiji Ikō no Wōkingu Kyōiku: Education of Walking after Meiji Era." *Wōkingu Kenkyū: Walking Research* 10 (2006): 63–67.

Nagatomo Chiyoji. "Edo Jidai Shomin no Dokusho" (Reading by the common people in the Edo era). *Bungaku* (September 1977): 99–109.

———. "Hon'ya no Kashihon, Kashihon-ya no Shuppan" (Rental library business by publishers and publishing business by rental libraries). *Bungaku* (November 1981): 83–94.

Nakamura Kankurō. *Kankurō Towazugatari* (Spontaneous talk by Kankurō). Tokyo: Shūeisha, 1994.

———. *Nakamuraya Sandai Yakusha no Seishun* (Three generations of the Nakamuraya, the springtime of actors). Tokyo: Kōdansha, 1987.

Nakamura Kankurō et al. *Nakamuraya Sandaiki: Kohinata no Ie* (Accounts of three generations of the Nakamuraya: The house at Kohinata). Tokyo: Shūeisha, 1998.

Nakamura, Karen, and Hisako Matsuo. "Female Masculinity and Fantasy Spaces: Transcending Genders in the Takarazuka Theatre and Japanese Popular Culture." In *Men and Masculinities in Contemporary Japan: Dislocating the Salaryman Doxa*, edited by James E. Robertson and Nobue Suzuki, 59–76. London: RoutledgeCurzon, 2003.

Nakamura Senjaku and Fujio Shin'ichi. "Beni to Oshiroi: Onnagata no Keshō" (Rouge and powder: Makeup of *onnagata*). *Kabuki* 12 (April 1971): 162–70.

Nakamura Shikaku. "Kabuki Haiyū no Hassei Shugyō" (Cultivation of elocution for kabuki actors). *Higeki Kigeki*, October 1972: 11–15.

Nakamura Tokizō. "Jibun no Monosashi o Motsu: Nakamura Tokizō" (Holding a ruler of one's own: Nakamura Tokizō). Interview by Komatsu Narumi. *Engekikai* (July 2008): 40–46.

Nakamura Utaemon [V]. "Geidan, Kaigyoku Yawa 1: Honchō Nijūshikō no Yaegakihime" (Accounts-on-*gei*, Night stories by Kaigyoku, part 1: Princess Yaegaki in *The Twenty-four Paragons of Filial Piety in This Country*). *EG* 27.10 (October 1933): 52–55.

———. "Nakamura Utaemon Kataru" (Nakamura Utaemon speaks up). *EG* 28.11 (November 1934): 33.

———. "Zoku Kaigyoku Yawa" (Sequel to the "Accounts-on-*gei*, Night Stories by Kaigyoku"). *EG* 32.7 (July 1938): 64–67.

Nakamura Utaemon V. *Kaigyoku Issekiwa* (One-night story by Kaigyoku). In Matsumoto Kōshirō VII et al., *Kabuki II* (Kabuki, part 2), 185–218. Vol. 2 of *NG*. Tokyo: Kyūgei Shuppan, 1979.

Nakamura Utaemon [VI]. "Watashi no Rirekisho" (My résumé). In *Watashi no Rirekisho*

14 (My résumé, vol. 14), edited by Nihon Keizai Shinbunsha, 333–410. Tokyo: Nihon Keizai Shinbunsha, 1984.

Nakamura Utaemon [VI] and Tobe Ginsaku. "Gendai o Ikiru 'Ayamegusa'" ("The Words of Ayame" Alive Today). In Hakii Kōzō et al., *Gendai no Geidan* (Contemporary accounts-on-*gei*), edited by Dentō Geijutsu no Kai, 28–52. Vol. 11 of *DG*. Tokyo: Gakugei Shorin, 1970.

Nakamura Yasuo. "Kaisetsu: *Hachijō Kadensho*" (Commentary: *The Eight-Volume Book of Transmission of Teachings on the Flower*). In *Kodai Chūsei Geijutsuron* (Theory on artistry from the ancient to medieval periods), edited by Hayashiya Tatsusaburō, 797–802. Vol. 23 of *NST*. Tokyo: Iwanami Shoten, 1973.

Nakarai Bokuyō. *Bokuyō Kyōka Shūi* (Bokuyō's *kyōka* supplement). In vol. 1 of *Kyōka Taikan* (Complete book of *kyōka*), edited by Kyōka Taikan Kankōkai, 339–51. Tokyo: Meiji Shoin, 1983.

Nakayama Seishichi. *Edo-ban Jōruri Hiden Shō* (The secret transmissions on *jōruri*, exegesis, the Edo version). Edited by Inobe Kiyoshi. In *Ningyō Jōruri* (The puppet theater), edited by Tsunoda Ichirō and Yokoyama Tadashi, 226–30. Vol. 7 of *NSBSS*. Tokyo: San'ichi Shobō, 1975.

Namino Yoshie. *Sannin Momotarō: Nakamura Kankurō Ikka Funsenki* (Three Momotarōs: Plucky fight of the Nakamura Kankurō family). Tokyo: Fusōsha, 1993.

Namura Jōhaku. *Onna Chōhōki* (Women's treasury). In *"Onna Chōhōki" "Nan Chōhōki"* (*Women's treasury* and *Men's treasury*), edited by Nagatomo Chiyoji, 9–196. Tokyo: Shakai Shisōsha, 1993.

Narukami (Saint Narukami). In *Kabuki Jūhachibanshū* (Eighteen great kabuki plays), edited by Gunji Masakatsu, 193–232. Vol. 98 of *NKBT*. Tokyo: Iwanami Shoten, 1965.

Nasutāsha/Nastazja (Nastasya). Directed by Andrzej Wajda, performed by Bandō Tamasaburō, Nagashima Toshiyuki. H.I.T./Say-To Workshop/TV Tokyo, 1994.

Natsume Sōseki. *Wagahai wa Neko de Aru* (I am a cat). Tokyo: Ōbunsha, 1965.

Nihon Geijutsu Bunka Shinkōkai (Japan Arts Council). "Deigan." *Bunka Dejitaru Raiburarī* (Digital library of cultures). http://www2.ntj.jac.go.jp/dglib/contents/learn/edc9/kouzou/mask_custome/mask/noumen20_b.html. Accessed 31 March 2014.

———. "Kōwakamai: Izumijō" (Kōwaka dance: Izumi castle). In *Bunka Dejitaru Raiburarī*. http://www2.ntj.jac.go.jp/dglib/edc4/index.jsp. Accessed 7 January 2014.

Nihon Kokugo Daijiten (Dictionary of the Japanese national language). 20 vols. Tokyo: Shōgakukan, 1972–76.

Nixon, Mark S., Tieniu Tan, and Rama Chellappa. *Human Identification Based on Gait*. New York: Springer, 2006.

Norizuki Toshihiko. "Okyōgenshi to Iu Edo no Joyū" (Edo actresses called theater-masters). *Geinō* 34.9 (September 1992): 10–16.

Obana Tsuyuko. "Joyū Rekihōroku 8: Morizumi Kikuko" (Records of visits with actresses, part 8: Morizumi Kikuko). *EG* 6.2 (February 1912): 25–29.

Ogawa Kyōichi. *Edo Bakuhan Daimyōke Jiten* (Dictionary of the shogunate and daimyo in the Edo era). Vol. 2. Tokyo: Hara Shobō, 1992.

Oka Onitarō. *Gidayū Hiketsu* (The secret of *gidayū* chanting). In *Kinsei Bungei Kenkyū Sōsho: Dai-2-ki Geinō-hen* (Studies of literary art in the Edo era, the second series, entertainment arts), edited by Kinsei Bungei Kenkyū Sōsho Kankōkai. Vol. 25, 1–189. Tokyo: Kuresu Shuppan, 1997.

Okada Mariko. "Inoue-ryū to Ningyō Jōruri" (The Inoue school and the puppet theater). *Waseda Daigaku Daigakuin Bungaku Kenkyūka Kiyō* 41.3 (1995): 81–93.

Okamoto Kidō. *Meiji Gekidan: Ranpu no Moto nite* (Theater circles in the Meiji era: Near a desk lamp). Tokyo: Iwanami Shoten, 1993.

Ōki Sentoku, ed. *Ochibashū* (Collected fallen leaves). In vol. 6 of *Nihon Kayō Shūsei* (Collection of Japanese *kayō*), edited by Takano Tatsuyuki, 401–521. Tokyo: Tokyōdō Shuppan, 1960.

Ōnishi Shigetaka. "Kudoki, Ningyōburi" (*Kudoki* acting and puppet-gesture acting). In *Shōwa Kabuki Taikan* (Encyclopedia of kabuki in the Shōwa era), edited by Wakei Shoten, 67–69. Kyoto: Wakei Shoten, 1948.

Onna Daigaku (Greater learning for women). In *Kaibara Ekiken Muro Kyūsō* (Kaibara Ekiken and Muro Kyūsō), edited by Araki Kengo and Inoue Tadashi, 201–27. Tokyo: Iwanami Shoten, 1970. Vol. 34 of *NST*.

"Onna Haiyū" (Female actors). *Tōkyō Nichinichi Shinbun*, 11 July 1888, 3.

Onoe Baikō VI. *Onnagata no Koto* (Matters on *onnagata*). In *Onnagata no Geidan* (*Onnagata*'s accounts-on-*gei*), 9–120. Tokyo: Engeki Shuppansha, 1988.

——. "Onnagata wa Ikitakutemo" (Even if *onnagata* wanted to go). *Kabuki* 110 (September 1909): 90.

——. *Ume no Shitakaze* (Wind beneath *ume* trees). In *Onnagata no Geidan* (*Onnagata*'s accounts-on-*gei*), 121–302. Tokyo: Engeki Shuppansha, 1988.

Onoe Baikō [VII], Mizutani Yaeko [I], and Kinoshita Junji. "Zadankai: Onnagata o Megutte" (Roundtable: On *onnagata*). *Teatoro* 118 (December 1951): 1–12.

Onoe Taganojō. "Watashi no Rirekisho" (My résumé). In *Watashi no Rirekisho* 12 (My résumé, vol. 12), edited by Nihon Keizai Shinbunsha, 147–216. Tokyo: Nihon Keizai Shinbunsha, 1984.

Onoe Taganojō and Andō Tsuruo. "Onoe Taganojō Geidan" (Accounts-on-*gei* by Onoe Taganojō). 6 parts. *Kabuki* 9–14 (July 1970–October 1971).

Onoe Taganojō, Fujiura Tomitarō, and Hakii Kōzō. "Seigaku Yawa to Yonsei Gennosuke" (*Night Stories by Seigaku* and Gennosuke IV). In Hakii Kōzō et al., *Gendai no Geidan* (Contemporary accounts-on-*gei*), edited by Dentō Geijutsu no Kai, 53–88. Vol. 11 of *DG*. Tokyo: Gakugei Shorin, 1970.

Onoe Umenosuke. "Onnagata: The Making of a Woman." Lecture and demonstration presented at the Ark, University of Michigan, Ann Arbor, 7 October 2003.

Oriyama Toshimi. *Suetsugu Shingo Takano Susumu Eikō eno Josō: Nihonjin demo Sekai to Tatakaeru!* (Suetsugu Shingo's and Takano Susumu's run-up to glory: Even the Japanese can fight with the world!). Tokyo: Shūeisha, 2003.

Ortolani, Benito. *The Japanese Theatre: From Shamanistic Ritual to Contemporary Pluralism*. Rev. ed. Princeton: Princeton University Press, 1995.

Osanai Kaoru. "Tsukiji Shōgekijō to Watakushi" (The Tsukiji Little Theater and Me). In *OKEZ*, edited by Sugai Yukio. Vol. 2, 43–44. Tokyo: Miraisha, 1965.

———. "Tsukiji Shōgekijō wa Nani no Tameni Sonzai Suruka" (For what purposes does the Tsukiji Little Theater exist?). In *OKEZ*. Vol. 2, 48–49.

Ōtani Takejirō. "Baikō no Kōfū o Omou" (Thinking of Baikō's dignified personality). *EG* 34.11 (November 1940): 26–27.

Ōtsuki Shigeru. *Ningen Kokuhō Onoe Taganojō no Nikki: Bita to Yobarete* (Diary of Living National Treasure Onoe Taganojō: Being called a bad coin). Tokyo: Seisō Shobō, 2010.

Ōya Yoshihiro. "'Nanba' Genryū-kō" (On the origins of *"nanba"*). *KKH* 26 (2000): 171–80.

Ozaki Hirotsugu. *Joyū no Keizu* (Genealogy of actresses). Tokyo: Asahi Shinbunsha, 1964.

Ōzasa Yoshio. *Nihon Gendai Engekishi: Meiji Taishō hen* (History of Japanese contemporary theater: The Meiji and Taishō eras). Tokyo: Hakusuisha, 1985.

Phelan, Peggy. "Feminist Theory, Poststructuralism, and Performance." *TDR* 32.1 (Spring 1988): 107–27.

Pola. *Utsukushii, no Uchigawa e* (Beauty, toward the interior of it). Directed by Tani Ichirō, performed by Bandō Tamasaburō and Kobayashi Mao. 2008.

Postlewait, Thomas, and Tracy C. Davis. "Theatricality: An Introduction." In *Theatricality*, edited by Tracy C. Davis and Thomas Postlewait, 1–39. Cambridge: Cambridge University Press, 2003.

Pronko, Leonard Cabell. *Theatre East and West: Perspectives toward a Total Theater*. Berkeley: University of California Press, 1967.

Ran. Directed by Kurosawa Akira, performed by Nakadai Tatsuya and Pītā. Tōhō, 1985.

Renchibō (Sadoshima Chōgorō). "Sadoshima Nikki" (The diary of Sadoshima). In *Yakusha Banashi* (The actors' analects), edited by Hachimonji Jishō. In *Kabuki*

Jūhachibanshū (Eighteen great kabuki plays), edited by Gunji Masakatsu, 364–77, 424–26. Vol. 98 of *NKBT*. Tokyo: Iwanami Shoten, 1965.

Robertson, Jennifer. "Gender-Bending in Paradise: Doing 'Female' and 'Male' in Japan." *Genders* 5 (Summer 1989): 50–69.

———. "The 'Magic If': Conflicting Performances of Gender in the Takarazuka Revue of Japan." In *Gender in Performance: The Presentation of Difference in the Performing Arts*, edited by Laurence Senelick. Hanover, NH: University Press of New England, 1992.

———. "Robo Sapiens Japanicus: Humanoid Robots and the Posthuman Family." *Critical Asian Studies* 39.3 (2007): 369–98.

———. "The Shingaku Woman: Straight from the Heart." In *Recreating Japanese Women, 1600–1945*, edited by Gail Lee Bernstein, 88–107. Berkeley: University of California Press, 1991.

———. *Takarazuka: Sexual Politics and Popular Culture in Modern Japan*. Berkeley: University of California Press, 1998.

Rose, Mark. *Authors and Owners: The Invention of Copyright*. Cambridge, MA: Harvard University Press, 1993.

Said, Edward W. *Orientalism*. New York: Vintage Books, 1978.

Sakai Naoki. "Joron: Nashonaritī to Bo/koku/go no Seiji" (Introduction: Nationality and the politics of mother/nation's/tongue). In *Nashonaritī no Datsukōchiku* (Deconstruction of nationality), edited by Sakai Naoki, Brett de Bary, and Iyotani Toshio, 9–53. Tokyo: Kashiwa Shobō, 1996.

———. *Voices of the Past: The Status of Language in Eighteenth-Century Japanese Discourse*. Ithaca, NY: Cornell University Press, 1991.

Sakata Tōjūrō. *Sakata Tōjūrō Kabuki no Shinzui o Ikiru* (Sakata Tōjūrō, living with the essential spirit of kabuki). Tokyo: Sekai Bunkasha, 2006.

Sakata Tōjūrō and Kameoka Noriko. *Yume: Heisei no Tōjūrō Tanjō* (Dream: The birth of Tōjūrō in the Heisei era). Kyoto: Tankōsha, 2005.

Sanford, James H. "Wind, Waters, Stupas, Mandalas: Fetal Buddhahood in Shingon." *Japanese Journal of Religious Studies* 24.1–2 (1997): 24.

Satō Chino. "Ganso Segawa Kikunojō no Geifū: Kyōhō no Onnagata" (Performance style of Segawa Kikunojō I: *Onnagata* in the Kyōhō era). *Kokugo to Kokubungaku* 74.4 (April 1997): 41–55.

———. "Ganso Segawa Kikunojō Shukkin Nenpu" (Chronological record of Segawa Kikunojō I's career). *KKH* 22 (December 1998): 163–87.

———. "Kakikae Onna Kyōgen 'Onna Narukami' o Megutte" (On a female version adaptation play, *Saint Narukami, the Female Version*). *Kokugo to Kokubungaku* 76.11 (November 1999): 69–82.

———. "Yakusha no Ikishini: Ganso Yoshizawa Ayame no Shōgai" (Life and death of an actor: The life of Yoshizawa Ayame I). *Kokubungaku Kaishaku to Kanshō* 73.3 (March 2008): 180–88.

Satō Yuki. "Bandō Tamasaburō Intabyū" (Interview with Bandō Tamasaburō). In *Bandō Tamasaburō Nasutāsha Shashinshū* (Collection of photographs of Bandō Tamasaburō in *Nastasya*), edited by Ishii Itsuko, no page numbers. Tokyo: Pia, 1994.

Sawai Manami. "Kyūsei Ichikawa Danjūrō to 'Ningyōburi': Ningyō-tsukai Yoshida Hacchō tono Kakawari o Chūshin ni" (Ichikawa Danjūrō IX and "puppet-gesture" acting: Mainly on his relations with puppeteer Yoshida Hacchō). *Minzoku Geijutsu: Ethno-Arts* 14 (1998): 156–61.

———. "Sansei Nakamura Utaemon no 'Ningyōburi'" ("Puppet-gesture" acting of Nakamura Utaemon III). *Geinōshi Kenkyū* 136 (January 1997): 15–34.

Sawamura Gennosuke [IV]. "Meiryū Geidan: Seigaku Yawa 8" (Accounts-on-*gei* by distinguished masters: Night stories by Seigaku, part 8). *EG* 21.6 (June 1927): 115–17.

———. *Seigaku Yawa* (Night stories by Seigaku). In Onoe Kikugorō V et al., *Kabuki I* (*Kabuki*, part 1), 227–312. Vol. 1 of *NG*. Tokyo: Kyūgei Shuppan, 1978.

Schalow, Paul Gordon. "Figures of Worship: Responses to Onnagata on the Kabuki Stage in Seventeenth-Century Japanese Vernacular Prose." In *Transvestism and the Onnagata Traditions in Shakespeare and Kabuki*, edited by Minoru Fujita and Michael Shapiro, 59–69. Kent: Global Oriental, 2006.

———. "Introduction." In Ihara Saikaku, *The Great Mirror of Male Love*, translated by Paul Gordon Schalow. Stanford, CA: Stanford University Press, 1990.

Scholl, Tim. "Queer Performance: 'Male' Ballet." In *Consuming Russia: Popular Culture, Sex, and Society since Gorbachev*, edited by Adele M. Barker, 303–17. Durham, NC: Duke University Press, 1999.

Scott, A. C. *The Kabuki Theatre of Japan*. London: George Allen & Unwin, 1955.

Scrubs. Directed by Bill Lawrence, performed by Zach Braff. ABC Studios, 2001–.

"Seinen Haiyū Taikan: Nakamura Kotarō" (Grand view of young actors: Nakamura Kotarō). *EG* 27.1 (January 1933): 87.

Seki Yōko. *Atarashī Kanzaburō: Gakuya no Kao* (New Kanzaburō: The face in the dressing room). Tokyo: Bungei Shunjū, 2005.

———. *Joyū de Arukoto* (To be an actress). Tokyo: Bungei Shunjū, 2004.

Sekine Shisei. *Tōto Gekijō Enkaku Shiryō* (Documents on the history of theaters in Edo/Tokyo). Edited by Sekine Masanao and Kokuritsu Gekijō Geinō Chōsashitsu. 2 vols. Tokyo: Kokuritsu Gekijō, 1983–84.

Senelick, Laurence. *The Changing Room: Sex, Drag and Theatre*. London: Routledge, 2000.

Sharaku. Directed by Shinoda Masahiro, performed by Sanada Hiroyuki, Iwashita Shima, and Nakamura Tomijūrō V. Shōchiku, 1995.

Shikitei Sanba. *Sanshibai Kakusha Hyōbanki* (Audience-critique booklet of the three theaters). Edited by Kumakura Isao. In *Kabuki*, edited by Gondō Yoshikazu, Munemasa Isoo, and Moriya Takeshi, 479–529. Vol. 6 of *NSBSS*, edited by Geinōshi Kenkyūkai. Tokyo: San'ichi Shobō, 1973.

Shinoda Masayuki. "Kenkyū Happyō Yōshi: 'Onna Danjūrō' ni tsuite" (Research report abstract: On "Woman Danjūrō"). *Nihon Engeki Gakkai Kiyō* 16 (1976): 98–100.

Shively, Donald H. "The Social Environment of Tokugawa Kabuki." In James R. Brandon, William P. Malm, and Donald H. Shively, *Studies in Kabuki: Its Acting, Music, and Historical Context.* Honolulu: University of Hawai'i Press, 1978.

Shuzui Kenji. "Tottori Ikeda-han Geinō Kiroku no Hakkutsu: Kinsei Shoki Geinō Shiryō (Kanbun-Jōkyō)" (Excavation of the records of performing arts at the Ikeda domain in Tottori: Documents of performing arts in the early Edo period [the Kanbun era and the Jōkyō era]). *Tōkyō Daigaku Jinbunkagaku-ka Kiyō* 9 (1956): 267–310.

———. "Zoku Tottori Ikeda-han Geinō Kiroku no Hakkutsu: Kinsei Shoki Geinō Shiryō (Genroku); Tsuketari Kanbun-hen no Hoi narabini Hochū" (Sequel to the excavation of the records of performing arts at the Ikeda domain in Tottori: Documents of performing arts in the early Edo period [the Genroku era]; along with supplement and notes for the Kanbun part). *Tōkyō Daigaku Jinbunkagaku-ka Kiyō* 13 (1957): 91–162.

———. "Zoku Zoku Tottori Ikeda-han Geinō Kiroku no Hakkutsu: Kinsei Shoki Geinō Shiryō (Hōei); Tsuketari Genroku-hen no Hoi narabini Hochū" (Second sequel to the excavation of the records of performing arts at the Ikeda domain in Tottori: Documents of performing arts in the early Edo period[the Hōei era]; along with supplement and notes for the Genroku part). *Tōkyō Daigaku Jinbunkagaku-ka Kiyō* 16 (1958): 153–344.

Shuzui Kenji and Ōkubo Tadakuni. "Kaisetsu" (Commentary). In *Chikamatsu Jōrurishū Ge* (Collection of *jōruri* by Chikamatsu Monzaemon, part 2), edited by Shuzui Kenji and Ōkubo Tadakuni, 3–19. Vol. 50 of *NKBT*. Tokyo: Iwanami Shoten, 1959.

Smith, Anna Deavere. *Fires in the Mirror.* PBS/American Playhouse. Directed by George C. Wolfe. PBS, 1993.

Sokō. "Kumehachi Ichiza no Wakatake-za o Miru" (Watching the troupe of Kumehachi at the Wakatake-za Theater). *Shizuoka Minyū Shinbun,* 23 November 1909: 3.

Sōma Akira and Torii Kiyokoto. *Kabuki: Ishō to Funsō* (Kabuki: Costume and makeup). Tokyo: Dai-Nihon Yūbenkai Kōdansha, 1957.

Sugimura Haruko. "Usotsuki Juban" (Deceptive underwear). *Engekikai* 45.1 (January 1987): 72.

Sugiura Zenzō. *Joyū Kagami* (The paragons of actresses). Tokyo: Sugiura Shuppanbu, 1912.

Sukeroku Yukari no Edo-zakura (Sukeroku, the flower of Edo). In *Kabuki Jūhachibanshū* (Eighteen great kabuki plays), edited by Gunji Masakatsu, 59–139. Vol. 98 of *NKBT*. Tokyo: Iwanami Shoten, 1965.

"Sukina Haiyū no Sukina Gei" (My favorite actors, my favorite *gei*). *EG* 6.7 (July 1912): 185–93.

Sunaga Asahiko. "Futanarihira no Keifu" (Genealogy of *futanarihira*). In *Ryōsei Guyū* (Androgyny), edited by Sunaga Asahiko, 208–14. Vol. 9 of *Shomotsu no Ōkoku* (Kingdom of monographs). Tokyo: Kokusho Kankōkai, 1998.

Suzuki Hiroko. "Genroku Kabuki Waka-onnagata (Waka-oyama) no Dōkō: Hantei Jōen Kiroku o Shiryō to shite" (The trend of *onnagata* for young women's roles in Genroku kabuki: Based on documents of performance records at samurai residences). *Kokubungaku Kenkyū Shiryōkan Kiyō Bungaku Kenkyū-hen* 34 (February 2008): 103–21.

———. "Kyōhō-ki Edo Kabuki ni okeru Yashikikata to Shibaimachi no Ichi-yōsō: Kaga-hantei Jōen Kiroku o Chūshin ni" (One aspect of Edo kabuki in the Kyōhō era at samurai residences and in the theater district: Based mainly on the performance record at the Kaga residence). *Geinōshi Kenkyū* 174 (July 2006): 24–40.

Suzuki Tadashi. "Ashi no Bunpō: The Grammar of Footwork." In Suzuki Tadashi, Isozaki Arata, Takahashi Yasunari, and Yamaguchi Masao, *Foot Work: Ashi no Seitaigaku*, 61–84. Tokyo: PARCO Shuppan, 1982.

Tadano Makuzu. "Solitary Thoughts: A Translation of Tadano Makuzu's *Hitori Kangae*." Translated by Janet R. Goodwin, Bettina Gramlich-Oka, Elizabeth A. Leicester, Yuri Terazawa, and Anne Walthall. *Monumenta Nipponica* 56.1 (2001): 21–38 (part 1); 56.2 (2001): 173–95 (part 2).

Taguchi Akiko. *Edo-jidai no Kabuki Yakusha* (Kabuki actors in the Edo period). Tokyo: Chūōkōronsha, 2002.

Taihei Rakukyo. *Hanakenuki*. Edited by Inobe Kiyoshi. In *Ningyō Jōruri* (The puppet theater), edited by Tsunoda Ichirō and Yokoyama Tadashi, 230–43. Vol. 7 of *NSBSS*. Tokyo: San'ichi Shobō, 1975.

Takahashi Hiroko. "Shosei Yoshizawa Ayame Nenpu" (Chronological record of Yoshizawa Ayame I). *Nihon Engeki Gakkai Kiyō* 21 (1983): 53–63.

———. "Shosei Yoshizawa Ayame ni okeru Tachiyaku no Gei" (Yoshizawa Ayame I's acquired artistic technique in male-role acting). *Engekigaku* 27 (1985): 28–43.

Takahashi Noriko. "Kurohon Aohon to Segawa Kikunojō: Kikugasane Onna Seigen no Kabuki Sesshu no Hōhō" (Black booklets, blue booklets, and Segawa Kikunojō:

Methodology of absorbing kabuki in *Double Chrysanthemums' Woman Seigen*). *Kinsei Bungei* 49 (November 1988): 33–48.

Takahashi, Yuichirō. "Kabuki Goes Official: The 1876 Opening of the Shintomi-za." In *A Kabuki Reader: History and Performance*, edited by Samuel L. Leiter, 123–51. Armonk, NY: M. E. Sharpe, 2002.

Takechi Tetsuji. *Bunraku Buyō* (The puppet theater and Japanese dance). Vol. 3 of *TTK*, edited by Ariki Daisaburō. Tokyo: San'ichi Shobō, 1979.

———. *Buyō no Gei* (*Gei* of dance). Tokyo: Tōkyō Shoseki, 1985.

———. *Dentō Ronkō* (Thoughts on traditions). Vol. 5 of *TTK*. Tokyo: San'ichi Shobō, 1980.

———. *Dentō to Danzetsu* (Traditions and discontinuation). Tokyo: Fūtōsha, 1989.

———. *Kabuki I*. Vol. 1 of *TTK*. Tokyo: San'ichi Shobō, 1978.

———. "Mai no Gijutsu" (Technique of *mai* dance). In *Mishima Yukio: Shi to sono Kabuki-kan* (Mishima Yukio: His death and his view of kabuki), 113–34. Tokyo: Nami Shobō, 1971.

Takechi Tetsuji and Tobe Ginsaku. "Kabuki ni Onnagata wa Fuyō ka: Osaka Mainichi Shinbun Shijō ni okeru Takechi Tobe Ryōshi no Ronsō" (Are *onnagata* unnecessary for kabuki?: Debates between Mr. Takechi and Mr. Tobe published in *Mainichi Shinbun*). *Engekikai* 14.4 (April 1956): 72–75.

———. "Taidan: Kabuki no Sekai Ura Omote" (Dialogue: The world of kabuki, both sides of it). *Engekikai: Zōkan* 39.12, special issue (October 1981): 50–61.

Takechi Tetsuji and Tomioka Taeko. *Dentō Geijutsu towa Nani Nanoka: Hihyō to Sōzō no tame no Taiwa* (What are traditional arts?: Dialogue for criticism and creation). Tokyo: Gakugei Shorin, 1988.

Takei Kyōzō. "Onnagata no So: Ukon Genzaemon" (The progenitor of *onnagata*: Ukon Genzaemon). *Bungaku* 55 (April 1987): 288–98.

———. *Wakashu Kabuki, Yarō Kabuki no Kenkyū* (Study of *wakashu kabuki* and *yarō kabuki*). Tokyo: Yagi Shoten, 2000.

Takemoto Harima-no-Jō. *Jōruri Hikyoku Shō* (The secret opuses of *jōruri*, exegesis). In *Ongyoku Sōsho Dai-2-hen* (Series on musical performances, part 2), edited by Kawakami Kunimoto, 1–38. Tokyo: Engei Chinsho Kankōkai, 1914.

Takemura, Kazuko. "Violence-Invested (non) Desire: Global Phallomorphism & Lethal Biopolitics." *F-GENS: Frontiers of Gender Studies* 3 (March 2005): 65–71.

Takenoya Shujin et al. "Ichikawa Kumehachi Tsuiokuroku" (In memory of Ichikawa Kumehachi). *EG* 7.9 (September 1913): 138–55.

Takeshiba Kisui. "Meiji Shonen no Onnagata" (*Onnagata* in the early Meiji era). *EG* 7.10 (October 1920): 36–44.

Takeshiba Kisui et al. "Ikeru Joyū Kumehachi" (The departed actress Kumehachi). *Kabuki* 159 (September 1913): 73–79.

Takeuchi Michitaka. "Ukon Genzaemon: Shoki Kabuki Haiyū Kō 2" (Ukon Genzaemon: On early kabuki actors, part 2). *Engekigaku* 2 (1960): 54–65.

Tamiya Kōon Shirogorō. "Zoku 'Nijinshū'" (Sequel to "The Dust in the Ears"). In *Yakusha Banashi* (The actors' analects), edited by Hachimonji Jishō. In *Kabuki Jūhachibanshū* (Eighteen great kabuki plays), edited by Gunji Masakatsu, 346–53, 426–34. Vol. 98 of *NKBT*. Tokyo: Iwanami Shoten, 1965.

Terajima Ryōan. *Wakan Sansai Zue 1* (Encyclopedia of heaven, earth, and humans in Japan and China, part 1). Edited by Tanigawa Ken'ichi. Vol. 28 of *NSSSS*. Tokyo: San'ichi Shobō, 1980.

Terakoya (The village school). Directed by Nagayama Takeomi, performed by Matsumoto Kōshirō VIII and Nakamura Ganjirō II. Shochiku, 2004.

Tian, Min. "Male *Dan*: The Paradox of Sex, Acting, and Perception of Female Impersonation in Traditional Chinese Theatre." *Asian Theatre Journal* 17.1 (Spring 2000): 78–97.

———. *Mei Lanfang and the Twentieth-Century International Stage: Chinese Theatre Placed and Displaced*. New York: Palgrave, 2012.

Tobe Ginsaku. "Kichō to Naru Shizensa: Shinsaku to Onnagata no Engi" (Naturalness as the basis : New pieces and the performance of *onnagata*). *Kabuki* 28 (April 1975): 52–61.

———. "Onnagata no Gihō to Seishin" (Technique and spirit of *onnagata*). *Kabuki* 12 (April 1971): 138–60.

———. "Shosei Yoshizawa Ayame to Onnagata-dō" (Yoshizawa Ayame I and the Way of *onnagata*). *Gekkan Bunkazai*, July 1976, 14–21.

Toita Yasuji. "Kyōgeki no Hana, Kabuki no Hana: 'Dan' to Onnagata to" (Flower of jingju, Flower of kabuki: *Dan* and *onnagata*). *Kabuki* 19 (January 1973): 56–64.

Torigoe Bunzō. "Kinsei Engeki no Shisō" (Thought of premodern theater). In *Kabuki to Bunraku no Honshitsu* (The essence of kabuki and the puppet theater), edited by Torigoe Bunzō, Uchiyama Mikiko, and Watanabe Tamotsu, 31–49. Vol. 1 of *IKKB*. Tokyo: Iwanami Shoten, 1997.

Tsuda Rui. *Kikigaki Joyū Yamada Isuzu* (Verbatim account, actress Yamada Isuzu). Tokyo: Heibonsha, 1997.

Uehara Teruo. "Geidan ni Miru Onnagata" (*Onnagata* in the accounts-on-*gei*). *Kabuki* 19 (January 1973): 36–43.

———. "Onnagata Geidan Tsunagi-kō" (Accounts-on-*gei* by *onnagata* and their transmissions). *Kabuki* 25 (July 1974): 50–59.

Ueno Chizuko. *Kafuchōsei to Shihonsei* (Patriarchy and capitalism). Tokyo: Iwanami Shoten, 1990.

———. "Orientarizumu to Jendā" (Orientalism and gender). In *Bosei Fashizumu: Haha Naru Shizen no Yūwaku* (Maternal fascism: The temptation of nature as that which is mother), edited by Kanō Mikiyo, 108–31. Vol. 6 of *Nyū Feminizumu Rebyū: New Feminism Review*. Tokyo: Gakuyō Shobō, 1995.

Uno, Kathleen S. "Women and Changes in the Household Division of Labor." In *Recreating Japanese Women, 1600–1945*, edited by Gail Lee Bernstein, 17–41. Berkeley: University of California Press, 1991.

Ushioda Tetsuo. *Mono to Ningen no Bunkashi: Hakimono* (The cultural history of humans and goods: Shoes). Tokyo: Hōsei Daigaku Shuppankyoku, 1973.

Wakita Haruko. *Chūsei ni Ikiru Onna-tachi* (Women living in the medieval period). Tokyo: Iwanami Shoten, 1995.

———. "Kankō ni Atatte" (Preface). In *Bosei o Tou: Rekishiteki Hensen* (To investigate motherhood: Historical trajectory), edited by Wakita Haruko. Vol. 1. Kyoto: Jinbun Shoin, 1985.

Watanabe Ichirō. "Heihō Densho Keisei ni tsuite no Ichi-shiron" (A working thesis on the formation of transmission books on swordsmanship and military science). In *Kinsei Geidōron* (Theory on the Way of arts in the premodern period), edited by Nishiyama Matsunosuke, Watanabe Ichirō, and Gunji Masakatsu, 645–73. Vol. 61 of *NST*. Tokyo: Iwanami Shoten, 1972.

Watanabe Tamotsu. *Kabuki ni Joyū o* (Actresses for kabuki). Tokyo: Maki Shoten, 1965.

———. *Onnagata no Unmei* (The destiny of an *onnagata*). Tokyo: Kinokuniya Shoten, 1974.

Watarai Kōji. "'Nanba' Aruki o Kangaeru" (A thought on "*nanba*" walking). *Gekkan Torēningu Jānaru: Training Journal* 253 (November 2000): 69–72 (pt. 1); 254 (December 2000): 68–72 (pt. 2).

Willis, Susan. "I Shop Therefore I Am: Is There a Place for Afro-American Culture in Commodity Culture?" In *Changing Our Own Words: Essays on Criticism, Theory, and Writing by Black Women*, edited by Cheryl A. Wall, 173–95, 238–39. New Brunswick, NJ: Rutgers University Press, 1989.

The Written Face/Kakareta Kao. Directed by Daniel Schmid, performed by Bandō Tamasaburō. First Run/Icarus Films, 1995.

"Yamada Isuzu san Shikyo" (Yamada Isuzu Passed Away). *Mainichi Shinbun*, 10 July 2012: 1, 31.

Yamai no Sōshi (The book of disease). In *Gaki Sōshi, Jigoku Sōshi, Yamai no Sōshi, Kusōshi Emaki* (The book of hungry ghosts, The book of hell, The book of disease, and The scroll painting of the nine stages from a corpse to the dust), edited by Komatsu Shigemi. Vol. 7 of *Nihon Emaki Taisei* (Collected Japanese scroll paintings). Tokyo: Chūōkōronsha, 1977.

Yamakawa Shizuo. "Onoe Taganojō Intabyū" (Interview with Onoe Taganojō). In *Yamakawa Shizuo Shibai Zuihitsu* (Essays on theater by Yamakawa Shizuo), 226–51. Tokyo: Engeki Shuppansha, 2003.

Yamamoto Jirō. "Ayamegusa" (On "The Words of Ayame"). *Nihon Engeki*, October 1944: 29–31.

Yamamoto Tsunetomo and Tashiro Tsuramoto. *Hagakure* (Hidden behind the leaves). Edited by Sagara Tōru and Satō Masahide. In *Mikawa Monogatari Hagakure (The story of Mikawa and Hidden behind the leaves)*, edited by Saiki Kazuma, Okayama Taiji, and Sagara Tōru. Vol. 26 of *NST*. Tokyo: Iwanami Shoten, 1974.

Yanagawa Shun'yō. "Joyū wa Ōi ni Yūbō" (Actresses are promising). *EG* 6.1 (January 1912): 45–48.

Yanagisawa Nobutoki. *Enyū Nikki* (Party diary). Edited by Nishiyama Matsunosuke and Hattori Yukio. In *Geinō Kiroku 2* (Records of performing arts, part 2), edited by Nishiyama Matsunosuke and Hattori Yukio. Vol. 13 of *NSBSS*. Tokyo: San'ichi Shobō, 1977.

Yang, X. Jie. "'Nanba Aruki' ni Miru Nihon to Chūgoku no Emaki" (Scroll paintings of Japan and China, seen from *"nanba* walking"). *Ajia Yūgaku: Intriguing Asia* 114 (September 2008): 176–82.

Yano Tatsuhiko, Kaneda Nobuo, Hasegawa Satoshi, and Koya Ichirō. *Nanba no Shintairon: Karada ga Yorokobu Ugoki o Tankyū Suru* (A theory on the body of *nanba*: Seeking the movements that please the body). Tokyo: Kōbunsha, 2004.

Yano Tatsuhiko, Kaneda Nobuo, and Oda Juntarō. *Nanba Bashiri: Kobujutsu no Ugoki o Jissen Suru (Nanba* running: Practicing the movements of ancient martial arts). Tokyo: Kōbunsha, 2003.

Yanone (Arrowhead). In *Kabuki Jūhachibanshū* (Eighteen great kabuki plays), edited by Gunji Masakatsu, 51–57. Vol. 98 of *NKBT*. Tokyo: Iwanami Shoten, 1965.

Yoshida Bungorō. *Bungorō Geidan* (Bungorō's accounts-on-*gei*). Edited by Nakayama Yasumasa. Tokyo: Sakurai Shoten, 1943.

Yoshida Setsuko, ed. *Edo Kabuki Hōrei Shūsei* (Collected laws and ordinances on kabuki theater in the Edo era). Tokyo: Ōfūsha, 1989.

———, ed. *Edo Kabuki Hōrei Shūsei Nenpyō* (Chronological table of the collected laws and ordinances on kabuki theater in the Edo era). Tokyo: Ōfūsha, 1997.

———, ed. *Zoku Edo Kabuki Hōrei Shūsei* (Sequel to the *"Collected Laws and Ordinances on Kabuki Theater in the Edo Era"*). Tokyo: Ōfūsha, 1997.

Yoshikawa Yoshio. "Genroku-ki no Onnagata" (*Onnagata* in the Genroku era). In *Engekishi Kenkyū, Dai-2-shū* (Study of the history of theater, part 2), 180–228. Edited by Engekishi Gakkai. Tokyo: Daiichi Shobō, 1932.

———. "Kabuki-geki no Onnagata" (*Onnagata* in kabuki theater). In *Engekishi Kenkyū,*

Dai-1-shū (Study of the history of theater, part 1). Edited by Engekishi Gakkai. Tokyo: Daiichi Shobō, 1932. 51–80.

Yuasa Yasuo. *Shintairon: Tōyōteki Shinshinron to Gendai* (Theory on the body: An Eastern mind-body theory and the present). Tokyo: Kōdansha, 1990.

Zeami Motokiyo. *Fūshikaden* (Transmission of teachings on style and the Flower). In *Zeami Zenchiku* (Zeami and Zenchiku), edited by Omote Akira and Katō Shūichi, 13–65. Vol. 24 of *NST*. Tokyo: Iwanami Shoten, 1974.

———. *Shikadō* (The path to the Flower). In *Zeami Zenchiku* (Zeami and Zenchiku), edited by Omote Akira and Katō Shūichi, 111–19. Vol. 24 of *NST*. Tokyo: Iwanami Shoten, 1974.

INDEX

Abe Yutaka [also "Bungo no Kami" and "Bungo" in bibliography], 197n85
abjection, ix, 19, 29, 43, 133, 137, 152, 162, 214n18
accounts-on-*gei* (*geidan*), 19, 59–60, 128–29, 132, 183n4, 197n85, 198nn89,91. See also *gei*
actor-critique booklets (*yakusha hyōbanki*), 27, 33, 38–39, 53, 57, 61, 67, 69, 115–16, 169–70n1, 170n3, 172n33, 176nn13,14, 183n4, 186n22. See also theater-related publications
Actors' Analects, The (Yakusha banashi), 37, 175n3, 177–78n34
actress (*joyū*), xiv, 9, 17, 80–81, 107, 120–21, 126–28, 134–36, 141, 145–47, 154, 156, 160–61, 181n70, 207–8n83, 208n84, 211n114, 216n35, 218n11
Aeba Kōson [also "Takenoya Shujin" in bibliography], 203n34
age-counting method, traditional East Asian, xv, 202n31, 215n23
all-female kabuki troupes (*onna shibai*), 117. See also woman-actor
Andō Tsuruo, 156
Arashi Yoshisaburō IV, 217–18n50
Arashi Yoshisaburō V, 156–57, 217–18n50
Ashihara Eiryō, 94, 96, 101, 195n48. See also *nanba* gait
Austin, J. L., 179n53
authentic traditions (*hongyō*; *honmon*; *honzetsu*), xiv, 10–11, 90, 123–24, 166n12, 186n12, 199n95, 207n72, 216n34

Bandō Matasaburō, 119, 148, 205n40
Bandō Mitsue, 117–19, 129, 132, 202n26, 203n32, 204nn36,38, 205n41. See also theater-master
Bandō Mitsugorō III, 202n26
Bandō Mitsugorō VII, 203n32
Bandō Mitsugorō VIII, 203n32
Bandō Tamasaburō III, 205n41, 211n119
Bandō Tamasaburō V, x, 6, 8–9, 150, 153, 155, 163, 205n41, 216n36; adoption, 144–45; ideas about *onnagata*, 157, 214n21; international collaborations, 50, 164, 167n18, 181n69; *Nasutāsha/Nastazja*, 50, 70, 164, 181nn69,70; *No Sleeve Wet upon Showering America*, 162; *The Peony Pavilion*, 167n18, 181n69
Barthes, Roland, 45, 189n71
big theaters (*ōshibai*) [also "three theaters" (*sanshibai*, also *sanza*)], 64–65, 68, 114, 116, 137, 147–48, 184n1, 185n10, 204n36, 205n40, 211n114. See also small theaters
bon festival dance, 93
Book of Disease, The (Yamai no sōshi), 28–29, 55, 173n42, 181–82n86
Brandon, James R., 162, 169n40, 202n30
Buddhism, 5, 25, 35–36, 56, 60, 72, 76, 78, 80, 98, 167n25, 171n17, 192n92
bunraku (puppet theater), xiv, 5–6, 49, 90, 92, 100–101, 104, 106–9, 126, 166n12, 175n8, 177n34, 181n69, 186n19, 193–94n17, 197n83, 198n91, 199n95. See also female *gidayū*; *gidayū* chanting; *jōruri* chanting
Butler, Judith, 70–71, 82, 210n108

[249]

Case, Sue-Ellen, 166n15, 176n21
Chikamatsu Monzaemon, 66, 83, 87, 105, 186n19, 193n99
citation, 14, 18, 45, 64, 70–73, 104, 192–93n98
Classified Glossary of Japanese Nomenclature (Wamyō ruijūshō, also Wamyō ruijushō), 29
Collected Fallen Leaves (Ochibashū), 29–30
Complete Book of Actors through All Ages, the New Edition, The (Shinsen kokon yakusha taizen), 61, 175n3, 200n11
Complete Book on Actors, The (Yakusha zensho), 69
constitutive other, the, 13, 18, 41, 54–55, 74, 83, 135–36, 147
constructionism and essentialism, the relation between, 3, 7, 20, 79, 83, 150, 158, 191n80
cross-gender performance, ix, 10–16, 20, 150; examples of, 11; theoretical problems of, 12–14
cultivation (*shugyō*), 17–18, 76–79, 87, 98, 103, 121, 136, 145–47, 149–50, 156, 192n92, 194n18, 207n74, 217n47

dance, 8, 25, 58–59, 61, 64, 88–94, 96–100, 104, 106–11, 118–19, 120–23, 127, 166n12, 170n9, 172n33, 183n5, 189n71, 198n89, 198–99n92, 199n101, 206nn67,68, 211n114, 212n124, 217n41; dancing and chanting, 6, 11, 64, 89–90; distinction between *odori* dance and *mai* dance, 106–10, 198–99n92; as part of kabuki grammar, 123. See also *bon* festival dance; *kagura* dance; *kōwaka* dance
dichotomy, 49, 55–56, 76, 103, 107–8, 121, 135, 173n38; artificial gender and natural gender, 135, 141, 145, 147, 149, 151, 163; modern dichotomies, 147, 149, 151, 157, 163
différance, 13, 41, 83, 191n78
disease, 28–29, 55, 80, 168n28, 181–82n86; intersex as, 28–29, 55, 181–82n86; metaphor of, 168n28
"Dust in the Ears, The" (Nijinshū), 76, 188–89n65

Each Month Exegesis (Maigetsushō), 78, 189n74

Edelson, Loren, 169n39
Ejima-Ikushima incident, the, 116, 184n1. See also kabuki history
Encyclopedia of the Heaven, Earth, and Humans in Japan and China, The (Wakan sansai zue), 29
Enomoto Shigetami, 9, 161, 200n2, 218n11
enunciation and enunciated, the relation between, 67, 72, 124, 182–83n3
epistemology, 22, 27, 76, 96, 136–38, 141, 144–47, 149, 153, 156, 158, 175n4, 177–78n34, 189n71
eras, names and duration of, xiii, 89
Ernst, Earle, 7, 44
esotericism (*hiden*; lit., "secret transmission"), 72, 76–78, 187n48, 189n74
exterior and interior, the relation between, 76–77, 79, 104, 158, 189nn68,71, 190n77, 190–91n78, 191–92n88, 201n24, 217n47

Famous-Product Journal, Actors' Sleeves, The (Yakusha meibutsu sode nikki), 62, 184n19
Fausto-Sterling, Anne, 12, 173n38
female *gidayū*, 123–25, 137, 206n69, 210–11n111, 207n78. See also bunraku; *gidayū* chanting
female masculinity, 123, 171–72n23, 176n21, 178n35, 207n70
female *onnagata*, ix–x, xiv, 8, 15, 19–21, 43–44, 112–38, 141, 152, 160–61, 163–64, 183n3, 209–10n108, 212n124, 212, 214n18. See also female masculinity; Ichikawa Kumehachi I; woman-actor; Yamada Isuzu
femininity: constructed essential femininity, 54; the degree of, 45–57; an eighteenth century notion of its essence, 46–54; an eighteenth century notion of the antithesis of its essence, 48–54, 176n13; in relation to class, 45–57; in relation to violence, 165n1, 172n23; of courtesans, 46–54; of samurai women, 48–54, 176n13
Foucault, Michel, 97–98, 138, 150, 157, 172n25, 180n65
Fukuchi Ōchi, 119, 133
futanari (intersex; androgyny), 27–36, 173nn41,42. See also *futanarihira*; intersex
futanarihira (androgynous beauties), 15,

27–36, 39, 55–56, 58, 172nn29,33, 173n41. See also *futanari*

gait, ix, 77, 88, 90–104, 110, 194n23, 195n39; as a biometric, 91–92, 103; modernization of, 97; school education, 96–98, 100. See also *nanba* gait
gei (acquired artistic technique), 19, 40–41, 59–60, 67, 72, 74, 76–79, 81, 83, 85, 87, 103, 105, 110, 118, 120–29, 132, 136, 143, 146, 154, 175n8, 177–78n34, 181n70, 183nn4,5, 185n3, 193n99, 198n89, 202–3n32, 207nn70,74, 207–8n83, 211n114, 216–17n39. See also accounts-on-*gei*
gidayū chanting, xiv, 90, 99–101, 104, 122–27, 129, 136–37, 186n19, 193–94n17, 194n18, 196n69, 199n99, 206nn67,69, 207nn70,78,81, 208–9n83, 209n84, 210–11n111. See also bunraku; female *gidayū*; *jōruri* chanting
Great Mirror of Male Eros, The (Nanshoku ōkagami), 26–27, 34–35, 39, 171n20
Greater Learning for Women (Onna daigaku), 20–21, 69–70, 79–80, 136
Gunji Masakatsu, 67, 89, 105–6, 175n3, 177nn28,34, 190–91n78, 198–99n92

Halberstam, Judith, 172n23
Hanayagi Shōtarō, 134
Hart, Lynda, 3, 200n2, 207n80, 210n108, 211n111; canonization, 182n3; on the principle of reverse, 168n27, 169nn38,42; violence and gender, 165n1, 172n23
Hattori Yukio, 58, 62, 65–66, 180n61, 182n91, 184n19, 185n12, 187n29. See also kabuki playhouses
Hayashi Kimiko, 114–16, 200n11
Hidden behind the Leaves (Hagakure), 172n25
History of the Takemoto and Toyotake Troupes (Chikuhō koji), 177–78n34
hongyō. See authentic traditions
honmon. See authentic traditions
honorary man, 19, 112, 125, 136, 200n2, 210–11n111
honzetsu. See authentic traditions

Ichikawa Danjūrō, the name of, 118–19, 148, 204n39, 205n40

Ichikawa Danjūrō II, 188n58
Ichikawa Danjūrō VIII, 139, 210n111
Ichikawa Danjūrō IX [also "Danshū" in text], 118–20, 123, 126, 129, 132–33, 142, 148, 197–98n88, 201n24, 205nn40,41, 208n88, 210n109, 211nn113,114, 214n23, 217n41
Ichikawa Danjūrō XI, 144, 201n24
Ichikawa Ennosuke III, 213–14n10
Ichikawa Ennosuke IV ["Ichikawa Kamejirō" in bibliography], 153, 215n26
Ichikawa Kamejirō II. See Ichikawa Ennosuke IV
Ichikawa Kumehachi I, 21, 116–17, 135–39, 161–62, 169n40, 202n30, 204n38, 210n108, 211n113, 212n127; accounts-on-*gei* of, 128–31; *Beloved Wife and Multicolored Reins*, 131; date of birth, 203–4n34, 212n124; in kabuki historiography, 130–33, 160, 162; "Instructions for *Onnagata*," 129; kabuki training and career of, 118–19, 122–23, 128, 205n41, 210–11n111; other names of, 118–19, 204n39, 205n41; performance reviews of, 120–22, 127, 206n52, 211n114; reputations of, 118–22, 125–28, 130–34, 208n88, 212n129; *Scandalous Comb in the World of Love Affairs*, 130; succession of *kata*, 130–31, 156. See also theater-master; woman-actor
Ichikawa Kumehachi II, 132, 211n112
Ichikawa Monnosuke VI, 82–83
Ichikawa Shōchō II, 155, 204n39, 216n38, 216–17n39
Ichikawa Shun'en II, 153, 213n10, 215n27
Ichikawa Suisen III, 201n24. See also *shinpa* theater
Ichimura Uzaemon XV, 144
ie (the stem-family household), 79–80, 143, 171n20, 172n25, 191n85, 198n89, 213n6; adoption, ix, 116, 121, 142–48, 156, 214n10; "art of the family" (*ie-no-gei*), 143, 145–46; family business, 143, 145, 148
iemoto (stem-family head), 108–11, 198n89, 198–99n92, 199n95
Ihara Saikaku, xv, 26, 171n20, 192n91
Ihara Toshirō [also "Ihara Seiseien" in bibliography], xv, 59, 170n4, 175n4, 183n8
Ikegami, Eiko, 77

Ikehata Shinnosuke [also "Pītā" in text], 97–99
Imao Tetsuya, 27, 29, 41, 46, 59, 172n29, 175n4, 177n28, 178n36, 180n58
Inoue Yachiyo II, 199nn95,98
Inoue Yachiyo III, 110, 199nn98,103
Inoue Yachiyo IV, 108–10, 198n92, 199nn98,101; on the gender restriction of the Inoue school, 199n101; on the Inoue school, 108–11, 198n92, 199nn95,98, 212n124; on puppet-gesture, 108–10
"Instructions for *Onnagata*" (Onnagata no kokoroe), 129
intersex, 12, 27–28, 30, 55, 149, 173nn38,39,41,42, 181–82n86. See also *futanari*
Irigaray, Luce, 25–26, 171n22
Itō Kodayū II, 70, 73
Iwai Hanshirō VIII, 83, 118, 135, 137, 142, 147, 152–53, 155–56, 204nn37,38, 205n41, 213n4, 214n15, 214–15n23

jōruri chanting, xiv, 69, 100, 115, 126, 193–94n17, 194n18, 196n69, 200n11, 207n81. See also bunraku; *gidayū* chanting
joshoku (female eros), 39, 171n20. See also *nanshoku*

kabuki: as a generic word, 5, 10, 180n66; as *kyūgeki* (old theater), 122, 184n2, 216n34; as *kyūha* (old faction and/or school), 216n34; masculinity-centric, 6; Tōhō-kabuki, 160–62, 218n9
kabuki history: ban on female performers (1629), 8, 12, 15–16, 23–24, 81, 110, 114, 170n9, 184n1; ban on *wakashu kabuki* (1652), 16, 23–24, 36, 170–71n12, 184n1; Ejima-Ikushima incident (1714), 68, 116, 184n1; *Genroku kabuki*, 168n31; Tōhō-kabuki, 160–62, 218n9; *wakashu kabuki* (young boys' kabuki), 16–17, 22–26, 34, 36, 81, 170n9, 170–71n12; women's kabuki (*onna kabuki*), 16, 19, 24–25, 110, 114, 170nn3,9; *yarō kabuki* (kabuki performed by adult men), 168n31
kabuki playhouses, 6, 16, 35, 57, 65–66; impact on acting, 66; the Kabuki-za Theater, 91, 119, 162, 185–86n12, 205n40, 212–13n1; the Kanamaru-za Theater, 66, 185n10, 187n28; meanings of the space, 64–66; the Nakamura-za Theater, 65, 184n1, 185n10; parts of a stage and a theater, 6, 66, 102, 114, 200n7, 214–15n23; ranking of, 119, 130, 148, 184n1, 205n40; religious connotations, 66; the Ryūsei-za Theater, 119, 148, 205n40; the size of a stage, 185–86n12; studies by Hattori Yukio, 65–66. See also big theaters; Hattori Yukio
kabuki publications. See theater-related publications
kabuku, 5, 10, 166n12, 216n34
kagura dance, 93
Kamiyama Akira, 117, 202n30
Kamiyo Nishiki, 126–27. See also Takarazuka theater
Kano, Ayako, 80–81, 120, 134, 145, 194–95n38
Karasuyakko [sic]. See Mishima Sōsen
kata ("direction" or "in charge of"). See *onnagata*: Chinese characters and meanings
kata ("form" or "pattern"), 10, 130–31, 142, 147, 156, 190–91n78, 197n85, 208n100, 213n4, 214n15
Kataoka Gadō XIII, x, 208n83
Kataoka Nizaemon XIII, 66, 144
Kawatake Mokuami, 67, 105, 133, 137
Kawatake Toshio, 47
Kitamura Rokurō, 129, 134
Kōdō Tokuchi, 118
Kokan Tarōji, 76
Kōno Yoshinori, 94, 96, 102–3, 195n45. See also *nanba* gait
kōwaka dance, 93
kunqu (also *kunju*), 11, 164, 167n18, 181n69
Kyōgen, xiv, 5, 49, 92, 109, 166n12, 175n8

Laqueur, Thomas, 173n38, 180n65, 206n53
Leiter, Samuel L., 47, 87, 166n1

male-role actors (*tachiyaku*), 6, 11, 39–40, 52–53, 75–76, 104, 108, 121, 126–27, 176n14, 177n25, 190–91n78, 192n91, 193n8, 206n67, 212–13n1
Marey, Étienne-Jules, 195n48
Matsui Sumako, 134
Matsumoto Kōshirō VII, 11, 144

INDEX [253]

Matsumoto Kōshirō VIII, xvi, 159
Mayama Seika, 120
Metropolis in the East, A (Tōyō daitokai), 120–21, 203–4n34
Mezur, Katherine, 43, 166n1, 167n22, 168–69n35, 178–79n41, 179n42, 199–200n1, 209n104, 209–10n108
"mind and body as one entity" (*shinshin ichinyo*), 78
Mishima Sōsen (psued. Udo) [also "Karasuyakko" [sic] in bibliography], 133, 203n34, 211n115, 212n124, 217n41
Mizuno Yūko, 125, 206n69
Mizutani Yaeko II, 201n24. See also *shinpa* theater
Mori Ritsuko, 128
Morita Kan'ya XIV, 144, 201n24

Nakamura Ganjirō II, 102–3
Nakamura Ganjirō III. *See* Sakata Tōjūrō IV
Nakamura Kankurō V. *See* Nakamura Kanzaburō XVIII
Nakamura Kanzaburō XVII, 144, 154, 201n24, 216n31, 218n50
Nakamura Kanzaburō XVIII ["Nakamura Kankurō" in bibliography], 89, 91, 93, 154, 202n25, 216n31
Nakamura Karoku III, 156, 218n50
Nakamura Kasen, 117
Nakamura Kichiemon II, 159, 161
Nakamura Senjaku II. *See* Sakata Tōjūrō IV
Nakamura Shikaku II, 194n18
Nakamura Shikan IV, 142, 217n41
Nakamura Shikan VII, x, 152–53, 202n25
Nakamura Sōjūrō, 131, 156, 209n106, 218n50
Nakamura Tokiko, 156
Nakamura Tokizō V, 206n67, 208n84
Nakamura Utaemon III, 197n87
Nakamura Utaemon V, xv–xvi, 60, 83, 123, 131, 156–57, 197n87, 212–13n1; accounts-on-*gei* of, 147, 197nn85,86, 208n97, 218n8; adoption, 142–44, 147; modern *onnagata*, a forerunner of, 113, 141; on puppet-gesture, 105–7; use of Hanshirō's *kata*, 147, 156, 213n4, 214n15
Nakamura Utaemon VI, x, xv–xvi, 60, 75, 142, 152–53, 155, 157, 159–61, 192–93n98, 207–8n83, 212n127, 213n1, 217n43

Nakarai Bokuyō, 27, 29, 39, 172n33
Namino Kuriko, 154, 201n24, 216n31.
  See also *shinpa* theater
nanba gait (also *nanban* gait), 77, 92–104, 109–10, 194–95n38, 195nn39,41,43,45, 196nn59,75; etymology of, 99, 196n65; in *gidayū*, 99–101, 196n69; Greek vases, 195n48; in high technology, 195n41; in martial arts, 93–96; in modern sports, 94–95; modernization, 97; in noh, 90–95; in swordsmanship, 94–96; school education, 96–98, 100; sliding steps (*suriashi*), 90, 93–95, 102–3; torso, 96–103. *See also* gait
nandan, 11, 167n18
nanshoku (male eros), 39, 171n20. *See also joshoku*
Nasutāsha/Nastazja (Nastasya), 50, 164, 181nn69,70. *See also* Bandō Tamasaburō V
nenja, 25–28, 35, 39, 171nn20,22. See also *wakashu*
Night Stories by Seigaku (Seigaku Yawa), 130–31, 205n40, 208n102, 209n103
No Sleeve Wet upon Showering America (Furu Amerika ni sode wa nurasaji), 162
noh theater, xiv, 5–6, 10–11, 49, 66, 72, 88–95, 103, 109–10, 115, 123–24, 133, 160, 163, 166n12, 174–75n8, 180n66, 181n69, 185–86n12, 193n8, 199nn95,98, 206n67, 207n72, 218n7. *See also* Zeami Motokiyo

Oka Onitarō, 99
Okamoto Kidō, 127, 208n88
onnagata: Chinese characters and meanings of, 174n2, 183n8; epithets of, 15, 82, 150, 152, 155; etymology of, 174n2; eye-raising, 128, 136; leading *onnagata* (*tate-oyama*), 6, 60, 89, 159, 161, 174n2, 191n88; shoulder blades, 103, 128, 136
Onoe Baikō VI, 11, 83, 113, 131, 134, 152–53, 155, 217nn41,43; accounts-on-*gei* of, 60–61; adoption, 143–44; on puppet-gesture, 105–6, 197n86; *Scandalous Comb in the World of Love Affairs*, 130, 208nn97,102
Onoe Baikō VII, 159, 161, 206n67
Onoe Kikugorō V, 143, 217n41
Onoe Kikugorō VI, 60, 113, 130, 148, 154
Onoe Kikujirō II, 130–31-

Onoe Taganojō III, 60, 82, 113, 127, 130–31, 148, 152, 156, 161, 205n40, 218n50, 219n13. *See also* small theaters
Orientalism, 95, 194–95n38. *See also* reverse Orientalism
Osanai Kaoru, 65, 184n2, 189n68
Overview and Details of Actors, the New Edition, The (Shinkoku yakusha kōmoku), 177n28
oyama. See *onnagata*

parlor-kabuki (*zashiki-shibai*; *zashiki-kabuki*), 114–15, 200nn10,11
parlor-theater (*zashiki-kyōgen*), 115–16, 200nn10,11
Party Diary (Enyū nikki), 114, 116, 200n10
Peony Pavilion, The, 164, 181n69. *See also* Bandō Tamasaburō V
performativity, 12, 14, 17–18, 20, 38, 42–43, 81, 92, 135–36, 146–47, 149–50, 179n53, 209–10n108, 212n123
Phelan, Peggy, 189n71
Pioneering Analects from Past and Present Actors, The (Kokon yakusha rongo sakigake), 37, 59, 61, 75, 175nn3,4, 183nn5,8
puppet-body (*ningyōmi*), 107–8, 198–99n92
puppet-gesture (*ningyōburi*), 88, 104–11, 119, 197nn83,85,86,87, 197–98n88, 198n91, 198–99n92

Ran (Kurosawa film), 97–98, 103
reverse Orientalism, 95, 101, 194–95n38. *See also* Orientalism; theory of Japaneseness
Robertson, Jennifer, 46, 70, 166n5, 169n36, 174n2, 192n93, 195n41, 210–11n111

Sakai, Naoki, 193–94n17, 194–95n38
Sakata Tōjūrō I, 76
Sakata Tōjūrō IV [also "Nakamura Senjaku" and "Nakamura Ganjirō" in citations and bibliography], 102, 199n101, 216n36; gait training, 88–93, 103, 109–10, 194n19; on puppet-gesture, 106–7, 198n91; success as an *onnagata*, 88, 103, 154–55, 194n23
Sawamura Gennosuke IV, 130–31, 152, 156, 208n102, 209n103, 214–15n23. *See also* small theaters
Sawamura Kodenji I, 192n91

Scandalous Comb in the World of Love Affairs (Yowanasake ukina no yokogushi), 130
second nature, 18–19, 64, 77–79, 81, 87, 98, 145, 147, 149–50, 157–58, 192n92
Secret of Gidayū Chanting, The (Gidayū hiketsu), 99
Secret Opuses of Jōruri, Exegesis, The (Jōruri hikyoku shō), 196n69
Secret Opuses of Jōruri, Supplement, The (Zōho jōruri hikyoku shō), 196n69
"Secret Transmissions of an *Onnagata*, The" (Onnagata hiden), 37–42, 44, 51, 59–60, 62, 64, 69–70, 73, 75, 77, 79, 183nn4,8, 188–89n65; bibliography of, 175n4; canonization of, 58–62, 182–83n3; differences from "The Words of Ayame," 190–91n78. *See also* Segawa Kikunojō I
Secret Transmissions on Jōruri, Exegesis, the Edo Version, The (Edo-ban jōruri hiden shō), 100
Segawa Kikunojō I, 11, 36–38, 43, 45–46, 58, 63, 70, 72, 75, 157, 183n5; differences from Yoshizawa Ayame I, 190–91n78; performance reviews of, 61–62, 76; studies of, 179n41, 181n78, 183n4. *See also* "The Secret Transmissions of an *Onnagata*"
"Sequel to 'The Dust in the Ears'" (Zoku "Nijinshū"), 76
shingeki, 122, 155, 184n2, 209n107, 216nn34,38
shinpa theater, 116–17, 119, 127, 129–30, 134, 154, 159, 162, 167n18, 201n24, 211n114, 216n34. *See also* Hanayagi Shōtarō; Ichikawa Suisen III; Kitamura Rokurō; Mizutani Yaeko II; Namino Kuriko
small theaters (*koshibai*), 68, 115, 119, 131, 137, 148, 205n40. *See also* big theaters
Sugimura Haruko, 154, 157, 162
Sunaga Asahiko, 27, 172n33
Suzuki Harunobu, 102
Suzuki Tadashi, 91

Tadano Makuzu, 190n77, 191–92n88
Takarazuka theater, 11, 117, 126–27, 178n35,

207n70, 216n35. See also *gidayū* chanting; Kamiyo Nishiki; Yorozuyo Mineko
Takechi Tetsuji, 77, 197n78, 203n32, 217–18n39; on dance, 109–10, 198n89, 198–99n92; on *nanba* gait, 93, 95, 97, 100–2, 196nn69,75; on the necessity of male *onnagata*, 155, 216n35; patronage of arts, 90, 93, 193n15, 199n101; on puppet-gesture, 106–10. See also *nanba* gait
Takei Kyōzō, 115, 168n31, 200n11, 201n15
Takemoto Tosahiro, 125, 207n78
Takemoto Tosatayū VI, 124–25
Takenoya Shujin. *See* Aeba Kōson
Takeshiba Kisui, 137, 203–4n34, 204n37
Tales of Actors through All Ages, The (Kokon yakusha monogatari), 27
Tamura Toshiko, 122, 138, 212n129
Theater under the Microscope (Gekijō ikkan mushimegane), 66, 68–69
theater-books (*gekisho*), 66–69, 75, 186nn22,24. See also theater-related publications
theatergoing, 68–69, 73, 114, 209–10n108; alternatives of, 68–69, 73, 114; virtual theatergoing, 68–69, 73, 114, 187–88n49
theater-master (*okyōgenshi*), xiv, 110, 114, 116–18, 132–33, 138, 202–3n32, 203–4n34, 204n36, 205n41, 206n69, 210n111, 212n124. See also woman-actor
theater-related publications, 22, 59–60, 62, 66, 68–69, 75, 186nn22,24. See also actor-critique booklets; theater-books
theory of Japaneseness, the (*nihonjinron*), 95, 101, 194–95n38. *See also* Orientalism; reverse Orientalism
three major cities, 38–39, 61, 185n10, 176n10
three theaters (*sanshibai*, also *sanza*). *See* big theaters
Throne of Blood (Kumonosu-jō), 157, 159–60. *See also* Yamada Isuzu
Tōhō-kabuki, 160–62, 218n9. *See also* kabuki history; Yamada Isuzu

Ueno Chizuko, 167n24, 201–2n25
ukiyo-e (woodblock prints), 102, 122, 128, 173n43
Ukon Genzaemon, 22, 25, 27, 33–34, 170nn3,4

Village School, The (Terakoya), 98–99, 102–3

wakashu, 16, 21, 23–30, 34–36, 38–42, 45, 52, 55–56, 58, 70, 81, 104, 110, 115–16, 171nn20,22, 172nn25,29; homogenderity of, 23–30; transience of, 23, 34–36, 38–42. *See also* kabuki history; *nenja*
Way of *wakashu* (*Wakashudō*), 16
Woman-Actor (Onna yakusha), 161
woman-actor (*onna yakusha*), xiv, 9, 112, 114, 117–18, 121–23, 127, 131–32, 137–38, 156–57, 160–61, 166n7, 203–4n34, 205n41, 206n69, 211n119, 212n127. *See also* all-female kabuki troupes; Ichikawa Kumehachi I; theater-master
women's *gidayū*. *See* female *gidayū*
Women's Treasury (Onna chōhōki), 69–70
"Words of Ayame, The," 7–8, 20, 37–42, 44–46, 48–49, 51–55, 58–62, 64, 69, 73–75, 77, 79, 88, 90–91, 175n8, 176n13, 177n28, 177–78n34, 178n36, 183nn4,8, 184n19, 188–89n65, 193n8; bibliography of, 175n3; canonization of, 58–62, 182–83n3; differences from "Secret Transmissions of an *Onnagata*," 190–91n78. *See also* Yoshizawa Ayame I

yagō (shop name), 65, 119, 185n3, 193n8, 204nn38,39
Yaji and Kita's Walking Tour on the Tōkaidō Highway (Yaji Kita Tōkaidōchū hizakurige), 159–61. *See also* Yamada Isuzu
Yamada Isuzu, 127, 137, 166n7, 208n84, 218nn5,8,10, 218–19n13; in kabuki plays, 127, 159–62; *Throne of Blood*, 159–60; Tōhō-kabuki, 162; *Yaji and Kita's Walking Tour on the Tōkaidō Highway*, 159–61
Yoda Gakkai, 118–19
Yorozuyo Mineko, 216n35. *See also* Takarazuka theater
Yoshida Bungorō III, 106–7, 198n91
Yoshimura Yūki, 99, 198n89; the Yoshimura school, 108
Yoshizawa Ayame I, 7, 22, 34–79, 87–92, 103, 157, 168–69n35, 176n13, 178–79n41, 184n1, 185n3, 188n59, 193n8; differences from Segawa Kikunojō I, 190–91n78; male-role acting of, 39–40, 176n14,

Yoshizawa Ayame I (*continued*)
177n25, 193n8; on the performance of courtesans' roles, 46–54; on the performance of samurai women's roles, 48–54, 176n13; performance reviews of, 38–40, 54–55, 61–62, 76, 87; studies of, 179n41, 183n4. *See also* "The Words of Ayame"

Yuasa Yasuo, 78, 190n75

Zeami Motokiyo, 11, 35, 48–50, 54, 72, 78, 89, 123–24, 163, 174–75n8, 181n69; on authentic traditions, 123–24, 207n72; on the performance of women's roles, 48–50, 163; "temporary bloom" and "the true Flower," 35. *See also* noh theater

www.ingramcontent.com/pod-product-compliance
Lightning Source LLC
Chambersburg PA
CBHW030614230426
43661CB00053B/1990